Developments in Psychotherapy

Developments in Psychotherapy

Historical Perspectives

edited by
Windy Dryden

SAGE Publications
London · Thousand Oaks · New Delhi

First published 1996

 SAGE Publications Ltd
6 Bonhill Street
London EC2A 4PU

SAGE Publications Inc
2455 Teller Road
Thousand Oaks, California 91320

SAGE Publications India Pvt Ltd
32, M-Block Market
Greater Kailash - I
New Delhi 110 048

British Library Cataloguing in Publication data

A catalogue record for this book is
available from the British Library.

ISBN 0 8039 7911 8
ISBN 0 8039 7912 6 (pbk)

Library of Congress catalog card number 96-069121

Typeset by Type Study, Scarborough, North Yorkshire
Printed in Great Britain by Biddles Ltd, Guildford, Surrey

To Brian Vale

Contents

Preface

While approaches to therapy change and develop over time, these developments are often not recognized, and when they are recognized they are often poorly understood. For this reason I decided to edit a book which had as its main theme the charting of developments in the major non-psychoanalytic approaches to psychotherapy. (The psychoanalytic approaches to therapy warrant a separate volume to themselves.)

Contributors to this volume were asked to detail and explain the major theoretical and practical developments in the approach under consideration. While I suggested several ways in which this could be done, I encouraged contributors to structure their chapters in order to highlight these developments. As such, this book contributes to our historical understanding of the developments in psychotherapy.

Windy Dryden, London

1

Person-Centred Psychotherapy: Twenty Historical Steps

Nathaniel J. Raskin

In this chapter a number of significant steps in the development of person-centred therapy will be described. These advances occurred in a special kind of atmosphere, which reflected the spirit of the person-centred movement and the characteristics of its founder. Carl Rogers formulated an approach to psychotherapy and human relations based on trust in the self-determining capacities of individuals and groups customarily seen as requiring direction, control and external authority – clients, children, students, workers. Rogers inspired his students and associates by hard work, conviction, intelligence, sensitivity and example. As a teacher, therapist and administrator, he was respectful, equalitarian, thoughtful, generous and unassuming. As a psychologist who was breaking new ground he confidently and skilfully debated with advocates of directive counselling, psychiatrists opposed to psychologists doing therapy and behaviourists who did not recognize the role of feelings or the concept of self. In his early forties he became the President of the American Psychological Association and later received that organization's highest scientific and professional awards.

Rogers's students and associates looked up to him and were aware that they belonged to a movement that was influencing traditional practices in a radical, even revolutionary, way. They were providing the building blocks of a new field of psychotherapy research, based on verbatim accounts of therapy cases, contributing to journals and publishing books. Programmes were organized at the annual conventions of the American Psychological Association. In 1948, for example, Rogers and some of his students organized a symposium on psychotherapy research and enlisted leaders from around the United States to lead small discussion groups on the subject. This was an entirely new concept in these national meetings. In 1949 an entire issue of the *Journal of Consulting Psychology* was devoted to a series of reports by Rogers and a group of students and staff making up the 'parallel studies' project, the first time a group of cases recorded verbatim were subjected to several different research analyses (Rogers et al., 1949). A strong *esprit de corps* has characterized the movement in the more than half-century of its history, during which time it has become more and more an international phenomenon. It is this kind of atmosphere that has given impetus to the growth and development described in this chapter.

The birth of the movement

Several of the significant steps in the development of the person-centred approach to psychotherapy were contained in the original formulation of the movement on 11 December 1940. On that date, towards the end of Rogers's first year as a psychology professor at Ohio State University, he addressed the University of Minnesota's chapter of Psi Chi, the national psychological honour society, on 'Some newer concepts of psychotherapy'. When, unexpectedly, the impact of the speech became clear, Rogers developed his ideas further into a book-length description of his approach entitled *Counseling and Psychotherapy* (Rogers, 1942). While he was presenting ideas and methods that were radically different, he gave credit to Otto Rank and some of his followers – Jessie Taft, Frederick Allen and Virginia Robinson – for supplying the roots of the newer concepts. The following are some of the historical steps contained in this early talk and book:

ONE. 'Therapy is not a matter of doing something to the individual, or of inducing him to do something about himself. It is instead a matter of freeing him for normal growth and development, of removing obstacles so that he can again move forward' (Rogers, 1942: 29).

The counselling programme at the University of Minnesota typified the prevalent concepts and practices of the time. These were based on gathering information through case histories and psychological tests and, on the basis of this data, guiding the client towards personal and vocational choices deemed by the counsellor to be appropriate and realistic.

In his talk, Rogers cited some of the techniques employed in this directive approach – ordering and forbidding, exhortation, suggestion, advice and intellectualized interpretation. Rogers quoted an advice-giving counsellor, who happened to be the programme chairman of the meeting he was addressing, describing his goal in working with a student: 'My job was to dissuade him from continuing in pre-business . . . I pointed out the competition in the professional School of Business . . . the courses in the . . . curriculum: statistics, finance, money and banking, theoretical economics. . . . He finally agreed to think it over. I outlined a plan of action' (Rogers, 1942: 24).

Rogers emphasized this way of trying to help people made the basic assumption that the counsellor knows best what the goals of the individual should be and he tries in various ways to get the client to achieve these goals. The goal of the newer approach was not to solve a problem; it was to promote the growth of the individual, to foster independence and integration so that the client would be able to solve not only this problem but future ones.

TWO. The newer approach stressed emotional or feeling aspects rather than intellectual elements, placed more emphasis upon the individual's immediate situation than upon the past, and valued the therapeutic relationship itself as a growth experience.

Rogers gave the example of a student who says, in his first interview, 'I've always realized that my methods of study, my study habits, are wrong. I don't feel as though I am a very brilliant person but I don't think I am as stupid as my grades indicate.' The traditional counsellor, rather than communicating recognition of the student's feeling that he can do better, responds to an aspect of content in the student's statement:

'Well, how bad are your grades? I thought they were pretty good' (Rogers, 1942: 133). This approach can also lead to focusing on the past and helps to structure a relationship of distance between therapist and client because the therapist is setting himself up as knowing more. If the therapist had responded to the client's expressed feeling, he would be staying with the student in the present and contributing to a relationship of equalitarian understanding and closeness, a relationship which could make a contribution to the client's personal growth.

THREE. Implicit in the therapist's attention to the client's attitudes and feelings was the idea that the client's frame of reference, which came to be referred to as the IFR (internal frame of reference), was the therapist's basic consideration, rather than his own appraisal of what was going on.

A few years later, in 1947, as outgoing president of the American Psychological Association, Rogers expressed the importance he attached to this point of view with some eloquence:

> Client-centered therapy has led us to try to adopt the client's perceptual field as the basis for genuine understanding. In trying to enter this internal world of perception . . . we find ourselves in a new vantage point for understanding personality dynamics. . . . We find that behavior seems to be better understood as a reaction to this reality-as-perceived. We discover that the way in which the person sees himself, and the perceptions he dares not take as belonging to himself, seem to have an important relationship to the inner peace which constitutes adjustment. (Rogers, 1947: 368)

FOUR. Rogers sought order in whatever he studied. In his 1940 talk and 1942 book, he described characteristic steps in the therapeutic process:

'*The individual comes for help.*' It might be added, on his or her own initiative. The client might be influenced by a parent, teacher or friend, but it is a deterrent to the client-centred process if he or she does not accept the responsibility for continuing in therapy.

'*The helping situation is usually defined.*' The counsellor conveys in various ways that she does not have the answers but will try to help the client work out his own solutions. This might be done explicitly, but for the most part is done implicitly by the therapist's concrete behaviour, e.g. concentrating on conveying an understanding of whatever the client volunteers, the fact that the therapist does not take a case history or probe for information, the therapist handling the next appointment by making it clear that this is the client's decision.

'*The counselor encourages free expression of feelings in regard to the problem.*' These feelings may be positive or negative, loving or hostile, clear or ambivalent. The counsellor is open to all of these, although negative feelings and ambivalence tend to predominate at the beginning of counselling, e.g. a mother describing her adolescent son as impossible to influence, or a child using play therapy to get rid of his baby sister.

'*The counselor accepts, recognizes, and clarifies these negative feelings.*' By being fully accepting of negative feelings, the therapist helps to create an environment which facilitates the client's ability to accept such feelings as part of himself.

'*When the individual's negative feelings have been quite fully expressed, they are followed by the faint and tentative expressions of the positive impulses which make for growth.*' Rogers described this change in direction as 'one of the most certain and predictable aspects of the whole process. The more violent and deep the negative expressions (provided they are accepted and recognized), the more certain are the positive expressions of love, of social impulses, of fundamental self-respect, of desire to be mature' (Rogers, 1942: 39). He gives the example of a mother who, having experienced the acceptance of feelings toward her son of desperation, hopelessness, annoyance and despair over the course of more than one interview, states that there were times when the boy could be 'good as gold'.

'*The counselor accepts and recognizes the positive feelings which are expressed, in the same manner in which he has accepted and recognized the negative feelings.*' The counsellor does this without praise, just as the client's negative feelings are not met with disapproval. This encourages a free exploration of self and creates an optimal environment for the promotion of insight and self-acceptance.

'*This insight, this understanding of the self and acceptance of the self, is the next important aspect of the whole process.*' Rogers cites a graduate student who says with a great deal of feeling, 'I'm really just a spoiled brat, but I do want to be normal. I wouldn't let anyone else say that of me, but it's true' (1942: 40). The mother who has been very critical of her son says, 'Perhaps what would do him most good would be for him to have some affection and love and consideration entirely apart from any correcting' (ibid.: 41).

'*Intermingled with this process of insight – and it should again be emphasized that the steps outlined are not mutually exclusive, nor do they proceed in a rigid order – is a process of clarification of possible decisions, possible courses of action.*' The counsellor communicates his or her understanding of the various options perceived by the client and his or her feelings (such as fear or uncertainty) about implementing them, but does not recommend particular choices or try to minimize any ambivalent feelings.

'*Then comes one of the fascinating aspects of such therapy, the initiation of minute, but highly significant, positive actions.*' Rogers gives the example of a very withdrawn secondary school boy who spends a whole session 'giving all the reasons why he would be too terrified to accept a social invitation', and leaves the office doubtful about going. The counsellor does not urge him, recognizing that he may not be able to take this step. The client goes to the party, which adds greatly to his self-confidence.

'*There is . . . a development of further insight – more complete and accurate self-understanding as the individual gains courage to see more deeply into his own actions.*'

'*There is increasingly integrated positive action on the part of the client. There is less fear about making choices, and more confidence in self-directed action. The counselor and client are now working together in a new sense. The personal relationship between them is at its strongest. Very often the client wants for the first time to know something of the clinician as a person.*'

'*There is a feeling of decreasing need for help, and a recognition on the part of the client that the relationship must end.*' The counsellor recognizes and accepts these attitudes, neither urging the client to leave nor trying to prolong the therapy. The client may express personal feelings of closeness and appreciation, which the counsellor may reciprocate.

Again, Rogers points out that the steps he has outlined may vary. But he maintains his belief that the therapy he has described is an orderly and 'even a predictable process in its major outlines', one which applies to a variety of problems and situations – parents and children, marital counselling, difficult vocational choice and other individual conflicts – and a process which 'has sufficient unity to provide suitable hypotheses for experimental tests' (1942: 44–5).

FIVE. This last statement points to another significant step taken by Rogers, systematically following up the way therapy was practised with research done to confirm or deny the validity of the hypotheses on which the practice was based.

Rogers's 1942 book, *Counseling and Psychotherapy*, summarized research projects on phases of psychotherapy in the treatment of adolescent girls, on the relationship between some basic capacities of the individual and the effectiveness of counselling, and on the development of a measure to compare directive and non-directive counselling interviews. The latter was part of E.H. Porter, Jr.'s 1941 PhD dissertation, 'The development and evaluation of a measure of counseling interview procedures', later summarized in a journal (Porter, 1943). Categorizing the statements in nineteen phonographically recorded interviews, Porter unveiled sharp contrasts between directive and non-directive counselling approaches.

A number of other graduate students at Ohio State University made contributions to the investigation of client-centred hypotheses.

Bernard J. ('Bud') Covner was a student of Rogers in Rochester, New York and followed him to Ohio State University, where he was indispensable in setting up the technology for making sound recordings of interviews. Covner (1942, 1944a, 1944b) also documented, in his doctoral dissertation and in four published articles, the inadequacy of notes compared with electronic recording.

William U. Snyder (1945) studied client and counsellor data in non-directive therapy. He found that 'the nondirective therapist uses a clearly defined method of counseling and . . . that there is a predictable process of therapy for the client' (Seeman and Raskin, 1953). Gump, Curran, Raimy and other Ohio State students also carried out significant studies, many of which were summarized by Seeman and Raskin. These individual investigations were pioneering efforts in the establishment of the field of psychotherapy research. Later, at the University of Chicago and the University of Wisconsin, individual students and staff members worked on different aspects of the same data, so that the research became cooperative and programmatic.

SIX. Rogers believed in the importance of using verbatim recordings of interviews in conducting research on the process of counselling and psychotherapy.

In a radical departure from the usual abbreviated and subjective accounts of therapy, approximately 40 per cent of *Counseling and Psychotherapy* was made up of the word-for-word transcript of the eight-interview case of Herbert Bryan. Rogers summarized the feelings and attitudes expressed by the client in the first and last interviews and made dozens of observations throughout the course of treatment but, having access to the verbatim account, the reader was able independently to judge the validity of Rogers's conclusions.

Move to the University of Chicago

Following the attack on Pearl Harbor, the United States declared war on Japan in December 1941. Rogers was asked to serve as Director of Counseling Services for the United Services Organization. Part of his job was to set up training courses for volunteers which included basic counselling principles. During his year of service on this job, in 1944–5, he conducted workshops or gave talks and demonstrations to perhaps 5,000 workers. In the summer of 1944, Rogers had been a visiting professor at the University of Chicago. He greatly impressed Dean Ralph Tyler, who offered him the opportunity to establish a university counselling centre, based on client-centred principles. Rogers accepted and he moved to Chicago during the summer of 1945, remaining there until 1957, when he accepted a position at the University of Wisconsin.

Several big steps were taken in the development of the client-centred approach during these years. Rogers's book, *Client-Centered Therapy*, published in 1951, documents these changes, and his Preface to the volume conveys their spirit:

> This book is about the suffering and the hope, the anxiety and the satisfaction, with which the therapist's counseling room is filled. It is about the uniqueness of the relationship each therapist forms with each client. . . . This book is about the highly personal experiences of each one of us. It is about a client in my office who sits there by the corner of the desk, struggling to be himself, yet deathly afraid of being himself – striving to see his experience as it is, wanting to *be* that experience, and yet deeply fearful of the prospect. The book is about me, as I sit there with that client, facing him, participating in that struggle as deeply and as sensitively as I am able. It is about me as I try to perceive his experience, and the meaning and the feeling and the taste and the flavor that it has for him. It is about me as I bemoan my very human fallibility in understanding that client, and the occasional failures to see life as it appears to him, failures which fall like heavy objects across the intricate, delicate web of growth which is taking place. It is about me as I rejoice at the privilege of being a midwife to a new personality – as I stand by with awe at the emergence of a self, a person, as I see a birth process in which I have had an important and facilitating part. It is about both the client and me as we regard with wonder the potent and orderly forces which are evident in this whole experience, forces which seem deeply rooted in the universe as a whole. The book is, I believe, about life, as life vividly reveals itself in the therapeutic process – with its blind power and its tremendous capacity for destruction, but with its overbalancing thrust toward growth, if the opportunity for growth is provided . . . the book also expresses our growing conviction that though science can never make therapists, it can help therapy; that though the scientific finding is cold and abstract, it may assist us in releasing forces that are warm, personal, and complex; and that though science is slow and fumbling, it represents the best road we know to the truth, even in so delicately intricate an area as that of human relationships.
>
> Again the book is about these others and me as we go about our daily tasks and find ourselves compellingly influenced by the therapeutic experience of which we have been a part. It is about each of us as we try to teach, to lead groups, to consult with industry, to serve as administrators and supervisors, and find we can no longer function as we formerly did. It is about each of us as we try to face up to the internal revolution which therapy has meant for us: the fact that we can never again teach a class, chair a committee, or raise a family without having our behavior profoundly influenced by a deep and moving experience which has elements of commonality for all of us. (Rogers, 1951a: x–xi)

This deeply felt Preface signals the following four (Seven to Ten) significant steps in the history of this orientation:

SEVEN. Therapy is conceived as being more than a practical way of helping people; it has the potential to be a deeply moving experience for both client and therapist.

Rogers's Preface demonstrates powerfully the depth of the experience for the therapist. *Client-Centered Therapy* includes a long Chapter 3 (pp. 65–130) on 'The therapeutic relationship as experienced by the client'. Rogers cites the observations of a number of clients in their own words. Here is part of one woman's account written after the conclusion of therapy:

> My memory of several interviews is so vivid that I have thought of them often since the final counseling session. I shall never forget the happiness, excitement,

elation, and peak of self-satisfaction I felt during the first part of the seventh interview when I had just come from proving to myself that I could face in the presence of someone other than the counselor the feeling that had been with me for years: that everyone thought I had expressed homosexual tendencies. I felt that it was the first evidence of the fact that I could find out what I was apart from what people thought I was – or rather, apart from what I thought they thought I was. I remember how keenly I felt my own pleasure reflected in the eyes of the counselor whom I was looking at directly for the first time in any interview. That in itself was something I had wanted to do very much since the first hour. During this interview I thought for the first time of the end of counseling; before that I could not believe that anyone would willingly remove himself from such a safe, satisfying situation. (Rogers, 1951a: 84)

EIGHT. The client's struggle is conceptualized as going beyond the search for solutions to problems. It has to do with the struggle to be oneself, and to live one's experience.

This represents a fundamental advance over the formulation of client progress contained in *Counseling and Psychotherapy* (1942), which was described in terms of gaining insight and taking actions to resolve problems with which the client began therapy or to redefine issues. *Client-Centered Therapy* (1951) puts forward in depth and detail, in theory and in practice, the idea that it is the modification of self-perception that represents the core change in psychotherapy. There were precursors. Rogers's (1931) doctoral dissertation, 'Measuring personality adjustment in children nine to thirteen years of age', relied heavily on the child's conscious attitudes toward self. Victor Raimy completed a doctoral dissertation in 1943 at Ohio State University on 'Self-reference in counseling interviews'. Seeman and Raskin noted that 'the main significance in Raimy's study is probably not to be found in his empirical results' (which showed a shift from self-disapproval to self-approval in successful therapy) 'but rather in the comprehensive formulation of an important aspect of self-theory. Raimy focussed on learnings about the self as being the key type of learning in therapy' (1953: 209).

When Barrett-Lennard (1979: 184) summarized the development of self-theory in client-centred therapy from the 1940s to the 1960s he wrote:

> The development of self-theory had begun with Raimy's dissertation and was first focussed on by Rogers in an address he gave in 1947 – as retiring President of the American Psychological Association – under the title, *Some Observations on the Organization of Personality*. By 1948, Raskin was able to say that 'The client's concept of self is now believed to be the most central factor in his adjustment and perhaps the best measure of his progress in therapy.' Two articles, by Elizabeth Sheerer and by Dorothy Stock, in the 1949 'parallel studies' project focussed directly on self-attitudes and feelings. . . . Rogers's nineteen-proposition statement was a further order of development and established his school of therapy as a new source of an articulated, psychological perspective on human personality and nature.

NINE. Rogers put forward a nineteen-proposition theory of personality to accompany his theory of therapy.

Barrett-Lennard was referring to the nineteen-proposition Theory of Personality and Behavior which constitutes Chapter 11 of *Client-Centered*

Therapy. Most of the nineteen propositions are directly related to the self-concept. An example is Proposition IX: '*As a result of interaction with the environment, and particularly as a result of evaluational interaction with others, the structure of self is formed – an organized, fluid, but consistent conceptual pattern of perceptions of characteristics and relationships of the "I" or the "me", together with values attached to these concepts.*' It is through this kind of interaction that a child may conclude, 'I'm a bad boy.'

Proposition XVII shows how psychotherapy can facilitate the alteration of elements of the self-concept: '*Under certain conditions, involving primarily complete absence of any threat to the self-structure, experiences which are inconsistent with it may be perceived, and examined, and the structure of self revised to assimilate and include such experiences.*'

In his 1951 preface, Rogers writes of the client's struggle 'to be his experience'. He equates this with striving to be oneself. Later in the book, he gives the example of a client who can't believe people who say they are impressed with her intelligence, because her self-concept is so inferior. He describes another client with a strict moralistic upbringing who fights against the admission of her sexual cravings. As therapy proceeds, 'by means of the relationship and the counselor's handling of it, the client is gradually assured that he is accepted as he is, and that each new facet of himself which is revealed is also accepted' (Rogers, 1951a: 517); these inadmissible experiences can be taken in as part of an expanded and positive self-concept.

TEN. Rogers sees the growth force in the client as rooted in a drive for order in the universe.

This idea was mentioned by Rogers in his Preface to *Client-Centered Therapy*, but was not developed in the main text of the book. In 1952 he participated in a conference on creativity at Ohio State University and later expanded his remarks into a paper which included the following: 'The mainspring of creativity appears to be the same tendency which we discover so deeply as the curative force in psychotherapy – *man's tendency to actualize himself, to become his potentialities*. By this I mean the directional trend which is evident in all organic and human life – the urge to expand, extend, develop, mature – the tendency to express and activate all the capacities of the organism, or the self' (Rogers, 1961: 350–1). The topic was taken up by him again in a 1963 paper on motivation, was stimulated by a conference on humanistic psychology in the early 1970s, and then articulated in a 1978 article on 'The formative tendency'. In *A Way of Being* (1980), Rogers cites the impact of other disciplines on his thinking, expressing a special indebtedness to the biologist Albert Szent-Gyoergyi, and Lancelot Whyte, a historian of ideas. He concludes:

> Thus, without ignoring the tendency toward deterioration, we need to recognize fully what Szent-Gyoergyi terms 'syntropy' and what Whyte calls the 'morphic tendency,' the ever operating trend toward increased order and interrelated complexity evident at both the inorganic and the organic level. The universe is

always building and creating as well as deteriorating. This process is evident in the human being, too. (1980: 126)

ELEVEN. The therapist's empathy for the client is seen as an absorbing struggle to appreciate the client's perceptions and feelings with as much depth and sensitivity as possible.

When I was a developing therapist, the endeavour to be empathic was very meaningful to me and I wrote a paper on 'The nondirective attitude', from which Rogers quoted in *Client-Centered Therapy*:

> There is [another] level of nondirective counselor response which to the writer represents *the* nondirective attitude. In a sense, it is a goal rather than one which is actually practiced by counselors. But, in the experience of some, it is a highly attainable goal, which . . . changes the nature of the counseling process in a radical way. At this level, counselor participation becomes an active experiencing with the client of the feelings to which he gives expression, the counselor makes a maximum effort to get under the skin of the person with whom he is communicating, he tries to get *within* and to live the attitudes expressed instead of observing them, to catch every nuance of their changing nature; in a word, to absorb himself completely in the attitudes of the other. And in struggling to do this, there is simply no room for any other type of counselor activity or attitude; if he is attempting to live the attitudes of the other, he cannot be diagnosing them, he cannot be thinking of making the process go faster. Because he is another, and not the client, the understanding is not spontaneous but must be acquired, and this through the most intense, continuous and active attention to the feelings of the other, to the exclusion of any other type of attention. (Rogers, 1951a: 29)

Rogers points out that what is intended is immersion in an empathic process without the counsellor experiencing the same emotions as the client.

Although the term was not used in *Counseling and Psychotherapy* (Rogers, 1942), empathy has been a core concept throughout the history of this approach. Rogers summarized empathy theory, practice and research in a paper which became Chapter 7, 'Empathic: an unappreciated way of being' in *A Way of Being* (1980: 137–63).

TWELVE. Client-centred principles were applied to the classroom, to the workplace, to administration, to group therapy, and to play therapy, in effect constructing a person-centred approach to areas of human relations outside of individual counselling and psychotherapy, even though the phrase 'person-centred approach' was not yet being used in 1951.

At Ohio State University in the early 1940s, the client-centred approach was employed just for one-to-one counselling. Rogers seemed interested in what worked in that context. In his preface to *Counseling and Psychotherapy*, he stated his conviction that 'counseling may be a knowable, predictable, understandable process, a process which can be learned, tested, refined, and improved' (1942: ix). He exhibited no interest in possible applications or implications of the non-directive approach, and gave the impression of being aphilosophical and apolitical. By contrast, some years later, he wrote of his teaching at the University of Chicago:

> I ceased to be a teacher. It wasn't easy. It happened rather gradually, but as I began to trust students, I found they did incredible things in their communication with each other, in their learning of content material in the course, in blossoming out as growing human beings. Most of all they gave me courage to be myself more freely, and this led to profound interaction. They told me their feelings, they raised questions I had never thought about. I began to sparkle with emerging ideas that were new and exciting to me, but also, I found, to them. I believe I passed some sort of crucial divide when I was able to begin a course with a statement something like this: 'This course has the title "Personality Theory" (or whatever). But what we do with this course is up to us. We can build it around the goals we want to achieve, within that very general area. We can conduct it the way we want to. We can decide mutually how to handle those bugaboos of exams and grades. I have many resources on tap, and I can help you find others. I believe I am one of the resources, and I am available to you to the extent that you wish. But this is our class. So what do we want to make of it?' This kind of statement said in effect, 'We are free to learn what we wish, *as* we wish.' It made the whole climate of the classroom completely different. Though at the time I had never thought of phrasing it this way, I changed at that point from being a teacher and evaluator, to being a facilitator of learning – a very different occupation. (1983: 26)

I was a student in Rogers's 'Personality Theory' class and other courses at Chicago. At first, I did not like having the responsibility for my learning shifted to me. But it did not take long for this to make sense to me. Soon after, I became a college teacher myself, and was a student-centred educator for about forty years, substituting student-chosen tasks for assignments and examinations, and using self-evaluation as the basis for grades. I learned that I could trust students as I did clients, and my educational career has been as gratifying and as validating of the person-centred approach as my work as a therapist.

THIRTEEN. The therapist was seen as participating as a whole person in the therapeutic relationship.

In an address at the Menninger Clinic in 1946, Rogers had stated, 'Client-centered counseling, if it is to be effective, cannot be a trick or a tool. It is not a subtle way of guiding the client while pretending to let him guide himself. To be effective, it must be genuine.' In the early 1950s, two graduate students and Counseling Center staff members, Oliver Bown and Eugene Streich, and Rogers himself, went further and described the therapist as entering into the relationship in a much more full and personal manner (Raskin, 1952: 240–1).

Streich (1951) put it this way:

> When the therapist's capacity for awareness is thus functioning freely and fully without limitations imposed by theoretical formulations of his role, we find that we have, not a person who must follow certain procedures, but a person able to achieve, through the remarkable integrative capacity of his central nervous

system, a balanced, therapeutic, self-growing, other growth-facilitating behavior as a result of all of these elements of awareness.

Oliver Bown, who died in July 1995, was bolder than other members of the Counseling Center staff half a century ago, believing that the term 'love' was the most useful 'to describe a basic ingredient of the therapeutic relationship'. I [Bown] use this term purposely to convey a number of things:

> First, that as therapist I can allow a very strong feeling or emotion of my own to enter the therapeutic relationship, and expect that the handling of this feeling from me by the client will be an important part of the therapy for him.
> Secondly, that a very basic need of the therapist can be satisfied legitimately (or I would rather say *must* be satisfied, if the relationship is to be healthy and legitimate) in his relationship with his client.
> And, thirdly, the therapeutic interaction at this emotional level, rather than therapeutic interaction at an intellectual cognitive level, regardless of the content concerned, is the effective ingredient in therapeutic growth.

This was quoted by Rogers in *Client-Centered Therapy* (1951a: 160). He thought so much of Bown's views that he devoted eleven pages of the book to quoting them. Rogers himself strongly supported the concept of the therapist being involved as a person in the therapeutic relationship:

> Shall we view this individual [the client] as a complex and as yet unresolved equation, or shall we enter into a warm, personal, human relationship with him, a relationship meaningful to ourselves as well as to the client? Do we gain our personal satisfaction from the correct understanding and manipulation of a complex set of factors in the case, or from the experience of relating to another individual in a deeply personal way? (1951b: 171)

FOURTEEN. William Stephenson's Q-technique was adopted as a methodology to measure the client's perceived self, ideal self, and the quantitative correspondence between the two, as therapy progressed. Other techniques were employed, such as using the clients as their own controls, in a waiting period prior to therapy, to achieve a state-of-the-art methodology for research on therapy process and outcome.

In the early 1950s a grant obtained by the Rockefeller Foundation allowed Rogers and his associates at the University of Chicago Counseling Center to set a new standard of sophistication for investigating psychotherapy process and outcome (Rogers and Dymond, 1954). When the results were published, they stimulated a wealth of other projects, within and outside of the client-centred orientation.

Stephenson, a British psychologist, was on the University of Chicago faculty at the time. When Rogers learned, from a graduate student, about the Q-technique as a way of quantifying self-concept, he was thrilled. The client sorted 100 statements such as 'I am a submissive person' and 'I am afraid of what other people think of me' into nine piles ranging from 'most characteristic of me' to 'least characteristic'. The number of cards permitted to go in each pile was fixed so that the frequencies approximated a normal distribution. Each time the client did a self-sort, another one was obtained for self-ideal. This was done prior to, at the beginning of, during, at the end, and at some point after therapy. Some of the findings were that:

- perceived self changes more during therapy than during a period of no therapy, and more than for control subjects;
- there is a significant increase in congruence between perceived self and ideal self, associated with therapy;
- after therapy, clients see themselves as more self-confident, understanding themselves better, experiencing more inner comfort, having better relationships with others, being less driven, and having less need to hide aspects of self;
- with therapy, perceived self changes much more than ideal self, while ideal self becomes more attainable.

FIFTEEN. Growth in the client was seen as going beyond increased self-esteem and involving openness to experience and the willingness to be engaged in a process of becoming.

Following the large-scale quantitative study of client perceptions of self carried out at the University of Chicago in the early 1950s, Rogers immersed himself in an intensive qualitative study of client transcripts and came out with a formulation on 'What it means to become a person', which included this cluster of concepts:

The experiencing of feeling
The discovery of self in experience
Openness to experience
Trust in one's organism
An internal locus of evaluation
Willingness to be a process. (Rogers 1961: 107–24)

Taken together, these concepts mean that the person is constantly evolving, taking in what happens as he or she interacts with people, and can make mistakes without general devaluation. There is an immersion of self in whatever is going on and less concern with the evaluation of others, consequently greater enjoyment of interaction with others, and more possibility of learning and growing. These ideas were contained in a talk given in 1954 by Rogers at Oberlin College in Ohio.

In 1957, after twelve years at the University of Chicago, Rogers accepted a position as a professor of both psychology and psychiatry at the University of Wisconsin, which he and his wife, Helen, had attended as undergraduates. 'Openness to experiencing' became the central concept in assessing client progress in the University of Wisconsin project which applied the person-centred approach to a schizophrenic population. The focus was on 'the degree to which the client is open to his feelings, able to own them, and to explore them in search of their personal meaning' (Rogers et al., 1967: 74).

SIXTEEN. Rogers formulated the 'necessary and sufficient conditions of therapeutic personality change' (1957).

There is probably nothing for which Rogers is better known than the triad of therapist-offered conditions of empathy, congruence and unconditional positive regard. Just as his very clear formulation of the client-centred approach had provided a basis for research, debate and discussion by therapists of diverse orientations, his 'necessary and sufficient conditions', a challenging set of concepts which were also carefully defined and capable of quantification, have stimulated hundreds of articles, convention programmes and research projects by theorists and practitioners of many different persuasions. Barrett-Lennard's Relationship Inventory, one of the instruments designed to measure these conditions, somewhat modified, has been used in hundreds of research projects, not just in the context of psychotherapy, but in parent–child, student–teacher, worker–employer, and other human relations applications (Barrett-Lennard, 1986).

SEVENTEEN. Rogers (1959) wrote 'A theory of therapy, personality, and interpersonal relationships, as developed in the client centered framework' for Sigmund Koch's *Psychology: A Study of a Science.*

This was the most rigorous exposition of Rogers's theories. In a diagrammatical representation of his formulation, 'A Theory of Therapy' is shown at the centre, with four other sets of theories surrounding the central theory on four sides and growing out of it. These are 'A Theory of Interpersonal Relationships', 'A Theory of Personality', 'A Theory of the Fully Functioning Person', and 'Theoretical Implications for Various Human Activities'. These include Family Life, Education and Learning, Group Leadership, and Group Conflict. This cluster of applications demonstrates the importance Rogers attached to the implications of the core principles of client-centred therapy and foretold the direction of his efforts during the remainder of his life, which ended in February 1987.

Move to California

After spending a total of twenty-three years at three major American universities (Ohio State 1940–44; Chicago, 1945–57; and Wisconsin, 1957–63) Rogers, a youthful sixty-one years of age, finally accepted the standing invitation of Richard Farson, who had been a student in Chicago, to join him at the Western Behavioral Sciences Institute (WBSI) in La Jolla, California. The institute was a non-profit organization devoted to humanistically oriented research in interpersonal relationships, and to facilitating constructive changes in these relationships. The inducement was freedom, and Rogers had been feeling quite constrained in academia. Kirschenbaum (1979: 316–17), in his important biography, *On Becoming Carl Rogers*, quotes Carl's second thoughts after rejecting still another invitation from Farson:

> What was a university, at this stage of my career, offering me? I realized that in my research it offered no particular help; in anything educational, I was forced to fit my beliefs into a totally alien mode; in stimulation, there was little from my colleagues because we were so far apart in thinking and in goals. On the other

hand, WBSI offered complete freedom with no bureaucratic entanglements . . . the opportunity to facilitate learning without becoming entrapped in the anti-educational jungle of credits, requirements, examinations, and . . . degrees.

In a letter addressed to friends, Rogers added:

It offers the complete and untrammeled freedom for creative thought of which every scholar dreams. . . . It means freedom from all routine responsibilities – committees, department meetings, budgets, requisitions, and the like. It fits my desire . . . to devote myself more to study, thinking, stimulating personal interactions, a modest amount of group or individual therapy, and writing. . . .

In the Institute we will also have the opportunity of approaching the whole problem of professional education (and perhaps education more broadly) from newer perspectives. Thus, personal experiential learning, as it is being developed in workshops, group dynamics labs and such, can be tried out experimentally . . . in a climate in which individuals are not subjected to the inhibiting effects of exams, grades, and degrees, which are so irrelevant to this type of learning. It should be an opportunity to develop a truly *integrated* professional learning, in which the cognitive and the affective are interwoven.

One of Rogers's last projects at Wisconsin was a week-long psychotherapy workshop in July 1963 in which 'the cognitive and the affective' were truly interwoven. The workshop represented a transition from the quantitative study of individual psychotherapy which had absorbed so much of Rogers's time and energy towards immersion in a group process, evaluated largely by the participants in their own terms.

EIGHTEEN. Rogers made group experiences and educational reform his primary foci.

In the foreword to *Carl Rogers on Encounter Groups* (1970: v), Rogers wrote:

For more than thirty-five years, individual counseling and psychotherapy were the main focus of my professional life. But nearly thirty-five years ago I also experienced the potency of the changes in attitudes and behavior which could be achieved in a group. This has been an interest of mine ever since. However, only in the past seven or eight years has it become one of the two primary foci of my work – the other being the crucial need for greater freedom in our educational institutions.

Rogers felt very strongly about the stultifying effects of traditional methods of education, with its top-down orientation. He was directly involved in efforts to transform two entire school systems, and published two editions of *Freedom to Learn* (1969, 1983). The first edition included a paper, 'Current assumptions in graduate education: a passionate statement', which had been rejected by the *American Psychologist* as being too controversial and potentially divisive! The second edition of the book, *Freedom to Learn for the '80s*, included a description of attempts to use person-centred principles to bring about changes in a number of educational organizations, including an inner city school system and a big city parochial complex. Rogers described himself as an active observer in the first and as one of a large group of facilitators from the Center for Studies of the Person in the second experiment.

In his 'passionate' paper on graduate education, Rogers was critical of the passive nature of the learning process, the emphasis on evaluation, the prevalence of orthodoxy and the lack of encouragement of creativity. With regard to the experiments in changing educational organizations, Rogers wrote in most detail about the two projects in which he had been most directly involved. He described his efforts and the others involved in a total of six undertakings as having short-lived success, offering this explanation of the disappointing results:

> When an organization is truly democratic, when persons are trusted and empowered to act freely and responsibly, this poses an enormous threat to conventional institutions. Our culture does not as yet believe in democracy. Almost without exception the 'establishment' – and the people – believe in a pyramidal form of organization, with a leader at the top, who controls his or her subordinates, who in turn control those further down the line. When some form of organization, other than authoritarian, flourishes and succeeds, it challenges a way of being that is deeply rooted in our society. (1983: 245)

The general encounter group movement had considerably greater success than the educational experiments. In this book, characteristically, Rogers looked for order in the phenomenon he was observing. Some of the steps he distinguished in intensive groups were:

- milling around;
- resistance to personal expression or exploration;
- description of past feelings;
- expression of immediate interpersonal feelings in the group;
- the development of a healing capacity in the group;
- self-acceptance and the beginning of change;
- the expression of positive feelings and closeness;
- behaviour changes in the group.

Rogers often wrote in a personal style. But Chapter 3 of *Carl Rogers on Encounter Groups*, 'Can I be a facilitative person in a group?', is unusually frank and self-disclosing. He writes that he delayed for more than a year in producing it, because he backed away from writing a homogenized chapter on 'The facilitation of encounter groups', or even one on 'My way of facilitating a group', because that still had the ring of an expert. He wanted to express his strengths, his weaknesses and his uncertainties, and the fact that he was involved in an ongoing process that could best be captured in a question.

Rogers states that, while his basic philosophy in a group does not differ from what it had been for years in individual therapy,

> my behavior is often quite different in a group from what it used to be in a one-to-one relationship. I attribute this to the personal growth experienced in groups. . . . My hope is gradually to become as much a participant in the group as a facilitator. This is difficult to describe without making it appear that I am consciously playing two different roles. If you watch a group member who is

honestly being himself, you will see that at times he expresses feelings, attitudes, and thoughts primarily directed toward facilitating the growth of another member. At other times, with equal genuineness, he will express feelings or concerns which have as their obvious goal the opening of himself to the risk of more growth. This describes me too, except that I know I am likely to be the second, or risking, kind of person more often in the later than in the earlier phases of the group. Each facet is a real part of me, not a role. (1970: 45–6)

Listening remains vital to Rogers in the group situation:

I listen as carefully, accurately, and sensitively as I am able, to each individual who expresses himself. Whether the utterance is superficial or significant, I *listen*. To me the individual who speaks is worthwhile, worth understanding . . . I wish very much to make the climate psychologically safe for the individual. I want him to feel from the first that if he risks saying something highly personal, or absurd, or hostile, or cynical, there will be at least one person in the circle who respects him enough to hear him clearly and listen to that statement as an authentic expression of himself . . . I would like the individual to feel that whatever happens *to* him or *within* him, I will be psychologically very much *with* him in moments of pain or joy . . . I think I can usually sense when a participant is frightened or hurting, and it is at those moments that I give him some sign, verbal or nonverbal, that I perceive this and am a companion to him as he lives in that hurt or fear. (1970: 47–8)

Later, Rogers declares that 'my attempt to understand the exact meaning of what the person is communicating is the most important and most frequent of my behaviors in a group' (ibid: 51). He also felt more free to express himself as a person in the group situation:

I have learned to be more and more free in making use of my own feelings as they exist in the moment, whether in relation to the group as a whole, or to one individual, or to myself . . . I trust the feelings, words, impulses, fantasies, that emerge in me. In this way I am using more than my conscious self, drawing on some of the capacities of my whole organism. For example, 'I suddenly had the fantasy that you are a princess, and that you would love it if we were all your subjects.' (ibid:52, 53)

This trust in self articulated by Rogers looks like a good example of historical step Thirteen above: 'The therapist was seen as participating as a whole person in the therapeutic relationship', with supporting statements by Streich, Bown, and Rogers himself in the context of the individual therapy situation. Twenty years later, with the move to California, and as a facilitator of groups, he was able to live the principle more fully.

NINETEEN. The concept of the 'person'.

A number of the historical steps described above have dealt with the concept of self – its use in theory, practice and research. Steps Eight, Nine, Fourteen and Fifteen begin with work done in the 1940s in which self-concept was deemed the most central construct for understanding clients. The concept occupied a substantial part of Rogers's nineteen-proposition Theory of Personality, and embraced a large body of quantitative research, much of it utilizing William Stephenson's Q-sort.

Step Fifteen marks a very significant development. It stemmed from Rogers putting aside the statistical data on self-concept and self-ideal and immersing himself in a qualitative study of client transcripts. The resulting formulation and talk at Oberlin College in 1954 were called 'What it means to become a person', and included a group of concepts which focused on a self becoming actualized, by reason of being increasingly open to the individual's experience of self and others, and trusting that experience. There was an image of an individual who is constantly evolving, taking in what happens as he or she interacts with people, who is able to make mistakes without self-disparagement. There is an immersion of self in whatever is going on and less concern with achievement and the evaluation of others.

A journal article by Rogers published in 1964, 'Toward a modern approach to values: the valuing process in the mature person', clarifies the link between the concepts of self and of person (the article was reproduced in *New Directions in Client-Centered Therapy*, 1970, edited by Hart and Tomlinson): The 'person' is an individual who is growing significantly in the ability to be more truly himself by virtue of changes in his value system. Rogers sees a 'surprising commonality' in the value directions of maturing clients:

- They tend to move away from facades . . .
- They tend to move away from 'oughts . . .'
- They tend to move away from meeting the expectations of others . . .
- Being real is positively valued . . .
- Self-direction is positively valued . . .
- One's self, one's own feelings come to be positively valued . . .
- Being a process [rather than desiring some fixed goal] is positively valued . . .
- Sensitivity to others and acceptance of others is positively valued . . .
- Deep relationships are positively valued . . .
- Perhaps more than all else, the client comes to value an openness to all of his inner and outer experience . . . (Rogers, 1964: 165–6)

The concept of 'person' connotes both an individual who deserves respect and who, being more fully realized, is more interested in and able to contribute to others. In 1978 I summarized some of the ways the person-centred approach had given meaning to the concept of the 'person'.

A person should be listened to, sensitively, respectfully.
A person merits a unique kind of respect regardless of age, degree of intelligence, or social status . . .
A person has strength, great capacities which can be loosed if he or she experiences empathy in a non-possessive, caring, and genuine relationship.
A person has choices which can represent increasingly the expression of her own unique self and which deserve to be supported.
Each person can be a rich source of experience for himself and others.
Each person has the potential to be a powerful social influence. (Raskin, 1978)

When Rogers wrote about 'the person' it was usually in the context of 'the emerging person' or 'the person of tomorrow'. In *A Way of Being* he lists the qualities of the 'person of tomorrow':

- Openness
- Desire for authenticity
- Skepticism regarding science and technology
- Desire for wholeness
- The wish for intimacy
- Process persons
- Caring
- Attitude toward nature
- Anti-institutional
- The authority within
- The unimportance of material things
- A yearning for the spiritual. (1980: 350–2)

Julius Seeman built a distinguished professional career for well over a quarter of a century investigating personality integration. In addition to carrying out his own research, often in collaboration with associates and graduate students, he studied a variety of sources, not restricting himself to investigators identified with the person-centred approach. He drew upon the work of Heinz Hartmann, Erik Erikson, Jane Loevinger, Marie Jahoda, Brewster Smith, Robert White and many others. His review of the literature and of his own research led him to an affirmation of 'the congruence between Rogers's original formulation [of the fully functioning person] and the subsequent empirical inquiry'. Consistent with Rogers's thinking, Seeman found that high-functioning persons are healthier, are more efficient in their perception of reality, have superior environmental contact, a high degree of self-esteem, confidence and trust in themselves, and possess a sense of autonomy that facilitates the development of caring and generative relationships (Seeman, 1984: 150–2)

TWENTY. The concept of community.

Just as the concept of self expedited the development of the concept of the person, the latter stimulated ideas about community in the person-centred approach. The person, or fully functioning person, is seen as someone who cares about others, is interested in close relationships and values open, experiential process. A natural result is a community with shared interests and values.

The term or concept of community is used in at least six different ways in the person-centred movement:

- At a particular workshop or conference, there may be fifty, a hundred, or several hundred individuals who have come together for the weekend, a week, or some other time span. In addition to the specific activities (individual presentations, panels, small group meetings, meetings of the entire group), there is *the possibility of the group as a whole developing a sense of community during the course of the workshop or conference*. At person-centred meetings, many or most of the participants would have that expectation. Some would have more individual and discrete goals.

- As part of most person-centred meetings, provision is made for times when all the participants meet with no agenda and can use the time in any way they wish. Typically, these would be daily meetings lasting one or two hours. These are called *community meetings*, and while they are often felt to be terribly frustrating, they continue to be valued as unique opportunities to create experiences or communities of the group's own design.

- *There are certain shared values regarding the organization of person-centred activities*. For example, the Association for the Development of the Person-Centered Approach has functioned for many years with no officers or elections. Different individuals volunteer to take the responsibility for future conferences, organization membership, the journal, the newsletter, etc. Any conflicts are negotiated. At most conferences, there is an assumption that the schedule may be altered, a participant may volunteer a presentation that is not in the programme, a new interest group may spring up, and so on. This is an aspect of person-centred community that has to do with organization.

- Barrett-Lennard (1994) has advanced a set of propositions on *a person-centred theory of community*, drawing upon a variety of sources, including questionnaire data collected after his participation in a 136-person, sixteen-day person-centred workshop led by Rogers and eight associates in August 1975.

- Personal relationships in the movement have developed over the course of years, stemming mostly from individuals getting to know each other in different conferences and training programmes, such as cross-cultural workshops starting in 1972, six international forums on the person-centred approach, three international conferences on client-centred and experiential psychotherapy, a series of Latin American conferences, annual meetings of the Association for the Development of the Person-Centered Approach since 1986, and a large number of training programmes in the person-centred approach in Eastern and Western Europe. These relationships have been furthered by collaboration on an article or programme, the discovery of a shared interest (e.g. poetry, children, music), visits to one another's homes, an e-mail network which started with five people in 1993 and exceeds 100 in 1996, with participants from Australia, Austria, Belgium, Brazil, Bulgaria, Canada, Denmark, England, Greece, Holland, Hungary, Italy, Japan, Mexico, Norway, Portugal, Russia, South Africa and Switzerland. Another important international stimulus has been the publications of people in the movement, particularly Carl Rogers. The result of this variety of activities and interactions is *a growing international person-centred community, with relationships that increase in breadth and depth, professionally and personally*.

• A discussion of the international aspects of the person-centred community must include the special area of *peace and conflict resolution*, Rogers's most passionate interest in his last years. In the autumn of 1986, a few months before his death, he and Ruth Sanford led highly successful workshops and large meetings in Moscow and Tbilisi, and were preparing for a third trip to South Africa, which was undertaken by Ruth Sanford in the summer of 1995.

Searching for peaceful ways to resolve conflict between larger groups became the cutting edge of the person-centered movement in the 1980s. . . . In some instances opposing groups have met in an intensive format with person-centered leadership. This has occurred with parties from Northern Ireland, South Africa, and Central America. . . . One notion is central to all these attempts at peaceful conflict resolution: When a group in conflict can receive and operate under conditions of empathy, genuineness, and caring, negative stereotypes of the opposition weaken and are replaced by personal, human feelings of relatedness. (Raskin and Rogers, 1995: 153–4)

An example is a weekend-long meeting of a group of four Roman Catholics and five Protestants from Northern Ireland facilitated by Rogers, Patrick Rice and Audrey McGaw. The early interaction was characterized by argumentative discussion of who was to blame for the violence, with different participants pointing their fingers at the wealthy class, the working class or the British Army. Then Tom recounted an incident in which his sister had been blown to bits in a street altercation and, grief-stricken himself, he had the task of informing his son of his aunt's death and then his parents of their daughter's death. 'No, it wasn't . . . , it was Margaret'. Margaret had been an especially dear member of her family. This story, told with great emotion, had the effect of transforming the group's interaction into an exchange of deeply felt fears, concerns and events, and resulted in the development of warm relationships among the participants lasting well beyond the weekend meeting. (This experience has become available as an hour-long videotape entitled *The Steel Shutter*, an expression which originated with a young teacher in the group who was describing his need to find a way to keep overwhelming emotions from interfering with his daily functioning.) (McGaw et al., 1973).

The person-centred approach as a movement

In 1990 I tried to take stock of the first fifty years of the person-centred approach, particularly in the United States (Raskin, 1990). I was of the opinion that, in the context of American academic and professional psychology, 'we are in a weak position. Compared to behavioral and psychoanalytic psychology, we have few adherents. We have hardly any doctoral training programs that allow a significant concentration in client-centered therapy and the person-centered approach. We have very little presence at general national meetings of psychologists. We are struggling to maintain a journal.' I went on to describe some positive aspects:

- The orientation is generally included in textbooks on theories of personality and approaches to psychotherapy.
- The concepts of self, self-image and self-esteem, which the movement developed in a seminal way, are in common usage.
- Programmes based on empathic listening and respect for the individual such as peer counselling and 'hotlines' for people in crisis are widespread.
- A large number of person-centred psychotherapists and educators have been successful and have won the respect of colleagues with other orientations.

I tried to account for the weakened position of the movement in the United States:

- Rogers's move from academia in 1964, and his distinctive position as a writer, leader, innovator and integrator, in relationship to other leaders of the person-centred approach who remained in university settings but did not have the same impact;
- the clarity, practicality and immediate usefulness of the techniques and research methodology of client-centred therapy in the 1940s and 1950s, affecting clinical practice and the stimulation of large numbers of doctoral dissertations;
- changes in values in recent years, causing psychotherapy and other fields to become more task-oriented and mechanized.

While the academic and professional position of client-centred therapy has declined in the United States, the same has not been true in other parts of the world. International meetings in this orientation attract significantly greater numbers than conferences in the United States. For many years, Charles Devonshire and Alberto Zucconi have had great success in organizing person-centred training programmes in Italy and other European countries. In recent years Devonshire has helped initiate new courses in Eastern Europe and his annual cross-cultural workshops, started in 1970, have been meeting in that part of the world and continue to be extremely well attended.

In personal communications, Brian Thorne and Dave Mearns have pointed out that there are 'flourishing person-centred associations in Holland, Belgium, Austria, and Switzerland', that there is a 'huge number of client-centred therapists in Germany' and that the approach is 'gaining ground in France, Greece, and Portugal'. They also cite the stronger position of the movement in European universities, such as Hamburg, Leuven, Vienna, the University of East Anglia in England, and Strathclyde University in Scotland. Thorne (1992) and Mearns (1994) are themselves responsible for training programmes at the latter two institutions and have made important contributions to the literature on the person-centred approach.

These advances in European academic and research activity are confounded by the tendency to make this orientation part of a more inclusive category, 'experiential psychotherapies'. Greenberg, Elliot and Lietaer

(1994: 510) write: 'Advocates of the experiential approaches emphasize the importance of active, process-directive intervention procedures oriented toward deepening experience within the context of a person-centered relationship. This implies that the relationship may not be sufficient for change'.

A directive dimension also characterizes the work of four Americans associated with the person-centred orientation who have had a major international impact:

- 'A felt shift' is a term for the bodily change and sense of release that accompanies the sudden new understanding of a previously unclear feeling (Gendlin, 1978).
- Tom Gordon's Effectiveness Training programs for parents, teachers and industrial managers are international in scope. Over a million parents enrolled in workshops since their inception in 1962 and more than 3.5 million books on parent effectiveness training have been sold. Effectiveness training programs have the purpose of teaching specific skills of listening and conflict resolution in various settings.
- Natalie Rogers's Person Centered Expressive Therapy Institute, based in California, also conducts programmes in other parts of the United States and in Russia, Greece, England, Mexico, Canada, and many other countries. Natalie (Rogers, 1995: 207) describes 'rebelling against . . . sitting and *talking* about life experiences and . . . *extending* the person-centered process to include the whole body and expression through the arts'. She describes the invention by herself and her associates of art projects, improvisations, guided visualizations and music to enact rage, grief, sorrow and celebration, and she has conceptualized a Creative Connection Process which makes use of different art forms to release layers of inhibitions leading to a sense of oneness.
- Garry Prouty of Chicago is well known in Europe for his pre-therapy work with difficult populations. He describes pre-therapy as a theory and methodology designed to develop or restore the reality, affective and communicative functions necessary for therapeutics with the psychotic/ retarded or chronic schizophrenic clients. It theoretically expands Rogers's contention that client and therapist need to be in psychological contact as the first necessary condition of a therapeutic relationship (Prouty, 1990). The techniques of contact reflections, contact functions and contact behaviours are utilized to achieve therapeutic readiness.

The introduction by Gendlin, Gordon, Natalie Rogers and Garry Prouty of systematic direction in their work raises an issue which divides adherents of the person-centred approach. This is true even though the interventions do not force any particular idea, feeling or action on their students or clients, and even though their purpose is to further some goal which is seen as a desirable outcome of client-centred work, such as heightened awareness, increased empathy, greater creativity and readiness for therapy. While these innovators believe they are being consistent with client-centred ideology and that they are furthering a person-centred process, other students of the approach are of the opinion that they do violence to basic person-centred tenets. Barbara Brodley (1995), Jerold Bozarth (1992), Tony Merry (1988), Ruth Sanford (1996), John Shlien (1967) and others argue with conviction that the belief in the client's capacities articulated with great eloquence by Rogers and others rules out intentional and systematic direction, strategies of confrontation or the devising of special methods for dealing with clients based on diagnostic or psychopathological assessment. Without accepting uncritically Rogers's own formulations such as the 'necessary and sufficient conditions', these individuals have done much to clarify and to shore up the importance of concepts like empathy with the client's world and self-actualization. Fred Zimring (1995) is a scientist-clinician who has creatively rethought and researched the therapy process using cognitive and experiential concepts without introducing therapist direction into the practice of therapy. C.H. Patterson (1984) has made important contributions towards validating the person-centred approach as a unique orientation.

The very first historical step articulated in this chapter was: 'Therapy is not a matter of doing something to the individual, or of inducing him to do something about himself. It is instead a matter of freeing him for normal growth and development, of removing obstacles so that he can again move forward' (Rogers, 1942: 29). While it has also been brought out here that Rogers himself became more free in his behaviour as a therapist or group facilitator, this activity did not take the form of systematic direction.

At the same time he made it clear that he was put off by the notion of creating 'little Rogerians'. He had great respect for those of his students and colleagues who departed from the client-centred approach in some form or other because of what made sense in their own experience. Many of them did, starting with William U. Snyder and Victor Raimy, Ohio State University students who made outstanding contributions to client-centred theory and research and who later became 'rational therapists', and continuing into his California period where, for example, collaborators Maureen Miller O'Hara and Betty Meador embraced the Gestalt and Jungian schools, respectively.

Other individuals like Bohart (1990) and Kahn (1994) have worked assiduously at the task of integrating person-centred theory with other orientations. G.T. (Goff) Barrett-Lennard (1986) is greatly respected across schools for his Relationship Inventory which has been used in research comparing diverse therapeutic approaches, as well as for his continuing contributions to community theory and the empathic process.

While there continues to be controversy about what is 'really' person-centred, the differing parties continue to meet together, respectfully and collegially, at the International Conferences on Client-Centered and Experiential Psychotherapy, which were held in Leuven in September 1988, then in Stirling, Scotland in 1991 and Gmunden, Austria in 1994, with Portugal scheduled as the next host in 1997. The meetings tend to be more cognitive in tone than the International Forums on the Person-Centered

Approach, which also attract participants with a range of ideologies. The forums, which schedule a daily meeting of the whole community, were initiated in the summer of 1982 by Alberto Segrera in Mexico and will assemble again in South Africa in 1998, for the seventh time.

Personal afterword

The twenty steps described here are necessarily somewhat arbitrary. The same material could have been apportioned differently, resulting in a different number. Zimring and Raskin (1992) divided the first fifty years of the person-centred approach into four major periods. Other equally qualified students of this orientation would differ about what is significant historically. Unavoidably, I was influenced by my own experience; each of us has a store of personal knowledge derived from our own participation and observation. The fact that I have been part of the movement from its beginning is advantageous in that not only do I know *about* the steps in its unfolding; I was present at or close to these events that have occurred over a span of fifty-five years. A close relationship with Carl Rogers for forty-seven years has provided a similar benefit.

Rogers's ideas, from the beginning, were revolutionary and, as a truly client-directed approach to counselling and psychotherapy, remain unique, perhaps even more than before, because of an increasing reliance on experts, and of pressures from insurance companies and health organizations to specify problems and treatments. Extremely impressive, too, is the fact that what began simply as a practical new way of trying to help an individual in therapy and seemed very much like an American phenomenon within a tradition of logical positivism, evolved into an international movement affecting education, organizational structure, and many other human relations settings, as well as a philosophy and a way of being for non-professionals. Notwithstanding a decline in influence in the United States, the importance of the concepts of self and of experiencing, of empathic listening, genuineness, and unconditional positive regard, and the usefulness of verbatim typescripts and tapes of individual interviews and group sessions, are unlikely to disappear from psychotherapy and other areas of human relations.

Support for this view comes from an unexpected source: psychiatrist Peter Kramer, author of the well-known book *Listening to Prozac* (1993). In an article called 'Rogers' due', Kramer (1995) asks, 'Why is he [Rogers] so much out of favor? Why, when we have adopted so many of his ideas, do we no longer read or teach Rogers? In his lifetime, peers rated Rogers the most influential American psychologist and the most influential psychotherapist. It seems odd that Rogers' star should be in eclipse today when his central belief, that empathy is the key to psychotherapy, is in the ascendant.'

Kramer goes on to express a profound appreciation for Carl as a person, crediting him with 'the massive infiltration of therapeutic concepts into ordinary life' and a lot more. After giving an example of one of Carl's very sensitive empathic responses, he writes, 'When we banish Rogers, we deprive ourselves of his music.'

An example of such music may be Rogers's answer to a statement by B.F. Skinner that 'The hypothesis that man is not free is essential to the application of scientific method to the study of human behavior.' The exchange occurs in 'The place of the individual in the new world of the behavioral sciences', the last piece in *On Becoming a Person* (Rogers, 1961). (Kramer is the author of the introduction to Houghton Mifflin's new edition of this work.) Rogers replied that

> we can choose to use the behavioral sciences in ways which will free, not control; which will being about constructive variability, not conformity; which will develop creativity, not contentment; which will facilitate each person in his self-directed process of becoming; which will aid individuals, groups, and even the concept of science, to become self-transcending in freshly adaptive ways of meeting life and its problems. The choice is up to us. (1961: 400)

Acknowledgement

Excerpts from Carl Rogers, *Client-Centered Therapy*, First Edition. Copyright © 1951 by Houghton Mifflin Company. Reprinted with permission.

References

Barrett-Lennard, G.T. (1979) 'The client-centered system unfolding', in F.J. Turner (ed.), *Social Work Treatment: Interlocking Theoretical Approaches*, 2nd edn. New York: Free Press. pp. 177–241.

Barrett-Lennard, G.T. (1986) 'The Relationship Inventory now: issues and advances in theory, method and use', in L.S. Greenberg and W.M. Pinsof (eds), *The Psychotherapeutic Process: A Research Handbook*. New York: Guilford. pp. 439–76.

Barrett-Lennard, G.T. (1994) 'Toward a person-centered theory of community', *Journal of Humanistic Psychology*, 34(3): 62–86.

Bohart, A.C. (1990) 'Psychotherapy integration from a client-centered perspective', in G. Lietaer, J. Rombauts and R. van Balen (eds), *Client-Centered and Experiential Psychotherapy in the Nineties*. Leuven, Belgium: Leuven University Press. pp. 481–500.

Bozarth, J.D. (1992) 'Coterminous intermingling of doing and being in person-centered therapy', *The Person-Centered Journal*, 1: 12–20.

Brodley, B. (1996) 'Carl Rogers' note on congruence', Presentation at 11th Annual Conference of the Association for the Development of the Person-Centered Approach, May, Kutztown, PA, USA.

Covner, B.J. (1942) 'Studies in phonographic recording of verbal material: I. The use of phonographic recordings in counseling practice and research. II. A device for transcribing phonographic recordings of verbal material', *Journal of Consulting Psychology*, 6: 105–13, 149–53.

Covner, B.J. (1944a) 'Studies in phonographic recording of verbal material: III. The completeness and accuracy of counseling interview reports', *Journal of General Psychology*, 30: 181–203.

Covner, B.J. (1944b) 'Studies in phonographic recording of verbal material: IV. Written reports of interviews', *Journal of Applied Psychology*, 28: 89–98.

Gendlin, E.T. (1978) *Focusing*. New York: Bantam Books.

Greenberg, L., Elliot, R. and Lietaer, G. (1994) 'Research on experiential psychotherapies', in A.E. Bergin and S.L. Garfield (eds), *Handbook of Psychotherapy and Behavior Change*. New York: John Wiley & Sons. pp. 509–39.

Hart, J.T. and Tomlinson, T.M. (eds) (1970) *New Directions in Client-Centered Therapy*. Boston, MA: Houghton Mifflin.

Kahn, E. (1994) 'Is client-centered therapy a one-person or a two-person psychology?' Presentation at 3rd International Conference on Client-Centered and Experiential Psychotherapy, September, Gmunden, Austria.

Kirschenbaum, H. (1979) *On Becoming Carl Rogers*. New York: Delacourt Press.

Kramer, P.D. (1993) *Listening to Prozac*. New York: Viking.

Kramer, P. (1995) 'Rogers' due', *Psychiatric Times*, May.

McGaw, W.H., Rice, P. and Rogers, C.R. (1973) *The Steel Shutter* (videotape). La Jolla, CA: Western Behavioral Sciences Institute.

Mearns, D. (1994) *Developing Person-Centred Counselling*. London: Sage Publications.

Merry, T. (1988) *A Guide to the Person-Centred Approach*. London: Association for Humanistic Psychology in Britain.

Patterson, C.H. (1984) 'Empathy, warmth, and genuineness in psychotherapy: a review of reviews', *Psychotherapy*, 21: 431–8.

Porter, E.H., Jr. (1943) 'The development and evaluation of a measure of counseling interview procedures', *Educational and Psychological Measurement*, 3: 105–26, 215–38.

Prouty, G.F. (1990) 'Pre-therapy: a theoretical evolution in the person-centered/experiential psychotherapy of schizophrenia and retardation', in G. Lietaer, J. Rombauts and R. van Balen (eds), *Client-Centered and Experiential Psychotherapy in the Nineties*. Leuven, Belgium: Leuven University Press. pp. 645–58.

Raskin, N.J. (1952) 'Client-centered counseling and psychotherapy', in E.L. Abt and D. Brower (eds), *Progress in Clinical Psychology*. New York: Grune & Stratton. pp. 236–48.

Raskin, N.J. (1978) 'A *Voices* editorial amalgam', *Voices*, 14: 12–13.

Raskin, N.J. (1990) 'The first 50 years and the next 10', *Person-Centered Review*, 5: 364–72.

Raskin, N.J and Rogers, C.R. (1995) 'Person-centered therapy', in R.J. Corsini and D. Wedding (eds), *Current Psychotherapies*, 5th edn. Itasca, IL: F.E. Peacock. pp. 128–61.

Rogers, C.R. (1931) *Measuring Personality Adjustment in Children Nine to Thirteen Years of Age* (Teachers College, Columbia University Contributions to Education, No. 458). New York: Bureau of Publications, Teachers College, Columbia University.

Rogers, C.R. (1942) *Counseling and Psychotherapy*. Boston, MA: Houghton Mifflin.

Rogers, C.R. (1947) 'Some observations on the organization of personality', *American Psychologist*, 2: 358–68.

Rogers, C.R. (1951a) *Client-Centered Therapy*. Boston, MA: Houghton Mifflin.

Rogers, C.R. (1951b) 'Where are we going in clinical psychology?', *Journal of Consulting Psychology*, 15: 171–7.

Rogers, C.R. (1957) 'The necessary and sufficient conditions of therapeutic personality change', *Journal of Consulting Psychology*, 21: 95–103.

Rogers, C.R. (1959) 'A theory of therapy, personality, and interpersonal relationships, as developed in the client-centered framework', in S. Koch (ed.), *Psychology: A Study of a Science*, Vol. 3: *Formulations of the Person and the Social Context*. New York: McGraw-Hill. pp. 184–256.

Rogers, C.R. (1961) *On Becoming a Person*. Boston, MA: Houghton Mifflin.

Rogers, C.R. (1964) 'Toward a modern approach to values: the valuing process in the mature person', *Journal of Abnormal and Social Psychology*, 68(2): 160–7.

Rogers, C.R. (1969) *Freedom to Learn*. Columbus, OH: Charles E. Merrill.

Rogers, C.R. (1970) *Carl Rogers on Encounter Groups*. New York: Harper & Row.

Rogers, C.R. (1978) 'The formative tendency', *Journal of Humanistic Psychology*, 18: 23–6.

Rogers, C.R. (1980) *A Way of Being*. Boston, MA: Houghton Mifflin.

Rogers, C.R. (1983) *Freedom to Learn for the '80s*. Columbus, OH: Charles E. Merrill.

Rogers, C.R. and Dymond, R.F. (eds) (1954) *Psychotherapy and Personality Change*. Chicago: University of Chicago Press.

Rogers, C.R., Raskin, N.J., Seeman, J., Sheerer, E.T., Stock, D., Haigh, G., Hoffman, A.E. and Carr, A.C. (1949) 'A coordinated research in psychotherapy', *Journal of Consulting Psychology*, 13: 149–220.

Rogers, C.R., Gendlin, E.T., Kiesler, D.J. and Truax, C.B. (eds) (1967) *A Study of Psychotherapy with Schizophrenics*. Madison, WI: University of Wisconsin Press.

Rogers, N. (1995) 'The creative journey', in M.M. Suhd (ed.), *Positive Regard: Carl Rogers and other Notables He Influenced*. Palo Alto, CA: Science and Behavior Books. pp. 175–224.

Sanford, R. (1995) 'On becoming who I am . . .', in M.M. Suhd (ed.), *Positive Regard: Carl Rogers and Other Notables He Influenced*. Palo Alto, CA: Science and Behavior Books. pp. 373–438.

Seeman, J. (1984) 'The fully functioning person: theory and research', in R.F. Levant and J.M. Shlien (eds), *Client-Centered Therapy and the Person-Centered Approach*. New York: Praeger. pp. 150–2.

Seeman, J. and Raskin, N.J. (1953) 'Research perspectives in client-centered therapy', in O.H. Mowrer (ed.), *Psychotherapy, Theory and Research*. New York: Ronald Press. pp. 205–34.

Shlien, J.M. (1967) 'A client-centered approach to schizophrenia: first approximation', in C.R. Rogers and B. Stevens (eds), *Person to Person: The Problem of Being Human*. Lafayette, CA: Real People Press. pp. 151–65.

Snyder, W.U. (1945) 'An investigation of the nature of nondirective psychotherapy', *Journal of General Psychology*, 33: 193–223.

Streich, E.R. (1951) 'The self-experience of the client-centered therapist', Unpublished paper, University of Chicago Counseling Center.

Thorne, B. (1992) *Carl Rogers*. London: Sage Publications.

Zimring, F.M. (1995) 'A new explanation for the beneficial results of client centered therapy: the possibility of a new paradigm', *The Person-Centered Journal*, 2: 36–48.

Zimring, F.M. and Raskin, N.J. (1992) 'Carl Rogers and client/person-centered therapy', in D.K. Freedheim (ed.), *History of Psychotherapy: A Century of Change*. Washington, DC: American Psychological Association. pp. 629–56.

2

The Existential-Phenomenological Movement, 1834–1995

Simon du Plock

An existential psychotherapist might append to Montaigne's adage 'To philosophize is to learn how to die', the observation 'and to begin to learn how to live'. Such an extension should serve to indicate the highly pragmatic and educative function of the existential approach, and its concern with the fundamental questions about how men and women may come to live their lives fully and in tune with what it means to be human, rather than deny this and seek to become like an animal or a stone.

We might expect such a project, the movement through which it has been expressed, and the model of therapy engendered by it, to have had a complex gestation and development and this is indeed the case. I intend, in this chapter, to begin by setting the scene for what has become existential-phenomenological psychotherapy by considering, briefly, the philosophical roots of the approach. I will go on to discuss the various ways in which the approach has manifested itself in, in turn, continental Europe, North America and Britain. After examining some of the variations in the approach as practised in each I will outline those aspects which existential therapists hold in common and utilize as the foundation of their therapeutic practice.

Philosophical roots

Virtually all therapeutic models are in agreement that it is the relationship at the heart of the therapeutic process which is of central importance. In particular, research suggests it is the extent to which the therapist is willing and able to be mindful of the etymological roots of the term 'psychotherapy' – that is, to be attendant upon the soul or, in modern parlance, the psyche – which is the crucial factor. The subject matter of this relationship is the relationship itself in so far as it facilitates, or fails to facilitate, an exploration of the very possibilities of being human. It should not be surprising that the existential-phenomenological approach – which is grounded in an examination of relationship and has taken questions surrounding the meaning-possibilities of 'being' as its primary defining characteristic – is seen as perhaps the most appropriate and efficient by a growing number of practitioners and clients.

Existential psychotherapy stands in marked contrast to the majority of the psychotherapies which have their roots in psychoanalytic concepts. These do not normally follow the classical Freudian model of sessions four or five times weekly with a therapist sitting out of sight of a recumbent patient. Nevertheless, they do broadly subscribe to the basic psychoanalytic model of psychological functioning: that unacceptable 'instinctual' wishes are 'repressed' into the 'unconscious', from which they may only emerge disguised – generally as a symptom – and that this disguise must be stripped away, the unconscious must be made conscious for the symptom to be removed. While this is, necessarily, an oversimplification it captures the essence of the psychoanalytic process still central to the psychotherapeutic endeavour.

Existential psychotherapy challenges this essentially biological theory with an account of human life grounded in philosophy and critiques Freud's presentation of the psyche as separate from the soma, a 'psychic apparatus' which is 'extended in space' and 'made up of several portions' (Freud, 1940). Existential psychotherapists have also developed critiques of key Freudian concepts such as 'projection', 'introjection' and 'transference' and have suggested new ways of understanding the notion of the 'unconscious' and of working with dreams.

Existential therapists have not, of course, been alone in their criticisms of the Freudian model. Many psychoanalysts and psychoanalytic theorists have over the course of time found the Freudian model too restrictive to account for the phenomenon they met in their practice. Cohn (1994) states that Donald Winnicott was not content to explore the mother–child relationship only in the light of 'object relations theory', while S.H. Foulkes thought the individual an 'abstraction', believed in the priority of the group and described communication as the therapeutic process *per se* – a radical revision of psychoanalytic theory which became the foundation of group-analytic therapy. While these new conceptualizations have extended the psychoanalytic base, existential psychotherapy has attempted to challenge it in its entirety with a comprehensive theory and an alternative method.

This theory, and the method it entails, is as difficult to state briefly as its psychoanalytic counterpart and for similar reasons, since it has a long and complex genealogy and has been understood and is practised in widely differing ways by different theorists. Perhaps rather more than the psychoanalytic approach, it eschews dogma, so has not taken the form of a specific creed or orthodoxy.

It would not be accurate, either, to speak of a number of distinct schools, regularly rent by conflict and schism. Though existential practitioners hold to a number of core beliefs, in practice these may be applied in different ways. Having emphasized the diversity among them we can offer a working definition of the approach which most existential therapists would recognize as a description of their own work. The existential approach is concerned with the exploration and understanding of people's orientation to the world, to themselves, and with the clarification of what it means to be alive. Existential therapists engage in descriptive, rather than analytic, examination and clarification of the client's issues, beliefs and world-views in a manner that respects the client's autonomy. They adopt a receptive rather than a directive stance and nurture an attitude of naivety in the face of the uniqueness of the client. In this way they call attention to significant questions regarding the possibilities and limitations not only of their own practice but of the practice of psychotherapy as a discipline.

As we shall see, the existential approach, grounded as it is in an analysis of relational issues, has as much to contribute to the practitioner, the profession and the wider community as it has to the individual client.

I began quite deliberately by drawing the reader's attention to the relationship between existential psychotherapy and philosophy – and, for that matter, to its close association with literature which, unique among the therapies, has provided a conduit for its ideas. While Freud made good use of classical mythology and literature to provide evidence for a number of his hypotheses, and some critics consider his own output to have attained the status of literature, he did not set out to write literature, and nor have his followers. It is equally unlikely that contemporary humanistic therapists would recognize a fellow traveller in Montaigne, with his focus on death.

At the heart of existential psychotherapy, though, lies an activity supremely philosophical. Existentialism focuses on human existence – a word derived from the Latin *existere* meaning 'to stand out' – and phenomenology, which provides existentialism with its way of investigating the world, is an approach which is open to the 'phenomena', to what 'shows' itself, independent of our presuppositions, explanations and theories. As Cohn has pointed out, when Freud, in his *Introductory Lectures*, states that 'The phenomena perceived must yield in importance to the trends which are only hypothetical', his aim is exactly the opposite to that of phenomenology.

It is a characteristic of human existence that we can 'stand out' of ourselves sufficiently to be able to reflect on *that* we are, *what* we are, and what we *do* in a way that the 'mere' existence of animals, plants and stones does not permit. Clearly it is this focus which we discover when we turn to consider the ancient philosophies.

As Rollo May, an American existential theorist (May et al., 1958) points out, the existentialist way of understanding human beings did not begin with the existential psychotherapists. He traces it back through Pascal and St Augustine to the Socratic Dialogues. Psychotherapy trainees in North America are given very little exposure to philosophy, since their profession is generally considered to be 'scientific'. It is thus comparatively easy for them to discount their philosophical heritage. They do so at a price, however, for to dismiss philosophy in favour of science may easily lead practitioners, as it has led Irvin Yalom, a well-known psychiatrist, to describe existential psychotherapy as rather much a homeless waif. It does not really 'belong' anywhere. It has no homestead, no formal school, no institution; it is not welcomed into the better academic neighbourhoods. It has no formal society, no robust journal (a few sickly offspring were carried away in their infancy), no stable family, no paterfamilias. It does, however, have a genealogy, a few scattered cousins, and friends of the family, some in the old country, some in America. (1980: 14)

Yalom is right in his assertion that existential psychotherapy, strictly defined, is a relatively recent development out of the existential 'tradition' in philosophy and the formal existential 'school'. We shall see the extent to which he (writing in 1980) has overlooked in some respects the considerable organized interest in this therapeutic approach and will attempt some understanding of the reasons why he did so. We may begin, though, by noting the marked similarity of both objectives and practices between contemporary existential psychotherapy and its Hellenistic antecedents. Applied philosophy was always meant to have the very practical function that psychotherapy and counselling are attempting to hold in the twentieth century. As Nussbaum expresses it: 'Aristotle and others knew that where the body had a need for medicine, the soul also had a need for an art that would heal diseases of thought, judgement and desire' (1994: 40).

This art of moral education had the practical objective of achieving *eudaemonia*, the good, or flourishing, life. What this was thought to be, and the methods required for its achievement, varied from one philosophical school to another. The guidelines for Aristotelian practice are strikingly similar to those of existential philosophy: in particular we may note the injunction that the philosophy teacher's (psychotherapist's) discourse with the pupil (client) should be a cooperative, critical one promoting the virtues of orderliness, deliberateness and clarity. Though the teacher is expected to be able to offer guidance from his or her own experience, teacher and student are both active and independent. The ethical inquiry that they engage in together is seen as a 'winnowing and sifting of people's opinions' (1994: 76). Pupils were taught to separate true from false beliefs and to modify and transform their passions accordingly. The idea that emotion could be educated, rather than ignored, or merely expressed or suppressed fits well with current theory in existential therapy. At the same time Aristotle's critique of Socrates's teaching that virtue is all and can overcome anything is powerful. It is a much more realistic acknowledgement of the realities of everyday life and the recognition that practical wisdom consists not of being sufficient unto oneself, but of being connected to the world and open to the range of emotions it evokes.

While the Epicureans and Sceptics, unlike Plato and Aristotle, rejected reason as a way out of difficulties, the Stoics accepted it, though they used it in a somewhat forceful and controlling manner. Here again there are important points of contact with existential therapy, and much can be learned from Stoicism both in terms of what might be helpful and what might be abusive. Many contemporary existential therapists would concur with the view that 'daily life is not so much evil as flaccid and lazy. We get truth by toning up the muscles of the mind' (Nussbaum, 1994: 335).

The educational aspect of this therapy, as of all the other Hellenistic therapies, is very strong, but this one also emphasizes the aspect of self-scrutiny, which includes an understanding of one's relationships with others. For the Stoics the student's goal is to become his or her own teacher and student, and again this fits well with the existential model. The objective is wisdom, which is the only ultimate value and virtue and leads to *eudaemonia*, the flourishing life.

Though there are many notable similarities between Hellenistic philosophy and existential psychotherapy it would, of course, be inaccurate and arrogant to claim that the ancient Greeks were involved in the practice of existential therapy in the way that practitioners have been during the past hundred or so years. Nevertheless, what we observe is more than coincidence. Clearly the existential tradition is ageless and all great thinkers have at some point turned their attention to life and death issues.

While this is surely true, the important point is not the wholly unremarkable one that people have always exercised their minds over existential matters but that the Hellenistic philosophical schools in Greece and, later, the Roman philosophers all conceived of their discipline as a way of addressing the most painful problems of human life. They saw the philosopher as a compassionate physician whose art could heal many pervasive types of human suffering and they practised philosophy not as a detached intellectual technique but as an immersed and worldly art of grappling with human misery.

There is a balance to be struck between the view that modern existential therapy can be traced back in an unbroken lineage throughout 3,000 years of philosophy and the view that the teachings of the ancient world are irrelevant and that existential therapy owes its existence to the work of Kierkegaard and Nietzsche in the last century. Perhaps van Deurzen-Smith, a leading contemporary theorist, expresses this most helpfully

> The whole philosophical tradition is relevant and can help us to understand an individual's position with regard to existential issues. The philosophers who are particularly pertinent are those whose work is directly aimed at making sense of human existence. But the philosophical movement that is of special importance and that has been directly responsible for the generation of existential therapy is that of phenomenology and existential philosophy. (1995: 1)

Nevertheless, existential therapists in Britain and continental Europe, mindful of the grounding of their tradition in philosophy, have been, and continue to be, more open to its wisdom and its lessons than those who owe their allegiance to other perspectives.

The development of existential psychotherapy in continental Europe

It is possible, if we should wish to do so, to establish a clearly demarcated beginning for the formal school of existential philosophy. Yalom does wish to do so and is surprisingly specific about it, tracing it back to the musings at a café table one Sunday afternoon in 1834 of a young Dane. Weighing on his mind this particular afternoon was the thought that he was approaching middle age and had not as yet made any great contribution to the world. He compared himself with his successful friends:

> benefactors of the age who know how to benefit mankind by making life easier and easier, some by railways, others by omnibuses and steamboats, others by telegraph, others by easily apprehended compendiums and short recitals of everything worth knowing, and finally the true benefactors of the age who by virtue of thought make spiritual existence systematically easier and easier.
>
> His cigar burned out. The young Dane, Søren Kierkegaard, lit another and continued musing. Suddenly there flashed into his mind this thought:
>
> You must do something but inasmuch as with your limited capacities it will be impossible to make anything easier than it has become, you must, with the same humanitarian enthusiasm as the others, undertake to make something harder. (1980: 15)

He realized that when all combine to make everything easier, then there is a danger that easiness will be excessive. Perhaps someone is needed to make things difficult again. It occurred to him that he had discovered his destiny: he was to go in search of difficulties – like a new Socrates.

While many shy away from reading Kierkegaard (1813–55), discouraged by his reputation as a difficult and enigmatic author, the short excerpt above should serve to indicate the irony to be relished on every page of his, frequently pseudonymous, texts. Unlike Socrates, though, Kierkegaard never had pupils to whom he might pass on his wisdom. In fact this is hardly surprising, since Kierkegaard was generally ridiculed or feared in his home town of Copenhagen for his violent railing against Christian dogma and the so-called objectivity of science (Kierkegaard, 1941, 1944). He thought that both were ways of avoiding the anxiety inherent in human existence. He had great contempt for the way life was being lived all around him. Truth, he said, could ultimately come forth only from being, not from thinking. What was most lacking was people's courage to live with passion and commitment from the depth of existence.

Nietzsche (1844–1900) took this philosophy of life further. He took as his starting-point the notion that God was dead (Nietzsche, 1961, 1974, 1986) and that it was incumbent upon people, in the absence of an ultimate law-giver, to decide how to live their lives. He formulated a philosophy of freedom that invited people to reject any rational or universal standard of morality and to discover their own will and, with it, a new power to live.

While much of the emotional impetus for existentialism is found in the work and lives of Kierkegaard and Nietzsche, its intellectual impetus is to be found in the phenomenology of Edmund Husserl (1960, 1962). Husserl (1859–1938) contended that natural sciences are based on the assumption that subject and object are separate, and that this kind of dualism can lead only to error and must be replaced by a new method of investigating the world. Prejudice and assumptions have to be put aside, in order to experience the world as if for the first time and to discover what is absolutely fundamental and directly available to us only through intuition. Instead of explaining and analysing things, we must describe and understand them.

Heidegger (1889–1976) applied this method of phenomenological investigation to reflect on the meaning of being (Heidegger, 1962, 1968). He argued that poetry and philosophy can bring greater insight into what it means to be in the world than can scientific knowledge. He also favoured hermeneutics, an art of interpretation which – unlike psychoanalytic interpretation, in which a person's experience is referred to a pre-established theoretical framework – is concerned to show how something is experienced by the individual human being.

The first direct application of Heidegger's philosophy to the treatment of psychological traditions came about with the work of Ludwig Binswanger (1881–1966), a psychiatrist who had become frustrated with the limitations of Freudian psychoanalysis. As he expressed it:

> The existentialist research orientation in psychiatry arose from dissatisfaction with the prevailing efforts to gain scientific understanding in psychiatry. . . . Psychology and psychotherapy as sciences are admittedly concerned with 'man', not at all primarily with mentally *ill* man but with *man as such*. The new understanding of man, which we owe to Heidegger's analysis of existence, has its basis in the new conception that man is no longer understood in terms of some theory – [be it] a mechanistic, a biological, or a psychological one. (May et al., 1958: 4)

Binswanger realized that an intellectual, systematic theory is not enough: what is needed is a new mode of understanding of what it is to be human. Binswanger was not simply antagonistic to Freud's work; indeed, Freud gives credit to Binswanger in his 'On the history of the psycho-analytic movement' (1914) for being among the first to practise psychoanalysis. It was during this practice at his clinic at Kreuzlingen in the early 1920s that Binswanger wrestled to bring together the insights of Husserl and Heidegger on the one hand and Freud on the other. The turning point came in 1922 when he read Brentano's descriptive phenomenology. Shortly after this, Husserl himself delivered a lecture on phenomenology at Kreuzlingen which Binswanger described as 'overpowering'. The application of phenomenology to psychiatry seemed to offer a great deal, particularly with regard to intersubjectivity. How, Binswanger (1963) asked, should the therapist act when patients' accounts of their own experience are confused and puzzling? The answer provided by phenomenology was that the therapist should project him or herself into the patient's experience. Such a radical answer to the problem could only have come about as a result of Heidegger's attempt in *Being and Time*, first published in 1927, to use the ontological structure of human existence as an access to the interpretation of the meaning of *being* itself. The crucial notion here was the characterization of human existence as essentially and fundamentally being-in-the-world.

While Heidegger was concerned with Being *per se* rather than with psychological issues, his work was to deeply influence both Ludwig Binswanger and the Swiss phenomenological psychiatrist Medard Boss. The 'intentional object' of Husserl's phenomenology now became a full world, and consciousness became *Dasein*. It is primarily, if not exclusively, by the analysis of a specific type of being, namely human being (*Dasein*), that Being can be understood. In Heidegger, Being assumes an active role, revealing itself to or hiding itself from thinking.

Binswanger was highly selective in his use of Heidegger's work: he made little use of being-towards-death, or guilt, but did take up the notions of facticity, thrown-ness (*Geworfenheit*) and care (*Sorge*). Interestingly, Heidegger wrote little on the social life of *Dasein* beyond a brief reference to coexistence, in which *der Mann* is a form of inauthenticity, but Binswanger was able to make use of the work of the theologist Martin Buber on relationship and the important idea that all human existence is based on encounter.

Binswanger emphasized imagery and metaphor as indispensable vehicles for phenomenology. In contrast to discursive and scientific language, these embody the authentic (*eigentliche*) language of phenomenology and Daseinsanalysis. However, unlike psychoanalysis, phenomenology does not require elaborate interpretations of dreams as being mere symbols for unconscious realities. Dreams can speak for themselves. This is a new and important emphasis in psychotherapy on the creative dynamics of the psyche. Binswanger also rejected any division between neurotic and psychotic disturbances. He believed that in the light of Heidegger's insights there were no completely meaningless experiences, since all are integral parts of the structure of being-in-the-world. This calls for a kind of interpretation that is no mere recording: it requires a theory of investigation (which in fact Binswanger was never to write, despite Heidegger's urgings) of the relationship between the symbol and the symbolized in psycho-analysis.

What of the 'unconscious'? Binswanger made use of the concept in his writing but could not, naturally, situate it within a Freudian model. The solution to this difficulty was, he felt, to be found in the generation of a better phenomenology of consciousness. 'Only he to whom the structure of consciousness is unknown talks of the unconscious.' Husserl said that the so-called unconscious 'is anything but a phenomenological nothing, but is itself a marginal mode of consciousness' (1969: 280).

Heidegger used the term *Dasein* of a being in relation to an entire world, not merely in relation to specific intentional objects. In his psychothera-peutic work Binswanger found this fruitful in interpreting the contexts of his patients' existence. *Dasein* for him involved a way of moving in the world. This may be seen in his analysis of dreams as ways of living and moving in space. To obtain a real understanding of a person one has to study primarily his or her world, not his or her organism or personality set apart from his world. The various 'worlds' for Binswanger are not separate, but regions within the comprehensive world of the person – the *Umwelt* or physical dimension, the *Mitwelt* or social dimension, and the *Eigenwelt* or psycho-logical dimension. (Van Deurzen-Smith has added a fourth dimension – the *Uberwelt*, or spiritual dimension.) Binswanger's existential analysis is not to be confused with the 'logotherapy' of Viktor Frankl which was for many years referred to by the same name. It is not unusual for commentators, particularly in America, to include logotherapy within the loose grouping of therapies they call the 'humanist-existential school', and Frankl has claimed that it constitutes the original existential psychotherapy. Certainly, this concern with meaning is of great importance to existentialists, who have even taken the position that it is only when life is experienced as devoid of all meaning that we can really begin to live (Camus, 1942; Sartre, 1938). Frankl's claim rests on his equation of existential anguish with lack of meaning and the notion that humans are essentially meaning-seeking. This thesis is an attractive one, though Frankl and his disciples have been unable to provide any coherent system whereby this insight might be used in therapy.

Logotherapy (*logos* = 'word' or 'meaning') originated in Frankl's work as a psychiatrist in Vienna in the 1920s and 1930s but is primarily derived from his experience of Auschwitz during the Second World War, where he observed that those who survived its horrors were those who were able to discover meaning in their lives. This concentration on meaning does indeed form a connection with existential psychotherapy, but Frankl's treatment methods (we might more properly call them techniques) and failure to engage with the majority of the concerns of existential phenomenology make this connection tenuous in the extreme. 'Dereflection', one of the two treatment methods most commonly occurring in the logotherapy literature, simply consists of urging patients to look for meaning outside themselves, as Frankl's own advice to a patient illustrates:

> Don't inquire into the source of your trouble. Leave this to us doctors. We will pilot you through the crisis. . . . Don't watch your inner turmoil, but turn your gaze to what is waiting for you. What counts is not what lurks in the depths, but what waits in the future, waits to be actualized by you. (1965: 365–7)

His other well-known treatment method, 'paradoxical-intention', requires phobic or obsessive patients to bring on, rather than avoid, their symptoms in order that they begin to experience themselves as in control of, and therefore responsible for, their illness. While such a technique may be effective in the context of brief therapy, it is difficult to place it in the context of an existential approach.

Frankl's own meaning, discovered in Auschwitz, was 'to help others find their meaning' (1969: 21). Paradoxically, his single-minded conviction of the importance of meaning provides the greatest obstacle to his inclusion in the ranks of the existential therapists, since it leads him to prescribe his own values and meanings to, often highly suggestible, patients rather than engage with them in an attempt to uncover their own. That this is not our only recourse when confronted by those who can find no meaning in an absurd world is illustrated by van Deurzen-Smith's account of working with an elderly and deeply depressed client (1988: 151–5). Given the opportunity to reflect on her life with a therapist prepared to challenge and to encourage her to recognize her choices and motivation, the client was able to see her life in a new light and to retrieve her basic sense of meaning.

Medard Boss (1903–90) began his medical career in Zurich and also studied in Paris, and in Vienna where he met Sigmund Freud. His scientific understanding and therapeutic career as a psychiatrist were decisively influenced by his contact with Heidegger soon after the Second World War. Already familiar with Binswanger's phenomenological understanding of the nature of being and illness, he was moved by *Being and Time* to renounce his hitherto psychoanalytically informed model of illness in favour of Daseins-analysis. His *The Analysis of Dreams* (1957b) extended enormously the possibilities of understanding human existence, both in health and illness. Yet more radical, *Psychoanalysis and Daseinsanalysis* (1957a) marked a decisive break not only with Freud's psychoanalysis and the influence of Carl Jung but even with Binswanger's psychiatric Daseinsanalysis, and Boss went on to claim that Daseinsanalysis should be used to denote only his own philosophically grounded approach.

His relationship with Heidegger entered a period of collaboration from 1959 to 1968, during which time the German philosopher held seminars for psychiatric registrars in Boss's home every few months – much of the contents of which Boss published in 1987 as the *Zollikon Seminars*. Boss's most influential work, translated as *Existential Foundations of Medicine and Psychology* (1979), provided a comprehensive critique of the traditional natural-scientific and medical way of understanding psychological illness and of human behaviour generally. When, in 1970, the Swiss Society for Daseinsanalysis was founded, followed in 1971 by the Daseinsanalytic Institute of Psychotherapy and Psychosomatics in Zurich, Boss became their lifelong president. He was also honoured abroad and was influential in the USA where, in 1971, he was awarded the 'Great Therapist Award' of the American Psychological Association.

We need to return for a moment to Binswanger's argument that dreams do not need to be deciphered but can be understood directly as part of the client's way of being-in-the-world, since this approach to dreams, and the view of the unconscious which it entails, comprises the most fundamental challenge to both Freudian and Jungian analysis. Heidegger himself, inspired by Hegel, used the term 'non-conscious', a term which immediately reminds us of Freud's unconscious; Binswanger continued to use the adjective 'unconscious', though by doing so he intended the meaning of 'unreflected upon'.

Boss jettisoned all of this, since he judged Freud's fundamental theory – that every dream has the same unconscious meaning, namely wish-fulfilment – to be incorrect. As Boss pointed out, dream phenomena do not enable us either to recognize infantile wishes as sources of dreams, nor to demonstrate the transformation of a wish into a dream. In other words, Boss's Daseinsanalysis, in rejecting the unconscious, rejects the wish-fulfilling intention of dreaming. Instead, true to the phenomenological injunction to stay with 'what shows', it considers the so-called 'manifest dream content', as this is what is actually dreamt, and ignores all the Freudian and Jungian paraphernalia of 'latent dream-thoughts', since these are added by the analyst.

As regards the 'unconscious', Daseinsanalysis discards such a hypothesis in favour of what can be observed of the behaviour of individuals. Gion Condrau, a colleague of Boss and now Director of the International Federation for Daseinsanalysis, has expressed it thus:

> The psychotherapeutic challenge is not, as is commonly thought, to make a theoretically informed guess about the unconscious motivations for such behaviours but rather to reveal phenomenologically the individuals' own lack of awareness and purposefulness in the conduct of their own lives. Following this approach, individual patients are shown, in purely phenomenological terms, how they remain closed not only to the inherent meaningfulness of all human behaviour but also, and especially, to meaningfulness of their own behaviours. (1993: 3)

So rather than talk of a hypothetical unconscious reason for the behaviour of clients, the existential psychotherapist, by staying at the level of what can be observed, can begin to explore those behaviours which are carried out carelessly and without due regard to their existential significance. The observation in the Socratic dialogues that 'the unreflective life is a life not worth living' can be seen to contain a great deal of wisdom. The area of dreams and the 'unconscious' continues to be debated among existential therapists. Young has recently argued that Boss and Condrau themselves reintroduce more than 'what shows'. Boss has been criticized for introducing a normative concept of health in *The Meaning and Content of Sexual Perversions* (1949) and *I Dreamt Last Night* (1977). Young (1993) also questions why trainee Daseinsanalysts should be examined on their ability to 'elucidate the unadulterated, essential meaning' of the dream phenomenon without reference to the dreamer's own meaning. It seems odd to suggest, as Boss does, that if several analysts analysed a single dream phenomenologically the same interpretation would be reached. As Spinelli has remarked, the notion of a single correct interpretation 'would presuppose we had access to, or knowledge of, an ultimate reality in any given situation' (Spinelli, 1989: 5). This debate continues, as does that between Smith (1994, 1995) and Spinelli (1994, 1995) on the relevance, or otherwise, of the concept of the unconscious.

Though Daseinsanalysis has achieved only a modest impact internationally, its influence in Switzerland grows apace. As we might expect, its continuing close relationship with psychoanalysis has profound implications for treatment, implications which sharply distinguish Daseinsanalysis from existential psychotherapy. From a Daseinsanalytic point of view, psychotherapy is a matter of disclosing to individuals the particular nature of the limitations and constrictions entailed by their way of being. This notion of 'disclosing *to*' the patient should alert us to a difference between Daseinsanalysis and existential psychotherapy. Daseinsanalysts speak of two different types of care which are to be found in their relationship with patients. The first, 'anticipatory care', describes the practitioner's work to enable patients to take care of themselves and is not unlike some elements of existential therapy. The second, 'intervening care', is rather dissimilar and involves the therapist in assuming responsibility for patients and giving advice, instruction and even medication – an interventionist position not found in existential psychotherapy.

Daseinsanalysts follow Freud's basic rule of free association for the patient and free-floating attention for the therapist. Terms such as 'transference' and 'countertransference' are still used, though they are understood as expressions of the patient's developing possibilities rather than as signs of the patient's unconscious wish to subvert treatment.

The most immediately obvious distinction between Daseinsanalysis and existential psychotherapy is the former's attempt to improve, rather than avoid, the use of psychopathology. Though it is highly significant that Daseinsanalysis insists upon the importance of understanding the individual in relation to their world, it continues to label the individual as schizoid, borderline or sexually perverted – classifications which seem to vastly diminish any possibility of fully engaging with the unique way of being of the other.

The European experience of the Second World War and the sweeping away of confidence in scientific progress, scientific certainty and the vestiges of religious faith, in the face of the tragic and absurd dimensions of human life, paved the way for a more widespread enthusiasm for existentialism. Nowhere was this more true than in disillusioned post-war France. Jean-Paul Sartre's famous formulation of an existential analysis in *Being and Nothingness* (1956) provided a critique of Freudian psychoanalysis and a philosophy suited to the times but does not really constitute a comprehensive method for practitioners to utilize in the way that the Daseinsanalysis of Binswanger and Boss does. While Heidegger emphasized that human beings are 'thrown' into the world, and that they must make a life for themselves using the situation, the time and the network of relationships in which they find themselves immersed, Sartre (1905–80) places greater importance on the freedom and responsibility of individuals for their existence. According to Sartre, each of us creates our own existence, and neurosis is understood as the result of attempts to hide from this frightening fact and to blame others or external circumstances for our discontent and suffering. Since mental dis-ease is, according to Sartre's analysis, simply the result of such self-deception, it follows that it is the task of the therapist to assist clients, by means of clarifying dialogue, towards an awareness of the choices on which they have based their life.

While Sartre, like Heidegger, never practised as a therapist, his ideas have been influential, and were taken up outside France by, among others, the Scottish psychiatrist R.D. Laing and his South African colleague David Cooper. It has to be said that these ideas do not make an easy read, unlike Heidegger, who uses language with Germanic precision (though his use of the hyphen may irritate rather than elucidate on occasion). Sartre employs the same terms to denote a variety of meanings at different times in his philosophical career. The untangling of these can present a formidable obstacle to the novice.

We cannot conclude our consideration of French existentialism without mention of Maurice Merleau-Ponty (1907–61) who, though overshadowed in the popular mind by his great contemporary Sartre, is regarded by some as the most important existential philosopher of all. If Sartre was influenced by Heidegger, Merleau-Ponty went back a step further to Husserl for much of the inspiration of *Phenomenology of Perception*, first published in 1945. His line of argument, though not expressed with the greatest clarity in many passages, may be summarized as an investigation of the way in which humans, through perception, attribute meanings to the world. In true existential fashion Merleau-Ponty emphasizes that since humans are actively engaged in the process of perception they can, to some extent, construct their own world. It should be stated immediately that his reasoning is very subtle and does not at all approximate the view that we can learn to take charge of our universe and order it as we wish, which is promulgated by some in the human potential movement. Merleau-Ponty's work may be better understood as a powerful critique of the behaviourist notion of a one-to-one correlation between stimulus and response. Since humans play an active role in the process of perception they are, as Merleau-Ponty puts it, 'condemned to meaning'.

More recent contributions to existential exploration continue to be based on Heidegger's work. There is a vast literature on the subject by many well-known authors such as Jaspers (1951, 1963), Tillich and Gadamer within the Germanic tradition, and Camus, Ricoeur and Minkowski (1970) as well as Sartre within the French tradition. Marcel, like Buber, has applied certain existential notions to a religious outlook.

The American therapist Betty Cannon has provided, in *Sartre and Psychoanalysis* (1991), a pioneering and comprehensive attempt to utilize Sartre's ontological (being-oriented) metatheory, primarily as he presented it in *Being and Nothingness*, to construe a system of therapy which is Sartrean rather than Heideggerian. Her objective is shared by many other practitioners who have regretted the lack of a systematic application of Sartre's ideas to depth therapy. In opening the way to such an application she has provided a service for Sartre similar to that provided for Heidegger by Binswanger and Boss.

The American scene

Much of Binswanger's work was translated into English in the 1940s and 1950s, and this – together with the immigration of Paul Tillich and other existential theorists to the USA – helped considerably in the adoption there of existential ideas as a possible base for psychotherapeutic practice (Valle and King, 1978). While the American appetite for therapy generally was expanding as never before during these years, it is unlikely that existential thought would have been taken up as widely but for the landmark publication by Rollo May, Ernst Angel and Henri Ellenberger in 1958 of *Existence*, an anthology of the work of a number of European authors, which for the first time offered US practitioners a comprehensive outline of the approach.

May's primary influence in this book was the work of Binswanger, and his two opening chapters attempted to correct the lack of awareness which Binswanger had been concerned about among American psychiatrists and psychologists of the work of their European antecedents, and in particular the philosophies of Husserl and Heidegger.

While this background knowledge was indeed missing – and continues to be so in both the USA and the UK to the extent that much important work of the European existentialists remains untranslated into English – we may trace the influence of European philosophy on the American scene via a different, and perhaps somewhat unexpected, route. As Spiegelberg (1971, 1972) notes, though the renowned American psychologist William James never refers to himself as a phenomenologist he is linked in an interesting way with Franz Brentano (1838–1917). Brentano gave a course of lectures on descriptive psychology at the University of Vienna in 1888 and 1889 in which he referred to the 'Descriptive Psychology of Describing Phenomenology'. Husserl called Brentano 'my one and only teacher in Philosophy'.

It is the concept of intentionality that links Brentano with William James, and perhaps helps to explain American receptivity to Husserl. Husserl freely acknowledged his debt to James: 'For the help and progress which I owe to this excellent investigator in the field of descriptive analysis have only aided my emancipation from the psychologist position' (Husserl, 1970). While Husserl took the term 'intentionality' and the general idea behind it from Brentano, critics have shown that his term 'intentionality' has a different meaning from that used by Brentano, for whom it indicated relatedness to an object. Husserl used it for the creativity in our acts, not a static directedness.

Spiegelberg argues that this concept of intentionality might well have had its origins in James's *Principles of Psychology* (1890), when he spoke of the goal of the mind as to take cognizance of reality, *intend* it and be 'about it'. James's chapter on conception was an important directive stimulus in the transformation of the Brentano motif (1971:116). This intellectual interchange is not at all improbable since there was well-documented contact between Stumf, a Brentano student, and Husserl and James in 1886 and 1889.

Though American interest in existentialism is apparent, practitioners in the USA have by and large given it a more pragmatic, more optimistic slant than that which the European writers intended to convey. Gordon Allport, a major figure in American psychology, illustrates this well in his comments on *Existence*:

Existential psychology tells us that Western man, in freeing himself from the drive-pressures of hunger, disease and fatigue, has run headlong into a vacuum where boredom and meaninglessness usurp his being. Only by transcending this existential vacuum can he fill his life with significance and motive. Alienation is a fact, the capacity for a self-transcendence is a fact: Man's potentiality to achieve a responsible world-design is a fact. (May et al., 1958: book jacket)

We may be reminded here of the ennui expressed by Kierkegaard in 'How Johannes Climacus became an author' (1946) and the tone of much of Nietzsche's writings. Allport's is a generally sophisticated appreciation of existential-phenomenological theory, yet his pragmatism and ebullience sit oddly alongside academic philosophy.

These few lines also serve to remind us of the difficulty of marrying the philosophical underpinnings of existentialism and phenomenology to the North American belief in the supremacy of medical science. To appreciate why this should be so, it is necessary to bear in mind that the continental tradition has been Leibnitzian, in contrast with the Lockean model which has enjoyed much influence in the Anglo-American world. The mind is represented by Locke as a passive *tabula rasa*, a conception which complements well the Cartesian-Humean model in which the object of attention is not the 'I' but mensurations, sense-impressions and cognitions. This is in direct contrast to the Leibnitzian model of the mind from which the dynamic theories of Freud, Adler, Jung, Binswanger and Boss sprang – a model which attributes to the mind a potentially active core and in which perception features as an active process.

Perhaps the most influential American to be inspired by existentialism and phenomenology was Carl Rogers, whose person-centred therapy now constitutes the prevalent humanistic therapy in the US. Rogers recognized the crucial importance in the therapeutic relationship of the patient's perception of the therapist's attitude, and his work has contributed much to the therapist's attempts to break through to those who experience themselves as radically separated from human contact. When the therapist tries to communicate to the client some of their (the therapist's) experience of the situation and of the client, the client becomes aware of the phenomenal world of the therapist – which includes them. In Rogers's theory the client, on seeing that they are 'reflected' in the world of the therapist, becomes aware of the possibility of being understood, and is, *ipso facto*, less isolated.

There are a number of such links between the phenomenological approach used by most existential therapists and person-centred therapy. Perhaps most fundamental, as Spinelli has shown, is the use Rogers makes of the phenomenological notions of *noema* and *noesis* as 'the primary means with which to maintain unconditional positive regard' (1990: 19). This unconditional positive regard is the keystone of Rogers's approach:

> I can state the overall hypothesis in one sentence, as follows. If I can provide a certain type of relationship, the other person will discover within himself the capacity to use that relationship for growth, and change and personal development will occur. (1961: 33)

This type of relationship can only be maintained if the therapist suspends judgement of the client's actions in favour of empathizing with the client's affects, or feelings, a distinction made by the phenomenologist Husserl. He posited that every act of intentionality (every mental act) is composed of two elements, the *noema* (the 'what') towards which we address our attention, and the *noesis* ('how' what happened is interpreted and 'felt'). By utilizing this contribution to existential-phenomenological theory Rogers was able to maximize the extent to which person-centred therapists are able to give unconditional positive regard.

There are also significant differences between the two approaches. While person-centred therapists generally believe that they suspend to a great extent their personal judgements of their clients, they do so against the background of a theory of human being which holds that humans are innately disposed to express their potential, and that change in the direction of expressing this potential – of self-actualizing – is central to the therapeutic process. It should be clear on even brief consideration that there are problems with this stance.

First, the underlying assumption of person-centred and other humanistic therapies that humans 'naturally' grow and develop, and struggle to do so even in the face of adverse environmental conditions, does not stand up to close scrutiny since while all living things struggle to live there is no reason to believe that they evince a predisposition of self-actualization. While we might agree with Rogers (1979) that potatoes will always shoot in the direction of light we should not confuse the growth of vegetables with the spiritual or psychological life of humans. Further, while person-centred therapists, like existential therapists, see human experience as one of constant change and variation, the importance they attach to self-actualization leads them to value clients for their ability to change in this direction – a very different thing from the existential therapist's attempt to engage with clients in order to explore their way of being in the world. As van Deurzen-Smith notes, 'people may evolve in any direction, good or bad . . . only reflection on what constitutes good and bad makes it possible to exercise one's choice in the matter' (1988: 56–7). She goes on to provide a helpful example of a client who is contemplating divorce as an answer to marital problems:

> One could implicitly encourage her to go ahead with divorce proceedings simply by consistent (and probably quite genuine) empathy. It would be easy to condone her new-found would-be authenticity and her desire for freedom by praising her for self-assertive behaviour even if it were ultimately quite destructive. Indeed, the client's discovery of her own ability to make choices rather than silently suffer and her discovery of the ability to express her feelings might seem like sufficiently valuable gains in themselves. . . . However, detaching oneself from the situation rather than evaluating it from the same position as the client clearly reveals how one-sided and erroneous such an approach would be. (1988: 57–8)

While the person-centred approach prides itself on its existential roots, it rarely pays due attention to the realities, limitations and consequences of human being in its overly-optimistic emphasis on freedom and potential. Person-centred and other humanistic theorists who attempt to dismiss

British and European existentialism as pessimistic are really missing the point – that these approaches provide a healthy corrective to a simplistic view of human nature. The more rounded perspective on what it is to be human which the European tradition, in particular, affords should not be discarded too readily.

Though Rogers has wholeheartedly adopted a number of existential insights on the importance in therapy of relationship, his inspirational, positive-reinforcement mode of working is at variance with basic existential philosophy and so his identification with this approach is necessarily problematic. His own understanding of this is clear when he remarks

> I was surprised to find, about 1951 . . . that the direction of my thinking and the central aspects of my therapeutic work could justifiably be labelled existential and phenomenological. It seems odd for an American psychologist to be in such strange company. Today these are significant influences in our profession. (1967: 378)

Rogers was not alone in consorting with 'such strange company': all the humanistic approaches have found themselves to a greater or lesser extent drawn to this philosophy and each has adopted and adapted those aspects of it with which they felt the greatest sympathy. Fritz and Laura Perls intended the Gestalt therapy which they developed in the 1940s to be a synthesis of various aspects of psychoanalysis, Gestalt psychology, and the existential/ humanistic tradition. It has been innovative in the importance it accords to the 'here and now', to feeling as well as thinking, and to active awareness rather than the passive reflection of analytic approaches.

It shares, though, many of the difficulties, from an existential perspective, of its fellow humanistic therapies – in particular with regard to its emphasis on self-actualization and in its conception of the self. Kovel, an American commentator, makes the position plain:

> Gestalt therapy is an avowedly existential approach, though with none of the gloom of 'being-in-the-world' that characterizes European existential analysis. Rather it is thoroughly, positively American – positive in its assumption (with Rogers) that the obvious, most consciously held fact is the guide to truth, positive in its assertion that excitement and growth are the key processes of the human organism, and positive in giving active permission for the patient to express, openly and in public, all felt needs and resentments. (1978: 168)

Fritz Perls expresses his contempt for Freudian concepts of regression and the unconscious even more crisply:

> A good therapist doesn't listen to the content of the bullshit the patient produces, but to the sound, to the music, to the hesitations. (1972: 57)

I share the view of many other existential therapists, though we may not express it so negatively, that a crucial part of therapy involves tuning into the client's world by attending closely not only to what is said but to the way in which it is said, and, beyond this, to the client's demeanour as a whole, but Perls's attitude to patients tended to be somewhat authoritarian and he largely discounted the dynamics of the therapist–client relationship, considered fundamental in existential practice.

Gestalt therapy has been open to the criticism that its concern with the 'here-and-now' (a term first used, in fact, by the psychoanalyst Otto Rank) precludes any consideration of past or of future. Such de-emphasis on the client's temporal context is fraught with difficulties, as the phenomenologist Merleau-Ponty pointed out:

> each present reasserts the presence of the whole past which it supplants, and anticipates that of all that is to come, and that by definition the present is not shut up within itself, but transcends itself towards a future and a past. (1962: 240)

The so-called Gestalt Prayer, with its exhortation that each individual should take responsibility for getting their own needs met, is certainly far removed from the 'gloom of being-in-the-world':

> I do my thing, and you do your thing.
> I am not in this world to live up to your expectations.
> And you are not in this world to live up to mine.
> You are you, and I am I,
> And if by chance we find each other, it's beautiful.
> If not, it can't be helped. (Perls, 1976: 4)

This, in fact, is just the point: the individual's relation to the world without which, from an existential perspective, human beings cannot be conceptualized, is swept away. To point this out is not to embark on a discussion of the merits or otherwise of selfishness or of 'doing one's own thing'; the difficulty is fundamental. As Misiak and Sexton, in their historical survey of the existential approach, state, it is a 'movement which focuses its enquiry on man as an individual person as being in the world' (1973: 84). Spinelli underlines the centrality of this when he says that one of the aims of the therapy which arises out of this understanding of human being is 'to examine, confront, clarify and reassess . . . the limits imposed upon the possibilities inherent in being-in-the-world' (1989: 127).

Being, then, is understood as boundaried by the limits of possibilities, not by their infiniteness. The Gestalt counter to these problems seems to be to have a foot in every theoretical camp and to hop about as required. The result is a merry dance but one which fails to address the concerns of existential therapists. There remains much work to be done to map precisely the areas of convergence and divergence of the two approaches. Readers are referred to the work of Yontef in the USA and Clarkson in Britain for important recent contributions to this debate.

May's work, beginning with *Existence* and going on to include *Love and Will* (1969) and *The Discovery of Being* (1983), has probably constituted the greatest authority on the approach in the USA, not least because of his unique ability among his contemporaries of bringing his personal experience (of tuberculosis as a child), his profound knowledge of the European writers – not just of Binswanger but of Kierkegaard and Nietzsche among others – and an urgent pragmatism to bear on his work. This last is particularly in evidence in his use of Tillich's *The Courage to Be* (1952) in formulating his philosophical approach to daily problems of living.

May was convinced of a continuity between Freudian psychoanalysis and the existential theorists. In particular, he traced Freud's indebtedness to Nietzsche, who showed how repressed emotions gave rise to 'bad conscience', and suggested that the territory explored by Freud had already been explored, and more deeply, by Kierkegaard. Unlike Kierkegaard and Nietzsche, who wished for no disciples, Freud had founded a secular religion. In the process, though, he systematically ordered his theories in scientific manner and made them disciplined, organized and communicable. May shared with Binswanger a frustration that, while Freud explored the *Umwelt*, he failed to examine the *Mitwelt* of man's relationship with others. Perhaps most crucially, May criticized Freud's model for objectifying the personality and reducing human beings to a collection of drives or tendencies to the extent that the individual who has these experiences vanishes.

One psychiatrist who recognized the importance to his own work of May's *Existence* is Irvin Yalom, for many years Professor of Psychiatry at Stanford University School of Medicine. In an effort to discover methods of deepening an existential approach to therapy he began using both individual and group therapy in the early 1970s with terminally ill cancer patients. Yalom declared that it was his 'belief that the vast majority of experienced therapists, regardless of their adherence to some other ideological school, employ many . . . existential insights' (1980: 5) and went on in his major text *Existential Psychotherapy* to demonstrate that these insights, far from being mere extra ingredients for effective therapy, were drawn from a rational, disciplined and comprehensive therapeutic approach. As he expressed it: 'the existential approach is a valuable, effective psychotherapeutic paradigm, as rational, as coherent, and as systematic as any other' (1980: 5).

Yalom has been a highly effective publicist of his approach to existential psychotherapy. He spoke for many when he said that 'professional existential philosophers surpass even psychoanalytic theoreticians in the use of turbid, convoluted language . . . I have never understood the reason for the impenetrable deep-sounding language' (1980: 16). Whether we view this as a shortcoming in Yalom or in the existential philosophers, it is obvious that they did not serve his purpose – the Americanization of existential psychotherapy. Few of the European thinkers whose work is included in May's *Existence* – among them writers of the stature of Binswanger, Boss and Minkowsky – have enjoyed much attention in the USA. Unfortunately Yalom may be accurate when he states the reason for this to be that 'they are steeped in a continental philosophical *Weltanschauung* far out of synchrony with the American pragmatic tradition in therapy' (1980: 17).

Only Frankl, the supremely pragmatic philosopher, earns Yalom's approbation. Though idiosyncratic, *Love's Executioner and Other Tales of Psychotherapy* (Yalom, 1989) has been enormously successful in bringing elements of the existential approach to the attention of the psychologically minded public. Its success highlights the difference between many of the European texts which are challenging – in the best sense – but discouragingly difficult for the lay reader, and the American popularization of elements of existential-phenomenological therapy which has immense appeal while frequently distorting or indeed ignoring much of the underlying philosophy or mixing it with behavioural and Sullivanian notions. Yalom's work provides an object lesson for British and continental European practitioners who should be encouraged to make their work as accessible as is consistent with the maintenance of its integrity.

It now appears that Yalom has ceased to hold the view that the existential approach constitutes a distinct way of working in the way that the psychoanalytic or person-centred approaches offer a distinct theory and methodology. Far from being the American existential therapist *par excellence* which many in Europe had understood him to be, he has confirmed that in his work as a psychiatrist he employs some existential concepts when he feels that it is necessary and, in his words, 'at some states of the therapy', and he describes existentialism as a philosophy which can underpin a variety of psychotherapeutic approaches, rather than a single approach.

Yalom's move in recent years away from psychotherapy and towards novel writing may do as much to popularize the existential approach as was achieved by him via his academic work. *When Nietzsche Wept* (1992), though based on an imaginary rather than a factual account, provides an interesting conception of the relationship between this philosopher and the other major figures of his period, among them Freud.

Clearly, while existential ideas have been enormously influential in the United States to the extent that the majority of practitioners would probably now agree that their work includes some awareness of existential issues, a radical existential approach based firmly in continental European ideas has not yet taken root. It remains unclear whether the American intellectual climate is unconducive to such an implant or whether it has simply never been presented in a sufficiently complete and systematic manner. The third option, of course, is that Yalom is correct in asserting that it is too 'un-American' to succeed, though this seems unlikely given the success of so many other imports. May himself, while continuing to refer to the existential-phenomenological tradition, moved, according to Kovel, 'towards an idiosyncratic blend of existentialism, psychoanalysis and a native American brand of pragmatism' (Valle and King, 1978: 145).

Moss reveals the reason for the uptake of what we might term a 'weak' existential approach when he states that since the publication of *Existence* introduced the existential and phenomenological perspectives to the USA 'the *meaning of the patient's experience* has been at the heart of new developments in the science and practice of psychotherapy' (Valle, 1989: 193; emphasis in original). A culture in which, paradoxically, the right of the individual to have his or her subjective experiences of the world validated, however odd or eccentric, is asserted alongside an unquestioned faith in the ability of science to make the world an ever better place, finds comfort in existentialism's concentration on individual experience and concern with rigorous methodology. So it is perfectly possible for American practitioners to take on board some aspects of the approach. There are, though, difficulties which discourage wider dissemination. The view held by many humanistic practitioners that the world is ours to manipulate and that it should, like a machine, be perfectible is anathema to existentialism, which warns against this attitude since it may lead so easily to our objectification of human beings and a belief that they can be repaired or perfected by some intervention, whether physical or psychological.

Though the work of academics at Duquesne University on the application of phenomenology and the work of other theorists such as George Gadamer and Clifford Gertz ensures the continuation of these ideas in the United States, the death in 1994 of Rollo May and the piecemeal use of aspects of the existential-phenomenological approach by many practitioners make a thoroughgoing application of it in the near future unlikely.

Developments in Britain

Britain became a fertile ground for the further development of the existential approach when Laing and Cooper took Sartre's ideas as the basis for a reconsideration of the notion of mental illness and its treatment (Laing, 1960, 1961; Laing and Cooper, 1964; Cooper, 1967). Laing studied medicine at Glasgow University but also undertook a detailed philosophical education, acquainting himself with the main contemporary thinkers, particularly in the continental tradition of existentialism and phenomenology. While training as a psychiatrist he planned to study with Karl Jsapers in Basle but was prevented by being called up for National Service. He began a psychoanalytic training at the Tavistock Clinic in 1957, entering analysis with Charles Rycroft (a member of the independent group), and supervised by Marion Milner and Donald Winnicott.

Throughout his career Laing was engaged in an intricate balancing act with a number of disparate creeds and philosophies, among which may be counted Sartrean existentialism. Freudian psychoanalysis, romantic-expressionist literature and transcendental meditation, and the meaning which he attributed to the disturbed behaviour of his patients naturally varied depending on the combination of these in ascendance at the time.

His first book, *The Divided Self: Existential Study of Madness and Sanity*, which he completed in 1957, focuses on the application of existential-phenomenological ideas to the so-called 'schizoid condition'. Laing recognized that the psychiatric terminology he had been trained to use prevented him from understanding the meaning of the patient's existence in any way other than as a clinical category. It is impossible to come to an understanding of patients when the technical terminology either isolates them or attributes a disproportionate importance to just one aspect of their being. Such false dichotomies as mind/body, psyche/soma, psychological/physical, and exaggerated attention to specific aspects such as the self or the personality encourage us to see the person in terms of abstract models. The individual is lost in this process of abstraction. As Laing expresses it:

> How can we speak in any way adequately of the relationship between me and you in terms of the interaction of one mental apparatus with another? . . . Only existential thought has attempted to match the original experience of oneself in relationship to others in one's world by a term that adequately reflects this totality. (1960: 19)

Further highly influential books were to follow in the years 1957–64. The companion volume to *The Divided Self*, *The Self and Others*, appeared in 1961, swiftly followed by three co-authored texts. *Sanity, Madness and the Family* (1964) with Aaron Esterson represents the results of joint phenomenological research on the families of 'schizophrenics' at the Tavistock Clinic and was the source of the common misunderstanding that they were claiming that families caused schizophrenia. This was to have major consequences, given the attention that Laing and Esterson paid to the role of mothers, and many feminist writers then and since have been concerned with the notion that it was in some sense the 'fault' of the mothers that 'caused' their children to become mentally disturbed. Elaine Showalter in *The Female Malady* (1985) charged Laing with being a 'manly physician-priest leading another explorer to the heart of darkness' whom he fails when 'faced with the obligation to play mother on the psychic journey'. Laing's characteristically direct response to this as 'total shit from beginning to end' was not helped greatly by his subsequent confession that he had never read the book.

Interpersonal Perception (1966), co-authored with A.R. Lee and H. Phillipson, is less remembered now but nevertheless contained important ideas about social (or interpersonal) phenomenology. *Reason and Violence: A Decade of Sartre's Philosophy 1950–60*, with David Cooper, first published in 1964, dealt with Sartre's later works, which provided one of the main theoretical influences on Laing's thinking in the early 1960s. Subsequent talks and papers were increasingly polemical and are collected in *The Politics of Experience* (1967).

The 'psychedelic model' of *The Politics of Experience* introduces the unique conceptualization of mental disturbance not as breakdown but as breakthrough, a stage in a healing process containing the possibility of entry into a realm of 'hyper-sanity' (1967: 129). Laing – with colleagues known as 'the brothers' (Cooper, Esterson, Briskin and Segal) – sought to provide true asylum for those in distress who would otherwise be admitted into a traditional psychiatric hospital. We should not understate the contrast between such asylums and the reality of psychiatric treatment at that time when insulin comas, electro-shock, physical restraint and lobotomies were often the treatment of (the psychiatrist's) choice. In comparison the asylum that was provided by Laing and his colleagues was, at least in theory, a supportive, democratic environment in which people could journey through their madness to emerge into the light of a greater sanity and self-awareness. Berke's explanation of the name 'Arbours' for the association he formed in 1970 illustrates well the philosophical and spiritual rather than intervention-ist medical goals which Laing and those around him were pursuing:

> The temporary dwelling places where the Israelites lived in the wilderness after the exodus from Egypt were called 'Arbours' – places of shade or shelter. Arbours communities aim to provide shelter and safe anchorage for people who have been buffeted by internal turbulence or external disturbance whether in fantasy or in actuality. (1979: 116)

The reality of the Philadelphia Association was often somewhat different – staff and residents were clearly distinguishable from each other, referral to psychiatric services was sometimes used in difficult situations, and those who did not make the journey might find themselves lost and alone in their despair.

The fame and notoriety of R.D. Laing acted as a magnet to students from the UK and internationally who flocked to take part in what by 1970 had become a formal training in psychoanalytic psychotherapy. Readers are referred to Robin Cooper et al., *Thresholds between Philosophy and Psychoanalysis: Papers from the Philadelphia Association* (1989) for a more detailed account of the development of the Association. Laing's appearance at the 1967 Dialectics of Liberation conference, held at the Round House in London under the auspices of the Institute of Phenomenological Studies (represented by Cooper, Berke and Redler), seemed to place him firmly in the New Left but the already volatile relationship which he had with Cooper was fractured irretrievably when Cooper identified him publicly with what he called 'anti-psychiatry'. The American psychiatrist Thomas S. Szasz rejected the term 'anti-psychiatry' on the grounds that it was 'imprecise, misleading, and cheaply self-aggrandising' (1977: 3). Not only did Szasz find it unhelpful; he also pointed out that it was not new, having first been employed by Bernhard Beyer in 1912. As a result of his disagreement with Cooper, Laing distanced himself from his erstwhile colleague and instead of going on to write the definitive politics of mental health as had been expected he withdrew from this field. His interests became progressively more introspective and concerned with schizophrenia, families and radical psychiatry. In his later work Laing was to move closer to humanistic psychology and the gulf between himself and his colleagues in the Philadelphia Association widened. He finally resigned as chairperson in 1981 and died in France in 1989.

Though it is not often acknowledged because of the vociferous attacks launched at Laing throughout most of his career by the British Medical Association and the radical myths which have grown up around his memory, he was unique in Britain in the 1960s and 1970s for his practice and his theories, both of which straddled the worlds of psychoanalysis and existentialism. Though it may initially have been useful to attain the status of a psychoanalyst (in order to attack the institution from within) he never wholly abandoned psychoanalytic theory, as we see when we read his struggle with 'unconscious phantasy' in *The Self and Others*.

Adrian Laing, in his recent study of his father (1994), claims that Laing's intention at the end of his professional training was to be able to speak authoritatively as a member of the medical establishment and, at the same time, to challenge in particular the conservative psychoanalytic movement by trying to persuade its members of the relevance of the existential-phenomenological perspective to the understanding of mentally disturbed patients. Zinovieff has asked recently whether

> R.D. Laing and his works (fifteen books, multi-various articles, the formation of the Philadelphia Association as an alternative place of care for psychiatric patients etc. etc.) were merely a symptom of the times? A 'reaction-formation' in tandem with the 60s climate of revolt and unrest? What lasting contribution, therefore, has Laing made to the study of human relations and, indeed, to the practice of psychotherapy? (1995: 184)

These are questions which must exercise any British existential psycho-therapist, particularly because for a large number of psychologists and practitioners from other orientations Laing *is* existential psychotherapy, just as Yalom personifies it in America.

Some aspects of his conceptualization of mental disturbance appear overly-optimistic now but they complemented the anti-psychiatry move-ment which sprang out of the radical and revolutionary political groupings of the late 1960s and the 1970s. As Sedgewick wrote in 1982, 'The thrust of Laingian theorising accords so well with the loose romanticism and libertarianism implicit in a number of contemporary creeds and moods that it can easily generate support and acquire plausibility' (1982: 6).

While he enjoyed limited success in influencing the stance of the medical establishment during his lifetime, his work has contributed greatly to changing the willingness of the major institutions to pay attention to alternative ways of viewing mental health. The recent commission by the *British Journal of Psychiatry* of a paper on existential-phenomenological therapy, and the national and international interest which this has aroused, seems to indicate the extent of these shifts (Cohn, 1994).

Curiously, Laing's work – treated reductionistically – might be as much use to the political Right as to the Left: like the theories of Thomas Szasz, Laing's work can be distorted to imply that there is no such thing as mental illness – an argument which would seem to support the closure of psychiatric hospitals and the growth of 'care in the community'.

Like Yalom, Laing wrote in an accessible, relatively jargon-free style (at least for his time) and the titles of his books intrigue and encourage the potential reader to take the plunge in a way that many of the scholarly tomes do not. More important, his work appeared in a period when conventional wisdom was being questioned on all fronts, especially by young people and students who were concerned to redress the wrongs with which they identified the capitalist system and its various agents of social repression and control. It is a tribute to his passion and accessibility that even today if the average psychology student or counselling trainee retains anything about existentialism in Britain it will more than likely have been culled from the pages of *The Divided Self* or *The Politics of Experience*.

So long as mainstream psychiatry and psychoanalysis are perceived as distant or disempowering, Laing's commitment to the individual and to the pain and importance of relationship will stand out as a beacon. The term 'Laingian' has taken its place in the *Oxford English Dictionary* and a whole Laing industry has been built up around his name which attests to the unabated public and professional interest in his life and work, an interest exacerbated by the 'guru' image Laing cultivated in the latter half of his career, by his enigmatic personality, and his comparatively early death.

As regards the continuing influence of his work on specific psychotherapy and counselling trainings, allegiance to some of his core ideas remains constant and many of his books are still in print (no small achievement in itself in a field in which the number of publications each year seems to grow exponentially and publishers' lists are rigorously pruned of dead wood) – a testimony to his enduring appeal.

An in-depth examination of Laing forms a significant part of the curriculum in only a few trainings – those offered by the Arbours Association, the Philadelphia Association and Regent's College (all in London). Appreciation of Laing's work is limited to a relatively small group of practitioners, trainers and advanced students. Abram, in her guide *Individual Psychotherapy Trainings*, puts Laing's influence in terms of numbers into perspective. The Arbours Association was established in 1970 by Dr Joseph Berke and Dr Morton Schatzman who had worked with R.D. Laing at the Kingsley Hall project from 1965 to 1968. Joseph Berke came to wide public attention because of his work with a patient called Mary Barnes which led to the publication of *Mary Barnes: Two Accounts of a Journey through Madness* (1971) and a subsequent play of the case first performed at the Royal Court Theatre in 1979. These, and his book *The Butterfly Man* (1977), later published as *I Haven't Had To Go Mad Here* (1979), have done much to bring the work of R.D. Laing and his associates into the public domain. Perhaps surprisingly, given these links with Laing, the training programme, which accepts no more than ten students annually and lasts between four and six years, is primarily concerned with the theory and practice of psychoanalysis. The aim is to provide both in- and out-patients with psychotherapeutic help within long-term communities as an alternative to psychiatric hospitalization.

The Philadelphia Association, like the Arbours Association, restricts the numbers of trainees who enter to approximately fifteen each year, and the full training takes four to six years to complete. This training pays attention to the work of psychoanalysts including Freud, Klein, Winnicott and Bion, as well as Laing, and to philosophers such as Socrates, Plato, Hegel, Kierkegaard, Nietzsche, Husserl, Heidegger, Sartre and Derrida.

Regent's College School of Psychotherapy and Counselling, probably the largest psychotherapy training institute in the UK after the Tavistock, is concerned to ensure that psychotherapy does not neglect its philosophical origins and encourages an appreciation of these philosophical underpinnings at all levels of training. Interest in Laing continues to be strong among a number of the staff, particularly on the MA in Psychotherapy and Counselling and on the specialist Advanced Diploma in Existential Psychotherapy, a post-Master's training in the existential and phenomenological approach. Between them, these two courses recruit approximately seventy students annually. Both take a minimum of two years to complete. A diploma programme was instituted in 1994 for students who wish to apply an existential approach in their work as counsellors.

While the interest generated by Laing et al. and the anti-psychiatry movement of the 1960s has never died away, its strong resurgence is evidenced by the number of major British publications over the last two decades, among them Jenner (de Koning and Jenner, 1982), Lederman (1984), van Deurzen-Smith (1988), Cooper (Cooper et al., 1989), Spinelli (1989, 1994), Cohn (1996) and du Plock (1966). Since the founding of the Society for Existential Analysis by Professor van Deurzen-Smith in 1988 the disparate, and not so disparate, bodies and individuals which we have considered in this chapter, however briefly, have had a forum for discussion and development of the existential-phenomenological approach. The journal of the Society numbers such distinguished practitioners as James Bugenthal and Thomas Szasz from the USA, and Gion Condrau of the International Federation of Daseinsanalysis in Switzerland on its editorial board, as well as Dan Burston of Duquesne University and, from Britain, John M. Heaton of the Philadelphia Association and Andrea Sabbadini of the Arbours Association.

In spite of these differences of approach it is possible to outline certain assumptions which most existential therapists are likely to see as the foundation of their therapeutic practice today. We may express them thus:

1. Human beings are 'thrown' into the world in the sense that they find themselves in a situation which is given rather than chosen. A baby cannot choose to be born into one family, with a different set of circumstances, rather than another, or to be born with particular physical attributes and genetic makeup. Similarly, as we are all born so shall we all die. While we cannot choose these givens we can choose our response to them and it is in doing so that we create our own values and our own life. As Sartre expresses it, men are condemned to be free. While this may seem quite clear, given some reflection many clients (indeed all of us at certain times) resist such an active view of their place in the world, preferring to attribute the shape of their life to fate, chance, economics, upbringing, or a hundred other 'external' factors which can be pressed into service.

2. Since human beings are thrown into the world it makes no sense to attempt to understand them without also coming to grips with their context. This is necessarily true also of human beings in the therapeutic relationship: neither client nor therapist is in the room as just client or therapist. As Cohn (1994) puts it: 'When we see a client his/her family, partner, social nexus etc.

are also present in the room. For the existential therapist, there is in fact no "individual" therapy.' This must also be the case for the therapist, though their context should not be permitted to impinge inappropriately on the client's work. In existential therapy, unlike psychoanalytic or psychodynamic therapy, it is understood that the therapist should not, indeed cannot, be a blank screen.

3. Since it is the 'phenomena' – those things which appear – that are of concern in existential therapy, the therapist should take care to be open to this and to engage with it as fully as possible. The therapist generally stays in the here-and-now of the client's experience rather than importing normative theories or gathering evidence from previous sessions to support the hypotheses which such theories entail.

4. Just as clients invariably bring their context into therapy, so they bring their past and their hopes and fears for the future as well as their experience of the present moment. Existential therapy is often misunderstood as discounting the past, but this is not so. However, it does reject the reductionistic notion so often encountered in therapy that the past 'causes' the present since such a deterministic approach denies the ability of humans to be creative and to make choices about their lives. Many clients restrict themselves to living only in the past, or the present or future, and in such cases much of the therapeutic work will be concerned with enabling them to experience themselves in relation to all three.

5. The existential approach is concerned with the whole being of the client and rejects dichotomies such as mind and body, or psyche and soma. The way in which we relate to our body cannot be split off from any other of the dimensions on which we encounter the world.

6. If we can choose our response to those aspects of our lives which are given, it follows that we can also fail to choose or can make choices which do not really reflect our needs. This necessitates the formulation of types of anxiety and guilt which are distinct from neurotic anxiety and guilt. The feelings we experience as a result of our attempts to evade authenticity are of a specifically existential nature and should be approached as such if they are to be worked with effectively.

Conclusion

The growth in the dissemination of the existential-phenomenological approach to therapy is likely to have exciting repercussions for the delivery of mental health care in the UK in future. Those who have chosen to pursue a career within the medical establishment, whether NHS or private, may be free to critique labelling and treatment but, in the final analysis, are expected to work as part of a team for whom the medical model provides, by and large, a bedrock of certainty about their role in relation to patients who are conceptualized as in need of treatment and, where possible, cure.

But in some important respects this approach, far from being out of step with current shifts in attitudes to both mental health and mental illness, can be seen to be prominent in the vanguard of such developments. A number of commentators, among them Samuels (1993) and Smail (1993), have noted that a better-educated, information-rich, largely secular society suffers as much if not more from psychological problems as did those of the century which witnessed the advent of psychoanalysis. As Smail notes, the origins of unhappiness are to be found among both the haves and the have-nots; anxiety, stress, depression, all seem endemic to our present ways of life. And so it is that we begin to recall Kierkegaard's hard-earned lesson that when everybody is bent on making life easier and easier perhaps the wisest, most authentic course is to make things more difficult, or at least to address the question of whether these endless examples of 'progress' really do add anything worthwhile to human existence. Life may be vastly easier for the majority in terms of the consumerist culture but the problem of how to live one's life is as burgeoning today when each is said to be free to invent him/herself as it was in ancient Greece 3,000 years ago. *Eudaimonia*, or the good life, is of concern to us as it has never been before and a philosophical approach to these problems is just as relevant.

As practical philosophers, existential psychotherapists are attuned to cultural changes and are able to engage with the problems synonymous with what Foucault (1972) termed the postmodern era. While other approaches, most notably the psychoanalytic, have altered immeasurably in response to these cultural changes and are now better able to address the social malaise rather than situate pathology in specific individuals or groups, the existential approach is increasingly recognized as the most relevant to address the era which Rieff has called that of psychological man (Rieff, 1966). Van Deurzen-Smith has said that

> A lot of distress is generated by post-modern society, now that humankind has reached a position of potential self-destruction through atomic war or overpopulation of the planet. Mass communication increasingly rules our lives, endangering personal relationships whilst little solace is expected from the old structures that used to safeguard human values. People often feel that they have a choice between either becoming commodities themselves as slaves in the production process or focusing so much on achievement in producing more commodities that they will not have time to enjoy the commodities that they have accumulated. (1994: 7)

The exhortatory tone of these words should by now be familiar: it is that of a tradition which we have traced from Kierkegaard and Nietzsche, through to Heidegger and Sartre and Laing. It may be found in the schools of ancient philosophy which inspired much of their work, and it is alive in the writings of Camus and De Beauvoir, among others. Each urges humans to rise above the herd, to use their talents to the full and to strive to live authentically. And recalling our opening remarks, to do so they must face the fact of their finitude, of the impending death which gives meaning to their actions in the world. This tone and tradition is in marked contrast to the technocratic style of much Anglo-American philosophizing, less abstract and distant from the problems of living with which we all struggle on a daily basis, and thus far better able to provide an intelligent guide to enable us to chart a course, though always open to what life brings, rather than stumble blindly from crisis to crisis.

Those aspects of the existential-phenomenological approach which are most often criticized – its willingness to speak of values and to make statements about moral actions, its flexibility and unwillingness to label and to pathologize – in fact constitute its best strengths. As people increasingly realize, particularly in the West, that no matter how much they concern themselves with 'feel-good factors' what is important is that what underpins these, in psychotherapy as in any other area of our society, is a genuine exploration and appreciation of what it means to be human. What matters is, as Husserl termed it, a return 'to the things themselves'.

Existential philosophers have always been concerned with the relationship between the individual and his or her context and existential psychotherapists have underlined, and their work has reinforced, the understanding that humans cannot be talked of meaningfully separate from their society – to attempt to do so, as some other approaches have, invariably impoverishes our understanding of what it is to be human and leads us down the cul-de-sac of labelling and pathologizing the individual. Just as it makes no sense to talk of human beings without their societies, so it is pointless to attempt a rigorous examination of life without a corresponding awareness of death. Similarly, any wish, no matter how well intentioned, to extend individual freedom without re-evaluating individual responsibility is deeply flawed. The debate between humanists and existentialists on the meaning of 'authenticity' is important here. Humanists think it is about self-assertive living – being true to the essential self. Existential therapists consider authenticity to be about being open and truthful to life: accepting its limitations and boundaries and allowing it to manifest as fully as possible through one's own transparency.

The result of such an approach as utilized in much humanistic therapy, and especially in the human potential movement, is that everybody loses: those with access to individual therapy become more egotistical, less connected to the wider society, and therefore more isolated from reality, while the poor and otherwise disadvantaged end up labelled as underachievers. Worse, in these dog days of political correctness, they are likely to attract the sort of euphonious terms which actually do violence to them in that they patronize and typecast while denying the political, philosophical or economic facts of their situation.

Psychotherapy and counselling are now in crisis as the conflict becomes more apparent between those who pursue 'feel-good' short cuts to psychological health, those who cling to intellectual theories of a functional kind, and those who are attempting to develop deeper philosophical foundations for their work in recognition of the creative dynamics in individuals. The ancient philosophies sought to know the world as a whole, by reason and by studying the nature of things in their entirety. Modern

science substitutes an abstract picture of the world for the world itself –
seeking to master it in this way, leaving nothing over, by a universal science.
As we have seen, the existential approach, though its core characteristics
endure, is articulated differently in Britain, the USA and continental
Europe. As it spreads to other parts of the world – flourishing practices are
now springing up in Australia and New Zealand – it is probable that new
strains will emerge as some aspects of the tradition are emphasized and
others relegated in keeping with the perceived needs of new client groups.

The work of the Society for Existential Analysis in facilitating contact and
debate between all existential theorists and practitioners will be an
important factor in the strengthening of this approach. The remit of the
Society – to provide a forum for the expression of views and the exchange of
ideas amongst those interested in the analysis of existence from philosophical and psychological perspectives – has, as might be expected, drawn those
whose approach is defined negatively by opposition to medically informed
psychiatry as well as those who seek to make connections between this and a
less doctrinaire approach; those, such as Thomas Szasz, who have a
right-libertarian perspective, and those, such as Cohn, van Deurzen-Smith
and Spinelli, who seek to operationalize a rigorous existential-phenomenological perspective on being.

Some have seen the Society as a place in which to resurrect the original
humanistic and philosophical content of Freud's theories and, in the spirit of
R.D. Laing, to draw parallels between this and some form of existential
analysis. While such a project may appear alien to many existential
psychotherapists, Sabbadini (himself an analyst) reminds us of Boss's
reinterpretation of Freudian psychoanalysis. For Sabbadini 'it is in that
intensely charged meeting of the analyst's Unconscious with that of his
analysand that lies the specific (and most special) "existential" quality of the
psychoanalytic rapport' (1990: 29).

This somewhat specialized use of the term 'existential' may provide an
insight into its use by the Arbours Association, of which Sabbadini is
Director of Training. It permits him to raise questions about the interface of
existential *Angst* and castration anxiety, and the place of the ego, id and
superego in a phenomenological description of the experience of mental
pain, questions which are of most pressing concern to those who seek to
import an attitude of openness to the other as a subject and free agent into
the analytic encounter while retaining a Freudian concept of the psyche.

The Society has been concerned to contribute to current debates within
psychotherapy and counselling generally, as well as within the existential-
phenomenological field. The very different perspectives on abuses of power
within therapy expressed at the Society's 1993 annual conference by Jeffrey
Masson and others, and papers by Masson and van Deurzen-Smith in a
subsequent Society journal, provide an effective illustration of the clarity
which a philosophically based analysis can provide on the most emotive and
fundamental questions.

The existential-phenomenological approach cannot be a panacea for all the social problems and schisms within the world of therapy and of social relations which we have noted. Nevertheless it, alone among the psycho-therapies, continues to offer, through its central concern with *being* itself, an encounter which reflects and clarifies the client's *being-in-the-world*, and thereby the potential for a radical shift in our approach to living out our relations with ourselves, our families, friends, neighbours and colleagues, and society itself. As Spinelli recently asked:

> if the client's experience and expression of 'being' is clarified and challenged from a therapeutic stance that accepts that being as it experiences and expresses itself through the therapist's attempts to 'enter' the client's experiential world-view, then could it not be that the consequences of these clarifications and challenges at the microcosmic level of encounter will resonate at the macrocosmic level? (1994: 372)

References

Abram, J. (1992) *Individual Psychotherapy Trainings*. London: Free Association Books.

Barnes, M. and Berke, J. (1971) *Mary Barnes: Two Accounts of a Journey through Madness*. London: Hart-Davis MacGibbon.

Berke, J. (1979) *I Haven't Had To Go Mad Here*. Harmondsworth: Pelican.

Binswanger, L. (1963) *Being-in-the-World*, trans. J. Needleman. New York: Basic Books.

Boss, M. (1949) *The Meaning and Content of Sexual Perversions: Daseinsanalytic Approach to the Psychopathology of the Phenomena of Love*. New York: Grune & Stratton.

Boss, M. (1957a) *Psychoanalysis and Daseinsanalysis*, trans. L.B. Lefebre. New York: Basic Books.

Boss, M. (1957b) *The Analysis of Dreams*. London: Rider.

Boss, M. (1977) *I Dreamt Last Night. . . .* New York: Gardner Press.

Boss, M. (1979) *Existential Foundations of Medicine and Psychology*. New York: Aronson.

Camus, A. (1942) *The Myth of Sisyphus*. Harmondsworth: Penguin.

Cannon, B. (1991) *Sartre and Psychoanalysis: An Existentialist Challenge to Clinical Metatheory*. Kansas: University of Kansas Press.

Cohn, H.W. (1994) 'What is existential psychotherapy?', *British Journal of Psychiatry*, 165: 699–701.

Cohn, H.W. (1996) *Existential Theory and Psychotherapeutic Practice*. London: Sage Publications.

Condrau, G. (1993) 'Dream analysis: do we need the unconscious?', *Journal of the Society for Existential Analysis*, 4: 1–12.

Cooper, D. (1967) *Psychiatry and Anti-psychiatry*. New York: Barnes & Noble.

Cooper, R., Friedman, J., Gans, S., Heaton, J.M., Oakley, C., Oakley, H. and Zeal, P. (1989) *Thresholds between Philosophy and Psychoanalysis: Papers from the Philadelphia Association*. London: Free Association Books.

Deurzen-Smith, E. van (1988) *Existential Counselling in Practice*. London: Sage Publications.

Deurzen-Smith, E. van (1994) *Can Counselling Help?* Durham: University of Durham Occasional Paper.

Deurzen-Smith, E. van (1995) *Existential Therapy*. London: Society for Existential Analysis.

du Plock, S. (ed.) (1996) *Case Studies in Existential Psychotherapy and Counselling*. Chichester: John Wiley & Sons.

Foucault, M. (1972) *The Archeology of Knowledge*, trans. A. Sheridan. London: Tavistock.

Frankl, V. (1965) 'Fragments from the logotherapeutic treatment of four cases', in A. Burton (ed.), *Modern Psychotherapeutic Practice*. Palo Alto, CA: Science and Behavior Books.

Frankl, V. (1969) *The Will to Meaning*. New York: World.

Freud, S. (1914) 'On the history of the psycho-analytic movement', in *The Standard Edition of the Complete Psychological Works of Sigmund Freud*, trans. and ed. J. Strachey. London: Hogarth Press and the Institute of Psycho-Analysis, 1953–74.

Freud, S. (1940) 'An outline of psychoanalysis' in *Standard Edition*, Vol. 23.

Heidegger, M. (1962) *Being and Time*, trans. J. Macquarrie and E.S. Robinson. New York: Harper & Row.

Heidegger, M. (1968) *What is Called Thinking?* New York: Harper & Row.

Heidegger, M. (1987) *Zollikoner Seminare*, ed. M. Boss. Frankfurt am Main: Klostermann.

Husserl, E. (1960) *Cartesian Meditations. An Introduction to Phenomenology*, trans. D. Cairns. The Hague: Martinus Nijhoff.

Husserl, E. (1962) *Ideas: General Introduction to Pure Phenomenology*. New York: Collier.

Husserl, E. (1969) *Formal and Transcendental Logic*. The Hague: Martinus Nijhoff.

Husserl, E. (1970) *Logical Investigations*. New York: Humanities Press.

James, W. (1890) *Principles of Psychology*. New York: Holt.

Jaspers, K. (1951) *The Way to Wisdom*, trans. R. Manheim. New Haven, CT and London: Yale University Press.

Jaspers, K. (1963) *General Psychopathology*. Chicago, IL: University of Chicago Press.

Kierkegaard, S. (1941) *Concluding Unscientific Postscript*, trans. D.F. Swenson and W. Lowrie. Princeton, NJ: Princeton University Press.

Kierkegaard, S. (1944) *The Concept of Dread*, trans. W. Lowrie. Princeton, NJ: Princeton University Press.

Kierkegaard, S. (1946) 'How Johannes Climacus became an author', in *A Kierkegaard Anthology*, ed. R. Brentall. Princeton, NJ: Princeton University Press.

Koning, A.J.J. de and Jenner, F.A. (1982) *Phenomenology and Psychiatry*. New York: Academic Press.

Kovel, J. (1978) *A Complete Guide to Therapy*. Harmondsworth: Pelican.

Laing, A. (1994) *R.D. Laing: A Biography*. London: Peter Owen.

Laing, R.D. (1960) *The Divided Self: Existential Study of Madness and Sanity*. London: Tavistock.

Laing, R.D. (1961) *The Self and Others*. London: Tavistock.

Laing, R.D. (1967) *The Politics of Experience*. New York: Pantheon Books.

Laing, R.D. and Cooper, D. (1964) *Reason and Violence*. London: Tavistock.

Laing, R.D. and Cooper, D. (1971) *Reason and Violence: A Decade of Sartre's Philosophy 1950–60*. New York: Vintage Books.

Laing, R.D. and Esterson, A. (1964) *Sanity, Madness and the Family*. Harmondsworth: Penguin.

Laing, R.D., Lee, A.R. and Phillipson, H. (1966) *Interpersonal Perception*. New York: Springer.

Ledermann, E.K. (1984) *Mental Health and Human Conscience*. Amersham: Avebury.

May, R. (1969) *Love and Will*. New York: W.W. Norton.

May, R. (1983) *The Discovery of Being*. New York: W.W. Norton.

May, R., Angel, E. and Ellenberger, H. (1958) *Existence*. New York: Basic Books.

Merleau-Ponty, M. (1962) *Phenomenology of Perception*, trans. C. Smith. London: Routledge & Kegan Paul.

Minkowski, E. (1970) *Lived Time*. Evanston, IL: Northwestern University Press.

Misiak, H. and Sexton, V.S. (1973) *Phenomenological, Existential and Humanistic Psychologies: a Historical Survey*. New York: Grune & Stratton.

Nietzsche, F. (1961) *Thus Spoke Zarathustra*, trans. R.J. Hollingdale. Harmondsworth: Penguin.

Nietzsche, F. (1974) *The Gay Science*, trans. W. Kaufmann. New York: Random House.

Nietzsche, F. (1986) *Human, All Too Human*, trans. R.J. Hollingdale. Cambridge: Cambridge University Press.

Nussbaum, M.C. (1994) *The Therapy of Desire: Theory and Practice in Hellenistic Ethics*. Princeton, NJ: Princeton University Press.

Perls, F. (1972) *Gestalt Therapy Verbatim*. New York: Bantam Books.

Perls, F. (1976) *The Gestalt Approach and Eye Witness to Therapy*. New York: Bantam Books.

Rieff, P. (1966) *The Triumph of the Therapeutic*. Harmondsworth: Penguin.

Rogers, C. (1961) *On Becoming A Person*. Boston: Houghton Mifflin.

Rogers, C. (ed.) (1967) *The Therapeutic Relationship and Its Impact: A Study in Psychotherapy*. Madison: University of Wisconsin Press.

Rogers, C. (1979) 'The foundations of the person-centered approach', unpublished manuscript.

Sabbadini, A. (1990) 'Existential analysis and psychoanalysis: some points of contact', *Journal of the Society for Existential Analysis*, 1: 29–32.

Samuels, A. (1993) *The Political Psyche*. London: Routledge.

Sartre, J-P. (1938) *Nausea*. Harmondsworth: Penguin.

Sartre, J-P. (1956) *Being and Nothingness: An Essay on Phenomenological Ontology*, trans. H. Barnes. New York: Philosophical Library.

Sedgewick, P. (1982) *Psychopolitics*. London: Pluto Press.

Showalter, E. (1985) *The Female Malady*. Princeton, NJ: Princeton University Press.

Smail, D. (1993) *The Origins of Unhappiness*. London: HarperCollins.

Smith, D.L. (1994) 'Riding shotgun for Freud: a reply to Ernesto Spinelli', *Journal of the Society for Existential Analysis*, 5: 142–56.

Smith, D.L. (1995) 'It sounds like an excellent idea! Episode four of a psychological cliff-hanger', *Journal of the Society for Existential Analysis*, 6(1): 149–59.

Spiegelberg, H. (1971) *The Phenomenological Movement*. The Hague: Martinus Nijhoff.

Spiegelberg, H. (1972) *Phenomenology in Psychology and Psychiatry*. Evanston, IL: Northwestern University Press.

Spinelli, E. (1989) *The Interpreted World: An Introduction to Phenomenological Psychology*. London: Sage Publications.

Spinelli, E. (1990) 'The phenomenological method and client-centred therapy', *Journal of the Society for Existential Analysis*, 1: 15–21.

Spinelli, E. (1994) 'Riding shotgun for Freud or aiming a gun at his head? A reply to David Smith', *Journal of the Society for Existential Analysis*, 5: 142–56.

Spinelli, E. (1995) '. . . Too bad it turned out the way it did: a further response to David Smith', *Journal of the Society for Existential Analysis*, 6(1): 157–65.

Szasz, T.S. (1977) 'Anti-psychiatry: the paradigm of the plundered mind'. London: The New Review.

Tillich, P. (1952) *The Courage to Be*. New Haven, CT: Yale University Press.

Valle, R.S. (1989) 'The emergence of transpersonal psychology', in R.S. Valle and S. Halling (eds), *Existential Phenomenological Perspectives in Psychology*. London: Plenum Press.

Valle, R.S. and King, M. (1978) *Existential Phenomenological Alternatives for Psychology*. New York: Oxford University Press.

Yalom, I. (1980) *Existential Psychotherapy*. New York: Basic Books.

Yalom, I. (1989) *Love's Executioner and Other Tales of Psychotherapy*. London: Bloomsbury.

Yalom, I. (1992) *When Nietzsche Wept*. New York: Basic Books.

Young, S. (1993) 'Everything is what it is, not something else', *Journal of the Society for Existential Analysis*, 4: 13–18.

Zinovieff, N. (1995) 'R.D. Laing: a biography by Adrian Charles Laing', *Journal of the Society for Existential Analysis*, 6(1): 183–5.

3

Developments in Transactional Analysis

Ian Stewart

Transactional analysis (TA) traces its history back to the mid-1950s. Like several other therapies, TA credits its origins to the work of one person. TA's founding father was Eric Berne (1910–70). Berne's original training was in psychoanalysis, and the roots of his theory lie firmly in psychodynamic thinking.

Like other therapies also, TA has seen a division in theory and practice into several sub-schools following the death of its founder. More recently there has been a period of consolidation, in which the discipline has made further progress that goes beyond the bounds of any one of these schools.

I have arranged this chapter in a simple chronological scheme. Its five sections trace five epochs in the development of TA. First, I review Berne's original thinking on the main concepts of TA, and suggest how his ideas developed from the work of earlier psychodynamic writers. This first section covers the period up to 1958, the year which saw the publication of the first journal paper to use the term 'Transactional Analysis'.

The second section describes the period of creative ferment that followed, in which Berne and his pioneer colleagues laid the foundations of TA. This phase ran from the late 1950s until around the time of Berne's death in 1970.

In the third section, covering the years from about 1970 until 1980, I describe the emerging differences in theory and practice that have given rise to the three main schools within TA. The fourth section outlines some major innovations in TA theory and practice during the period between about 1980 and 1990.

In the final section, I suggest the emergence of a 'psychodynamic renaissance' in current TA, beginning in the 1980s and still in progress today.

Eric Berne and the origins of TA

Eric Berne was born and brought up in Canada, where he qualified as a doctor in 1935. Shortly afterwards he moved to the USA and began psychiatric residency. In 1941 he began training as a psychoanalyst, becoming an analysand of Paul Federn.

This was interrupted by the outbreak of the Second World War, during which Berne served in the US army as a psychiatrist. During this period, he began practising group therapy. He had already started compiling critical notes on psychiatry and psychoanalysis that were to form the basis for later writings.

Following his release from the army in 1946, Berne resumed his psychoanalytic training, this time under Erik Erikson. His first book, *The Mind in Action*, was published in 1947; it was revised in 1957 as *A Layman's Guide to Psychiatry and Psychoanalysis*.

In 1949 Berne published the first of six journal articles concerning the nature of intuition. Appearing from that year until 1958, these presented the emerging ideas on which Berne was to found his development of TA (Berne, 1977).

In November 1957, Berne read a paper to the American Group Psychotherapy Association. It was entitled 'Transactional analysis: a new and effective method of group therapy'. In this article, which appeared in print the following year (Berne, 1958), Berne described the four main concepts that provided the foundation for his theory. In the description that follows, I give additional references to Berne's later work, where each idea is more fully explained.

Berne's original theory

The four central concepts in Berne's theory are arranged in a logical sequence, in which the ideas in each part of the theory develop from those that went before. They are:

the structural model of ego-states
the analysis of transactions
games
script

The structural model of ego-states   Berne's principal intent was to construct a model of the structure of personality. The building-blocks of this model were *ego-states*, defined as 'consistent patterns of feeling and experience directly related to corresponding consistent patterns of behavior' (Berne, 1966: 364).

Berne did not invent the concept of ego-states. He drew it, with acknowledgement, from the work of his first psychoanalytical mentor, Paul Federn (1952), and Federn's pupil Edoardo Weiss (1950). In the ego-psychology of Federn, an 'ego-state' meant the totality of a person's mental and bodily experience at any one moment. Federn had suggested that the person might sometimes re-experience ego-states dating from earlier stages in her life. The difference between current ego-states and archaic ego-states, however, would be evident only in the person's internal experience.

Berne made two significant amendments to Federn's model. First, he asserted that each category of ego-states was shown in a distinctive and observable set of *behaviours*, as well as being experienced internally.

Second, he suggested that there was a third distinct category of ego-states, additional to the two in Federn's model.

Berne introduced the third category of ego-states because he believed there were certain experiences and behaviours that Federn's model did not fully explain. As well as the current and archaic ego-states that Federn had noted, Berne observed a third set of ego-states in which the person's experiences and behaviours seemed to have been copied from someone else. This 'someone else' was most often a parent or parent-figure (Berne, 1961: xx).

By this reasoning, Berne arrived at the tripartite model of ego-states that is now the trademark of TA: the *Parent–Adult–Child (PAC)* model. *Parent* ego-states are those 'borrowed' (introjected) from parents or parent-figures. *Child* ego-states are archaic, that is, replayed from epochs in the person's own childhood. When in an *Adult* ego-state, the person is responding to here-and-now stimuli as her age-appropriate self (Berne, 1961: 66–9; 1966: 366).

The analysis of transactions Berne was then able to model the possible patterns of communication between people, in terms of the ego-states that each person employs. This he called the *analysis of transactions* (Berne, 1972: 20).

Years earlier, Freud had written in general terms of 'transference' and 'countertransference'. Berne adopted these ideas direct from Freud. But in Berne's model, it was possible to specify *observable* patterns of communication – transactions – that reliably indicated the presence of transference and countertransference (or their absence). This followed from Berne's premise that ego-states were behaviourally observable. For example, a Parent–Child transaction is by definition transferential; an Adult–Adult transaction is transference-free.

Games Berne next addressed one of the perennial questions of psychotherapy: why do people so often go on doing things that are painful for them? *Games* were portrayed in Berne's system as stereotyped, repetitive sequences of transactions leading to a predictable, dysfunctional outcome.

This idea also built upon one of Freud's general concepts, in this case the 'compulsion to repeat'. The element added by Berne's model was again that of behavioural observability: he postulated that every game followed a sequence of six distinctive and observable steps, which indeed defined the process known as a 'game' (Berne, 1972: 24).

Script Games themselves were then framed as but one expression of a wider life pattern, the *script*. This Berne defined as: 'a life-plan based on a decision made in childhood, reinforced by the parents, justified by subsequent events, and culminating in a chosen alternative' (Berne, 1972: 445). He described the script also as a 'transference drama' (Berne, 1958: 155–6), and pointed out that it is 'preconscious' (Berne, 1972: 25).

Berne cited several post-Freudian writers as sources for his ideas on script. He suggested that it was Alfred Adler who 'comes closest to talking like a script analyst' (Berne, 1972: 58–9; Adler, 1963). Berne quoted Adler's concept of the 'life goal' and his suggestion that the person would unconsciously direct her entire life plan towards this goal, just as a drama is directed towards its final act. Berne also cited the work of his second analyst, Erik Erikson, who had suggested that people follow a sequence of developmental stages lasting from birth till death (Erikson, 1950).

Berne's concept of script, like Adler's 'life-style', is a theoretical construct that cannot itself be observed. But Berne specified several ways of judging by observation whether a person was acting out her script at any given moment (Berne, 1972: 315–17).

In all these ways, Berne constructed a theory that was psychodynamic in concept, yet that could be checked directly against real-world observations.

Berne's original views on practice

Throughout his career, Berne kept up a keen interest in the function of intuition, which had been the subject of his original and seminal series of journal articles. In Berne's practice, this was reflected in the stress he laid on understanding covert as well as overt messages. Berne spoke of this as 'thinking Martian'.

One of Berne's ideals was to cure people quickly, rather than having them 'make progress' during years of therapy. His contemporaries recount that Berne often urged his students to 'cure their patients in one session' (Cheney, 1971). Like many of Berne's contributions, this may be seen as a reaction to what he saw as the overly slow and cumbersome procedure of traditional psychoanalytic therapy.

To further his objective of speedy cure, Berne advocated the merits of open communication between client and practitioner. He chose to use colloquial language for the terms in his theory (game, script, racket, etc.) instead of the Latin- and Greek-derived terms often favoured in other psychological approaches.

The early years of TA

Beginning in the early 1950s, Berne and his psychiatric associates had been holding regular clinical seminars. In 1958 they formed the San Francisco Social Psychiatry Seminars, meeting each Tuesday at Berne's home. These seminars provided a fertile breeding ground for the emerging ideas of TA.

Berne's *Transactional Analysis in Psychotherapy*, the first book entirely devoted to TA, appeared in 1961. It was followed in 1963 by *The Structure and Dynamics of Organizations and Groups*. The *Transactional Analysis Bulletin* began publication in January 1962, with Berne as editor; after his death it was to continue in existence as the *Transactional Analysis Journal*.

The membership of the San Francisco seminars included many who later became well-known figures in what would be known as the classical school of TA. Prominent among them were Claude Steiner, Jack Dusay, Stephen Karpman and Franklin Ernst.

Another of the participants in the early seminar meetings was Jacqui Lee Schiff, latterly the co-founder of the Cathexis school of TA. Robert Goulding entered clinical supervision with Berne in the early 1960s, and Mary McClure (later to become Mary Goulding) began attending the clinical seminars a few years later. The Gouldings were to be the originators of the redecision school of TA. Thus the seeds of development of the three main schools of current TA were already being sown in these early seminars.

The year 1964 saw a landmark in TA's history: the publication of *Games People Play* (Berne, 1964). Berne had intended the book to be a reader for a small circle of professionals. Instead, it became a bestseller. As its sales boomed worldwide, so the language and ideas of TA caught the imagination of a mass audience. This began a period of media popularity for TA, which was to last from the late 1960s until the mid-1970s.

With hindsight, this period emerges as something of a diversionary cul-de-sac for both the theory and the practice of TA. I have discussed this episode in detail elsewhere (Stewart, 1992: 120–8; Stewart and Joines, 1987: 18–20). In the final section of the present chapter I shall review the impact of some of the oversimplified versions of TA theory that were in circulation at that time. For now, however, I shall focus on the continuity of TA's development before and after the 'pop psychology' phase that rode on the mass success of *Games People Play*.

Theory in the early years

Within the professional group who attended the San Francisco Seminars, theoretical ideas were bandied around freely, so it is not always easy to distinguish who was the originator of which idea. Here, I shall simply credit each piece of theory to the writer under whose name it first appeared in print. In Berne's final writings he cited and acknowledged the work of Steiner and others along with his own.

Several concepts developed in the early seminars did not see the light of print until after 1970; I shall discuss them under the heading of the 'classical school' in the next section. However, some of the best-known ideas of TA date from articles published before 1970. For example, 1966 saw the appearance of Claude Steiner's seminal article on 'script and counterscript' in the *TA Bulletin*. In this, Steiner presented his *script matrix*, a model that analyses script in terms of the person's own ego-states and those of his parents (Steiner, 1966).

In an article that appeared two years later, Stephen Karpman introduced his now famous model of the *Drama Triangle* (Karpman, 1968). He pointed out that in the everyday dramas of life – as in ancient Greek drama – each player would typically take up one of three roles: Persecutor, Rescuer or

Victim. At the climax of the dramatic action, each player would switch suddenly from one of these roles to another.

Practice in the early years

Berne's *Principles of Group Treatment* appeared in 1966. Addressed to a professional audience, it set forth some of Berne's central recommendations on therapeutic practice. Despite its title, it does not deal exclusively with treatment in group settings, and much of the practice that Berne describes is relevant not only to TA but also to other modalities.

In this book, Berne voiced his view that the effective therapist had to be a 'real doctor' (Berne, 1966: xviii). Berne was not suggesting that only medically qualified persons should become therapists. On the contrary, he meant that *any* therapist had to accept the responsibilities expected of a medical doctor. The 'real doctor', said Berne, is always oriented above all towards curing his patients. He must plan his treatment so that at each phase he knows what he is doing and why he is doing it.

In his 1966 book Berne also set forth his thinking on another foundation stone of TA practice: *contractual method*. He defined a contract as 'an explicit bilateral commitment to a well-defined course of action' (Berne, 1966: 362). For Berne, the effective therapist needed to work within the terms of explicit contracts, negotiated with the client and with any other parties who might be concerned.

The same year saw the publication of an article on 'Permission and protection' by Pat Crossman. A crucial function of the therapist, suggested Crossman, was to give the client *permission* to go against the prejudicial commands of the Parent 'in her head'. To do this, the therapist needed to convince the client that she had more *potency* – more power – than that internal Parent. Crossman added the suggestion that, at the same time, the therapist needed to provide the client with appropriate *protection* from the wrath of the internal Parent, at least until the client could develop her own protection. This trilogy – of permission, protection and potency – is now usually referred to in TA simply as the 'three Ps'.

By June 1970 Eric Berne had completed the manuscripts of two more books, *Sex in Human Loving* (Berne, 1970a) and *What Do You Say After You Say Hello?* (Berne, 1972). However, he was never to see them in print: Berne died of a heart attack on 15 July 1970.

A perspective on the early years   It is intriguing to realize that the history of TA now counts more years since Berne's death than it did during his life. Beginning with his 1958 article, Berne's personal contribution to TA spanned twelve years. Since his death, TA has seen more than twenty-five years' further development. The first professional fruits of this development materialized during the decade 1970–80, with the emergence of three main schools of TA theory and practice.

The three schools of TA

The three main streams of TA theory and practice that emerged during the 1970s are still recognized today as clearly distinguishable schools within the discipline. They are:

the classical (Bernian) school
the redecision school
the Cathexis (Schiffian) school.

The three schools had begun to diverge before Berne's death in 1970. In 1965 the Schiffs, now based in the eastern USA, had already begun their work with psychotic clients (Schiff, 1970). In the mid-1960s, too, the Gouldings had begun building up their combined experience of the therapeutic work of Berne and of Fritz Perls (Goulding, 1985: 9–10). The decade of the 1970s emerges with hindsight as the period in which each school made its most distinctive innovations. However, it was not until 1977 that the formal distinction between the three schools of TA was first made in print in an article by Barnes (1977).

In TA, unlike some other areas of psychotherapy, relations between the various schools have remained cordial. The differences between the schools lie in emphasis and interpretation, and in the differing contributions to theory and practice that practitioners have added to Berne's system. Despite these differences, all three schools agree on some common features of theory and practice that define TA as a discipline. The theoretical foundation of all the schools rests upon two of Berne's fundamental concepts: *ego-states* and *script*. The practice of all three TA schools also has one common feature: the use of *contractual method*.

The classical (Bernian) school

The classical school of TA is so called because it has remained closer than any other school to Berne's original theory and practice. As well as Berne's theory, practitioners in the classical school have developed contributions of their own. Following Berne's example, they have devised various diagrammatic models to help understand personality and communication. Like Berne also, they have often given their models colloquial names.

Classical theory   This includes Claude Steiner's *script matrix* (Steiner, 1966), and Stephen Karpman's *Drama Triangle* (Karpman, 1968), mentioned in the previous section. Steiner also developed his theory of the *stroke economy* (Steiner, 1971). The term 'stroke' here implies any form of attention, recognition or touching. Steiner postulated that parental and cultural influences conspired to set up the illusion that strokes were in short supply.

Karpman also was busy in the 1970s with new theoretical ideas, among which was that of *ego-state options* (Karpman, 1971): here he suggested how, with knowledge of ego-states, the person can achieve various desired outcomes in communication by deliberately choosing particular patterns of transacting.

Franklin Ernst was the inventor of the *OK Corral* (Ernst, 1971). This is a four-way matrix that depicts the four alternatives in what Berne had called the 'theory of positions' (I'm OK – you're OK, and so on). Ernst's diagram relates each position to corresponding social strategies the person may use in adult life.

Jack Dusay devised the *egogram* (Dusay, 1972). This takes the form of a 'bar chart' diagram. The relative heights of the bars show an intuitive assessment of the relative energy the person invests in different ego-states.

Fanita English added an important extra dimension to Berne's concept of 'racket feelings'. Berne had drawn attention to these, which are feelings that the person sometimes uses manipulatively to further her script; he had suggested that they formed the payoff for every psychological game. English extended Berne's model by suggesting that every racket feeling was a *substitute* for another, authentic, feeling that had been prohibited in the person's family of origin (English, 1971, 1972, 1976a, 1976b).

Classical practice   In a classical TA approach, the therapist will emphasize the forging and strengthening of an Adult alliance. The initial aim is for the client to *decontaminate* her Adult. This implies separating out her grown-up thoughts, feelings and beliefs from those she borrowed from her parents or carried forward from her childhood. To aid this process, the typical intuitive diagrams of classical theory have the role of engaging the client's Adult functioning, while also enlisting the attention and energy of the Child.

Traditionally, the classical TA practitioner favours group treatment rather than individual therapy. In group, she works by following the transactions between group members, coming in where appropriate to offer interpretations or confrontations. She may or may not phrase these interventions in TA's colloquial language. In these ways, she follows the example that Berne set in his own therapeutic work (e.g. Berne, 1970b).

The redecision school

The founders of the redecision school are Robert and Mary Goulding (see e.g. Goulding, 1977; Goulding and Goulding, 1972, 1976, 1978, 1979; Kadis, 1985). Their approach combines the theory and practice of TA with that of Gestalt therapy.

The Gouldings (1978: 211) have described their reasons for developing this combined approach. In their early work with TA during the 1960s, they had been using Berne's model of structural, transactional, game, and script analysis. They had found this an excellent way of helping clients to develop self-understanding. Often, too, the client would move on to make be-havioural change. Yet sometimes, the Gouldings found, the person still seemed to experience some bad feeling or some unresolved conflict. In terms of ego-states, it was as though the Child were still struggling against whatever new Adult decision the person had made (Goulding, 1985: 10).

The solution to this problem that the Gouldings proposed was to invite the person to make their new decision *from Child* as well as from Adult. To facilitate this, they incorporated into their work some of the actionistic, feeling-oriented techniques of Gestalt therapy. They did not abandon the cognitive TA approach that they had learned from Berne; instead, they combined it with their affective Gestalt-based work. This combination of thinking and feeling work became a central principle of the redecision approach.

Redecision theory   Fritz Perls had already set forth his theory of *impasses*. These he saw as 'stuck places' in which two different aspects of the person were pushing in different directions with equal force. The result was that the person expended much energy but stayed in the same uncomfortable place.

Combining this with Berne's structural analysis, the Gouldings suggested that these conflicted 'parts of the person' often corresponded to different ego-states (Goulding and Goulding, 1979: 44–9; see also Mellor, 1980). The resulting impasses, they suggested, could be of three different types, depending upon the developmental stage from which the relevant ego-states derive.

In a *Type I impasse*, the conflict was between Parent and Child ego-states dating from later childhood. Thus therapeutic issues here would centre on the *counterscript*. For example, the person might be conflicted between a counterscript decision to 'work hard' and a Child desire to take some rest.

For a *Type II impasse*, the struggle was between Parent and Child ego-states from an earlier, pre-verbal stage of development. Thus the issues at stake would centre on decisions that the child had made in response to injunctions. For example, the early decision 'I must never be close to people' might conflict with the person's desire for closeness.

A *Type III impasse* entailed a conflict between primitive Parent and Child ego-states from early infancy. Here the issues would turn around self-worth or worthlessness, basic trust or mistrust.

Redecision practice   The redecision therapist may often invite the client to put the 'two sides' of the conflict on cushions in imagination and conduct a conversation between them (McNeel, 1976; Pulleyblank and McCormick, 1985). The objective is that the client find a way of resolving the conflict and moving on. Alternatively the therapist may ask the client to return in imagination to a childhood scene in which the conflict was being played out in reality. The client then has the chance to re-experience the scene and finish it in a new way.

Often such work entails the release of emotions that the client felt in the original situation but has since repressed. A central principle of redecision technique is that such emotional release is backed up by cognitive analysis. Here, client and therapist will often use the familiar TA pictures of transactions, Drama Triangle, games, and so on. The therapist will also ask the client to contract for behavioural change, practising whatever new pattern she has now decided upon.

Redecision therapists do not step into transferential roles during their work. Instead, they invite the client to 'put the transference out where it belongs' – that is, upon the projected parental figure that the client has placed on the cushion. A similar principle applies in group work. The group process is acknowledged, but it is not used in the therapy; the group members work one to one with the therapist. The function of the group is to bear witness to the work done and to stroke the achievement of desired change.

The Cathexis (Schiffian) school

The founder of this school is Jacqui Lee Schiff (working initially with her husband, Morris Schiff). Like the Gouldings, Schiff was a regular attender at Berne's early seminars. She and her associates developed a particular interest in using transactional analysis in the treatment of schizophrenic clients (Schiff, 1970). The Cathexis Institute, founded by the Schiffs in 1972, gave its name to their school of TA. The principles of their approach are set out in *The Cathexis Reader* (Schiff et al., 1975).

Cathexis theory   As a product of their original focus on psychotic disturbance, members of the Schiffian school have made several important contributions to TA's repertoire of analytical models. Schiffian theory starts from the premise that, when in script, the person distorts his perception of self, others and the world so that it appears to fit his script beliefs. This process of distortion, always carried on without conscious awareness, is called *redefining* (Mellor and Sigmund, 1975b).

The person redefines intrapsychically. Thus to judge whether someone may be redefining, the therapist needs to go on the evidence of certain clues that the person shows externally. Among these clues are certain patterns of communication called *redefining transactions*. In such a transaction, the person who responds 'shifts the ground' of what is being discussed. He does this without awareness. His motive always is that, in Child, he perceives the original topic as a threat to his script beliefs.

There are two types of redefining transaction, *tangential* and *blocking*. In a tangential transaction, Person B 'shifts the ground' by addressing a different issue from the one that Person A originally raised. A blocking transaction is one in which Person B avoids the issue by disagreeing about its definition.

As part of the process of redefining, the person may engage in *discounting* (Schiff and Schiff, 1971; Mellor and Sigmund, 1975a). Shea Schiff has defined this as 'unawarely ignoring information relevant to the solution of a problem' (S. Schiff, workshop presentation 1983, unpublished). In discounting, the person typically underestimates his own or other people's resources, or ignores some options available in the real-life situation.

In Schiffian theory, a *symbiosis* is said to occur when two or more individuals behave as though between them they form a single person. The people concerned in such a relationship will be *discounting* some of their available ego-states. Typically, one of them will be using only Parent and Adult ego-states while excluding Child. The other will take the opposite position, staying in a Child ego-state while shutting out Parent and Adult.

Every symbiosis, the Schiffs suggest, is an attempt to get developmental needs met which were not met during the person's childhood. Psychological games, in this framework, are seen as ways in which the person repeatedly attempts to work through unresolved symbioses from her early life.

Cathexis practice   In the early stages of the Schiffs' work, therapy with psychotic clients was carried on only in a long-term residential setting. The Schiffs' thesis was that the source of their clients' disturbance lay in destructive and traumatic messages in the content of a Parent ego-state. The remedy, they reasoned, might lie in decommissioning this Parent and replacing it with new and healthy Parent messages. The means lay in the spontaneous age-regression of which some of their schizophrenic clients were capable. Instead of trying to head this off or mute it with drugs, the Schiffs set up a safe environment and then encouraged the client to regress to early infancy. The task of the therapist then was to step in and be a new parent for the client, while the client re-ran the process of growing up. This form of therapy was termed *radical reparenting*.

In this original form of Cathexis work, the therapist deliberately and actively steps into a Parental role in relation to the client. It is not as though she were merely giving permissions in Crossman's sense, battling for power with the client's negative Parent. During radical reparenting, the Schiffian therapist 'becomes' the client's parent; she offers her own Parent ego-state as a *replacement* for the client's original destructive Parent.

Practitioners in present-day Cathexis work seldom use radical reparenting. Schiffian therapists now prefer modified forms of the technique that require a less extreme commitment of time and relationship by client and therapist. Cathexis methods are now widely used also in work with non-psychotic clients. The Cathexis approach, with either client group, still emphasizes an assertively Parental stance by the therapist.

In Cathexis group work, the therapeutic function of the group lies in 'caring confrontation'. All the members of the group, including the therapists, are expected to confront any discounting or redefining, while themselves being open to confrontation.

Beyond the 'three schools'

In this section I shall describe some advances in TA theory and practice that go beyond the boundaries of any one school. Broadly speaking, these developments came to prominence during the 1980s. However, just as the emergence of the 'three schools' began around the mid-1960s, so the beginnings of these more recent developments can be traced back to about the mid-1970s.

Of the many advances in TA theory and practice during the 1980s, I shall focus here upon three in particular. I have chosen these three because I believe they all offer useful contributions to psychotherapy generally, not only to transactional analysis; and because they are all now well-established parts of theory and practice within TA itself.

All these innovations have clear connections to Berne's original work, and specifically to his concept of *script*. The first, the *Process Model*, builds upon Berne's observation that the person might live out her script within very short time periods. Next, the *Racket System* reformulates script: instead of the linear progression that Berne pictured, the script is modelled as a self-reinforcing closed system. The third topic takes the form of a practical advance in therapy: an approach to the management of suicide risk known colloquially as *closing the escape hatches*. This too is directly related to the Bernian concept of script: both Berne (1972) and Steiner (1974) had written of 'tragic scripts', in which suicide might be one of the script outcomes.

Personality adaptations and the Process Model

The advances I shall describe under this heading are primarily the work of two men, Taibi Kahler and Paul Ware. Working at first independently, and subsequently together, they have developed a comprehensive framework for assessing personality and planning therapeutic intervention. This employs the linked concepts of *personality adaptations* (Ware, 1983) and the *Process Model* (Kahler, 1979).

Ware (1983) suggests that as part of the process of script formation, every child decides on a set of basic strategies for surviving and getting needs met. The person may sometimes replay these strategies in grown-up life, especially in stress situations. They then represent various ways of adapting to the world. Ware proposes that six main sets of strategies can be distinguished. They correspond to his list of six *personality adaptations*.

The main thrust of the Process Model (Kahler, 1979) is that many features of a person's script can be reliably diagnosed within the first few minutes' acquaintance, through the second-by-second observation of *driver behaviours*. These are specific sets of short-lived behavioural clues, five in number. To observe driver behaviours, the therapist's focus must be on the *process* of the client's communication, the 'how', rather than on its content, the 'what'; hence the name 'Process Model'.

In particular, a person's driver order gives a highly reliable prediction of her personality adaptation. This diagnosis does not require formal 'history-taking'.

Personality adaptations Ware's six personality adaptations correspond broadly to certain formal diagnostic categories. He labels them with names drawn from clinical psychodiagnosis. However, Ware stresses that his use of these labels does not necessarily imply psychopathology in a clinical sense. A person can show the characteristics of one or more of Ware's categories while still being clinically 'normal'. A formal clinical diagnosis will only be attached if a person shows a particular adaptation at such high intensity as to disrupt his day-to-day functioning. The therapist can apply the Ware scheme to 'normal' clients simply by noting the same traits as he would assess for a clinical diagnosis. However, the 'normal' person will show these traits *at a lower intensity* than do clients who would merit the clinical diagnostic label.

To underline this, I shall also give an alternative set of labels for the six personality adaptations, suggested by Vann Joines (1986). I list these names below, following the traditional diagnostic labels that Ware applied to each of them.

> obsessive-compulsive (*responsible workaholic*)
> paranoid (*brilliant sceptic*)
> schizoid (*creative daydreamer*)
> passive-aggressive (*playful critic*)
> hysteric (*enthusiastic over-reactor*)
> antisocial (*charming manipulator*)

By the adjective he adds to each name, Joines underlines the important point that each adaptation has its advantages as well as its problems.

All 'normal' people, suggests Ware, display all six adaptations to some degree. However, most individuals have one adaptation that is dominant. Sometimes a person will show two adaptations more or less equally.

Knowledge of the client's personality adaptation gives the therapist important guidance both in assessing the client and in planning treatment direction. Each adaptation carries with it a typical set of script beliefs about self, others and the world. Along with these go typical emotions and patterns of behaviour that the person is likely to show while in script. All these features find their origins in developmental issues that are also typical of that adaptation. This knowledge helps the practitioner select the treatment direction that will most effectively meet each client's needs.

Further, knowledge of someone's personality adaptation gives the therapist guidance on how best to make and keep effective rapport with that person. This entails making a systematic choice of the sequence in which she addresses the person's thinking, feeling or behaviour. This is the 'Ware sequence'.

The Ware sequence   Ware (1983) distinguishes three possible areas of contact between therapist and client:

> thinking
> feeling
> behaviour

Ware suggests that to make and keep effective contact with any given client, the therapist needs to address these three areas in a specific sequence. We can imagine, says Ware, that each person has three *contact doors*, corresponding to the three possible contact areas. The 'doors' are:

open door
target door
trap door

The sequence of the contact doors will vary systematically according to personality adaptation. For example, for the person with the paranoid adaptation the open door is thinking, the target door is feeling, and the trap door is behaviour. By contrast, the schizoid's open door is behaviour, his target door thinking and his trap door feeling.

When first making contact with her client, the therapist needs to address their open door. Once she has established communication at the open door, she can move to the client's target door. The trap door is the area in which the person is most heavily defended and is most likely to get stuck; but it is also the area in which the most profound personal changes can be made.

If the therapist addresses the doors out of order, the person is likely to retreat into a defence. This is especially likely if the therapist attempts to make first contact at the client's trap door. These considerations apply both in planning the longer-term treatment sequence (strategy) and choosing interventions from second to second (tactics).

Driver behaviours   One of the most significant developments in modern TA has been the discovery of *driver behaviours* (Kahler, 1974). These are distinctive sets of behavioural clues that the person exhibits over a very short time span (about half a second at a time). They act as highly reliable indicators to personality adaptation, and to other features of personality and of the life-script.

Taibi Kahler's work on drivers was first presented in a 1974 journal article. Kahler had been exploring Eric Berne's assertion that the person might often show her script over short periods, as well as within a longer time frame (Berne, 1972: 203–12). Extending this to its logical conclusion, Kahler had been observing the behavioural clues that his clients showed from one split second to the next. He made the intriguing discovery that, just *before* engaging in any scripty behaviour or feeling, the person would show a distinctive set of short-lived behaviours (Kahler, 1974, 1979). Further observation revealed that there were five different sets of these behaviours. They seemed quite independent of such factors as cultural or educational background. Kahler called these 'driver behaviours' because of their compulsive, 'driven' quality.

Each driver comprises a distinctive set of behavioural clues, shown in the person's words, tones, gestures, postures, and facial expressions. There are five different sets of these behavioural clues. Each set defines one of the driver behaviours. In traditional TA fashion, Kahler uses colloquial names to label the five drivers. They are:

Be Perfect
Be Strong
Try Hard
Please Others
Hurry Up

Kahler stresses that the practitioner should not base judgement on observation of just one behavioural clue. For reliable diagnosis of the driver, it is necessary to observe several clues to that driver *occurring together*.

Everyone, says Kahler, shows all five of the driver behaviours from time to time. However, most people have one driver that they show most often. Usually it will also be the one they show first in any interaction. This is called the *primary driver*. A minority of people have two or more drivers about equal in intensity. By noting a person's primary driver, the therapist can make a reliable diagnosis of his main personality adaptation (Kahler, 1979; Ware, 1983). For each adaptation, the primary driver may often be accompanied by secondary drivers. For example, the person whose primary driver is Try Hard will have passive-aggressive as her primary personality adaptation. The paranoid adaptation is marked by a combination of Be Perfect and Be Strong driver signals, shown with about equal intensity.

Because driver behaviours are displayed over such a short time scale, the observer can readily make an assessment of the person's primary driver on the evidence of no more than two minutes' conversation. Further, because driver observation is based on process, not on content, it is immaterial what the subject of the conversation may be. Thus the Process Model, linked with Ware's set of personality adaptations, lends an entirely new dimension to the task of psychodiagnosis.

The Racket System

Richard Erskine and Marilyn Zalcman (1979) are the co-developers of a model known as the *Racket System*. It illustrates the way in which the person, when in script, enters a closed, self-perpetuating system of beliefs, actions and perceptions. Erskine and Zalcman used the word 'racket' in a sense similar to that employed by Berne. It means a repetitive pattern of behaviours, thoughts and feelings that the person engages in while in script.

Berne and Steiner, in their earlier work, had viewed the script either from a historical perspective (e.g. in the script matrix) or as a linear progression, a 'story' that developed in various successive episodes through time. Erskine and Zalcman, by contrast, wished to explain how the script is maintained from moment to moment in the here and now.

Script beliefs and feelings Erskine and Zalcman begin by viewing the formation of the script in a developmental context. They focus on the infant's attempts to 'make sense of' unmet needs and unfinished feelings. For every infant, they suggest, there are times when the expression of feelings does not bring the hoped-for response from the caretaker. When this happens over a period, the infant is likely to use *cognitive mediation* to alleviate the discomfort of the unmet need. That is, he finds a means of 'explaining away' the fact that his needs are not being met. He then uses this 'explanation' to make himself feel better temporarily. The young child arrives at his 'explanation' non-verbally, using the magical thinking typical of infancy.

Erskine and Zalcman suggest that the person may carry these infant 'explanations' forward into adult life, without awareness, and that they will then constitute the person's *script beliefs* about self, others and the quality of life.

Suppose next that in adulthood the person meets a stress situation that in some way resembles the unfinished situation of his infancy. As he begins to re-experience the discomfort of that situation he attempts to deal with it in the same way as he did when he was an infant. Internally he restates his script beliefs in a renewed attempt to 'explain' to himself how he feels. By thus replaying his script beliefs, he 'justifies' the fact that the original feeling remains unfinished. This interplay of script beliefs and repressed feelings takes the form of a *feedback loop*. The entire process takes place intraphysically, and remains outside the person's conscious awareness.

This is a closed system, in that the person is not making his script beliefs available for updating against here-and-now reality. Each time he replays his script beliefs, the person achieves his infant objective of 'explaining away' his unmet needs. But in so doing, he blanks out other possible explanations of the situation that are more appropriate to present reality.

Rackety displays   When the person is engaged in this intrapsychic process, he manifests it externally in various ways that Erskine and Zalcman call *rackety displays*. These may include *observable behaviours, reported internal experiences* and *scripty fantasies*. As well as showing the overt behaviours included in rackety displays, the person may report internal sensations such as tension or muscle pain, or somatic disturbances like blushing or indigestion. He may also engage in fantasies that depict some scripty outcome, often in the form of 'the worst that could happen' or 'the (grandiose) best that could happen'.

All these reflect strategies that the infant decided to adopt as a means of getting needs met when the expression of his original feeling had failed to do so. When in script as an adult, the person replays these old strategies, along with their accompanying emotions. So long as the script beliefs remain unconfronted, these behaviours and feelings will be replayed over and over again as the person attempts to deal with the unfinished needs of childhood.

Reinforcing memories   Each time the adult person in script reruns a childhood strategy, it is likely to bring results similar to those it brought in childhood. Along with these will go the same emotions the person felt as a child. Thus each time the process is repeated, the person can say to herself without awareness: 'Yes, the world *is* like I thought it was.'

The person typically builds up a store of emotional memories of these outcomes. When in script, she consults these memories and re-experiences the stored emotions that go with them. They provide 'evidence' in support of the script beliefs, and so serve to strengthen those beliefs. Erskine and Zalcman thus call these *reinforcing memories*. By this repeating process of reinforcement, another closed feedback loop is formed on the Racket System.

Interventions in the Racket System   Erskine and Zalcman suggest that, in terms of the Racket System, the aim of intervention is to help the client break out of the old feedback loops and replace them with new options.

They stress that there is a difference between *interrupting* the flow of the Racket System and *breaking free* from it permanently. To escape the Racket System permanently, they suggest, the person must do two things. First, she must update her script beliefs; second, she must resolve the script feelings that accompany these beliefs. As the person changes in these ways, say Erskine and Zalcman, she can go on to achieve permanent changes in the behaviours, thoughts, feelings and bodily patterns that make up the rest of the system.

This said, there are good reasons for paying attention to all the other parts of the system as well (Erskine and Moursund, 1988). The client's presenting problem will often lie in her rackety displays. The therapist may choose to make an *initial* intervention by asking the client to interrupt the system at any point. He can do this by asking the client to change her thinking, her feelings, her behaviour, or the way she uses her body. This initial change can often act as a 'key' into the more fundamental change of script beliefs and feelings.

Blocking tragic script outcomes: 'closing the escape hatches'

In his early work on script, Steiner (1974) had written of 'tragic' script outcomes. Holloway (1973) coined the term 'escape hatches' to describe three of these possible outcomes: suicide, homicide, or going crazy. Holloway's term conveys the way in which the person in Child may regard these three outcomes, tragic as they are, as possible 'ways out' of a situation that the Child otherwise regards as insufferable.

A major development in current TA practice has been the introduction of the therapeutic procedure known as *closing the escape hatches*. In this, the client takes an Adult decision to renounce all three of the tragic script outcomes. She decides and declares that she will never, in any circumstances, kill or harm herself, kill or harm others, or go crazy.

Crucially, this statement is not a *promise* to the therapist. It is a *decision* made by the client by herself, for herself. The therapist's role is to act as witness. He must also watch for, and reflect back, any incongruity the client may show when stating her decision.

The concept of closing escape hatches was first advanced in a seminal paper by William Holloway (1973). In the same year, Drye, Goulding and Goulding (1973) published an article on the management of suicide risk in hospital settings. They had used a procedure similar to that now known as escape-hatch closure. Harry Boyd and Laura Cowles-Boyd (1980) set forth a detailed method for facilitating the closure of escape hatches; they also explained the script theory that accounts for its therapeutic importance. A further contribution came from Ken Mellor (1979), who focused on the way in which the three tragic script outcomes might act as substitutes for each other.

The role of escape-hatch closure in script change   Why should closing escape hatches be central to script change? In script terms, the option of killing self is seen as the most fundamental escape hatch. The other two escape hatches act as alternatives to suicide. The child may decide: 'I'll kill someone else instead of killing myself.' For go-crazy the decision is: 'Instead of ceasing to exist altogether, I'll cease to exist as a thinking person' (Boyd and Cowles-Boyd, 1980; Mellor, 1979).

When she closes the escape hatches, the client makes a commitment from Adult to renounce all three tragic options. She accepts she is responsible for her own situation, and acknowledges she has power to alter that situation. She thus becomes free to experience and own a full range of feeling responses without fear of losing control.

She no longer needs to maintain a store of bad feelings that she can use to 'justify' her tragic script payoff, so she can also stop setting up the painful situations from which she had gathered those feelings. The energy she was previously using to maintain her bad feelings now becomes available for other uses. If she wishes, she can employ it to achieve change in psychotherapy.

Experience shows that when the person closes escape hatches, he may find he begins to change his behaviour in constructive ways, even without conscious intent. This process can be given more direction by contractual work in therapy.

By contrast, what happens if therapy goes ahead while one or more of the client's escape hatches remain open? It is likely that the client will covertly 'sabotage' his stated contract goals. In reality, what is going on below the client's awareness is not 'sabotage'. In Child, it appears the exact opposite. The person is still clinging to the possibility that one day, if things get bad enough, he may go through an escape hatch. So long as he clings to that option, he is also likely to cling to the familiar patterns he has used to 'justify' the options of killing or harming self or others or going crazy.

The practice of closing escape hatches   To close escape hatches, the client's undertaking not to kill or harm self or others or go crazy must be *permanent and unconditional*. The client commits herself congruently to keep the hatches closed for the remainder of her natural life, no matter what may happen. Anything less – including any incongruity in the statement of closure – means the hatch in question is not fully closed. The therapist will then proceed as though there had been no statement of closure for that hatch.

Closure of the escape hatches is properly described as a *decision*, not a *contract*. A contract can be reviewed, renegotiated and changed if client and therapist so agree. By contrast, the essence of closing escape hatches is that the client's decision is irrevocable and non-negotiable.

All three escape hatches must be closed at one time. Mellor (1979) has stressed that if the client has more than one hatch open, closure of one will increase the likelihood that she may opt for another or others. If the client is not ready to close all three escape hatches, then that becomes the priority for therapeutic attention, whatever the apparent 'presenting problem'. It is also important for the therapist to set up short-term protection against whatever tragic outcome the client may have left open (Drye et al., 1973; Stewart, 1989: 90–1).

Closing escape hatches as protection   Closing escape hatches also serves as a practical safeguard against the possibility that the client will kill or harm self or others or go crazy. Experience shows that the decision to close escape hatches, *if taken congruently from Adult*, does effectively guard against the three tragic outcomes. Drye, Goulding and Goulding (1973) support this finding by reference to the results of a survey of psychiatric patients, with whom they had employed the escape-hatch procedure as a test for suicide risk as well as a means of risk management.

By facilitating the client to close the escape hatches, the therapist provides a central element of *protection*, in the sense of the word suggested by Crossman (1966).

The psychodynamic renaissance

The years since the late 1980s may be too close historically for us to view them in clear perspective. Perhaps these years have already seen the emergence of a new school of TA, or of a major new diagnostic model like the Process Model or the Racket System. If so, then this has still not become obvious in the TA literature.

However, I think there is one stream of change in TA that does distinctively mark the present decade. That is a return to, and re-evaluation of, the psychodynamic ideas that provided the original basis for TA.

I call this a 'renaissance' because, of course, these psychodynamic ideas were not newly born in the TA of the late 1980s. They had already been alive in the work of Berne, as in that of Federn, Weiss and Freud before him. Nor were these concepts even 'brought back' into TA in the present decade; in reality, they had never been away. It was simply that throughout the middle decades of TA's history, most theorists and practitioners had been busy looking in other directions.

The impetus for this renaissance has come via two distinct currents of activity within TA. Both these trends began as long ago as the early 1980s, but they have taken a long time to work through into the full awareness of transactional analysts generally, and all of their implications are still emerging.

First, TA theorists have revisited Eric Berne's original formulations of his theory, particularly the theory of ego-states. They have drawn attention back to the psychodynamic and transferential implications of Berne's thinking. Second, many transactional analysts have been taking a keen interest in the writings of object-relations theorists. They have been considering how they could reconcile these writers' work with TA theory and practice.

But why did this re-evaluation need to be done at all? Was not Berne's original theory couched in terms that were both psychodynamic and easily compared with object-relations thinking?

Berne did develop his theory of ego-states directly from the post-Freudian 'ego-psychology' of Federn and Weiss. As regards the influence of the object-relations school, Berne acknowledged Melanie Klein as the source from which he had derived several elements of his script theory (Berne, 1966: 291; 1972: 134n; Klein, 1949). Berne also cited Fairbairn, calling him 'one of the best heuristic bridges between transactional analysis and psychoanalysis' (Berne, 1972: 134n; Fairbairn, 1954).

It was not for any lack of psychodynamic components in Berne's writing, then, that current theorists felt the need for this re-evaluation. Rather, it was because of rising dissatisfaction with a degraded version of the ego-state model that had become commonplace in TA writing. To trace the origins of this down-at-heel model, we need to look back temporarily to a few years earlier in TA's history.

The oversimplified model of ego-states   The genesis of the 'oversimplified model', as Vann Joines and I have called it, can be traced to the period of TA's mass popularity in the 1970s (Stewart and Joines, 1987: 18–20; Stewart, 1992: 122–6). In brief, the oversimplified account made it seem as though ego-states were *defined* purely by the manner of the person's behaviour. If the person were seen to behave in a 'childlike' manner, then this was deemed equivalent to 'being in a Child ego-state'. If the person behaved in any way 'like a parent', then, according to this degraded model, he or she was by that token assumed to be 'in a Parent ego-state'. The 'Adult ego-state', on this account, was signalled by an emotionless style of behaviour, concerned only with dispassionate reality-testing.

In the hands of some writers, this 'model' underwent an even more bizarre oversimplification. It now simply stated: 'Child is feelings, Adult is thinking, and Parent is oughts and shoulds.' Presumably, this was reasoned out by extension: childlike behaviour often does entail expressing feelings, parental behaviour often means laying down the law, and grown-up behaviour often involves thinking about things.

This oversimplified model, with its three easily recognized 'ego-states', had immediate simplistic appeal. Also, because it focused purely on overt behaviour, it had (and still has) heuristic value in some straightforward applications of TA, for example in communications and management training. However, it will be clear that the oversimplified model totally lost sight of the psychodynamic element that was inherent in Berne's original formulation. Further, because this model also ignored the *time* dimension, it robbed the other elements of TA theory – transactions, games and scripts – of the transferential implications that had been so crucial to Berne's thinking (Stewart, 1992: 122–6).

During the years when the oversimplified version of the ego-state model held wide currency within TA, it was clearly difficult to build bridges between TA thinking and that of post-Freudian or object-relations theorists. By contrast, as the full psychodynamic meaning of Berne's ego-state theory has once again been brought to light, it has become correspondingly easier for transactional analysts to cross-fertilize their thinking with that of their colleagues in the object-relations school.

The ego-state model reappraised   In fact, this reappraisal had already begun by the early 1980s. Journal papers by Trautmann and Erskine (1981) and Hohmuth and Gormly (1982) drew attention to the various mutually inconsistent versions of the ego-state model that were vying for attention in the TA literature. The latter authors in particular highlighted the psychodynamic implications of Berne's original model. They stressed that in the oversimplified 'values-thoughts-feelings' formulation, 'a theory of personality structure arises that is quite different from that proposed by Berne' (Hohmuth and Gormly, 1982: 141).

Haykin: object relations and the ego-state model   Meanwhile, even before these writers reopened the discussion of ego-state theory, a journal paper had appeared that began the reconciliation of TA and object-relations theory. Its author was Martin Haykin (1980). His article genuinely deserves both those overworked adjectives, 'seminal' and 'pathbreaking'.

Haykin's purpose was to review the contemporary literature of psychotherapy, 'especially as it relates to the borderline and narcissistic personality disorders, and to integrate these trends with the theories of . . . Eric Berne' (Haykin, 1980: 355). He began by reminding his readers how Berne had drawn some of the key ideas for his script theory from Melanie Klein, and had acknowledged the work of Fairbairn. Haykin then went on to review more recent contributions in the field of object relations. He focused particularly on the writings of Bowlby (1960), Masterson (1968), Winnicott (1975), Mahler (1979), and the 'self-psychologist' Heinz Kohut (1971, 1977).

Starting from the premise that mental dis-ease can be traced to 'arrests in development' during the person's early years, Haykin used the work of these writers to synthesize a sequence of developmental stages. From Berne's familiar picture of structural ego-states, Haykin constructed a model to show how arrests in development at each stage could be expressed in terms of ego-state pathology.

In a significant addition to Berne's theory, Haykin then suggested that the borderline and narcissistic pathologies were best modelled by focusing on an early Child ego-state which was *split*. The traditional three-part ego-state model, argued Haykin, related to too late a stage of development to be meaningful for these pre-Oedipal arrests in development.

Building on Haykin's work, Woods and Woods (1981, 1982) further developed the idea of ego-state splitting. Citing also the work of Otto Kernberg (1975), these authors went on to suggest practical strategies for carrying out therapy with the borderline client.

Except for this response, however, Haykin's article largely sank from sight in the years immediately after its publication. Perhaps this was partly because of its strangely uninformative main title, 'Type-casting'. It was not until 1985 that Haykin's idea of the split Child ego-state reappeared in the literature. This time, however, it was to make a much greater impression on the development of TA theory.

Moiso: transference and early Child ego-states   Carlo Moiso (1985), like Haykin, started from a standard Bernian model, in this case the analysis of transactions. He pointed out that if ego-states were defined in Berne's original terms, then the theory of transactions was also by definition a theory of transference. Combining this with Haykin's concept of the split Child ego-state, Moiso constructed a transactional model of the therapeutic relationship, particularly as it applied to the treatment of borderline and narcissistic clients.

This paper was one in a series of articles by Moiso and his compatriot Michele Novellino, in which they have described what they call the 'TA-psychodynamic approach' (Novellino, 1984, 1987; Novellino and Moiso, 1990). Their approach is both a model of psychopathology and a methodology for intervention. It combines the explanatory models of TA with a technique of 'working within the transference' in group-analytic style. However, Moiso and Novellino disown any notion that they may have founded a new 'school' of TA. Their approach is avowedly Bernian; they see themselves as simply making developments in a theory and technique that were already implied in Berne's original work (Novellino and Moiso, 1990: 192).

Since Moiso's 1985 article appeared, the themes of object relations and transference have been frequent topics in the TA literature. The influential theorist Richard Erskine has continued since the later 1980s to urge a return to Berne's original definition of ego-states (e.g. Erskine, 1987, 1988). Petruska Clarkson and Maria Gilbert (e.g. 1988, 1990) have argued a similar case.

When Vann Joines and I wrote our textbook *TA Today* (Stewart and

Joines, 1987), our aim was to present an introductory account of TA that was built 'from the ground up' on Berne's original theory of ego-states.

Theory in the 1990s   In 1991 the *Transactional Analysis Journal* devoted two successive issues to the topic of 'Transactions and transference' (*TAJ*, April and July 1991). Among the articles was a wide-ranging review by Richard Erskine (1991) in which he brought together the three themes that were by now major foci in TA. He showed how these three topics – transference, object relations, and the reconstruction of the ego-state model – were logically interdependent.

Another of the contributors to the symposium was Stephen Karpman: the same Stephen Karpman who, twenty-five years earlier, had worked alongside Berne to develop the original ideas of TA. Offering a critique of the various articles on transference, Karpman made a plea for the authors to use crisp TA language and to express their psychodynamic notions in terms of TA theory. He warned against the notion that TA people needed to use traditional psychoanalytic language or theory to get their ideas across (Karpman, 1991: 137). For example, every instance of transference or countertransference could readily be analysed using the language of TA game theory. Karpman concluded:

> Freud's work has a dynamic base, but transference is often presented as an inevitable unconscious occurrence in therapy. With TA, transference can also be seen behaviourally. . . . Thus Berne added the sociodynamic model to Freud's psychodynamic model.
>   The possibilities of an idea may seem exhausted in its own system, but can be expanded when approached by a new system, particularly if the full power of the new system is explored. Thus we can see how TA offers many new perspectives to the concept of transference. (Karpman, 1991: 140)

Karpman here underlines one lesson that is emerging from the psychodynamic renaissance in TA. It is that while TA has learned a great deal from reviving its psychodynamic roots, it can also offer some useful learning back to other psychodynamic therapies. As I have argued elsewhere, Berne's system offers a quality of *behavioural observability* that cannot be found in any other psychodynamic approach (Stewart, 1992: 17–20).

And I would agree with Karpman, as with Berne: if any observation can be expressed in traditional psychoanalytic language, it can be expressed just as precisely in the shorter language of TA. Verboseness and theoretical rigour are not the same thing.

TA practice in the 1990s

The renaissance of psychodynamic ideas in TA theory has not yet been matched by any distinctive shift in TA practice. Certainly, TA psychotherapists now routinely think in terms of a client group that includes persons with the narcissistic and borderline disorders. The many authors who have written on these disorders in the TA literature have made detailed suggestions about treatment planning and the choice of interventions, yet there is no unanimity among their recommendations. This may mean that we are still feeling our way towards a clearly agreed treatment strategy for these disorders. Alternatively, it may mean that there are as many different 'good strategies' as there are borderline and narcissistic clients. In this area, the jury is still out.

Adding a third dimension to the Process Model A more significant innovation in practice since the late 1980s has been in the field of psychodiagnosis rather than of intervention. In the previous section I described the Kahler–Ware Process Model and how it can be used to diagnose six 'personality adaptations'. As the practice of transactional analysts has broadened to deal with the narcissistic and borderline disorders, so this diagnostic model has been extended to take account of those pathologies.

Divac-Jovanovic and Radojkovic (1987) have proposed a combined diagnostic model, drawn on three dimensions instead of two. Suppose that the Process Model's six personality adaptations are placed on a two-dimensional map. This map can then be considered to relate to developmental issues from around the Oedipal stage of development. These authors then add a third dimension, depicting the 'stages of developmental arrest' proposed by Haykin (1980). The earlier stages of arrest that give rise to the borderline and narcissistic disorders lie 'behind' the Process Model map on this third dimension. The origins of symbiotic psychosis, earlier still, lie still 'further back' on this same developmental axis.

Joines (1988) also proposes a model that adds a third dimension to Ware's diagnostic system. However, instead of the developmental stages outlined by Haykin, Joines uses a sequence suggested by Vaillant (1977). This focuses primarily on the individual's current level of functioning, which Vaillant categorizes as 'psychotic, immature, neurotic and mature'. Of course this refers also, by implication, to stages of developmental arrest.

Joines then ranges Ware's personality adaptations around the traditional 'OK Corral' diagram (Ernst, 1971), building on earlier work by Kaplan, Capace and Clyde (1984) on interpersonal distancing. We can then visualize Vaillant's sequence of stages of functioning as a 'third dimension' coming outwards from the page, through the centre of the OK Corral diagram. (This is my own interpretation; the diagram is not drawn thus by Joines in his paper.) The locus of the narcissistic and borderline disorders will, again, lie 'behind' the two-dimensional map of personality adaptations.

These three-dimensional models of diagnosis alert us to the necessity to make a combined diagnosis on several *different* developmental levels, rather than only on the currently presenting level. For example, the client bringing a problem that traditionally would be called 'neurotic' may also have unresolved issues at the borderline or narcissistic level, and these issues may be expected to surface at some stage in the therapy.

By extension, these three-dimensional models help us realize that nobody 'is' borderline or narcissist, any more than anyone 'is' paranoid or histrionic. In reality, everyone – including all of us well-functioning 'normal' people – is likely to be somewhat borderline or a little bit narcissistic.

On the widest plane of diagnostic activity, these models allow us to reconceptualize the whole process of script analysis. We can now see that the traditional three-person script matrix (Steiner, 1966) relates primarily to the Oedipal stage of development. To make a meaningful diagnosis of borderline and narcissistic issues, it is necessary to gather evidence about pre-Oedipal developmental arrests – in a sense to go 'before the script'.

Working with the transference in current TA   The rebirth of interest in transference in TA theory has not bred any unanimity when it comes to deciding how to work with the transference. Current TA is a wide church in this respect. Clarkson (1991: 174) points out that in TA psychotherapy: 'transference may be allowed, invited, resolved, temporarily interrupted, avoided, or minimised, depending on the patient's diagnosis and needs and the nature of the psychotherapeutic contract'. This wide range of attitudes to transference is not the result of mere 'eclecticism' among TA practitioners. It reflects a focus on treatment planning that is designed to meet the needs of each client, based on psychodiagnosis and contract-making. To be sure, there is room for individual preference, based on diversity of experience and training, and on differing models of personal change.

Some TA practitioners today, as Clarkson says, favour working 'intentionally and actively' with the transference. Among these she numbers herself as well as Moiso and Novellino. This preference may often give rise to a relatively leisurely, relationship-based therapeutic style. In a recently published paper, Phil Lapworth says simply: 'For me, the relationship *is* the psychotherapy' (Lapworth, 1995: 47). Interestingly, Lapworth then goes on to describe how he uses a detailed intake procedure, completes a life-script questionnaire, and makes diagnoses using the structural model and the Process Model, before embarking on his relationship-based therapy.

Other transactional analysts, including myself, favour a style of working in which the practitioner recognizes the transference but sidesteps it (Stewart, 1989; cf. Kadis, 1985). This is often reflected in a therapeutic style that is relatively technique-based, closely bounded in time, and founded on a clearly specified contract and treatment direction. Yet the therapist–client relationship is always in account; no matter how virtuosic the technique, it will come to nothing unless it is supported by 'what's going on' at the psychological level of the relationship.

As Clarkson (1991) points out, this diversity of approaches to transference in TA is not new. On the contrary, it has been embodied in the differing emphases of the 'three schools' of TA over the past two decades. It is simply that, with the revival in awareness of transference in TA theory, transactional analysts in recent years have given more specific attention to the ways in which they work with transference.

I reflect also that Eric Berne himself said hardly anything in his writings about the 'therapist–client relationship' as such. Yet Berne's thinking, and the entire TA approach that arose from it, is inseparably bound up with the analytic concept of transference and hence with the notion of the therapeutic relationship.

Coda   With the 'psychodynamic renaissance', the theory and practice of TA have in a sense 'come full circle' from their beginnings some forty years ago. Yet, of course, the circle is not truly a circle: it has not led us back to that early starting-point. Four decades of learning and development separate us from Berne's first intuitions.

The TA writer Pam Levin (1982) has suggested that the process of personal growth follows a series of cycles. As the person moves through these cycles of development, he may feel at times as though he is indeed 'going round in circles'. Yet when viewed from the outside, the path of development is seen to be not a circle, but an ever-expanding spiral. Each time the person revisits old issues, he does so with new knowledge and new experience. He is then able to set off on the next cycle of development in a way that is familiar, yet always new.

Perhaps psychotherapies, like people, grow in cycles. Does TA today stand at the beginning of a new cycle of development?

References

Adler, A. (1963) 'Individual psychology', in G. Levitas (ed.), *The World of Psychology*. New York: George Braziller.

Barnes, G. (1977) 'Introduction', in G. Barnes (ed.), *Transactional Analysis after Eric Berne*. New York: Harper's College Press. pp. 3–31.

Berne, E. (1947) *The Mind in Action*. New York: Simon & Schuster.

Berne, E. (1958) 'Transactional Analysis: a new and effective method of group therapy', *American Journal of Psychotherapy*, 12: 735–43. Reprinted in E. Berne (1977).

Berne, E. (1961) *Transactional Analysis in Psychotherapy*. New York: Grove Press.

Berne, E. (1963) *The Structure and Dynamics of Organizations and Groups*. New York: Lippincott.

Berne, E. (1964) *Games People Play*. New York: Grove Press.

Berne, E. (1966) *Principles of Group Treatment*. New York: Oxford University Press.

Berne, E. (1970a) *Sex in Human Loving*. New York: Simon & Schuster.

Berne, E. (1970b) 'Eric Berne as group therapist', *Roche Report: Frontiers of Hospital Psychiatry*, 7(10). Reprinted in *Transactional Analysis Bulletin*, 9(35): 75–83.

Berne, E. (1972) *What Do You Say After You Say Hello?* New York: Grove Press.

Berne, E. (1977) *Intuition and Ego-States*, ed. P. McCormick. San Francisco: TA Press.

Bowlby, J. (1960) 'Grief and mourning in infancy', *Psychoanalytic Study of the Child*, 15(9): 52.

Boyd, H. and Cowles-Boyd, L. (1980) 'Blocking tragic scripts', *Transactional Analysis Journal*, 10(3): 227–9.

Cheney, W. (1971) 'Eric Berne: biographical sketch', *Transactional Analysis Journal*, 1(1): 14–22.

Clarkson, P. (1991) 'Further through the looking glass: transference, countertransference, and parallel process in transactional analysis psychotherapy and supervision', *Transactional Analysis Journal*, 21(3): 174–83.

Clarkson, P. and Gilbert, M. (1988) 'Berne's original model of ego-states: some theoretical considerations', *Transactional Analysis Journal*, 18(1): 20–9.

Clarkson, P. and Gilbert, M. (1990) 'Transactional analysis', in W. Dryden (ed.), *Individual Therapy: a Handbook*. Milton Keynes: Open University Press.

Crossman, P. (1966) 'Permission and protection', *Transactional Analysis Bulletin*, 5(19): 152–4.

Divac-Jovanovic, M. and Radojkovic, S. (1987) 'Treating borderline phenomena across diagnostic categories', *Transactional Analysis Journal*, 17(2): 4–10.

Drye, R., Goulding, R. and Goulding, M. (1973) 'No-suicide decisions: patient monitoring of suicidal risk', *American Journal of Psychiatry*, 130(2): 118–21.

Dusay, J. (1972) 'Egograms and the constancy hypothesis', *Transactional Analysis Journal*, 2(3): 37–42.

English, F. (1971) 'The substitution factor: rackets and real feelings', *Transactional Analysis Journal*, 1(4): 225–30.

English, F. (1972) 'Rackets and real feelings, part II', *Transactional Analysis Journal*, 2(1): 23–5.

English, F. (1976a) 'Racketeering', *Transactional Analysis Journal*, 6(1): 78–81.

English, F. (1976b) 'Differentiating victims in the drama triangle', *Transactional Analysis Journal*, 6(4): 384–6.

Erikson, E. (1950) *Childhood and Society*. New York: W.W. Norton.

Ernst, F. (1971) 'The OK Corral: the grid for get-on-with', *Transactional Analysis Journal*, 1(4): 231–40.

Erskine, R. (1987) 'A structural analysis of ego: Eric Berne's contribution to the theory of psychotherapy', in *Keynote Speeches Delivered at the EATA Conference, July 1986*. Geneva: EATA.

Erskine, R. (1988) 'Ego structure, intrapsychic function, and defense mechanisms', *Transactional Analysis Journal*, 18(1): 15–19.

Erskine, R. (1991) 'Transference and transactions: critique from an intrapsychic and integrative perspective', *Transactional Analysis Journal*, 21(2): 63–76.

Erskine, R. and Moursund, J. (1988) *Integrative Psychotherapy in Action*. Newbury Park, CA: Sage Publications.

Erskine, R. and Zalcman M. (1979) 'The racket system: A model for racket analysis', *Transactional Analysis Journal*, 9(1): 51–9.

Fairbairn, W. (1954) *The Object-Relations Theory of Personality*. New York: Basic Books.

Federn, P. (1952) *Ego Psychology and the Psychoses*. New York: Basic Books.

Goulding, M. and Goulding, R. (1979) *Changing Lives through Redecision Therapy*. New York: Brunner/Mazel.

Goulding, R. (1977) 'No magic at Mt. Madonna: redecisions in marathon therapy', in G. Barnes (ed.) *Transactional Analysis after Eric Berne*. New York: Harper's College Press. pp. 77–95.

Goulding, R. (1985) 'History of redecision therapy', in L. Kadis (ed.), *Redecision Therapy: Expanded Perspectives*. Watsonville, CA: Western Institute for Group and Family Therapy.

Goulding, R. and Goulding, M. (1972) 'New directions in transactional analysis', in C. Sager and H. Kaplan (eds), *Progress in Group and Family Therapy*. New York: Brunner/Mazel. pp. 105–34.

Goulding, R. and Goulding, M. (1976) 'Injunctions, decisions and redecisions', *Transactional Analysis Journal*, 6(1): 41–8.

Goulding, R. and Goulding, M. (1978) *The Power is in the Patient*. San Francisco: TA Press.

Haykin, M. (1980) 'Type casting: the influence of early childhood experience upon the structure of the Child ego state', *Transactional Analysis Journal*, 10(4): 354–64.

Hohmuth, A. and Gormly, A. (1982) 'Ego state models and personality structure', *Transactional Analysis Journal*, 12(2): 140–3.

Holloway, W. (1973) 'Shut the escape hatch', *Monograph IV*, William D. Holloway MD.

Joines, V. (1986) 'Using redecision therapy with different personality adaptations', *Transactional Analysis Journal*, 16(3): 152–60.

Joines, V. (1988) 'Diagnosis and treatment planning using a Transactional Analysis framework', *Transactional Analysis Journal*, 18(3): 185–90.

Kadis, L. (ed.) (1985) *Redecision Therapy: Expanded Perspectives*. Watsonville, CA: Western Institute for Group and Family Therapy.

Kahler, T. (1974) 'The miniscript', *Transactional Analysis Journal*, 4(1): 26–42.

Kahler, T. (1979) *Process Therapy in Brief*. Little Rock, AR: Human Development Publications.

Kaplan, K., Capace, N. and Clyde, J. (1984) 'A bidimensional distancing approach to TA', *Transactional Analysis Journal*, 14(2): 114–19.

Karpman, S. (1968) 'Fairy tales and script drama analysis', *Transactional Analysis Bulletin*, 7(26): 39–43.

Karpman, S. (1971) 'Options', *Transactional Analysis Journal*, 1(1): 79–87.

Karpman, S. (1991) 'Notes on the transference papers: transference as a game', *Transactional Analysis Journal*, 21(3): 136–40.

Kernberg, O. (1975) *Borderline Conditions and Pathological Narcissism*. New York: Jason Aronson.

Klein, Melanie (1949) *The Psycho-Analysis of Children*. London: Hogarth Press.

Kohut, H. (1971) *The Analysis of the Self*. New York: International Universities Press.

Kohut, H. (1977) *The Restoration of the Self*. New York: International Universities Press.

Lapworth, P. (1995) 'Transactional Analysis', in M. Jacobs (ed.), *Charlie: an Unwanted Child?* Buckingham: Open University Press.

Levin, P. (1982) 'The cycle of development', *Transactional Analysis Journal*, 12(2): 129–39.

McNeel, J. (1976) 'The parent interview', *Transactional Analysis Journal*, 6(1): 61–8.

Mahler, M. (1979) *The Selected Works of Margaret Mahler*. New York: Jason Aronson.

Masterson, J. (1968) *Psychotherapy of the Borderline Adult*. New York: Brunner/Mazel.

Mellor, K. (1979) 'Suicide, being killed, killing and dying', *Transactional Analysis Journal*, 9(3): 182–8.

Mellor, K. (1980) 'Impasses: a developmental and structural understanding', *Transactional Analysis Journal*, 10(3): 213–22.

Mellor, K. and Sigmund, E. (1975a) 'Discounting', *Transactional Analysis Journal*, 5(3): 295–302.

Mellor, K. and Sigmund, E. (1975b) 'Redefining', *Transactional Analysis Journal*, 5(3): 303–11.

Moiso, C. (1985) 'Ego states and transference', *Transactional Analysis Journal*, 15(3): 194–201.

Novellino, M. (1984) 'Self-analysis of countertransference in integrative Transactional Analysis', *Transactional Analysis Journal*, 14(1): 63–7.

Novellino, M. (1987) 'Redecision analysis of transference: the unconscious dimension', *Transactional Analysis Journal*, 17(1): 271–6.

Novellino, M. and Moiso, C. (1990) 'The psychodynamic approach to Transactional Analysis', *Transactional Analysis Journal*, 20(3): 187–92.

Pulleyblank, E. and McCormick, P. (1985) 'The stages of redecision therapy', in L. Kadis (ed.), *Redecision Therapy: Expanded Perspectives*. Watsonville, CA: Western Institute for Group and Family Therapy. pp. 51–9.

Schiff, J. (1970) *All My Children*. New York: Jove.

Schiff, A. and Schiff, J. (1971) 'Passivity', *Transactional Analysis Journal*, 1(1): 71–8.

Schiff, J., Schiff, A., Mellor, K., Schiff, E., Schiff, S., Fishman, J., Wolz, L., Fishman, C. and Momb, D. (1975) *The Cathexis Reader: Transactional Analysis Treatment of Psychosis*. New York: Harper & Row.

Steiner, C. (1966) 'Script and counterscript', *Transactional Analysis Bulletin*, 5(18): 133–5.

Steiner, C. (1971) 'The stroke economy', *Transactional Analysis Journal*, 1(3): 9–15.

Steiner, C. (1974) *Scripts People Live: Transactional Analysis of Life Scripts*. New York: Grove Press.

Stewart, I. (1989) *Transactional Analysis Counselling in Action*. London: Sage Publications.

Stewart, I. (1992) *Key Figures in Counselling and Psychotherapy: Eric Berne*. London: Sage Publications.

Stewart, I. and Joines, V. (1987) *TA Today: a New Introduction to Transactional Analysis*. Nottingham: Lifespace.

Trautman, R. and Erskine, R. (1981) 'Ego-state analysis: a comparative view', *Transactional Analysis Journal*, 11(2): 178–85.

Vaillant, G. (1977) *Adaptation to Life*. Boston: Little, Brown.

Ware, P. (1983) 'Personality adaptations', *Transactional Analysis Journal*, 13(1): 11–19.

Weiss, E. (1950) *Principles of Psychodynamics*. New York: Grune & Stratton.

Winnicott, D. (1975) 'Transitional objects and transitional phenomena', in *Through Paediatrics to Psychoanalysis*. New York: Basic Books.

Woods, M. and Woods, K. (1981) 'Ego splitting and the TA diagram', *Transactional Analysis Journal*, 11(2): 130–3.

Woods, K. and Woods, M. (1982) 'Treatment of borderline conditions', *Transactional Analysis Journal*, 12(4): 288–300.

4

Developments in Gestalt Therapy

Malcolm Parlett and Judith Hemming

In writing about the historical developments of Gestalt therapy there is a difficulty in that readers may well have certain images of what the approach is, which are themselves not accurate. In discussions with psychotherapists who are not Gestalt trained, we come across common misconceptions about the approach, which colour all discussion of it. That such misunderstandings exist is mostly the fault of Gestalt theorists and practitioners themselves, who collectively have failed over the years to communicate clearly the nature of this radical approach, and who have allowed false or incomplete pictures to circulate unchallenged.

We find that there still exist, despite a welter of recent writing, some of it very good (e.g. Clarkson and Mackewn, 1993), images of Gestalt as a therapy primarily geared to heightening emotional expressiveness, with particular techniques that involve empty chairs and the beating of cushions, and a view that the theory of Gestalt therapy is rudimentary and infinitely less sophisticated than, say, that of object relations. There are, as in all stereotypes, some explanations as to how these images have become so durably implanted. And they take us to the core of the approach and to its genesis.

When Gestalt therapy was first articulated as a unified approach and named 'Gestalt therapy' – that is around 1950 – there was one small core group, in New York. A group of writers, artists, therapists and political activists clustered around two German Jewish psychoanalysts – Frederick (later Fritz) Perls and his wife, Laura – who had recently arrived from South Africa where they had spent the years since fleeing from Nazi Germany. The group was characterized by vigorous discussion and expression of differences. No one view or person dominated the group entirely. And in 1951 when the book, *Gestalt Therapy: Excitement and Growth in the Human Personality*, which signalled the 'launching' of the new approach, was published, it was the product of two specific minds and outlooks, although it was actually written by three co-authors: Frederick Perls, Ralph Hefferline and Paul Goodman.

Fritz Perls – who had already written a book in 1942 which challenged a number of orthodox psychoanalytic ideas (Perls, 1947) – had a fifty-page manuscript which he asked Paul Goodman to expand to book length. Goodman did much more than that. He was a quirky, brilliant thinker, very widely read, who overflowed with his own ideas. His writing style has been pilloried and also lauded. Some say it is unintelligible, others point to the fact that he was also a poet and his prose, like poetry, is dense with layered meaning.

The outcome of the collaboration, the first book of Gestalt therapy, included a section of practical do-it-yourself exercises that the third author, Ralph Hefferline, a university teacher, had tried out on his students. The book – known familiarly as 'Perls, Hefferline and Goodman' – still remains a primary focus for theoretical debate within Gestalt therapy. Undoubtedly it reflected the long-term revisionist thinking of Fritz and Laura Perls with regard to Freudian orthodoxy. It also included the basic philosophical outlook which characterized – and still does – the Gestalt approach: holistic, phenomenological, experimental and field theoretical. But there were major additions from Goodman which it is not absolutely clear that even Fritz Perls fully understood. If he did he seemed to make little reference to them subsequently, and even in some respects to repudiate or replace some of the ideas with others. This aside, the book represented an overview of an extraordinary synthesis of ideas and theoretical outlooks, which continues to underpin and constitute the Gestalt philosophy and method. Moreover, this synthesis – involving (as we would say nowadays) a shift of paradigm – had to be appreciated as far more than a conceptual model, but as a 'way of experiencing' (what the authors described as the 'Gestaltist mentality'), without which the ideas and theories cannot be understood.

Prominent in the mix of influences were several outcast sons of psychoanalysis – notably Wilhelm Reich and Otto Rank, but also Sullivan and Jung and Ferenczi. Added was an existential-phenomenological outlook, at variance with the then still dominant positivistic philosophy; a recognition of the overall context (or field) and a critique of Cartesian dualism in favour of a holistic perspective (commonplace in the 1990s but remarkable in the 1950s); and a view of neurosis based on a different model of learning and change (including not locating the source of 'problems' solely within the individual sphere but in the culture).

There were other influences too which were apparent in the original mix. Fritz Perls's love of theatre, and his awareness of Moreno's work in psychodrama, was one of them; another was Laura Perls's background in the expressive arts and body awareness techniques, and her interest in yoga. Paul Goodman was greatly interested in Taoism (Stoehr, 1994).

The theoretical diversity and the clash of strong opinions which characterized the approach from its inception was reflected in more than the arguments which surrounded the contents of the book. There was disagreement even over a name for the new approach, with Laura Perls not wanting the 'Gestalt' label, as it embodied ideas from sources other than those of the Gestalt psychology she had herself been trained in. She also knew that surviving Gestalt psychologists, like Wolfgang Kohler, would object to the use of the name. They did.

Alongside the writing of the book, the first training institute was being set up in New York. The spirit of the first discussion/peer therapy group was continued in the Institute's somewhat anarchic procedures. It resisted establishment, permanence and conformity. To this day the New York Gestalt Institute does not have its own building but meets in various places. This is indicative of a wider pattern which has profound implications for understanding the development of Gestalt therapy.

For what has arisen is not a single unified school, with its adherents all following a circumscribed practice laid down from the centre. While there is undoubtedly a core synthesis of ideas and a broadly conceived method to hold on to, there is immense scope for interpreting these distinctively. Indeed, Laura Perls has expressed the view that there is not a single Gestalt therapy but as many therapeutic approaches as there are Gestalt therapists – and that the Gestalt therapist needs to be open to finding unique ways of working with individuals – which implies almost inventing a new therapy for that person and situation (Rosenblatt, 1995). This, of course, is impossible in practice and taken to its logical conclusion would suggest that there is no such thing as Gestalt therapy as a distinctive, recognizable entity – yet there undoubtedly is one. But the lack of fixed orthodoxy and penchant for variation was present from the beginning.

Needless to say, the fundamental opposition to permanent organization and orthodoxy dictated from the centre has not been followed uniformly! Indeed, there have been many attempts to organize, to establish institutes and training procedures, and stark warnings (From, 1984) about the need to circumscribe Gestalt therapy theory, delineating its boundaries and holding to them, so that it cannot be bent into any shape by any individual wishes, regardless of its fundamental ideas. There has been recognition that for the approach to continue to exist as a separate entity, the *gestalt* of Gestalt therapy (its overall form and distinctive qualities) cannot become too diffuse and all-inclusive. Thus the fresh and anarchistic nature of the approach has been tempered with some continuing struggles over 'maintaining the essence' of Gestalt therapy, and steps have been taken towards institutional-ization, though a leaning towards diversity remains.

The important point for the present discussion is that when we talk of the developments of Gestalt therapy we are having to discern overall patterns within a field of great variation, spread over two or three generations. Not only did the original core group tolerate a lot of differences between themselves, but when *Gestalt Therapy* was written and teaching began to spread out centrifugally, differences of emphasis appeared from the outset, with no 'national association' or franchising authority to provide a centri-petal counterbalance. As happened, for instance, in the spread of Buddhism – where there was never a central enforcing agency and ample scope for reinterpretation of the original teachings – numerous individual teachers and Gestalt training institutes all around the world have developed versions of Gestalt therapy largely out of immediate contact with others – though, as we shall see, this state of affairs is now being challenged.

While there has been much publishing in recent years, there was until the

1980s very little new writing, and therefore little scope for further development of the approach collectively and internationally. During the long period of theoretical quiescence, with core teachings being passed on predominantly via the oral tradition linked to experiential learning, the separate 'schools' of Gestalt therapy proceeded more or less independently. Many of the differences found across the globe can be traced to which original American teacher first travelled there, and where and with whom this teacher him/herself was trained, or which 'sphere of influence' he or she came from. (Gestalt therapy is represented in developed countries all around the world, with a strong presence, for instance, in Germany, France, Italy, Brazil, Australia, Russia and Spain, to name a few. The exact number and distribution of Gestalt institutes is unknown, as there is – as yet – no international coordinating agency to gather such data.)

'Lineages' within Gestalt therapy

In order to appreciate the developments that have occurred it is necessary to trace some of the major 'lineages', particularly in America, since that is where all the teaching originally sprang from, although there have been separate developments since then in other countries (like Germany) which can be regarded as truly 'home grown'.

The first lineage is that of the New York Institute, where Laura Perls and Isadore From remained as prominent 'traditionalists' (though they would have hated being so described, considering their anarchistic leanings and Bohemian backgrounds) until the late 1980s. They deplored grandiosity, never forgot the psychoanalytic roots of Gestalt therapy, engaged assidu-ously in long-term individual Gestalt therapy, were profoundly sceptical towards simplified and popular versions of Gestalt therapy (including those Fritz Perls propagated), and travelled a lot overseas, especially in continen-tal Europe, where they were greatly loved and respected. The New York Institute itself has had a turbulent history, with not always much cohesiveness, but still remains a historically focal point. However, there are no less than four other Gestalt trainings being offered in Manhattan at the present time, evidence in itself of the capacity for Balkanization of Gestalt therapy.

Soon after the New York Institute was established in 1951, a group of mainly clinical psychologists in Cleveland, Ohio, began to invite members of the New York group to come and teach them. Though an outgrowth from New York beginnings, with Isadore From its main visiting teacher, the Cleveland Institute developed in a very different manner, true to its Midwestern milieu. It acquired its own buildings and developed over the years a large training programme (now with many hundreds of graduates) and many local links with hospitals and universities. The Gestalt Institute of Cleveland has continued to develop theoretically and practically along its own lines, rather in isolation – though again, this is changing fast. Three members of that community, however, have had international impact from the early days. Joseph Zinker's teaching on creativity and experiment (1977) has been a major influence worldwide. Erving and Miriam Polster (1973) wrote the first book articulating the original theory of Gestalt into its clinical applications. They moved to San Diego in the mid-1970s and many Gestaltists from around the world have attended their summer training programmes. All three have also frequently visited as trainers for Gestalt programmes outside the USA.

The greatest diverging influence was, of course, that of Fritz Perls himself. Almost before the ink was dry on the manuscript of the founding book, he left New York and began travelling extensively and living away from his wife, for longer and longer periods. He spent periods of years living in Florida, California and British Columbia. Particularly during his Esalen years (at the famed growth centre) he had immense influence. By this time he appeared almost to have repudiated some of his earlier work, and in his enthusiasm to disseminate his ideas seemed also to simplify them. In keeping with the times (the early 1970s), he favoured vivid direct experience over intellectualized discussion, and he also gathered a huge personal following. In his last years he was clearly disturbed by the massive oversimplification of the approach, as displayed by followers, though he had been largely responsible for this.

There is a case to be made that Fritz Perls's charismatic and brilliant style of demonstrating and interpreting Gestalt therapy put it durably on the therapy map. But there were costs. Many of the stereotypes we have referred to – for instance the use of empty chairs – arose from the huge visible exposure of Gestalt therapy at that time. Other lineages, while still proceeding, were not capturing the public imagination in the same way. They offered a practice different in kind from what has been termed 'Perlsism'. In the long term, however, it was the steady growth within these traditions which has kept Gestalt therapy on the map. Had there not been these other ongoing centres, in New York and Cleveland, and a continuing lineage in California through Jim Simkin and later the Los Angeles Gestalt Institute, Gestalt therapy might have died out altogether, regarded as another brilliant comet which briefly lit up the sixties sky.

The superseding of 'Perlsism'

As we have indicated, generalizations which apply right across the field of Gestalt therapy are suspect, given the variations to be found on the ground. Yet one or two can be advanced with confidence. One is that there has been a definite swing away from the kinds of Gestalt therapy which Fritz Perls promulgated at the height of his popularity, with other strands and traditions – especially the New York, Cleveland and Los Angeles influences – remaining relatively intact, certainly by comparison.

Some of the most popular images of Gestalt derive from Fritz Perls's films and popular books, such as *Gestalt Therapy Verbatim* (Perls, 1969). The film which has had the most lasting impact is the one in which Perls, Carl Rogers and Albert Ellis work with a woman called 'Gloria'. Many Gestalt therapists today view this with mixed feelings since Perls's confrontational style is no longer regarded as a model.

Although 'Perlsism' (Dublin, 1976) is not easy to encapsulate, it represents a style of work which fitted the needs of the 1960s, whereas a wholly different synthesis of Gestalt ideas and methods of work is required today. It is not so much what Perls actually thought, wrote and did himself that needed to be superseded, as what was imitated and misrepresented by all sorts of inadequately trained and intellectually disinclined 'therapists' who were drawn to him. That is not to let Perls himself off the hook altogether. He sometimes acted unethically and he was abusive. He also swallowed the anti-intellectualism of the Californian growth scene and provided easy slogans (e.g. 'Lose your head and come to your senses', 'Shit or get off the pot') which set a particular tone, popular and shocking at the time, that did not endear him to serious-minded mental health professionals. Nevertheless, many flocked to work with this extraordinary, brilliant and provocative therapist/teacher, and were inspired by him.

What was rarely understood – and this is what made him dangerous for imitators with little clinical experience – was that Perls's skill was not a magic which could be picked up in a few weekends of observing it: it grew out of, and relied upon, clinical acumen and subtle diagnostic work which Perls had accumulated through decades of psychoanalytic training and professional practice as a psychiatrist. So when he confronted someone, or refused to work with certain people, or made an outrageous suggestion for a behavioural change, or did something else extraordinary which seemed to unlock a person's energy in some utterly beautiful way, he was taking the short cuts of the master therapist. Yet it was a style which, if copied with no understanding, was a blunt instrument or even an abusive one.

Copying Perls had other results. For instance, when – adapting a technique from Moreno (characteristically without attribution) – Fritz Perls began to work regularly with two chairs, asking his volunteers to move from one to another in order to explore their polarized selves, he was experimenting, as do all great artist/craftsmen who seek to innovate and extend the boundaries of what they do. He would have been appalled if he had thought that this technique would somehow in time become identified for a lot of people as 'the way Gestalt therapists work'. (It has been suggested that it was possible, with some poorly trained therapists, to identify the date of their limited exposure to Fritz Perls by noting the specific technique they employed and which they had religiously copied from Perls, given that he was constantly changing the way he worked and 'the phases' can be dated.)

The reaction against Perlsism – which Gestalt writers have been writing about for ten years now (e.g. Clarkson, 1991; Yontef, 1993) – has been so profound and widespread that there is danger of Fritz Perls's contributions being undervalued. As Clarkson and Mackewn (1993) point out, that would be as much a mistake as arguing that Perls's 1960s version of Gestalt therapy is all there was on offer. What has been rejected – widely if not universally – is the legacy of anti-intellectualism, which meant that many people who were phobic towards articulating their ideas or having any intellectual discourse were sustained in their limitation (and that Gestalt therapy disappeared from most therapy textbooks). A concentration on 'Gestalt techniques' has been abandoned in favour of a deeper appreciation (at least within the Gestalt community itself) of how important it is to ground experimentation in the unique conditions of the field, and not to use 'off the shelf' methods in some automatic ritual (we recall the days when, if someone said they felt angry, the therapist or a group member would reach for a cushion). There has been a strong repudiation of the ethical transgressions, notably the sexual exploitation of patients and trainees, for which Perls was notorious (as were some other 'gurus' of the same era, of course). There has been a shift away from the workshop format that Perls favoured – where a group of strangers came together for a few days, often only a weekend, and where the therapist worked with one person at a time in the so-called 'hot seat' (which evidently Perls, not being an American, did not realize was also slang for the electric chair). Now most practitioners work long term with individuals and groups, and in groups there is attention to the group process, not just to individuals. Lastly, the 'therapist in theatre director' role, which Perls often exemplified, has been substituted in most places with the role of 'therapist as someone with whom to relate, to connect, or to dialogue'.

Fritz Perls was an extreme man, colourful, a maverick, and undoubtedly a brilliant, theatrical demonstrator of Gestalt therapy. In moving away from Perlsism, there have been recent suggestions that the pendulum may have swung too far. Daniel Rosenblatt, a friend and colleague of Laura Perls, has suggested that the quintessential Perlsian Gestalt therapist could be said to have the following qualities: 'charismatic, rebellious, anarchistic, chaotic, primitive, sexual, vulgar, creative artist, playful bohemian, intuitive, personal, aggressive, destructive, visceral, gutsy and lively' (1995: 47). He goes on: 'What I am pleading for is that Gestalt therapists do not become pious, smug, routinized, scholastic and academic. . . . Gestalt therapy has become successful and copied to the degree that it has maintained a tradition of "the Outsider", somewhat unpredictable, subversive of received truths and conventional beliefs about oneself and society' (ibid.: 48).

Rosenblatt suggests the possibility of a counter-reaction to the counter-reaction in Gestalt, reminding the present generation of Gestalt therapists of their subversive roots. There is support for this view just as there is for the opposite trend, of continuing to question received Gestalt ideas, of practitioners and teachers becoming more intellectually sophisticated, and more involved in the mainstream of psychotherapy. It is to these developments that we now turn.

From 'figure' to 'field'

As Resnick has recently pointed out, one of Fritz Perls's most important contributions was that he popularized the fact that 'any living organism, including a person, cannot be understood by merely looking at the organism; the organism must be seen in its environment, of its context, of its field' (in Resnick and Parlett, 1995). This recognition of the continuous relationship between organism and environment, and of their shared field, has existed right from the beginning of Gestalt. It was always understood that even in a theoretical sense different parts of the field cannot be separated; inevitably individuals and events are context bound and exist in an ever-changing relation to one another.

In their essence, these ideas of field and function are embodied in the Gestalt concepts of figure and ground, which offer a scaled-down description of the field as being the 'figure and ground in relationship'. This notion, taken over from Gestalt psychology, is a cornerstone of Gestalt therapy. However, as Beaumont (1993) and others (Wheeler, 1991; Parlett, 1991) have pointed out, Gestalt practice has tended to focus almost exclusively on what is figural rather than what is in the ground, on what is present and most vivid in the moment rather than on the background factors in a person's life. Beaumont has even suggested that much Gestalt therapy might be called 'figure therapy', so oriented does it tend to be to what is immediate and obvious. Wheeler has written about 'the structured ground' of long-term relationships and commitments, and the necessity to look at people's constructions of their overall lives, not just to 'the issues' which they bring to therapy (Wheeler, 1991).

The 'here and now' emphasis of Gestalt represented a radical shift in the practice of psychotherapy as it was, and to this day remains a priority. However, like any powerful and useful insight it opened up the possibility of overlooking the very insights it replaced. And Gestalt therapists are now allowing much more of the ground of a person's experience to become part of the therapeutic exploration. Rather than concentrating on offering an intense learning experience of great immediacy, they also pay attention to the question of whether the learning can be carried over into the person's everyday life and be fully integrated. An event produced in the setting of a therapy session may need recontextualizing. If, for example, a person has, within a therapy session or a group, the experience of releasing and expressing his anger, it is not necessarily helpful for the individual if he is unable also to manage his anger effectively when he returns to his workplace or family. Releasing anger as he 'learned' to do in therapy could have unanticipated and destructive consequences. A field theory perspective underlines the importance of attending to the transferability of experience.

Erving Polster (1987) made a similar 'correction' to over-attending to the present moment when he argued that there was a place for Gestalt therapy clients to be allowed 'to tell their stories'. Again, it is not at all clear that such a corrective would be required of all Gestalt therapists – it depends largely on where they trained. Some of the original practitioners would naturally have honoured the whole context of individuals, their developmental history and culture. But certainly such a wider perspective was often lost to view in the Fritz-Perls-dominated 1960s and 1970s.

Another facet of earlier forms of Gestalt therapy was its emphasis on action in the moment; its popularity stemmed partly from the fact that participants experienced such liveliness when they came fully into the present and actually did something. It offered all those ingredients that can still create an electrifying experience, cutting through poor contact and stories that have become old and stale or repetitious. The emphasis was on immediate action and experiment: *Client*: 'I want to feel closer to people.' *Therapist*: 'How could you do that now? In this room?'

Such interventions raise energy and riskiness, nudging people into new territory. They build on the key truth that change can only take place in the present, and that change means redefining boundaries, moving into the unknown. People also require support so that new emergencies can be safe enough to be embarked upon. This liveliness, and the pursuit of closure that fuelled the urgency to express feelings or develop a new pattern of behaviour, has latterly been set against other important needs, for instance the need to develop a relationship with the therapist, who is a major part of the field of the client.

Let us digress for a moment on to the key place of field theory in modern Gestalt, as recognized by an increasing number of practitioners and theorists. Its principles are basic to the theory of Gestalt therapy (Parlett, 1991). Elements of the field may be thought of as anything that affects meaning. A piece of furniture only has meaning within a specific context in time and space: a table can easily be used as a seat, or as a room divider, and we need to understand *how* it is being used and what *for*, before we can understand how the table is experienced by any particular individual. And an even fuller description of a person's experience of the table might take us into how it has been advertised, described in craft journals, remembered from the past, or compared to other furniture in the present moment. In a similar way we give meaning to a couple relationship in the context of its enactment – e.g. is the couple in 'dutiful parent' mode, preparing to visit a school, or are they 'free of the kids' and on a second honeymoon? Single events (like a handshake) are interpretable only in relation to a vast number of cultural, familial and other influences. With a set of rules, we would need to know the whole field in which that set of rules is operating before judging whether the rules were oppressive or light, useful or irrelevant. To investigate and find such meaning takes the Gestalt therapist away from exclusive attention to the immediate and observable. In ongoing therapy – as opposed to therapy demonstrations – such attention to the wider field is essential.

Another principle of field organization relates to time. Although it is undeniable that we can only act or be in the present, what we engage in may, significantly, be remembering the past or anticipating the future. This emphasis on the importance of remembering and planning has had to be relearned, as it were, by Gestalt therapists. Many of the early Gestaltists were steeped in psychoanalytic theory and ways of working. In reacting against 'talking about' and the 'there and then', some Gestalt therapists (who did not have the taken-for-granted common sense of the originators), were inclined to take the principle and make it a rule, even to the point of sometimes urging clients not to speak of last week.

Wheeler (1991) has referred to the 'structured ground' of a person's life as having organization and continuity, with constraints of past habits and future plans embedded in her ground, or to use Lewin's phrase, her 'life space'. When we attend to what is figural we are only looking at a fraction (fractal) of the total picture, and not necessarily accessing what might be useful perspectives from the wider ground of that person.

From individual to system

Historically there have been changes in the forms in which Gestalt therapy is practised. There was – especially among those from the numerically dominant Fritz Perls lineage – a tendency for Gestalt to be seen as a form of brief therapy, conducted mainly in groups but with a focus on 'individual interaction with the therapist'. Over the past twenty years the focus has shifted, with more organic, group-focused ways of conducting group therapy now being more common. Longer-term individual therapy has been recognized as essential, especially for working with individuals with personality disorders (Yontef, 1993).

Regarding groups, the Gestalt Institute of Cleveland has played a leading part. For example, the faculty there has developed a Gestalt theory of groups, elaborating the process of the group as a whole – how it interacts, creates and completes group *gestalts* (or fails to do so) (Kepner, 1980). The therapist – in this approach a facilitator of the group, thinking of him/herself almost as a consultant to the group – will intervene on various levels, either at an individual intrapsychic level (e.g. suggesting an experiment a participant might make with breathing deeply and slowly), or interpersonally (e.g. inviting two participants to address one another) or at the level of the group as a whole (e.g. commenting that the energy of the group has dropped) (Kepner, 1980). While this way of running groups has not superseded groups based primarily on individuals working sequentially and individually with the group leader, there has been undoubted acknowledgement of the need to attend to group process. There is also more interest in and discussion of the systemic impact of a group, its culture and norms, on the participating individuals.

Gestalt philosophy and methods have also been applied in other settings, particularly in work in organizations. There are now many people working at a large system level, mainly as organization development consultants, exploring management styles, resistance to change, blocks to communication, and so on (e.g. Nevis, 1987; Merry and Brown, 1987). The Centre for the Study of Intimate Systems in Cleveland has also pioneered applying (and teaching) Gestalt therapy principles and methods to working with couple and family systems (Zinker, 1994).

Gestalt thinking has also been applied to education. *Gestaltpädogogik* is a specialist area of educational theory and practice in Germany. George and Judith Brown, in the USA, have developed a training programme in 'confluent education' which is based on Gestalt principles (Brown, 1971). In post-communist Russia numerous educational innovations are being influenced by Gestalt principles (Pauline Rose Clance, personal communication).

The therapy relationship

As with all therapy, effective Gestalt therapy needs to provide a bounded and supportive context in which the therapeutic relationship can flourish. Although the notion of support was always part of Gestalt thinking and central to the teaching of Laura Perls, the emphasis (especially, but not exclusively, among those greatly influenced by Fritz Perls) had been more on the challenging skill of the therapist (the *provocateur*) than on his or her supportive presence (the *évocateur*) (see Nevis, 1987). Laura Perls taught that a good therapist should provide support for the client, but no more was to be given than 'just enough' so that the client could continue. Too much support and the value position of Gestalt therapy – that people can learn to take responsibility, and realize that they have choice, concerning their lives – could be undermined.

Altogether the bias has traditionally been towards what Erving Polster has informally termed 'business as unusual' – that is, favouring what is novel and fresh, extending boundaries, and choosing the experimental alternative. Encouraging risk-taking feeds into a particular therapeutic style. While lip service has been paid to respecting and working with resistance rather than trying to promote change, the full elaboration of the 'paradoxical theory of change' (Beisser, 1970) did not come until the 1970s. Beisser's view, fundamental to Gestalt, was that full acceptance of 'where one is now' – including the so-called resistant factors – allows for possible moves from that position. In other words, change occurs as a result of awareness rather than from attempts by one part of the self to manipulate another in the service of intentional change. Resistance was crucial, and to be honoured.

Some of the strongest reactions to earlier excesses have been voiced by Gestalt therapists associated with the Los Angeles Institute of Gestalt Therapy (perhaps not surprisingly, given that the worst 'excesses' of the post-Fritz-Perls 'fad' for Gestalt therapy were occurring in California). Both Yontef (1993) and Resnick (in Resnick and Parlett, 1995) have reacted against the theatrical and cathartic kinds of display which characterized this manifestation of Gestalt therapy – which they have described as 'Boom-Boom' therapy. Such demonstrations, often provided by flamboyant and charismatic practitioners (some of whom dressed and spoke like Fritz Perls and grew similar beards), not only contributed to Gestalt therapy's one-time reputation as a 'dangerous' therapy, but also of course wholly misunderstood that personal change is incremental and rests on assimilation of many learnings rather than on a single explosion which may not always be followed up. As Resnick says: 'There was something about catharsis alone, about valuing pyrotechnics and abrasiveness where emotional expressiveness was considered the ultimate therapeutic success [but] heat without light is usually a waste of time. One sometimes needs the abreaction, the catharsis, but without awareness, assimilation and integration, it is mostly useless' (in Resnick and Parlett, 1995: 5).

The pattern of longer-term individual therapy – always a feature of versions of Gestalt therapy which derived from New York or Cleveland lineages – is now probably the predominant form of therapy, its most common medium. One-off weekend workshops have declined in number. Thus, in superficial appearance, Gestalt therapists proceed in ways more like those of psychodynamic psychotherapy. And with the management of therapy in this format have come some of the concerns of analytical therapists. For instance, Gestalt therapists are now more inclined than any time previously in their history to reflect on the need to avoid blurred roles between training and therapy, and other questions about boundaries. Moreover, interest in the longer-term reparative functions of therapy and of the developmental stages of the therapeutic relationship (Shub, 1992) has increased, as has understanding and beginning elaboration of a Gestalt theory of psychological development. Stern's (1985) insights into infant development, in particular, have been recognized as compatible and useful.

Although transference is not a widely used Gestalt concept, in many quarters more attention has been paid to the phenomena of complex fixed projections on to the therapist. Whereas 'in psychoanalysis the data of the analysis of transference is used primarily to explicate the past', in Gestalt therapy it is used to 'further the dialogue and experiential phenomenology of the present relationship with the patient' (Yontef, 1991: 6).

That Gestalt therapists emphasize the real relationship in the room, as opposed to focusing on its past evocations, and value personal phenomenology over interpretation of its meaning, distinguishes them from psychoanalytical psychotherapists. There is a growing recognition among many Gestalt therapists of how long it takes a client to re-own projections and to come into a present relationship. This recognition supports the move away from short-term episodic work and into a greater depth of attention to the therapeutic relationship, based on a more inclusive and broader methodological range.

Another way in which Gestalt is changing relates to the interest in language forms and the way that clients frame their experiences. Gone is the earlier didactic stance on language use, which characterized Perlsian Gestalt and its aftermath; the old Gestalt 'rules' (e.g. 'Say "I" rather than "it"') are downplayed, seen as belonging to a more authoritarian era.

Again associated with the Los Angeles lineage, the importance accorded to the function of dialogue has increased. Whereas in the 1970s, much influenced by Fritz Perls, Gestalt therapists were likely to be playing the part of the observer or orchestrator of experiments, the director of dialogue between aspects of the self, the 1990s Gestalt therapist is far more likely to be bringing his or her own relationship with the client into central focus. Hycner (1985, 1988) and Jacobs (1989), among others, have taken the original ideas of Martin Buber, always influential within Gestalt therapy (though interestingly almost absent from *Gestalt Therapy* (Perls et al., 1951)), and given them much higher prominence. The therapist is now seen as a central participator in the contact, facilitating genuine meeting, encouraging the healing acceptance and recognition of what Buber called the 'I–Thou' encounter. Central to this has been the development of therapists' willingness to reveal aspects of themselves in appropriate ways that may not only further the relationship but also model the process of phenomenological sharing as an additional form of support and education. The importance of appropriate and timely therapist self-disclosure constitutes one of the major defining characteristics of Gestalt therapy today.

Buber's ideas on dialogue focused on the importance of existential acknowledgement and begin: 'when each person regards the other ". . . as the very one he is. I become aware of him, aware that he is different, essentially different from myself, in the definite, unique way which is peculiar to him, and I accept who I thus see, so that in full earnestness I can direct what I say to him as the person he is"' (Buber, 1965, quoted in Hycner, 1988: 43).

The various concerns we have alluded to in this section have together pointed the way to the development of a more respectful and sensitive relationship between the Gestalt therapist and his or her client than was evident in at least some of the earlier lineages. Zinker (1994: 34) has written about the importance of the therapists' 'apperceptive mass' (life experience, wisdom, depth of being) being of equal value to their 'clinical technology', and has also written eloquently and influentially about the therapist's presence as the ground against which the figure of another self can flourish: 'Presence hints at that special state of being fully here with all of oneself, one's body and soul. It is a way of being with, without doing to' (Zinker, 1994: 158). Latner goes further and encourages therapists to recognize that love plays a central role in their work: 'If we cannot trust in love, how can we expect it to transform our work and the ones who have come to us for help? We must serve (love) . . . allow our craft and our wits to be informed and fashioned by it, make a place for it to dwell' (1995: 49).

This is a far cry from the unbounded relationships, abrasive confrontations and sexual promiscuity of much of the early humanistic movement, including Gestalt therapy. Nevertheless it was always implicit in the philosophy of Gestalt therapy, given the latter's attentiveness to phenomenology and to authentic relationship, to the necessity to acknowledge that the therapist is not a 'doer to' but, as part of the field, an inevitable full participant in the 'co-creation of the therapeutic dance' (Parlett, 1991).

Diagnosis

In the early years of Gestalt therapy there was a pronounced disinclination to make use of psychiatric diagnostic systems: 'Historically Gestalt therapy, as well as the whole humanistic movement, have rejected the very idea of diagnosis as being depersonalising, anti-therapeutic and politically re-pressive' (Delisle, 1991: 42). The criticism was that labels were applied to the person rather than to the process they were engaged in, and did not take into account the relationship to the specific context – they were rarely 'field sensitive' in their descriptions. Indeed Gestaltists are mostly still careful to refer to a client as having a 'borderline process' rather than 'being' a borderline. However there has been a marked swing in recent years towards accepting the general importance of diagnosis as a way of illuminating the appropriate path forward; as a differential approach towards clients; and also as a way of furthering contact with fellow professionals in the psychotherapeutic field.

Diagnostic skill allows for different aspects of Gestalt to be offered at different times rather than unhelpfully treating all with the same method-ology. When rethought as a way of identifying recurring patterns of process, it can indicate to the Gestalt practitioner, for instance, in which part of the 'cycle of awareness' (Zinker, 1977; Clarkson, 1989; Melnick and Nevis, 1992) it is most useful to work and which aspects of contact should be focused on. As Delisle (1991: 49) writes:

> Gestalt therapists who sufficiently understand the dynamics of personality disorders are in a position of greater receptivity to those characteristics which are present in their client. . . . If we allow ourselves to make use of the trans-theoretical language of empirical psychiatry, it is my opinion that we will promote the recognition of Gestalt therapy . . . as a powerful contemporary clinical approach to the understanding and treatment of human suffering.

Other practitioners have also written about the value of differential diagnosis and differential use of Gestalt methods. For example, Stratford and Brallier (1979) describe how, when working with client populations such as schizophrenics or those experiencing an overload of change or loss, it is necessary to strengthen what is familiar: the need is to add more 'glue'. Other populations, not fragmented but very stuck, may require not glue but 'solvent' – something to challenge and dislodge an overload of the familiar.

Yontef (1993) is one of several writers who have detailed important guide-lines for working with clients with borderline and narcissistic processes, making it clear that some of the more challenging kinds of intervention in the Gestalt therapist's repertoire could be dangerous for such individuals, and that boundary strengthening and containment are vital. Beaumont (1993) has described the process of working with 'self-fragility' – clients whose sense of self can easily fragment and who can lose contact with the continuity of themselves, their wider 'ground' of self.

Melnick and Nevis (1992) have explored the concept of character entirely in terms of the paradigm of the cycle of experience, exploring appropriate strategies of intervention for different types of dysfunctioning at the contact boundary.

Although it is now clearly recognized that Gestalt therapists do diagnose and should do so, it remains an activity that must be set against the creativity required to practise Gestalt therapy – the flexibility and sensitivity to search for what Zinker (1994) calls 'good form', that ability to be in skilful relationship with each unique person or system appropriately; the opposite to clinging to any set procedures even if they are cast in a Gestalt framework. If the movement is too far in the direction of clinical deliberation, Fritz Perls's insight that 'therapy is all play' (quoted by Rosenblatt, 1995) can be lost.

Attending to the wider field

Gestalt therapy arose in part as a post-war reaction to authoritarianism at a political, social and clinical level. Paul Goodman's thinking was always focused on social conditions and not only on psychopathology; he even coined the term 'sociotherapy' to describe his later work. But the impact of the wider context has received comparatively little attention in Gestalt circles, despite the centrality in its theory that neurosis is as much a function of society and social context as it is of the person as an individual.

If attention has been overwhelmingly on the individual, there is nevertheless growing recognition of the need for a more field-sensitive outlook. It has become more common to speak of the relationship between organism and environment (e.g. person and other) as 'co-created': a person's experience of herself cannot be separated from her experiencing of her environment, and vice versa.

Compared to when Gestalt therapy began, there is more appreciation of holistic and relativistic perspectives in general, so it is not surprising that these parts of the Gestalt philosophy and outlook are now better appreciated. In their clinical work Gestalt therapists are likely today to be thinking along many dimensions – conscious not only of the personal realm but also of the boundaries between the individual and the wider system, as well as the relationship between one *gestalt* and another. Any part of the field which is focused on is always the subset of a larger field, and, as Resnick says:

> a system at whatever level – biochemical, cellular, individual, couple, family, organisational, community, national, planet or cosmos – is simply a subset of the field that concerns us at any given time. The interrelatedness between parts of the field and the effects that all have on each other means that the field is constantly in flux, constantly relational, constantly in process. (Resnick and Parlett, 1995: 3)

Another change that has occurred is that the Gestalt preoccupation with styles of contact has traditionally included a bias against what has been termed 'confluence' – the weakening of the boundary with 'other', allowing merging and loss of separate identity; and also against 'introjection' – where the boundary is transgressed by aspects of other in a way which suggests 'swallowing whole' rather than 'chewing and spitting out what is unpalatable'. Yet, as Polster (1993) has pointed out, all social organization, stable living arrangements and collaborations within community require a willingness to be confluent and to accept unquestioningly some societal norms.

Here we see the questioning of some of the most subtle and pervasive Gestalt therapy values and priorities, or – perhaps more accurately – a redressing of an imbalance that was planted at the beginning, not least as a result of the personal styles and predilections of Paul Goodman and Fritz Perls. Both men were notably sceptical towards conventional lifestyles and social conformity of any kind, and even phobic towards intimacy and familial stability.

Erving Polster, as we have noted, has argued that confluence and introjection can be valuable. His concern to rescue them from being invariably pathologized is indicative of a wider questioning of the whole language of 'disturbances' or 'interruptions' of contact – a language which lies, along with the 'restoration of ego-functions', at the very centre of Gestalt therapy theory. These notions derive from Goodman and have been kept very much alive by Isadore From, the notable New York Gestalt therapist and trainer (who died in 1994).

Gordon Wheeler (1991) has pointed out that the original writers were unclear in suggesting 'disturbances' (thus reintroducing the language of pathology) when the various contact boundary transactions could be more appropriately seen as 'styles' or modes of contact, disturbing or useful only according to the field's needs and conditions.

In the terminology of 'disturbance', 'interruption' and 'resistance' to contact there is an obvious high value placed on contact *per se*. In both theory and practice, Gestalt therapists do also value withdrawal, just as they purport to honour resistance as an agent of creativity and change. But the subtle pathologizing implied in the terminology, which Wheeler, Polster and others have been seeking to correct, runs deep. The more the principles of field theory are placed centre stage, and are fully understood, the more it is appreciated that every quality or action, depending as it does on the immediate and wider circumstances, can never be described as inherently pathological or healthy.

The de-pathologizing of introjection and confluence has become commonplace. Retroflection, a uniquely Gestalt concept, is also a candidate for rethinking. Although it is obvious that there are many occasions when holding back, or being extremely self-reliant, may be damaging to the individual's ability to flow and make good contact, there are also occasions when it would be more significant, from a learning point of view, to interrupt an impulsive action rather than express it. Only an infant would be considered healthy who lacked retroflective ability. From the point of view of the liveliness of individuals, their ability to be self-organizing, engaging with full sensory awareness, neither habitual retroflection nor habitual expressiveness would be serviceable. What is needed is an overall appreciation of the person and their full circumstances; support for awareness and therefore choice, rather than for any particular style of contact. Again, this kind of thinking requires an appreciation of how profoundly all phenomena are comprehensible only in relation to the total situation existing at the time – i.e. the field.

Gestalt as a movement

There has been an enormous change in Western society since 1951, when Gestalt therapy was first formulated as an approach in its own right. It has matured and developed along with the whole profession of psychotherapy generally, in Britain, Europe and the United States. There is now a vast proliferation of different psychotherapeutic approaches; although Gestalt therapy was one of the first of the non-psychoanalytic therapies to gain a footing in the psychiatric and clinical psychological world. At one point it was thought to be the third most frequently practised therapy, after psychoanalysis and behaviour therapy: this was at the height of what we have called the 'Gestalt as fashionable fad' phase, and in the United States there was a dramatic decline in the popularity and in the number of adherents and practitioners when the fashion inevitably changed.

However, Gestalt therapy survived, not least because several lineages had well-established roots in theory and practice. The efforts of one individual in the United States also played a key part: Joe Wysong began publishing *The Gestalt Journal* in the mid-1970s, and also organized an annual conference which began the process of talking and writing. This has grown steadily in the intervening years and communication between different centres and traditions is now flourishing as never before. Similar movements have occurred elsewhere, for instance in Britain, where the number of trainees and practitioners has increased in the years 1980–95 at least tenfold.

Gradually Gestalt therapy has shifted from being a new synthesis of many different ideas to itself being incorporated in syntheses made by other therapeutic approaches. Aspects of Gestalt have been integrated, particularly into Neuro-Linguistic Programming, process psychology, Transactional Analysis, psychosynthesis, and humanistic psychology generally. It is hard to remember how unusual and revolutionary Gestalt concepts once seemed, as they have been extensively borrowed, or in the case of psychoanalytic theory reinvented, in ways that have rarely been acknowledged.

A very big change has occurred with regard to Gestalt training – at least in Britain – over the past decade. It is now accepted that the education and clinical training of Gestalt therapists needs to be very rigorous indeed. In the UK, for example, the accreditation procedure for Gestalt therapy trainees within the Gestalt Psychotherapy Training Institute is one of the more

stringent in the United Kingdom Council for Psychotherapy. The requirements, in terms of training, practice, supervision and personal therapy, are
equal to or more than those of most other training organizations. The
examination procedure, involving in the case of GPTI both a written and
oral component, cannot be successfully completed by most candidates
without at least five years of immersion in study and practical learning.

The development of Gestalt training worldwide has been held back
because institution building and the maintenance of routine systems are not
activities to which many Gestalt therapists have felt drawn. Gestalt has
sometimes stayed out of the mainstream of psychotherapy developments,
especially during the 1970s. However, this trend has, in Britain at least, been
stopped. Two Gestalt therapy organizations were part of the original group
that came together to form the United Kingdom Council for Psychotherapy.
There is now widespread acceptance of Gestalt as a serious form of
psychotherapy with strong intellectual foundations. This has furthered the
aim of practitioners who seek to move out from private practice settings into
work in hospitals, or units for drug treatment or disturbed adolescents.
These more conservative settings have required practitioners to modify
aspects of the radicalism of Gestalt as part of the need to be sensitive to their
particular field conditions. Gestaltists have also found it within their scope to
influence the environment of such settings in the public sector, rather than
confining themselves to influencing clients alone. Through the work of
clinical practitioners and organizational consultants the ideas of Gestalt
have fed into many aspects of the helping professions and the delivery of
care for disturbed populations. However, the majority of Gestalt therapists
still work in private practice settings.

The notion of Gestalt as standing aloof from the mainstream is being
replaced by a willingness to think ecumenically, acknowledging that the
overall trend is towards the integration of previously distinct branches of
psychotherapy. Many of the key ideas of Gestalt are now integrated into
good therapeutic practice generally. Resnick has even said, 'One of the
great tributes to Gestalt therapy would be if we did not have to exist as a
separate entity or an "ism"' (Resnick and Parlett, 1995: 7).

There has also been a strong move over the past decade to establish links
within and between Gestalt communities, creating a much richer forum for
dialogue and mutual support. Both national and international meetings
have become common. There is now a four-yearly European Gestalt
Conference as well as regular national conferences in Britain and abroad. A
recently founded international body, the Association for the Advancement
of Gestalt Therapy, held its inaugural conference in 1995 in New Orleans.

The anti-intellectual bias has definitively been rebalanced and there is a
renaissance of intellectual enquiry and debate. The *British Gestalt Journal*
began publishing in 1991 and has achieved a high reputation for publishing
new ideas. Germany and Italy both have several Gestalt journals; in the
USA a second publication, the *Gestalt Review*, is being established
alongside *The Gestalt Journal* which has been published twice-yearly for

more than twenty years. Thus there is now much more contact between different branches of the Gestalt world, with all the possibilities that this brings from cross-fertilization and expansion of range and expertise.

Nevertheless the anarchistic trend in Gestalt remains alive and well. For instance, there is often reluctance in the Gestalt community to take part in systems that are either large scale or formal – like accreditation systems – on the grounds that such participation leads to conformity, blunts the questioning edge, and sacrifices independence and creativity. The move has been towards establishing levels of organization and professionalization that might have seemed unsettling to Gestalt therapy's founders, but which are obviously necessary if Gestalt therapy is to be understood as a mature therapeutic approach of significant value.

References

Beaumont, H. (1993) 'Martin Buber's I–Thou and fragile self-organisation: Gestalt couples therapy', *British Gestalt Journal*, 2(2): 85–95.

Beisser, A.R. (1970) 'The paradoxical theory of change', in J. Fagan and I. Shepherd (eds), *Gestalt Therapy Now*. Palo Alto, CA: Science & Behavior Books.

Brown, G.I. (1971) *Human Teaching for Human Learning: An Introduction to Confluent Education*. New York: Viking Press.

Clarkson, P. (1989) *Gestalt Counselling in Action*. London: Sage Publications.

Clarkson, P. (1991) 'Gestalt is changing: Part 1 – from the past to the present', *British Gestalt Journal*, 1(2): 87–93.

Clarkson, P. and Mackewn, J. (1993) *Fritz Perls*. London: Sage Publications.

Delisle, G. (1991) 'A Gestalt perspective of personality disorders', *British Gestalt Journal*, 1(1): 42–50.

Dublin, J.E. (1976) 'Gestalt therapy, existential-Gestalt therapy, and/versus "Perls-ism"', in E.W.L. Smith (1976) *The Growing Edge of Gestalt Therapy*. New York: Brunner/Mazel.

From, I. (1984) 'Reflections on Gestalt therapy after thirty-two years of practice: a requiem for Gestalt', *The Gestalt Journal*, 7(1): 4–12.

Hycner, R.H. (1985) 'Dialogical Gestalt therapy: an initial proposal', *The Gestalt Journal*, 8(1): 23–49.

Hycner, R.H. (1988) *Between Person and Person*. Highland, NY: Gestalt Journal Press.

Jacobs, L.M. (1989) 'Dialogue in Gestalt theory and therapy', *The Gestalt Journal*, 12(1): 25–68.

Kepner, E. (1980) 'Gestalt group process', in B. Feder and R. Ronall *Beyond the Hot Seat – Gestalt Approaches to Group*. New York: Brunner/Mazel.

Latner, J. (1995) 'Love in Gestalt therapy – a reply to Staemmler', letter in *British Gestalt Journal*, 4(1): 49–50.

Melnick, J. and Nevis, S. (1992) 'Diagnosis: the struggle for a meaningful paradigm', in E. Nevis (ed.), *Gestalt Therapy*. New York: Gardner Press (Gestalt Institute of Cleveland Press).

Merry, U. and Brown, G. (1987) *The Neurotic Behaviour of Organisations*. New York: Gardner Press (Gestalt Institute of Cleveland Press).

Nevis, E. (1987) *Organisational Consulting – A Gestalt Approach*. New York: Gardner Press (Gestalt Institute of Cleveland Press).

Parlett, M. (1991) 'Reflections on field theory', *British Gestalt Journal*, 1(2): 69–81.

Perls, F. (1947) *Ego, Hunger and Aggression*. London: Allen & Unwin.

Perls, F. (1969) *Gestalt Therapy Verbatim*. Moab, UT: Real People Press.

Perls, F., Hefferline, R. and Goodman, P. (1951) *Gestalt Therapy: Excitement and Growth in the Human Personality*. New York: Julian Press.

Polster, E. (1987) *Every Person's Life is Worth a Novel*. New York: Norton.

Polster, E. (1993) 'Individuality and communality', *British Gestalt Journal*, 2(1): 41–3.

Polster, E. and Polster, M. (1973) *Gestalt Therapy Integrated*. New York: Brunner/Mazel.

Resnick, R. and Parlett, M. (1995) 'Gestalt therapy: principles, prisms and perspectives', Robert Resnick interviewed by Malcolm Parlett. *British Gestalt Journal*, 4(1): 3–13.

Rosenblatt, D. (1995) Letter in *British Gestalt Journal*, 4(1): 47–8.

Shub, N. (1992) 'Gestalt therapy over time: integrating difficulty and diagnosis', in E. Nevis (ed.), *Gestalt Therapy*. New York: Gardner Press (Gestalt Institute of Cleveland Press).

Stern, D. (1985) *The Interpersonal World of the Infant*. New York: Basic Books.

Stoehr, T. (1994) *Here Now Next. Paul Goodman and the Origins of Gestalt Therapy*. San Francisco: Jossey-Bass.

Stratford, C.D. and Brallier, L.W. (1979) 'Gestalt therapy with profoundly disturbed persons', *The Gestalt Journal*, 2(1): 90–104.

Wheeler, G. (1991) *Gestalt Reconsidered*. New York: Gardner Press (Gestalt Institute of Cleveland Press).

Yontef, G.M. (1991) 'Recent trends in Gestalt therapy in the United States and what we need to learn from them', *British Gestalt Journal*, 1(1): 5–20.

Yontef, G.M. (1993) *Awareness, Dialogue & Process – Essays on Gestalt Therapy*. Highland, NY: Gestalt Journal Press.

Zinker, J. (1977) *Creative Process in Gestalt Therapy*. New York: Brunner/Mazel.

Zinker, J. (1994) *In Search of Good Form*. San Francisco: Jossey-Bass.

5

Developments in Transpersonal Psychotherapy

John Rowan

If we try to give a brief definition of the transpersonal, the most succinct version I have come across is by Stanislav Grof. He says that transpersonal experiences can be defined as: 'experiences involving an expansion or extension of consciousness beyond the usual ego boundaries and beyond the limitations of time and/or space' (Grof, 1979: 155).

This at least put us into the right general area. Just as paying attention to conscious verbal content puts us into one realm, and paying attention to the underlying emotional content puts us into another realm, and paying attention to the unconscious aspects of a person's discourse and actions puts us into another realm of consciousness, now we are saying that there are other realms, of which the transpersonal is one.

If you have had a peak experience, as described by Maslow (1973), you will understand this chapter very well. If you have had an experience of the numinous, as described by Otto (1958), you will get it easily. If you have not had any such experience, it will seem a bit strange and you may reject it. Abraham Maslow was the great writer about peak experiences, and in several of his books, he goes into the question in some detail. There is no space for much of that here, but here is an example of a peak experience:

> I was walking across a field turning my head to admire the Western sky and looking at a line of pine trees appearing as black velvet against a pink backdrop, turning to duck egg blue/green overhead, as the sun set. Then it happened. It was as if a switch marked 'ego' was suddenly switched off. Consciousness expanded to include, *be*, the previously observed. 'I' was the sunset and there was no 'I' experiencing 'it'. No more observer and observed. At the same time – eternity was 'born'. There was no past, no future, just an eternal now . . . then I returned completely to normal consciousness finding myself still walking across the field, in time, with a memory. (Hay, 1990: 50)

It can be seen how this fits with the definition of 'transpersonal' which we noted from Grof.

It is hard to write about the transpersonal in a way that will communicate to everyone. The essence of the transpersonal approach is that it is something which goes beyond the ego. But the language in which we write books is an ego function, speaking from the ego to the ego. Hence this ordinary language becomes a barrier and a problem if we want to talk about anything which goes beyond the ego. So it is an unfortunate fact that some of this chapter will communicate very well to those who have experienced what it is talking about, but not very well to those who have no such experience.

A second reason why this chapter will be difficult for many readers is that it has to do with spirituality, and our culture has a curious attitude to spirituality (the holy, the divine), either dismissing it altogether as a primitive misunderstanding, or regarding it as something very religious and very special, the domain of the yogi, the priest or the saint. According to this understanding, this is a field populated largely by fakers and frauds claiming to be spiritual in their efforts to exploit people. For those who go along with this view, the transpersonal would be dangerous and difficult territory, best left alone (Ellis and Yeager, 1989).

One of the most succinct statements of what we are talking about here was laid down by Frances Vaughan (or Clark as she was then) in an article which appeared about twenty years ago:

> One of the underlying assumptions of transpersonal psychotherapy is that each human being has impulses toward spiritual growth, the capacity for learning and growing throughout life, and that this process can be facilitated and enhanced by psychotherapy. In this respect, it has much in common with growth-oriented humanistic approaches such as client-centred therapy, but goes beyond them in affirming the potentiality for self-transcendence beyond self-actualization. (Clark, 1977: 70)

This means that in transpersonal psychotherapy we have a place for all the normal, usual things dealt with in other forms of psychotherapy, but also a place for spirituality – for the divine spark within every human being.

The main commitment is to the spiritual, by which we mean the core of the person, the deepest centre within. It is here that the person is open to the divine, both in an immanent and in a transcendent form. It is here that the person experiences ultimate reality. In other words, this is the realm of mysticism, if by mysticism we mean the immersion in authentic spirituality which people have for themselves. It is the character of mystics down the ages that they must have their spiritual experiences for themselves – they cannot get them simply from reading books or following leaders or participating in ceremonies. It is for this reason that mystics throughout history have been remarkable for their practicality, their down-to-earth quality (Underwood, 1961).

How can mysticism be brought usefully and practically into psychotherapy? That is one of the questions which the transpersonal approach tries to answer. But as we shall see, it is an answer which is complex and at times unexpected. Even in my own work (Rowan, 1993) I made some mistakes about this which are corrected in the present chapter, particularly in the area of the pre/trans fallacy.

History

It can be said that transpersonal psychotherapy has been known from ancient times: there is an Egyptian document of approximately 2200 BCE which contains a dialogue of a suicidal man with his soul. This is quoted in full and explained at length by Barbara Hannah (1981), who makes some very interesting comments on it.

More recently, the classic psychologist William James had a great deal of value to say about spiritual experiences of one kind and another, though he never applied this to psychotherapy.

But so far as anything actually named transpersonal psychotherapy is concerned, we can only go back as far as Jung and Assagioli, and the discussions which led to the founding of the *Journal of Transpersonal Psychology* in 1967–69. So this is a recent speciality, in so far as it has an identity of its own. It was Abraham Maslow, himself no therapist, who inspired the modern movement: Roberto Assagioli says that the term 'transpersonal' was

> introduced above all by Maslow and by those of his school to refer to what is commonly called spiritual. Scientifically speaking, it is a better word: it is more precise and, in a certain sense, neutral in that it points to that which is beyond or above ordinary personality. Furthermore it avoids confusion with many things which are now called spiritual but which are actually pseudo-spiritual or parapsychological. (Quoted in Assagioli, 1991: 16)

It was taken up in various countries in the years after 1969. In England, the Centre for Transpersonal Psychology, under Ian Gordon-Brown and Barbara Somers, was founded in 1973. It put on a series of workshops that combined structured experiential work with some theory. Out of these workshops developed a full training in transpersonal perspectives and techniques. A good account has been published (Gordon-Brown and Somers, 1988) of its work.

The California Institute of Transpersonal Psychology has offered a doctoral programme since 1975, combining professional training in psychology with spiritually focused inner work.

The Belgian Transpersonal Association was formed in 1984, and it was this team which held the first European Transpersonal Conference in the same year. Following on from this, the French Transpersonal Association (AFT) was founded in February 1985. It emerged from various currents, and in particular from a Commission on the Transpersonal which existed within the French Association for Humanistic Psychology (AHP) from 1978 to 1984; this included people like Allais, Barbin, Biagi, Descamps, Donnars, N'Guyen, de Panafieu, Philippe, Sandor, Sée, Stacke and others. The transpersonal approach was also to be found in the Society for Psychotherapy Research with Pélicier, Descamps, Guilhot and others, who put on a colloquium as early as March 1980. Other currents of the transpersonal in France flow from Marie-Madeleine Davy, Graf Dürckheim, Lilian Silburn of the *Hermés* review, Pir Vilayat Inayat Khan, the Yoga Federations and the Buddhist Centres. This shows rather clearly how, in Europe as in the USA, the personnel involved in the early days had a good deal to do with the AHP, and that in both cases transpersonal psychology emerged out of humanistic psychology, picking up a good deal of Eastern material along the way. Marc-Alain Descamps is a prominent member of the AFT, and has brought out, with other members, several books in the area (Descamps et al., 1987, 1990).

Also in 1985 the German Transpersonal Association was established, and another early entrant was the International Transpersonal Association of the Netherlands; here Rumold Mol is well known.

In 1989 the Italian Association of Transpersonal Psychology was set up, which includes an Institute of Meditation. Laura Boggio Gilot is widely known as a representative of this group.

Assagioli was developing the theory and practice of psychosynthesis throughout the 1920s and 1930s (when two articles of his were published in the *Hibbert Journal* in England) and 1940s, but it was only in the 1950s that it emerged from Italy and encountered the wider world, material starting in the 1960s to be published in the USA and in France. The history is well described in Hardy (1987). The Psychosynthesis Research Institute was opened in Valmy near Delaware in 1957, soon after that the Psychosynthesis Association of Argentina came into being, and in 1960 the Greek Centre for Psychosynthesis was founded by Triant Triantafyllou. In 1965 the Psychosynthesis and Education Trust was founded in England: it lapsed in 1969, but was revived in 1980 by Diana Whitmore. In 1974 the Institute of Psychosynthesis was founded in London by Joan and Roger Evans.

Psychosynthesis training centres now exist in many countries, including Canada, Holland and Switzerland, and are opening up in other countries.

In 1993 the Polish Transpersonal Association was established, taking advantage of the new opening up of Eastern Europe. Other beginnings around this time include the Croatian Transpersonal Association, the Czech Transpersonal Association and the Spanish Transpersonal Association, where Manuel Almendro is a leading figure.

A British training school broadly within the purview of the transpersonal is the Karuna Institute in the West of England, which has been teaching core process psychotherapy under the able guidance of Maura and Franklyn Sills since 1980. The focus on awareness and presence in this work derive from a Buddhist perspective. This approach draws on deeper levels of unconditioned awareness to penetrate the processes involved in the arising of consciousness itself. In Core Process work, this understanding, and ways of working, distilled from Buddhist awareness practice, have been integrated with Western practice to form the basis of a practical psychotherapy (Donington, 1994).

In 1993 the Association for Accredited Psychospiritual Psychotherapists was formed in the UK, as a body serving the Institute of Psychosynthesis, the Psychosynthesis & Education Trust, the Karuna Institute, ReVision and the

Centre for Transpersonal Psychology. They choose to call themselves psychospiritual rather than transpersonal, but this organization is clearly within the purview of this chapter.

It does illustrate one of the most important facts about the transpersonal: it has no centre, no founder, no basic texts, just a number of people who are all trying, in their various ways, to make sense of what Maslow called 'the farther reaches of human nature'. They do, however, fall into certain natural groupings, as we shall see later.

The primary interest of all these organizations is in transpersonal psychology generally, not just in psychotherapy: in fact, some of them are not very interested in psychotherapy at all. The transpersonal field includes psychiatry, anthropology, sociology, ecology and altered states of consciousness – particularly as attained through meditation (Walsh and Vaughan, 1993). To these we might add transpersonal management theory (e.g. Ray and Rinzler, 1993) as well as transpersonal psychotherapy.

One of the most important developments in the field of the transpersonal was the publication in 1980 of *The Atman Project* by Ken Wilber. This was followed up by *No Boundary* (1981), which applies the same thinking to psychotherapy in particular. This puts the transpersonal on a much better theoretical footing, showing how it represents a specific stage in psychospiritual development, linking psychology with spirituality in a convincing manner. Wilber has since published a detailed study (Wilber et al., 1986) of how different forms of therapy relate to problems that emerge at different stages on the psychospiritual journey. I myself have tried to relate all this to actual practice in the field (Rowan, 1993).

But perhaps Wilber's most challenging contribution to the field, which has still not been digested by many practitioners, is the idea of the pre/trans fallacy. And it is this which we now need to examine.

The Pre/Trans Fallacy

One of the greatest mistakes made by those who are interested in these matters has been to imagine that there is just one thing called the transpersonal or the spiritual. This is usually identified as ultimate states, illumination, mystical union, transcendence or cosmic unity (Sutich, 1980); the highest state of consciousness (White, 1972); maximum or optimum consciousness (Walsh and Vaughan, 1980); consciousness of the awakened one (Boorstein, 1980); cosmic consciousness (Havens, 1982; Keutzer, 1982); Divine Ground and eternal Self (Huxley, 1993); or unity with God, or unitive consciousness, or the Supreme Identity – in other words, the highest or deepest spiritual state which can be obtained or imagined. There are two ways in which this is absurd:

First, to call something the Ultimate or the Highest is to say that there is nothing further, that this is the end of the line of spiritual development. But how can we possibly know this? Our existing experience is that every time we thought we had come to the end of the line, it turned out that there was more to do, somewhere further to go. Why should this not continue? The fact that we can't see how it could possibly continue may just be our own limitation. We don't know, and we shouldn't pretend to know.

Second, to think that once we pass beyond the conventional ego we immediately enter the highest state of all is to ignore the possibility that there are stages or steps which are more than the ego and less than the highest. And in fact, as we shall see in a moment, it has been possible not only to say that there are these intermediate stages, but also to name and describe them. People like Rolf von Eckartsberg (1981) have shown that writers in the past and present have found evidence of these graduations. But probably the most extensive and adequate version of this has been produced by Ken Wilber (1995).

In following his cartography of the stages of psychospiritual development we shall also be able to sort out another problem for the transpersonal, thus killing two birds with one stone.

Ken Wilber has thrown a great deal of light on transpersonal matters, and is very highly regarded within the transpersonal world. One of his greatest contributions to the field is the idea of the pre/trans fallacy. At first this seems a very simple idea, not worthy of much comment because so obvious. But its implications are enormous. Here is his basic statement as to what it is:

> The essence of the pre/trans fallacy is easy enough to state. We begin by simply assuming that human beings do in fact have access to three general realms of being and knowing – the sensory, the mental, and the spiritual. Those three realms can be stated in any number of different ways: subconscious, self-conscious and super-conscious; or prerational, rational and transrational; or prepersonal, personal and transpersonal. The point is simply that, for example, since prerational and trans-rational are both, in their own ways, nonrational, then they appear quite similar or even identical to the untutored eye. Once this confusion occurs – the confusion of 'pre' and 'trans' – then one of two things inevitably happens: the transrational realms are reduced to prepersonal status; or the prerational realms are elevated to transrational glory. Either way a complete and overall world view is broken in half and folded in the middle, with one half of the real world (the 'pre' or the 'trans') being thus profoundly mistreated and misunderstood. (Wilber, 1983: 202)

Just to spell this out even more clearly, Wilber is saying that there is a path of psychospiritual development which we are all on, whether we know it or not and whether we like it or not. The earlier stages in this development are common to us all and we are encouraged to progress through them by everything in our culture; the middle stages are reached almost as if we were on an escalator – they are almost impossible to avoid because our culture urges them on to us so much. But the later stages are voluntary: we have to choose them, and society does not help us in doing so (though there are some cultures, today and historically, which have actively helped people in these later stages of development).

If we draw a line representing the path of psychospiritual development, the middle of this line would be the personal, the rational, the self-conscious: in other words, the normality envisaged by our Western culture, where we can play our roles and understand the roles of others. This is the realm of the mental ego. Before it, in terms of time and development, would come the pre-personal realms of childhood and picture-thinking, common to all of us before we come to adolescence and maturity. After it, in the same terms, would come the transpersonal realms of the superconscious, the transrational and authentic spirituality.

Wilber has gone further than this very basic layout, however, which I suppose most of us could agree with. He has named the stations on the way, and described each of them quite carefully. Most of his work has been on individual development, but he has also (with the help of Jean Gebser and others) made a case for the development of whole cultures along similar lines. Because we are most interested here in psychotherapy, we shall stick to the individual. In his most elaborate versions, he has many stages and sub-stages, but for our purposes here it will be sufficient to deal with ten, in order of development: (1) primary matrix or pleroma; (2) body as sensoriperceptual; (3) magical; (4) mythic-membership; (5) mental ego; (6) centaur or bodymind; (7) psychic; (8) subtle or high archetypal; (9) causal or spirit; and (10) nondual. Let us look at each in turn.

Level one: primary matrix or pleroma

This is the first state of consciousness we have, the first notion of self we possess: and it is contentless. There is no environment, there is no self to experience an environment. This is an empty form of consciousness, more like the possibility of consciousness rather than anything formed at all concretely. It has been described in such terms as objectless, spaceless, protoplasmic, oceanic, omnipotent, paradisal, desireless, choiceless, time-less. One with *materia prima* as described in alchemy. The most primitive of unities, on a material and physical level. Aurobindo (1973) has outlined these stages in his own way, and he calls this the subconscient level. In Vedanta this is the *annamayakosa*.

Level two: body as sensoriperceptual

The areas of sensation and perception treated as one general realm; simple sensorimotor cognition as Piaget has described it. Wilber (1980) describes this as the typhonic body ego. This is a self which is acutely conscious of threats to its existence, oriented towards survival. Acausality is still present, though even at this early stage there are some built-in expectations. Dreams and images are important, and elementary emotions (pleasure, pain, terror, greed, rage). The pleasure/unpleasure principle reigns. Time is experienced as a concrete, momentary passing present. This is the classic stage of primary narcissism in psychoanalysis. Klein's early stages of paranoid/schizoid, depressive, good breast and bad breast. Non-reflexive body image, the first kind of self-image. Aurobindo calls this the physical-vital-emotional level. In Vedanta this is the *pranamayakosa*.

A great deal of research has shown that the infant is more competent and more rational than some of the earlier theories had supposed (Bremner, 1988), and we must not downgrade this level too much, but it is still the simplest beginning of a separate consciousness.

Level three: magical

The beginning of the mental realms; this includes simple images, symbols, and the first rudimentary concepts, or the first and lowest mental productions, which are 'magical' in the sense that they display condensation, displacement, confusion of image and object, 'omnipotence of thought', animism, and so forth. There is some difficulty with perspectivism, the ability to clearly perceive and understand the role of another person. This is Freud's primary process thinking, Arieti's paleologic, Piaget's pre-operational thinking. It is correlated with Kohlberg's pre-conventional morality, Loevinger's impulsive and self-protective stages, Maslow's safety needs, and so forth.

This level develops in two stages – that of symbols (2–4 years), and that of concepts (4–7 years), as both Arieti and Piaget have suggested. A symbol goes beyond a simple image in this essential respect: an image represents an object pictorially, while a symbol can represent it non-pictorially or verbally. This is very similar to what Aurobindo calls the will-mind.

There is a distinct shift during this period from a more magical to a less magical conception of the world. At the earlier stage the child believes in Santa Claus; at the later stage this is more doubtful. The child moves from having a self-image to having a self-concept.

Level four: mythic-membership

Time binding really begins, time structuring, past and future start to be consciously realized. The self at this stage is a verbal, tensed, membership self. Language is becoming extremely important. Gratification can be postponed. This is the beginning of higher representational thought, but still incapable of formal-operational insight; still anthropomorphic; mixture of logic with previous magic.

More advanced than magic, with a beginning of concrete operational thinking (Piaget) and a beginning of perspectivism (or communal role-taking), but still incapable of the simplest hypothetico-deductive reasoning. In Vedanta this is the beginning of the *manomayakosa*. It is correlated with Loevinger's conformist and conscientious-conformist stages, Maslow's belongingness needs, Kohlberg's conventional morality, and so forth.

Mythic-membership ranks intermediate; it is aware of others, and can begin to take the role of others, but because it is something of a learner's stage in perspectivism, it tends to become captured by a conformist or traditional attitude: the culture's codes are its codes, the society's norms are its norms, what they want is what I want.

Wilber sometimes calls this the rule/role mind. It is the first structure that can clearly perform rule operations, such as multiplication, division, class inclusion, hierarchization, etc., as Flavell and Piaget have shown. Aurobindo describes this structure as the mind that operates on sensory or concrete objects – very similar to Piaget. The key feature of the membership structure is language itself.

Level five: mental ego

This is where we are fully in the realm of Freud's secondary process thinking. This is verbal-dialogue thinking. We acquire willpower, self-control, temporal goals and desires, esteem needs. Time is now seen as linear, extended, past–present–future. Awareness of ego-splits and ego-states, subpersonalities. Ego and consciousness experience their own reality by distinguishing themselves from the body. We have passed through adolescence and have now reached egoic rationality.

This is the level of Piaget's formal operational thinking. In Vedanta it represents the culmination of *manomayakosa*. It is the first structure that cannot only think about the world but think about thinking; hence, it is the first structure that is clearly self-reflexive and introspective, and it displays an advanced capacity for perspectivism. It is also the first structure capable of hypothetico-deductive or propositional reasoning ('if a, then b'), which allows it to apprehend higher or purely noetic relationships. Aurobindo calls this level the reasoning mind, a mind that is not bound to sensory or concrete objects, but instead apprehends and operates on relationships.

The self places itself above the body, like a rider on a horse, and attempts to direct it. The body becomes a mechanism to be controlled and disciplined. This is the characteristic consciousness of our own period of history. We all know it well.

Level six: centaur or bodymind

This is the stage of the real self, the authentic self, the existential self. The splits in the personality between mind and body, left and right, intellectual and emotional, have been healed. This represents the synthesis of primary and secondary process; trans-consensual cognition. What we find here are the things the humanistic tradition talks about: creativity, spontaneity, fully owned emotion, the opening of the heart. Intentionality is fully recognized here, and we speak of action rather than of behaviour; this is the realm of integration, self-actualization and genuine autonomy. Conscious emergence of the real self; 'I create my world.' Highest point in the existential realm. Blissful states experienced and labelled as peak experiences. Cosmic love felt. Ability to transcend the ego and accept its death.

Psychologists have pointed out there is evidence for a cognitive structure beyond Piaget's 'formal operational'. It has been called 'dialectical', 'integrative', 'creative synthetic' and so forth. Wilber prefers the term 'vision-logic'. In any case, it appears that whereas the formal mind establishes relationships, vision-logic establishes networks of these relationships. This is what Aurobindo called the higher mind. It is, as it were, on the cusp dividing the personal from the transpersonal: this is presumably why in some of Wilber's accounts it is not mentioned.

Wilber uses the analogy of the centaur to refer to the difference between the horse-and-rider separation of the previous stage and the unification of the present stage. At this level we have the experience of authenticity; a combination of self-respect and self-enactment. At this level we get what Maslow calls self-actualization, what Rogers calls the fully functioning person and what Perls calls the self as opposed to the self-image.

Now up to this point we are within the range of experience which most of us have had some dealings with, though not many people have fully digested this sixth level. If we want to go on further, we have to recognize that this is rare. We are now about to move outside the range of what is generally acceptable in the Western culture of the twentieth century. We are now entering the realm of the transpersonal proper.

Level seven: psychic

This is the level of the *Ajna* chakra – third eye. It is very important, however, to distinguish this from merely unusual talents which may occur to anyone. The results here are due to spiritual development, not to accidental gifts. They may often be experienced as strange or even horrific invasions of consciousness – what are now called spiritual emergencies (see p. 135ff. on this). The residue of this kind of crisis may be out-of-body experiences, the ability to sense auras, clairvoyance, healing, etc. In yoga, these are called the *Siddhis*.

This means going beyond 'meaning in my life'; giving up intentionality and self-actualization; letting go of self-autonomy. Various traditions call this the lower soul or psychic level. Intuition, openness, clarity are all to be found here in greater measure than before. The transpersonal awareness of others is greater because of the dropping of ego boundaries: the self is not encapsulated as in the previous stage. In Eastern systems, this is the beginning of *manas*; in Kabbala, it is *tipareth*. Those adepts mastering such states, via body manipulation and mental concentration, are generally known as yogis. This is the level of what Aurobindo calls the illumined mind.

Level eight: subtle or high archetypal

This is where we may experience higher presences or guides, guardian angels, the higher self, the transpersonal self, the inner teacher, the overself. It is the home of personal deity-forms such as *ishtadeva*, demiurge, or *yidam* in various systems. It is important to realize that the notion of the divine at this stage is often polytheistic rather than monotheistic. The deity has many names, and this is the realm of the Great Goddess, just as the mythic-membership level was the realm of the Great Mother. The person is likely to experience rapture and bliss in meditative experiences. High religious inspiration and literal inspiration belong here. Symbolic visions may be experienced at this point, and be very important for later life. Blue, gold and white light may appear in visions. Audible illuminations and brightness upon brightness may come. Compassion develops here in a very rich emotional way. Experience of high archetypes. The *dhyani*-Buddha. Insight into, and eventual absorption as, Archetypal Essence. The full entry into the realm of what is called the *sambhogakaya* in Tibetan Buddhism.

In Kundalini yoga this is the beginning of the seventh chakra, the *sahasrara* at the crown of the head. Those adepts who master such subtle structures – nicely symbolized (both East and West) by halos of light at the crown of the head – are generically known as saints.

It is what Aurobindo calls the intuitive mind; in the Kabbala it is *geburah* and *chesed*. Vedanta this is called the *vijnanamayakosa*. It is experienced in a state of consciousness called *Savikalpa samadhi*.

Level nine: causal or spirit

Deity-archetypes condense and dissolve into final-God, the Source of all archetypes. Perfect radiance and release may be experienced. *Ananda* (bliss). *Karuna* (loving-kindness). Formless consciousness, boundless radiance. Final-God self dissolves into its own Ground of formlessness. Samadhi of voidness. Both man and *dharma* forgotten. Coalescence of human and divine; the Depth, the Abyss, the Ground of God and soul; I and the Father are One; *nirguna* Brahman. The Ground of God and the Ground of the soul are one and the same. My *me* is God.

This is what Aurobindo calls the overmind or supermind. It is realized in a state of consciousness known variously as *nirvikalpa samadhi* (Hinduism), *nirodh* (Theravada Buddhism), *jnana samadhi* (Vedanta). This is the *anandamayakosa* (Vedanta) or the *alayavijnana* (Mahayana), and so forth.

Here we have left behind the symbols and images and divine visions of the previous stage, and are out in the deep water of spiritually where no symbols or words will do.

The subject–object duality is radically transcended, so that the soul no longer contemplates Divinity, it becomes Divinity, a release the Sufi calls the Supreme Identity. If the subtle is the home of communion with the divine, the causal is the home of divine identity. The adepts who realize this adaptation are generally known as sages.

Level ten: nondual

Here we can only speak of total Unity-Emptiness. Nothing and All Things. The world at this level is seamless, not featureless. This level transcends but includes *all* manifestation. Identity of the entire World Process and the Void. Perfect and radical transcendence into and as ultimate Consciousness as Such. Aurobindo describes this as absolute Brahman-Atman. The state of consciousness where this is all experienced is known as *sahaja samadhi*. Nirvanic level. *Cittamatra* (mind-only). In the Kabbala, this is *Kether*. The state of *turiya* (and *turiyatita*), absolute and unqualifiable Consciousness as Such, Zen's 'One Mind'.

Strictly speaking, the nondual is not one level among others, but the reality, condition or suchness of all levels. *Svabhavikakaya* is the culmination of Dharmakaya religion.

Having outlined the ten levels, it only remains to point out the four easiest confusions. It is easy to confuse:

the primary matrix or pleroma with the causal;
the body as sensoriperceptual with the centaur or bodymind;
the magical with the psychic;
the mythic-membership with the subtle or archetypal.

This is shown in Figure 5.1.

But it is important not to fall for these confusions if we want to retain any kind of clear map of these states. The primary matrix can be looked on as a kind of void, a kind of nothingness – but it is an ignorant nothingness, an

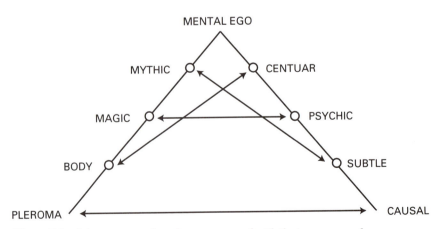

Figure 5.1   *It is easy to confuse the pre-personal with the transpersonal, and this is called the pre/trans fallacy. In particular, certain confusions are very common, as shown in this figure*

empty void, which is prior to any kind of content. The causal level is also often looked on as a kind of void, a kind of nothingness – but it is a pregnant void, a rich void: it is only a kind of nothingness because all the limitations have been removed. In other words, the causal self has been through all the prior stages and is beyond them: the primary matrix has not yet been through anything. The primary matrix or pleroma is pre-personal: the causal is transpersonal.

Similarly, the body as sensoriphysical is an important stage where we really own and are our bodies. All our experience is reflected in and through our bodies: we put everything into our mouths to make sense of them, we explore the world with our bodies and make discoveries every day. We climb on things and then climb off them again, just to prove that we can do it. We are our bodies. The centaur or bodymind stage is also very important. We rediscover our bodies, which we had disowned. We make amazing discoveries – 'I am my body!' We acquire a new respect for our child selves, and want to go back and rescue them in many cases. We can rediscover and rethink our relationship with our bodies. But it is very important to keep the realization that the sensoriphysical body is pre-personal, while the centaur or bodymind self is transpersonal.

The magical is a state of mind where we really believe that magic is possible, because we have not yet advanced to the stage where we understand the logic of three-dimensional space and time. And because all these stages are like Chinese boxes, one inside the next, we all have this magical self still within us: we watch the stage magician and can hardly believe that he or she is only performing a trick, and that we are being cheated. We believe that people can fly. But the divine is not like the amazing tricks of the stage magician. At the psychic stage we begin to have a vision of how the division between subject and object may be transcended.

The mythic-membership level is where we use myth to cement the group and avoid progressing to the next level. We use ritual to stay where we are. We avoid death through celebrations and ceremonies. Often these observances are tied to a place and cannot be carried out in some other place. Often they are tied to a season and cannot be carried out in some other season. They are limited. And in psychology when we find rituals being compulsively carried out we call it obsessional behaviour – again it keeps us where we are. The subtle self goes beyond logic, and beyond the ego, and beyond the limits of time and space, but it does so by recognizing the divine – by having genuine experiences not provided by someone else. Sometimes the divine may seem to be invoked from outside, and sometimes it may seem to be evoked from inside – but it is the real thing, not a substitute. And if rituals are used, as they often are, it is to focus the energies involved, and to take us further away from the fixed positions we held earlier. We can begin to distinguish the low inherited archetypes of the mythic-membership level, which come from the less developed structures of the human race, from the high archetypes which, far from lying in the past, are in fact drawing us on into the future.

As for the tenth level, Wilber says that it could be imaged, in the case of Figure 5.1, as the paper on which the whole diagram is written. It is the ground on which the whole edifice rests.

Finally, we are not just and only interested in the differentiation of these structures of consciousness. Because we have been through all of them, because they are all present, nested within us, we can gain more understanding and control of our internal world by going back and doing them justice. Just as with the usual picture of psychotherapy, where we can gain by going back and re-owning what we had previously disowned – our child, our Shadow, our deeper potentials – so in this sphere as well we can gain by re-owning the stages we had disowned. We can get in touch with our roots, and that process too can be empowering and enriching and energizing.

Similarly, there is a temptation to think that reaching the highest state is the aim of the whole thing. But there is a second journey, back down the levels with the new realizations which have been achieved. Within the transpersonal perspective there is both a movement from the Mental Ego through to the Nondual and a movement of the Nondual (and the Causal, the Subtle and the Centaur) back to the Mental Ego to manifest its nature there. That is why there are ten 'Ox-Herding Pictures' (Suzuki, 1950) and not eight. The eighth picture is about reaching the Nondual, the ninth and tenth are about the return to the everyday world.

The point of this whole section, the heart of this chapter, is to say that the transpersonal is a potentially deceptive and confusing realm, and that unless we pay attention to the map that Wilber has provided we are likely to go astray. In my experience most practitioners do not pay enough heed to all this.

The transpersonal field

Let us now look at some of the detail within the field. The first question to dispose of is – where does Jung fit in? The answer is that Jung hardly fits in at all, but some of his followers and successors do. He opened up a very ambiguous field in a remarkable way, and we have to salute him for this, but he is not a good guide in the transpersonal area. The reason for this is that Jung was seduced by his concept of the collective unconscious into thinking that everything spiritual had ultimately to be reduced to the psychological. As soon as something went out of the realm of the psychological, he refused to recognize it as valid. The evidence for this is well discussed by Clarke (1995). In other words, Jung is a magnificent gateway, but not a good terminus. But let us look at some of his followers.

James Hillman

Later Jungians are clearer about some of the ambiguities in this field, and James Hillman in particular has come out strongly in favour of the idea that

Jungians should stick to the soul (the Psychic and the Subtle in our terms), and steer clear of the spirit (the Causal):

> Within the affliction is a complex, within the complex an archetype, which in turn refers to a God. (Hillman, 1975: 104)

Note that he says 'a God' not 'God', as Jung might have done. Hillman has a polytheistic vision, which is very much a part of the Psychic and the Subtle levels as they are understood today (Hillman, 1981).

One idea which Hillman took from Jung was the notion of an archetype. It is not an easy concept to get hold of, and some of the explanations given seem to me seriously flawed, as for example that they are of the nature of biological instincts.

> One more word we need to introduce is *archetype*. The curious difficulty of explaining just what archetypes are suggests something specific to them. That is, they tend to be metaphors rather than things. We find ourselves less able to say what an archetype is literally and more inclined to describe them in images. We can't seem to touch one or point to one, and rather speak of what they are like. Archetypes throw us into an imaginative style of discourse. . . . By setting up a universe which tends to hold everything we do, see, and say in the sway of its cosmos, an archetype is best comparable with a god. And gods, religions sometimes say, are less accessible to the senses and to the intellect than they are to the imaginative vision and emotion of the soul. (Hillman, 1989: 23–4)

This is a view which comes close to the general orientation of the present chapter. We do not look for biological explanations, which perhaps could be seen as a reductionist way of going on, but rather trust to the mythopoetic mind itself as its own explanation.

June Singer

Singer (1990) speaks of 'the archetypal matrix in which we are all embedded', and this is perhaps more like it – archetypes are not things we have, but more like a sort of home in which we partake, or a goal towards which we are drawn. This fills out the picture somewhat, and helps us to see how useful this concept can be in the actual process of psychotherapy.

Jean Shinoda Bolen

The processes of active imagination and the imaginal world, pioneered in a cautious way by Jung, are strongly related to the archetypal vision. And one of the most important aspects of this is the way in which archetypes can be personalized:

> These patterns can be described in a personalized way, as gods and goddesses; their myths are archetypal stories. . . . They ring true to our shared human experience; so they seem vaguely familiar even when heard for the first time. . . . Myths from Greece that go back over 3,000 years stay alive, are told and retold, because the gods and goddesses speak to us truths about human nature. Learning

about these Greek gods can help men understand better who or what is acting deep within their psyches. (Bolen, 1989: 6–7)

I do not entirely agree with Wilber (1995) when he says that Bolen's gods and goddesses 'are not transpersonal modes of awareness, or genuinely mystical luminosities, but simply a collection of typical and everyday self-images (and personae) available to men and women. Collective typical is not transpersonal.' I agree that they are a bit ambiguous, and could be taken in that way, but I am convinced that some people can take them as entry points into the transpersonal, because I have seen them do it. Using symbols in this way does enable us to think non-ordinary thoughts, and in that way to transcend the normal channels and patterns of thought characteristic of our society. And this makes it possible for the transpersonal to crash into our lives and transform them.

Roger Woolger

Woolger wrote a book (Woolger, 1990) subtitled 'A Jungian psycho-therapist discovers past lives', which expresses quite succinctly what the book is all about. Woolger is beautifully clear about working in a psychotherapeutic way, and not otherwise. It is not his job, he says, to make his client feel better, but to deal with painful realities:

> While there are some psychotherapists who believe that the summoning of beautiful and transcendent imagery – spirit guide figures, gurus, angels, the Higher Self, etc. – is sufficient to alleviate psychological distress, I must confess I am not among them. (Woolger, 1990: 86)

This is something we have to remember all the time when working in this field. It reminds us of Jung's saying – 'We do not become enlightened by imagining figures of light but by making the darkness conscious.'

There are of course a number of other Jungians and ex-Jungians who have made contributions to the transpersonal field, including Mary Watkins (1986), Robert Johnson (1986), Liz Greene and Howard Sasportas (1989), Hal Stone and Sidra Winkelman (1989), Thomas Moore (1992) and others.

Psychosynthesis

There is a curious connecting link between Jung and Assagioli, who is the next name we have to consider. A wealthy woman named Olga Fröbe-Kapteyn was at first very interested in Assagioli and Alice Bailey, and ran three annual meetings for them. It is interesting, however, that although Hardy (1987) mentions Alice Bailey (whose channelled work is still published by the Lucis Trust), she never makes the point that Assagioli knew her well, appeared on platforms with her, and adopted her doctrine of the Seven Rays in his own account of the seven psychological functions (Assagioli, 1974: 49). Later Olga Fröbe (as she was more usually known) transferred her loyalties to Jung and helped develop the gatherings that led

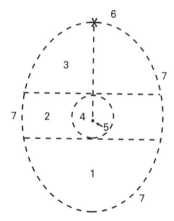

1 Lower unconscious – psychodynamic realm
2 Middle unconscious – usually called preconscious
3 Higher unconscious or superconscious
4 Field of current awareness or consciousness
5 Conscious self or 'I'
6 Higher self or transpersonal self or greater self or deeper self
7 Collective unconscious – source of archetypes

Figure 5.2 *The Assagioli egg (Assagioli, 1975)*

to the Eranos meetings, which she hosted, and the Eranos yearbooks, which she edited (Wehr, 1987; Gordon-Brown, personal communication, 1995).

Roberto Assagioli was a great pioneer in this area, taking off from Freud and Jung and developing his own approach, which he called psychosynthesis. In many ways this is an advance on Jung, and is certainly much more approachable and understandable.

One way of using symbols deliberately is in the form of symboldrama, also known as a guided fantasy, directed daydream or pathworking. What we do is to use a simple scene or story to enter what Hillman has called the imaginal world. The very form of the symboldrama will help the person to open up to the transpersonal realm. It gives a hint, as it were, on the symbolic level, of how we can go beyond words (Whitmore, 1991).

It seems that the honour of first using the word 'transpersonal' in relation to psychotherapy has to go to Roberto Assagioli (1975). He introduced his system of psychosynthesis, which in some ways follows Jung and in some ways goes further, in the years after 1910, and opened up his institute in Italy in 1926. In 1927 the Institute published a book in English called *A New Method of Treatment – Psychosynthesis*. In 1934 an article entitled 'Dynamic psychology and psychosynthesis' appeared in the British *Hibbert Journal*, and this contained Assagioli's 'egg diagram' which mentions the 'Higher Self'. This higher self was later called the Transpersonal Self. But the essential feature can easily be seen in Figure 5.2: the Higher Unconscious (sometimes called the Superconscious) is not the same as the collective unconscious.

In other words, it was Assagioli who first made the distinction between the collective unconscious and the transpersonal. The collective unconscious is something much wider and more inclusive. In the terms we have been using so far, the archaic archetypes within it are pre-personal, while the superconscious archetypes are transpersonal.

> In reality, there exists not only a difference but an actual antagonism between these two conceptions of 'archetypes' and from this confusion between them arise various debatable consequences, debatable at the theoretical level and liable to be harmful in therapy. (Assagioli, 1967: 8)

Here Assagioli is distinguishing between the pre-personal and the transpersonal contents of the collective unconscious.

> To have a true experience of the Self, however, it is necessary to disidentify also with the superconscious. This is very difficult because superconscious states can be so joyous and meaningful that we easily become attached to and identified with them. (Whitmore, 1991: 116)

This then enables Assagioli to distinguish between different kinds of mystical experiences. *Savikalpa samadhi* is the ecstatic experience of the archetypes, which may at this level be god-forms (Aphrodite, Cernunnos, etc.) or experiences of the higher self (inner teacher, etc.) or communion with saints (Mary, Luke, etc.) or angels (as Wilber, 1995, has described in the case of St Teresa of Avila) or high archetypes (as we saw in the previous section) – all these symbolic entities belonging to the transpersonal realm. *Nirvikalpa samadhi* goes beyond this into the realm of the spirit, where there are no symbols. It is a direct experience of Universal Mind. All dualities and images are totally and cleanly removed, and one no longer contemplates or contacts reality – one becomes reality. This important distinction can be made in terms of psychosynthesis, but not in terms of the Jungian theory.

The recent work in psychosynthesis has concentrated on showing how it is a full form of psychotherapy, comprising all the requirements of a full training. But it never loses its connection with the transpersonal. Diana Whitmore tells us:

> In supervision with Assagioli, when I told him that I felt impatient with a client's progress, he suggested that I meditate on 'eternity' and tune into the timeless unfoldment of human evolution. Strangely enough, doing this enabled me to approach the client with a wider and more inclusive vision which allowed me to affirm her reality, as well as see her potential to change. This is not a technique, but a holistic attitude which addresses long-term potential rather than short-term goals. (Whitmore, 1991: 24)

This is to use meditation as an aid to therapy, in a way which seems to me perfectly legitimate, and not to reduce it in any way. The point of meditation, as of any other spiritual discipline, is not to engage in contact with the divine for its own sake – though this may be valuable too – but to engage with it for the sake of fuller living and deeper awareness in the here and now. As Jean Hardy points out:

> Like most twentieth century mystical writers, Teilhard saw that mysticism must be deeply related to action. The sense of urgency about the need to change the world and the consciousness of the human beings within it is felt by many writers this century. (Hardy, 1987: 212)

She goes on to foresee a world in which people are truly awake, and where the unity between people, the animal world and the environment will be completely conscious, and the uniqueness of each creature will be enhanced by the unity of the whole.

We must not confuse this with a blue sky approach which ignores the shadow side, what Unamuno used to call 'the tragic sense of life'. Douglas Mathers has told us recently:

> Though transpersonal experiences are positive in themselves they can be a source of problems if a person is not well enough prepared or mature enough to handle them. There is also a pathology of the sublime. (Mathers, 1994: 76)

This is true, and has been well described at greater length by Wilber et al. (1986) in his discussion of the fulcrums of development. But it does seem as if psychosynthesis is one of the main vehicles for the transmission of transpersonal approaches to psychotherapy.

The academic stream

But there is a third stream, emanating directly from Abraham Maslow, someone else who is a good gateway but a poor terminus. He had initiated the formation of the *Journal of Humanistic Psychology* (*JHP*) in the early 1960s, and in the late 1960s set about initiating the *Journal of Transpersonal Psychology* (*JTP*) in a set of discussions which involved Anthony Sutich (first editor of the *JHP*), Stanislav Grof and others. Sutich became the first editor of the new journal, and wrote its statement of aims. The *JTP* has developed over the years into the prime source of information about the transpersonal, though it still only appears twice yearly. Maslow and Sutich were not practitioners, and so we need say no more about them here, but Stanislav Grof is of great interest as one of the primary practitioner/writers in this area.

Stanislav Grof

Born in 1931 in Prague, Grof studied at the Charles University School of Medicine and received his PhD from the Czechoslovakian Academy of Science. In 1956 he had his first experience of LSD, under the guidance of Dr George Roubicek, Associate Professor of Psychiatry at CUSM. In 1960 he began research into the psychotherapeutic uses of LSD at the Psychiatric Research Institute in Prague. He moved to the United States in 1967, where he continued his work as Chief of Psychiatric Research at the Maryland Psychiatric Research Centre in Baltimore (1967–73) and as Assistant Professor of Psychiatry at the Henry Phipps Clinic of Johns Hopkins University.

The original idea was that LSD could give people the same symptoms as schizophrenia, and that therefore LSD could be used to study schizophrenia from the inside, as it were. But what the researchers found was that the LSD experience was nothing like the schizophrenic experience – indeed, if anything, it was just the opposite.

The clearest demonstration of this was given not by the Grof research but by some work of Bernard Aaronson. He put volunteer subjects into a deep hypnotic trance, and then told half of them that there was no depth of vision in their world; the dimension of depth would be gone. The other half were told that the dimension of depth would be expanded. As people talked about their experience (and as their bodies expressed various postures) in each of these conditions, psychiatric observers categorized them as schizophrenic or as healthy. Those in the 'no depth' condition reproduced many of the characteristics of schizophrenia; those in the 'expanded depth' condition seemed not only to be healthy, but to be having experiences which went beyond the ordinary. 'All six subjects responded to this condition with an expanded awareness of the world similar to the experiences described by Huxley in *The Doors of Perception*' (Aaronson, 1971: 286). In other words, schizophrenia brings with it experiences of the world closing in, while psychedelic states bring with them experiences of the world opening out.

What Grof began to notice, as the experiments went on, was that many of the visions that people had with the psychedelic drugs seemed to have to do with their inner problems and conflicts. Not only that, but these inner phenomena seemed to come out more vividly and more explicitly with these drugs than they did in the normal analytic session:

> LSD appeared to be a powerful catalyst of the mental processes activating unconscious material from various deep levels of the personality. Many of the phenomena in these sessions could be understood in psychological and psychodynamic terms; they had a structure not dissimilar to that of dreams. (Grof, 1979: 19)

This was an exciting time, and many discoveries were made. One of the most interesting things that happened was that much of the thinking in psychoanalysis (particularly the early phantasy postulated by Melanie Klein and her followers) was verified by spontaneous re-experiencing of events under LSD.

When LSD was banned, Grof and his second wife Christina found that breathing techniques, accompanied by carefully chosen music, could bring about the same kinds of experience as had been reached through LSD. He called this holotropic therapy, and has described it in some detail (Grof, 1988). What Grof has done is to show that transpersonal experiences can be obtained quite readily, and can be extremely useful in therapeutic terms.

Grof later became Scholar in Residence at the Esalen Institute, and

President of the International Transpersonal Association, which he helped to create in 1978.

He has some interesting things to say about Wilber's idea of the pre/trans fallacy:

> My own observations suggest that, as consciousness evolution proceeds from the centauric to the subtle realms and beyond, it does not follow a linear trajectory, but in a sense enfolds into itself. In this process, the individual returns to earlier stages of development, but evaluates them from the point of view of a mature adult. At the same time, he or she becomes consciously aware of certain aspects and qualities of these stages that were implicit, but unrecognized when confronted in the context of linear evolution. Thus, the distinction between pre- and trans- has a paradoxical nature; they are neither identical, nor are they completely different from each other. (Grof, 1985: 137)

This is well worth thinking about. It would be a pity to be too dogmatic about these matters at this early stage in the game.

Grof has been writing in this field since the mid-1970s, and has insisted on the connection of the transpersonal with the unconscious and with perinatal experience. In his latest book (Grof, 1992) he gives a number of case studies which exemplify therapeutic work at this level. He describes very well, for example, the experience of dual unity, where all boundaries between client and therapist are dissolved. In an earlier book (Grof, 1988) he gives the fullest list I have seen of the whole range of transpersonal experiences. One of Grof's main points is that clients often do not mention bizarre experiences they are having because they do not trust the therapist to listen to them or make sense of them. We shall come back to this point in more detail later.

Frances Vaughan

Vaughan, another important writer/practitioner in transpersonal psychology, has been involved with transpersonal conferences and other events for many years now. Her most influential book (Vaughan, 1985) presents a convincing rundown of the theory of transpersonal work. The process of therapy in this frame of reference may be defined as one of expanding consciousness, allowing the client to discover and integrate the inner wellsprings of experience. Like most of the transpersonalists, she takes dreams seriously and works with them a good deal.

Seymour Boorstein

Boorstein is a great contributor to the field, starting work in the 1970s and editing the biggest book of readings to date (Boorstein, 1980). He felt that his psychoanalytic training enabled him to deal with Oedipal material, and his meditation practice enabled him to have a wider perspective and a fuller sense of possibilities.

David Lukoff

Lukoff has written very clearly about the distinction between transpersonal experiences and psychosis. He says that if we ask some simple questions we can distinguish between pure psychotic experiences, pure mystical experiences, and mixtures of the two (Lukoff, 1985, 1988). He makes it possible to escape from the romanticism of the old fallacy that 'The psychotic and the mystic are swimming in the same sea; but the psychotic is drowning while the mystic is swimming.'

John Nelson

Nelson has used the model of the seven chakras described in Kundalini yoga to tackle the question of madness as opposed to transcendence. He integrates biochemical and neuroanatomical findings with transpersonal theories of consciousness. His recent book (Nelson, 1990) lays out an original and challenging view of mental illness, with a number of fascinating case histories.

Group work

Another group of practitioners come from the encounter tradition. It is not always realized that encounter groups and marathon groups are well suited to the emergence of transpersonal material.

At first this sounds very unfamiliar and unusual, until we realize that virtually all group leaders rely on their *intuition* a great deal. Intuition takes many forms (Goldberg, 1983), but can be one of the faculties of the higher unconscious and as such takes us into the realm of the transpersonal.

Again, many group leaders use *imagery and fantasy*, and these too can sometimes take us into the transpersonal realm. When we ask a participant to bring to mind an image of his or her inner conflict, or suggest that they imagine what their opponent might turn into or invite them to bring to mind a certain scene, we are invoking the imaginal world (Corbin, 1970), which is the realm of the Psychic and the Subtle.

Will Schutz

Schutz tells the story of a British woman in one of his groups who was asked to become very small and go inside her own body (Shaffer and Galinsky, 1989: 218). He was working in a way which may or may not have been directly transpersonal, but opened up a potential path into the transpersonal. Imagery very often involves playing with the normal limitations of time and space. In other work, Schutz (1981) explicitly uses meditation, prayer, chanting and spiritual exercises.

James Elliott

Another important writer/practitioner on encounter, Elliott says that human beings are not just physical objects but are best characterized by such words as freedom, choice, growth, autonomy and mystery. He also refers to *creativity* and liberation (Elliott, 1976: 58).

Another phenomenon noted by Elliott is the Fusion Experience, which often happens after primals and similar cathartic experiences. The whole person is involved, and often seems to be taken outside their ordinary world. 'Looking back on the experience, [one has] the feeling that one was outside time and space. Typical comments are "The world fell away"' (Elliott, 1976: 198).

Elizabeth Mintz

Mintz (1983) talks of countertransference of such a kind that the group leader actually feels inside her own body the next thing that needs to happen for the participant. This links directly with the research on countertransference mentioned by Samuels (1989) in his valuable book, which again ties in with the Psychic, and with the Hillman idea of the imaginal world, and with Grof's discovery of dual unity.

Louise Rockman

Rockman ran groups in which it was common to organize funerals in a ritual manner to mourn losses which are often unrecognized in our culture: this might include abortions, or the loss of a partner, or the loss of a subpersonality which had been prominent up to its loss in the process of therapy.

> Funerals had set props – a corpse, a sheet, candles. Music, usually Fauré's Requiem. Often a recital of the Kaddish, regardless of whether or not people were Jewish. Usually an object had to get buried, the knife that had killed the person, or some symbol of rage or fear or whatever emotions were being buried. There was a procession to a hole outside. The person was asked to say everything he wanted to say to the dead person, speaking directly, as in gestalt therapy. We repeatedly asked, 'Is there anything you need to do before you say goodbye, or in order to say goodbye?' Often a candle was left burning on the grave. There were post-funeral rites – placing a branch, or flowers daily, or three times a day on the grave. (Rockman, 1984: 39)

Rites of healing and rites of rebellion were also enacted in these groups, particularly when they were led by a therapist who was also an Anglican priest, who seemed to have a gift for this sort of thing, and whose status seemed to help the process.

The people who went through these experiences seemed to become not only more individual, as in the ordinary encounter group, but also more connected with others, more overlapping with others. This is one of the distinguishing features of work at the transpersonal level.

Some might feel that this is all quite ordinary, and that there is no need to mention the transpersonal, but I don't agree. I think we can get a much more accurate sense of what we are doing in group work by recognizing that we are working on many different levels all the time.

Jean Houston

Houston has been working in this field since before 1965, and has written two major books (Houston, 1982, 1987). All her work is grounded in the body and in taking the whole unity of body-feelings-intellect-soul-spirit seriously. Houston talks about her work as sacred psychology, and says that in our day this must involve some element of initiation; this is why 'the ritualization of rebirth plays so key a role in sacred psychology'. She is particularly good on guided fantasy, and has originated a number of extraordinary exercises to illuminate various aspects of sacred experience.

Starhawk

Another person who has written well about group work, Starhawk comes from a pagan tradition and sometimes calls herself a feminist witch. Her main reverence is for the religion of the Great Goddess:

> Earth-based spirituality values diversity, imposes no dogma, no single name for the sacred, no one path to the centre. But at this moment in history, the mythology and imagery of the Goddess carry special liberating power. (Starhawk, 1987: 21)

Her whole book is about group work conducted at this level and with this spirit, and it cannot be summarized in a few words. It needs to be read.

The Erickson tendency

A final group of practitioners come from the background of hypnosis, particularly as developed by Milton Erickson and modified by the exponents of Neuro-Linguistic-Programming.

Jacquelyn Small

Small is a transpersonal therapist who has taken a particular interest in addiction. In her book (Small, 1982) she offers a model of the transpersonal, and uses it to good effect. She has some good remarks about time, suggesting that we stand at a junction between the horizontal dimension of time, where our personal life takes place between past and future, and the vertical dimension of timelessness, where our transpersonal life partakes of the nature of Being, of the eternal now. A complete human being has the power of choice to move into one or the other as necessary. There are some good exercises in her book, and she gives hints as to how and when to use them well.

Connirae Andreas

With her sister Tamara (1994), Connirae Andreas has contributed a very interesting exercise called 'Core Transformation' which has a lot to offer in taking a symptom and using it to enter the transpersonal realm. This is a brilliantly simple idea and deserves to be more widely known.

Spiritual emergencies

A very important issue which has come to prominence in recent years is the appreciation of the difficulties that can arise when people move into the transpersonal area. This is especially difficult when people are suddenly exposed to spiritual experiences which they are not ready for. This has to do with the backward movement from the highest, illuminating earlier stages, which we noticed in an earlier section. Energies that have been activated in the higher levels as a means of awakening the sleeping Mental Ego may be just too much, and go over the top. Christina and Stanislav Grof (1990) have outlined ten specific problems which can come out of such events.

Peak experiences   These can be so overwhelming for someone who has never been ecstatic before that there can be fears of going crazy. To be out of touch with ordinary reality, even for a short period of time, is for some people an impossibly worrying event. These may be at the level of the Centaur or Bodymind, or the Psychic or the Subtle. It is important at this point not to get into the hands of a psychiatrist or a mental hospital.

Kundalini energy awakening   Sometimes through yoga, body work or even quite spontaneously, the energy of the chakras can combine to give an overwhelming experience. Again this tends to be at the level of the sixth or seventh chakra. Probably this is worst for people who have no conception of such a thing, and who live in a social context which is unsympathetic to it. But it is essentially a healing experience if it can be contained and lived through.

Near-death experiences   These are the experiences when people are declared physically dead, and are then revived. Even an approximation to this, through an accident for example, can result in a full-blown near-death experience. This is often at the Subtle level. The difficulty may come from the people around at the time, who may be very worried by what the person says, and perhaps later for the person involved, in owning it and in talking about it.

Past-life memories   If a person has, for any reason, a vivid memory which appears to refer to a previous life, this may be very disturbing for the person, particularly if they do not believe in reincarnation. Often such memories have a life-or-death quality to them, which may make them hard to take, at the same time as they make them very meaningful. They can be at any level from the lowest to the highest.

Opening to life myth   Here the person seems to go on a journey to the centre, to the central meaning of life. But because it takes place on a Psychic or Subtle level, the whole process can be dramatic and overwhelming. The person may feel that they are at the centre of global or even cosmic events. Death and rebirth, masculine and feminine energies – these can be central concerns on a grand scale. There are here great dangers of ego inflation, and this state needs to be handled very carefully and with real understanding, so as not to fall into the error of assuming that it is a manic episode. It can be healing and very positive, if handled correctly. Emma Bragdon (1990) makes the point that these experiences usually last no more than forty days. Interestingly enough, they often last exactly forty days.

Shamanic crisis   This is an initiatory crisis often involving a visit to the underworld, where annihilation takes place, followed by a rebirth and perhaps an ascent to heaven. Power animals are often involved, sometimes in quite horrifying ways. But if the person can be encouraged to stay with the experience and work through it, it can be genuinely initiatory, taking the person to a Psychic or Subtle level of consciousness.

Psychic opening   This is the arrival of psychic powers of one kind or another, perhaps quite suddenly and surprisingly. All sorts of paranormal phenomena may be involved here, including poltergeist phenomena. Out-of-body experiences are quite common – apparent journeyings through space, leaving one's solid body behind. Loss of identity may be experienced, and this can be frightening, too. There may be experiences of synchronicity, which may be confused with delusions of reference. The Psychic level has to be handled here.

Channelling   The arrival of spirit guides or discarnate entities offering to use one as a channel for communication can be very disconcerting. This can be a healing and transforming experience for the recipient, and other people may also feel benefited. The dangers of ego inflation are large here too, and so it is very important to discriminate what is pre-personal from what is transpersonal. Jon Klimo (1988) has written well about this.

UFO encounters   Contact with UFOs can be frightening and challenging, and such an experience often carries with it, as do many of these other experiences, the feeling that one cannot talk about this. One might be regarded as crazy, or at least as self-deluding. Yet such experiences can be genuinely illuminating for the person involved. They can partake of the nature of initiations. Again ego inflation may result, and has to be watched out for.

Possession   Here there is a sense that one has been taken over completely by an entity which may be good or evil. If it is voluntary, as in some rituals where the participant is supposed to be taken over by a god or goddess, there is usually no problem. But if it is involuntary, and particularly if the entity seems to be evil, it can be very frightening, both to the person and to those around. But 'when the person is given an opportunity to confront and express the disturbing energy in a supportive and understanding setting, a profound spiritual experience often results, one that has an extraordinary healing and transformative potential' (Grof and Grof, 1990: 99).

There is now a worldwide network of therapists who are willing and able to handle such states, and this is something which all those involved in the transpersonal may be able to help with.

Conclusion

This is a fast-developing field. In 1994 the new edition of the standard diagnostic manual called *DSM-IV* included for the first time a category of spiritual disorders. Many of the articles in the *Journal of Transpersonal Psychology* tell of ground-breaking work, and the recently founded *Transpersonal Review* reviews a mind-shaking number of new books in each issue. There is talk of a possible journal in Europe. Who knows what the next few years may see?

References

Aaronson, B. (1971) 'Some hypnotic analogues to the psychedelic state', in B. Aaronson and H. Osmond (eds), *Psychedelics: The Uses and Implications of Hallucinogenic Drugs*. London: Hogarth Press.

Andreas, C. and Andreas, T. (1994) *Core Transformation*. Moab, UT: Real People Press.

Assagioli, R. (1967) *Jung and Psychosynthesis*. New York: Psychosynthesis Research Foundation.

Assagioli, R. (1974) *The Act of Will*. London: Wildwood House.

Assagioli, R. (1975) *Psychosynthesis*. Wellingborough: Turnstone Press.

Assagioli, R. (1991) *Transpersonal Development*. London: Crucible.

Aurobindo (1973) *The Life Divine* and *The Synthesis of Yoga* (XVIII–XXI). Pondicherry: Centenary Library.

Bolen, J.S. (1989) *Gods in Everyman*. San Francisco: Harper & Row.

Boorstein, S. (ed.) (1980) *Transpersonal Psychotherapy*. Palo Alto, CA: Science & Behavior.

Bragdon, E. (1990) *The Call of Spiritual Emergency: From Personal Crisis to Personal Transformation*. San Francisco: Harper & Row.

Bremner, J.G. (1988) *Infancy*. Oxford: Basil Blackwell.

Clark, F.V. (1977) 'Transpersonal perspectives in psychotherapy', *Journal of Humanistic Psychology*, 17(2): 69–81.

Clarke, J.J. (ed.) (1995) *Jung on the East*. London: Routledge.

Corbin, H. (1970) *Creative Imagination in the Sufism of the Ibn'Arabi*, trans. R. Manheim. London: Routledge.

Descamps, M-A., Alfille, L. and Nicoleson, B. (1987) *Qu'est-ce-que le transpersonnel?* Paris: Editions Trismégiste.

Descamps, M-A., Cazenave, M. and Filliozat, A-M. (1990) *Les psychothérapies transpersonelles*. Paris: Editions Trismégiste.

Donington, L. (1994) 'Core process psychotherapy', in D. Jones (ed.), *Innovative Therapy: A Handbook*. Milton Keynes: Open University Press.

Elliott, J. (1976) *The Theory and Practice of Encounter Group Leadership*. Berkeley, CA: Explorations Institute.

Ellis, A. and Yeager, R.J. (1989) *Why Some Therapies Don't Work: The Dangers of Transpersonal Psychology*. Buffalo, NY: Prometheus Books.

Goldberg, P. (1983) *The Intuitive Edge*. Los Angeles: Jeremy Tarcher.

Gordon-Brown, I. and Somers, B. (1988) 'Transpersonal psychotherapy', in J. Rowan and W. Dryden (eds), *Innovative Therapy in Britain*. Milton Keynes: Open University Press.

Greene, L. and Sasportas, H. (1989) *Dynamics of the Unconscious*. London: Arkana.

Grof, S. (1979) *Realms of the Human Unconscious*. London: Souvenir Press.

Grof, S. (1985) *Beyond the Brain*. Albany, NY: SUNY Press.

Grof, S. (1988) *The Adventure of Self-discovery*. Albany, NY: SUNY Press.

Grof, S. (1992) *The Holotropic Mind*. San Francisco: Harper.

Grof, C. and Grof, S. (1990) *The Stormy Search for the Self: A Guide to Personal Growth through Transformational Crisis*. Los Angeles: Jeremy Tarcher.

Hannah, B. (1981) *Encounters with the Soul*. Boston, MA: Sigo Press.

Hardy, J. (1987) *Psychology with a Soul*. London: Routledge.

Havens, R.A. (1982) 'Approaching cosmic consciousness via hypnosis', *Journal of Humanistic Psychology*, 22(1): 105–16.

Hay, D. (1990) *Religious Experience Today*. London: Mowbray.

Hillman, J. (1975) *Re-visioning Psychology*. New York: Harper Colophon.

Hillman, J. (1981) 'Psychology: monotheistic or polytheistic?', in D.L. Miller (ed.), *The New Polytheism*. Dallas, TX: Spring Publications.

Hillman, J. (1989) *The Essential James Hillman*, introd. and ed. Thomas Moore. London: Routledge.

Houston, J. (1982) *The Possible Human*. Los Angeles: J.P. Tarcher.

Houston, J. (1987) *The Search for the Beloved: Journeys in Sacred Psychology*. Los Angeles: J.P. Tarcher.

Huxley, A. (1993) 'The perennial philosophy', in R. Walsh and F. Vaughan (eds), *Paths beyond Ego*. Los Angeles: J.P. Tarcher.

Johnson, R. (1986) *Inner Work*. San Francisco: Harper & Row.

Keutzer, C.S. (1982) 'Physics and consciousness', *Journal of Humanistic Psychology*, 22(2): 74–90.

Klimo, J. (1988) *Channeling*. Wellingborough: Aquarius.

Lukoff, D. (1985) 'The diagnosis of mystical experiences with psychotic features', *Journal of Transpersonal Psychology*, 17(2): 155–81.

Lukoff, D. (1988) 'Transpersonal perspectives on manic psychosis: creative, visionary and mystical states', *Journal of Transpersonal Psychology*, 20(2): 111–39.

Maslow, A.H. (1973) *The Farther Reaches of Human Nature*. Harmondsworth: Penguin.

Mathers, D. (1994) 'Psychosynthesis', in D. Jones (ed.), *Innovative Therapy: A Handbook*. Milton Keynes: Open University Press.

Mintz, E. (1983) *The Psychic Thread*. New York: Human Sciences Press.

Moore, T. (1992) *Care of the Soul*. London: Piatkus.

Nelson, J.E. (1990) *Healing the Split, Madness or Transcendence?: A New Understanding of the Crisis and Treatment of the Mentally Ill*. Los Angeles: J.P. Tarcher.

Otto, R. (1958) *The Idea of the Holy*. London: Oxford University Press.

Ray, M. and Rinzler, A. (1993) *The New Paradigm in Business*. Los Angeles: Tarcher/Perigee.

Rockman, L. (1984) 'Ritual enactments in primal-encounter groups', *Aesthema*, 4: 36–43.

Rowan, J. (1993) *The Transpersonal in Psychotherapy and Counselling*. London: Routledge.

Samuels, A. (1989) *The Plural Psyche: Personality, Morality and the Father*. London: Routledge.

Schutz, W. (1981) 'Holistic education', in R. Corsini (ed.), *Innovative Psychotherapies*. New York: John Wiley.

Shaffer, J. and Galinsky, M.D. (1989) *Models of Group Therapy*, 2nd edn. Englewood Cliffs, NJ: Prentice-Hall.

Singer, J. (1990) *Seeing through the Visible World*. London: Unwin Hyman.

Small, J. (1982) *Transformers: The Therapists of the Future*. Marina del Ray, CA: De Vorss.

Starhawk (1987) *Truth or Dare*. San Francisco: Harper & Row.

Stone, H. and Winkelman, S. (1989) *Embracing our Selves*. San Rafael, CA: New World Library.

Sutich, A.J. (1980) 'Transpersonal psychotherapy: history and definition', in S. Boorstein (ed.), *Transpersonal Psychotherapy*. Palo Alto, CA: Science & Behavior Books.

Suzuki, D. (1950) *Manual of Zen Buddhism*. London: Rider.

Underwood, E. (1961) *Mysticism*, 12th edn. New York: E.P. Dutton. (Other editions available, from 1930 onwards.)

Vaughan, F. (1985) *The Inward Arc*. Boston, MA: New Science Library.

von Eckartsberg, R. (1981) 'Maps of the mind', in R.S. Valle and R. von Eckartsberg (eds), *The Metaphors of Consciousness*. New York: Plenum Press.

Walsh, R.N. and Vaughan, F.E. (1980) 'Comparative models of the person and psychotherapy', in S. Boorstein (ed.), *Transpersonal Psychotherapy*. Palo Alto, CA: Science & Behavior Books.

Walsh, R. and Vaughan, F.E. (1993) *Paths beyond Ego*. Los Angeles: Tarcher/Perigee.

Watkins, M. (1986) *Invisible Guests*. Hillsdale, NJ: Analytic Press.

Wehr, G. (1987) *Jung: A Biography*. Boston, MA: Shambhala.

White, J. (1972) *The Highest State of Consciousness*. Garden City, NY: Anchor Books.

Whitmore, D. (1991) *Psychosynthesis Counselling in Action*. London: Sage Publications.

Wilber, K. (1980) *The Atman Project*. Wheaton, IL: Quest.

Wilber, K. (1981) *No Boundary*. London: Routledge.

Wilber, K. (1983) *Eye to Eye*. Garden City, NY: Anchor Books.

Wilber, K. (1995) *Sex, Ecology, Spirituality*. Boston, MA: Shambhala.

Wilber, K., [Engler, J. and Brown, D.P.] (1986) *Transformations of Consciousness*. Boston, MA: New Science Library.

Woolger, R. (1990) *Other Lives, Other Selves*. Wellingborough: Crucible.

6

Looking Back, Looking Forward: Personal Construct Therapy in Sociohistorical Perspective

Robert A. Neimeyer and Joel M. Martin

If we examine human beings through the wide-angle lens of historical or cultural enquiry rather than through the microscope of individuals in psychotherapy, we are immediately struck by the immense diversity of human beliefs and cultural practices, as well as their mutability across time. Of course, there are countless ways of theorizing about these differences – are they the result of environmental factors or visionary leaders? Religious inspiration or genetic predetermination? Scientific progress or sociological forces? The very multiplicity of possible explanations for the diversity of belief systems reinforces the point that human beings, whatever limitations they may possess, are inveterate theorists, weavers of cultural narratives that explain, constrain and shape their experience of themselves in physical and social contexts. Moreover, the apparent boundlessness of belief systems and their never-ending refinement, revision or reconstruction cautions us against the simple conclusion that any one form of human belief can comfortably claim to be true, while all others are judged to be in varying degrees of error. Like it or not, we as a species seem to be in the unique position of living our lives on the basis of alternative assumptions that are all too often shifting, provisional and inconsistent with those of other members of our species.

In a sense, personal construct therapy (PCT) is the clinical implementation of this essential philosophical insight: 'all of our present interpretations of the universe are subject to revision or replacement' (Kelly, 1955: 15). As a system of psychology, personal construct theory attempts to understand and study this human penchant for assigning meanings to things by examining the structure of personal belief systems, their processes of change over time, and the social embeddedness of even our most private convictions (R. Neimeyer, 1987). As an approach to psychotherapy, PCT instils in the therapist a basic respect for the structural constraints on changes in the client's constructions of self and circumstances, helps both client and therapist map the meanings that make up the client's experiential world, identifies conditions and strategies that can help facilitate experimentation with alternative world-views, and engages the person of the therapist inextricably in the renegotiation of the client's (inter)personal realities. Our goal in this chapter will be to review some of the major concepts and techniques associated with this approach to psychotherapy by placing their development in sociohistorical perspective, and by considering how they are continuing to evolve some forty years after their first formal presentation by George A. Kelly in 1955.

Historicizing PCT: a sociological framework

There is a common belief among academics that intellectual history should be written in the abstract, as if the success of a particular school of thought is ensured by the strength of its ideas alone, independent of the concrete persons and groups that originate, debate and elaborate them. But in keeping with our social constructivist orientation, it seems more appropriate to account for the development of personal construct therapy in *sociohistorical* terms, embedding our discussion of conceptual developments in the theory in the broader perspective of the social factors that facilitated or impeded them. We hope that this account will illuminate some of the developmental twists and turns of the theory's past, foster an appreciation of its present status, and offer a glimpse of its possible future.

How to 'punctuate' the history of any person, group or set of ideas is a tricky question that is often glossed over by historians of psychology. For example, identifying stages in the development of a therapeutic school by relying solely on identifiable shifts in the published thought of its founder risks ignoring the larger social and intellectual context in which he or she was working, minimizes the impact of other contributors to the perspective, and neglects the critical role of communication *between* people in the dissemination and evolution of ideas.

As an alternative to such a one-sided emphasis on a 'great man' behind an evolving theory, Nicholas Mullins (1973) formulated a sociological model for analysing aspects of a discipline's social functioning. The target of Mullins's analysis was the emerging *theory group*, defined as a coherent band of scientists sharing a common theoretical orientation and interest in a related set of problems, as it gradually differentiated from its parent discipline and matured to become a specialty in its own right. The basic feature of this process was the group's changing *communication structure*, as revealed by its institutional context, its published literature, and the extent and formality of apprentice and colleague relations among those who were identified with the perspective.

According to Mullins, as a new theory group differentiates from its parent discipline, it progresses from a *normal science* stage characterized by few colleague, apprentice and co-author relations among group members to the *network* stage, when such relations begin to appear. Simultaneously, the group begins to rally around an exciting intellectual product and reaches an agreement on research style and direction, which is reflected in a published programme statement. Training and research centres begin to develop. The *cluster* stage is often ushered in by a 'publication explosion', facilitated by the greater concentration of (co-authoring) faculty and students at a few major centres. Communication with scientists outside the cluster declines, and a social organizational leader emerges to promote the group's further development. As a result of this increased level of activity, the theory group becomes more visible to members of the parent discipline, who may come to regard it either as revolutionary or elite. Finally, as the group members are hired away from successful clusters, the theory gradually progresses into the *specialty* stage. Although the output of the group may continue to grow as it produces texts, reviews and further research, its communication structure gradually weakens as members re-establish ties with scientists in other fields. Institutionalizing the work of the group becomes a concern at this stage, with elite specialties gaining prominence through established journals and positions, and revolutionary specialties creating new ones. Eventually, in the late specialty stage, the communication pattern of the group begins to approximate that of normal science, as different factions of the group begin to elaborate their work in different directions.

Because this model has proven helpful in identifying phases in the development of personal construct theory in previous studies (R. Neimeyer, 1985; R. Neimeyer et al., 1990), we will adopt it as an organizing framework in this chapter. Such a framework has the advantage of being 'data-based', in the sense that 'objective' data on publication patterns, co-authorship, training centres and so on have been used to describe some of the major shifts in the history of personal construct therapy in this chapter and in the broader and more detailed studies of the theory group that preceded it. However, we undoubtedly have introduced into this history our own selection biases in drawing upon these data, and have interpreted them in ways that probably reveal as much about our outlooks as they do about the history we are attempting to describe. Indeed, from a personal construct perspective, any account is inevitably saturated with the perspectives of those who offer it; no 'God's eye view' is possible of the living histories in which we are immersed. We have tried to deal with our own immersion in this history by referring the reader to alternative formulations of the issues confronted by the theory group where these are available, and by citing a broad range of literature that the motivated reader can consult to form her or his own conclusions regarding the scope and direction of this therapeutic tradition. We will begin by considering the origins of personal construct therapy in the solitary work of its founder, George Kelly, and then move on to discuss extensions and revisions of the approach as it has matured to become an international specialty.

Normal stage (to 1955): the shape of things to come

Born in 1905 to parents who were literally among the last homesteaders of the American frontier, George Alexander Kelly gradually broadened his horizons from his small Kansas farming community through his educational achievements (R. Neimeyer, 1985; R. Neimeyer and Jackson, 1996).[1] After receiving his PhD from the University of Iowa in 1931, George Kelly started his career as an academic psychologist in the fall of that year in a small public college in the western half of Kansas – Fort Hays Kansas State College (Zelhart et al., 1982). Although Kelly began as an experimental psychologist, he was soon diverted to clinical work when a fourth-grade teacher referred a 12-year-old boy to the Psychology Department for help because of his 'shifty eyes', which she feared were the outward signs of a latent criminality. Adopting the case as a class project, Kelly began a decade of work in rural consultation to the children, families, schools and communities that were reeling under the economic and environmental impact of the Great Depression and the American 'Dust Bowl'.

While historically unique, the popular case-based classes and travelling clinics that Kelly and his students offered were at first fairly conventional in their emphasis on detailed psychometric assessment of the children and formulation of practical recommendations for remediating any difficulties detected. However, by the late 1930s Kelly had also begun to explore the implications of some rather esoteric theories in the classroom. In particular, he was drawn to Korzybski's (1933) general semantics, with its proposition that human thought and action was shaped by the personal and cultural 'abstractions' through which human beings label or name objects in the world. In addition, he was intrigued with Moreno's (1937) use of psychodramatic techniques of self-presentation and improvisation to promote apparently rapid and sustained personality change (Stewart and Barry, 1991).

These interests were soon melded in some of the earliest recorded psychotherapy research, which was carried out by two Master's students under Kelly's direction (Edwards, 1943, and Robinson, 1943). These theses addressed issues of central and abiding concern to Kelly, and articulated a set of concepts and procedures that later formed the basis of personal construct theory and its most novel clinical procedure, *fixed-role therapy*. Recognizing the untenability of long-term psychoanalytic psychotherapy as an efficient treatment for large numbers of people, Kelly devised a dramatically different form of therapy designed to help clients achieve substantial personality changes in as few as five or six sessions. This emphasis on providing therapy for a 'fixed' (or time-limited) period, while radical at the time, followed from Kelly's growing conviction that one's 'social role' (or self-identity) was essentially a 'semantic self-description' that could be enlarged or supplemented by enacting a carefully constructed alternative role after dramatizing it in the protective context of psychotherapy. Thus, like later, more developed expressions of personal construct therapy, Kelly's pioneering experimentation with this form of brief treatment embodied several key constructivist assumptions: (1) that 'personality' was a mutable social construction rather than a fixed intrapsychic entity; (2) that the language or semantics that individuals used to depict their social role could channel their interactions with others in sometimes dysfunctional ways; (3) that narrative means of assessment such as unstructured 'self-characterizations' could reveal the client's self-constructions; and (4) that effective therapy did not require a direct cognitive assault on dysfunctional ways of constructing one's identity, so much as action-oriented experimentation with an alternative outlook.

Edith Edwards's and Alexander Robinson's theses were direct tests of role therapy. In this procedure, the client was coached to adopt a new, hypothetical social role drafted by the therapist and a consulting team, one that introduced novel ways of viewing oneself and one's relationships. To titrate the client's level of discomfort, care was taken to write an alternative sketch that was markedly different from his or her current, problematic outlook and behaviour, yet not completely opposite from them. For example, for one young man who viewed himself as a 'non-participant' in life, and whose 'cynicism' in opposite-sex relationships was compensated for by his being 'too closely integrated' with his family, Edwards, Kelly and other members of the consultation team developed an alternative role emphasizing his intelligence, social responsibility, and a shift from 'sitting on the sidelines' to 'achieving his ambitions'. These abstract features of his identity were then anchored in concrete behavioural assignments, such as writing a story for the school newspaper on the architecture of the university (building design was one of his special interests). Similarly, in the case of an immigrant student who felt ostracized because of his ethnicity, the team drafted an alternative role emphasizing his being a 'cultural pioneer in a school of pioneers' who could 'set an example for others to follow' while 'regaining his educational heritage'. Alternative roles were modified through negotiation with the client and then enacted over several sessions of contact with the therapist, who assumed the parts of parents, classmates, and others as necessary to prime generalization of the new role to real-life contexts. These procedures were refined in the subsequent study by Robinson, who stressed the critical importance of writing a new role that would 'thoroughly satisfy the case's inner needs, not merely modify his external behavior' (Robinson, 1943). Remarkably comprehensive assessments of intellectual, personality and social functioning showed substantial gains for most cases across both the Edwards and Robinson studies.

Interestingly, the seeds of Kelly's most influential contribution to clinical assessment could also be discerned in his original but isolated activity at Fort Hays in the pre-war years. Having a keen interest in attitudinal components of personality, Kelly used several bipolar adjective scales in his measurement of the progress of the students evaluated at the travelling clinics (Jackson et al., 1988), as well as using these scales in the Psychology Clinic at Fort Hays. In their general form of requiring self-ratings on such concepts as 'liberal vs. conservative', these efforts foreshadowed Kelly's development of the *role construct repertory grid*, or repgrid, in the post-war period. The repgrid (discussed in the next section) was later to become the workhorse for clinical research within the theory (Winter, 1992), being used in approximately 90 per cent of published studies (R. Neimeyer, 1985).

After the Second World War, Kelly briefly served on the faculty of the University of Maryland before being hired by the Ohio State University as a professor and Director of Clinical Psychology. It was during these years that Kelly laboured to realize the ambitions of the recently enunciated scientist-practitioner model of clinical psychology training (Committee on Training in Clinical Psychology, 1947). He also began to articulate more explicitly his own distinctive theoretical commitments, which had gradually led him farther and farther from the pale of the psychodynamic and behaviouristic psychologies of his day (R. Neimeyer, 1995). By the early 1950s the general outlines of personal construct theory had taken sufficient shape to prompt Kelly to begin presenting papers on it at professional meetings, foreshadowing the publication of his major position statement in 1955.

The normal stage in sociological terms

In Mullins's (1973) view, theory groups often have their origins in the efforts of one or more solitary figures, who begin their work within the conventional paradigms of established disciplines, only to gradually develop a more distinctive set of concepts, procedures and research programmes. During this 'normal' stage of disciplinary development, few colleague, apprentice or co-author relationships support the work of those within the theory group, and its emerging originality is often recognized only in retrospect. And so it was with personal construct theory. From his forays into rural mental health at Fort Hays to his early years at Ohio State, Kelly was basically alone in his world, having few students and only one co-authored paper (Howard and Kelly, 1954). Furthermore, few publications in PCT appeared during this stage. However, the articles that were published were influential in shaping clinical heuristics and research for subsequent generations of construct theorists. For example, Landfield's (1954, 1955) examination of *threat* contributed to the repertoire of clinical concepts that informed personal construct therapy. In his analysis, an individual's foreboding sense of an impending shift in central identity constructs could arise in interaction with others who exemplified the polar contrasts of favoured self-constructions. For example, a former alcoholic meeting an old 'drinking buddy' can feel threatened in this sense, as can a therapist encountering in a client ways of thinking, feeling or acting that represent clear, but undesired possibilities for the therapist as well. In both cases, the threatening individual's embodiment of these all-too-plausible characteristics, outlooks or behaviours can shake the moorings of the perceiver's sense of self, and lead to contemptuous rejection of the other, regressive behaviour in the self, or other dysfunctional outcomes. This consistent emphasis on the (re)construction of social role in the context of significant relationships continues to distinguish personal construct therapy from other 'cognitive' approaches, as represented in more recent work on the concept of interpersonal validation

(Landfield, 1988), and systemic extensions of Kelly's original approach (Feixas, 1992; Procter, 1987).

Late 'normal stage' research carried out by Kelly's students also foreshadowed progressive research programmes on clinical assessment that followed the formal publication of Kelly's novel theory. One example was the work of Jones (1954) on self–other distances, the notion that dissimilarity between a person's construing of self and relevant others on the repgrid represents the degree of 'identification' with or 'isolation' from significant others in that person's world. Like the trend-setting research of Landfield, Jones's early work continues to influence contemporary psychotherapy research drawing on personal construct concepts and methods, such as recent process-outcome studies of identification with therapists and group members as predictors of treatment response in group therapies for incest survivors (R. Neimeyer et al., 1991).

While Kelly himself published little during this time, many of the students he mentored during the normal stage eventually became eminent figures in PCT specifically and clinical and personality psychology more generally (e.g. Boyd McCandless, David Hunt, Al Landfield, James Bieri, Brendan Maher, Leon Levy, Walter Mischel, Lee Sechrest). Kelly seemed to be saving himself for the publication of his *magnum opus*, which was to mark the beginning of the next stage in the development of personal construct therapy.

Network stage (1955–66): the new paradigm

With the publication of Kelly's *Psychology of Personal Constructs* in 1955, the tenets of personal construct psychology were succinctly outlined and then painstakingly elaborated in over 1,200 pages of theory, methods and clinical illustrations. In this seminal programme statement, Kelly developed his central metaphor of the *person as scientist* with a level of systematicity that was unique in the field of social science. Beginning with his *fundamental postulate* that 'a person's processes are psychologically channellized by the ways in which he anticipates events' (1955: 47), Kelly grounded his theory in both a Korzybskian semantics and the nascent cognitive movement in psychology. He asserted that the central goal of each individual is to formulate a unique *construct system* that renders experience interpretable, and to some degree predictable, while also suggesting avenues for active engagement with the world and others. Like incipient scientists, individuals were viewed as testing their theories or constructions for their validity, and undertaking the sometimes deeply perturbing revision of their systems when faced with invalidation of their core assumptions. However, unlike more 'objectivist' clinical theories, Kelly endorsed a philosophy of *constructive alternativism*, arguing that there was no 'correct', 'logical' or 'rational' construction of events against which others were viewed as deficient (R. Neimeyer, 1993a). Instead, he emphasized the multiplicity of workable interpretations of human experience, and placed inflection on the importance of bold experimentation with possible worlds in science and life more generally.

Kelly extended his fundamental postulate with eleven *corollaries* that further elaborated on the *process* of construing, the *structure* of personal knowledge systems, and the *social embeddedness* of our construing efforts (R. Neimeyer, 1987). This theory, emphasizing the person's inherent 'effort after meaning', the structural integrity of core constructions of self and world, and the quest for the enactment of meaningful role relationships predicated on the construing of others' outlooks, formed the grounding for Kelly's clinical theorizing. In particular, his respect for personal meanings led him to reject extraspective (or 'other-referenced'), classificatory systems of psychiatric diagnosis in favour of *transitive diagnosis*, a more process-oriented conception of psychological disturbance that focused on current or impending changes in the individual's system of meaning (Raskin and Epting, 1993). Similarly, Kelly eschewed the time-honoured distinction between cognition and emotion, respecting the inherent passion of personal knowledge rather than attempting to 'logically restructure' it to bring feelings into line with rational appraisals (Bannister, 1977). Finally, Kelly's emphasis on the critical importance of social role gave rise to therapeutic enactment procedures whose goal was not to 'train' clients to behave more 'skilfully', but to thrust them into situations in which they could view events through the eyes of real or hypothetical others. These techniques, ranging from casual in-session role-plays to carefully scripted fixed-role therapies (Epting, 1984), embodied the spirit of Moreno, while instantiating an approach to change in keeping with Kelly's constructivist convictions.

A distinctive feature of Kelly's theorizing was his definition of personal constructs as fundamental *contrasts* or *distinctions* that embodied and constrained one's perceived alternatives, at every level ranging from one's core values to one's behavioural options in concrete situations. Thus, if a client in therapy repeatedly construed others in terms of their being 'successes versus failures', 'social butterflies versus loners', 'loving versus hostile', and so on, one could assume that these constructs also functioned as significant themes for organizing the client's own social identity and actions. To assess such personal meanings and the implications they carried, Kelly (1955) devised the role construct repertory grid (repgrid), which presented the respondent with a set of elements (e.g. family members, liked and disliked acquaintances, and the self), and encouraged the person to compare and contrast them systematically in terms of personally meaningful bipolar adjectives (cf. R. Neimeyer, 1993c; see Figure 6.1 for an example). This methodological innovation in the measurement of meaning paved the way for hundreds of subsequent repertory grid studies on clinical topics, giving members of the nascent theory group a distinctive method as well as a theory around which to rally. In the context of psychotherapy as it was practised in the 1950s, the combination of a sophisticated theory of personal meanings, an empirical means of assessing such constructions, and a set of techniques

MAC GRID		ELEMENTS										Grid Type
		1	2	3	4	5	6	7	8	9	10	SCALE (1 to 5)
C1	serious	2	4	1	5	2	4	1	1	3	3	silly
C2	fun to be around	4	1	4	1	5	1	5	5	1	1	not fun...
C3	unattractive	2	3	2	5	3	5	1	1	3	5	physical appeal
C4	strong	4	4	1	4	1	1	1	5	2	1	weak
C5	loud-mouthed	5	3	2	2	3						soft-spoken
C6	cultured											vulgar
C7	kind											mean
C8	happy											sad
C9	liberal											conservative
10	good with hands											clumsy

E1 Self
E2 Mom
E3 Dad
E4 Brother
E5 Boss
E6 Jimmy
E7 Big Edna
E8 Jeff Gillooly
E9 Self in 10 years
E10 Self as I wish I were

Elements are listed across the top of the grid (E1–E10) and may be supplied by the therapist or the client or developed conjointly. They may be of any quantity deemed necessary and may be persons (as in the figure), relationships, jobs, or any other nouns the client and therapist wish to compare. Constructs are listed down the sides of the grid (C1–C10). Each is of a bipolar nature ('serious' contrasts with 'silly', etc.) and may be supplied by the therapist or the client. The client then rates each element on each construct. In the case of the figure, a scale of 1–5 was used, where a '1' indicates that the client views the element as aligned with the left pole of the construct, while a '5' indicates a greater perceived affinity with the right pole. The completed grid may be mathematically analysed to yield qualitative information about the terms in which the client construes his or her world.

Figure 6.1 *The repertory grid. This grid was generated using a beta version of MacGrid, a computer programme developed by Ken Ford, Jack Adams-Webber, John J. Brennan, Jr. and Alberto Cañas*

for fostering their therapeutic elaboration was unique, offering a core of concepts and methods that began to attract adherents in the USA and abroad.

The network stage in sociological perspective

An examination of apprentice, colleague and publication patterns in the network stage reveals the critical shifts that were beginning to occur in the social communicative structure of the growing personal construct network. The burgeoning group of students attracted to Kelly at Ohio State and to personal construct theorists at other institutions by the publication of Kelly's master work were beginning to contribute to research on the clinical applications of PCT. The major thrusts of these networks were, at this stage, rather narrowly focused, drawing on repertory grid technique to study a range of clinical conditions and their responses to treatment. Sechrest (1962) investigated clients' construing of their therapists, and Tyler and Simmons (1964) examined such construing on the part of psychiatric in-patients. But the most influential American work in the clinical area during the network stage was probably performed by Landfield and his students at the University of Missouri, who produced some of the first psychotherapy outcome studies employing constructivist assessment techniques. Focusing on the pre- and post-therapy construct systems of clients, these investigators examined the similarity between clients' and therapists' systems and related the degree of that similarity to improvement (Landfield and Nawas, 1964; Nawas and Landfield, 1963). They discovered that commonality in the *content*, but dissimilarity in the structural *complexity* of construct systems was associated with therapeutic progress, suggesting that clients and therapists, to be most successful, needed to be able to 'speak the same language' but organize their world-views differently. Thus, these and subsequent investigators began to focus attention on the way in which client and therapist meaning systems interacted to facilitate change in the client's outlook and level of functioning.

Within the American core of the theory group, Kelly continued to function as its indisputable intellectual leader. But Kelly's iconoclasm in relation to mainstream psychology, particularly of the behavioural orientation, placed him in an ambivalent position with respect to social/organizational leadership of the nascent movement. On one hand, Kelly's prominence in American psychology led to his election to consecutive presidencies of the consulting and clinical divisions of the American Psychological Association (in 1954–55, and 1956–57, respectively). On the other hand, his uneasiness about assuming the mantle of authority was suggested by his response to the invitation to become the editor of clinical psychology's most prestigious journal. When asked if he would take the helm of the *Journal of Consulting and Clinical Psychology*, Kelly reportedly replied that he would be happy to do so, provided he could rename the publication *The Ten Worst Journal Articles of the Year* (Bannister, 1979, personal communication). Needless to say, this sort of irony did not endear Kelly to the psychological establishment! Thus, while he remained a passionate exponent of the scientist-practitioner model within the Ohio State programme and in the APA, Kelly did not build a pulpit from which to preach the personal construct 'gospel'. Instead, he preferred to facilitate the development of students and younger colleagues in their own distinctive directions.

A very different style of leadership was displayed by Don Bannister, who imported personal construct theory to Great Britain in the late 1950s. In contrast to Kelly, who was somewhat formal in public meetings, Bannister playfully lampooned traditional psychoanalytic, behavioural and, later, cognitive perspectives alike in dozens of conference settings, rhetorically creating a space for the very different vision of psychology offered by PCT. This occasionally took the form of invidious comparisons of the images of humanity implicit in dominant models, as in his remark that psychoanalytic theories portrayed man as:

> a dark cellar in which a well-bred spinster lady and a sex-crazed monkey are forever engaged in mortal combat, the struggle being refereed by a rather nervous bank clerk. Alternatively, learning theory seems to suggest that man is basically a ping-pong ball with a memory. Along these lines some types of information theory hint at the idea that man is basically a digital computer constructed by someone who has run out of insulating tape. (Bannister, 1966: 21)

In the atmosphere of British psychology in the 1960s, Bannister's radical and irreverent approach quickly found adherents among a generation of psychologists and psychiatrists who were disaffected with the deterministic and pathologizing tendencies of the dominant models, but who sought a more disciplined approach to clinical research and practice than was afforded by more vaguely formulated humanistic approaches then available.

Intellectually, the prominence of a personal construct perspective during the network phase was reinforced by Bannister's programmatic line of repertory grid research into the construct systems of thought-disordered schizophrenics. Bannister and his colleagues discovered that schizophrenics were prone to 'loose' construing, that is, to disorganized and inconsistent interpretations of the social world (Bannister, 1960; Bannister and Fransella, 1966). Moreover, Bannister and Salmon (1966) discovered that schizophrenics manifested construing that was looser in relation to people than objects, arguing for specific deficits in their conceptual structure that affected certain domains of thinking more than others. Supplementing these clinical studies, a parallel series of experiments investigated the genesis of schizophrenia via the 'serial invalidation' of the affected individual's construct system by his or her social environment (Bannister, 1963, 1965). This research programme was instrumental in demonstrating the relevance of Kelly's theory to serious psychopathology, establishing an exemplar for research into the conceptual structures associated with other psychological disorders.

In summary, during the network phase, developments in personal construct therapy *per se* took a back seat to the promotion of PCT as a theoretical perspective and the application of grid technique to clinical research. This theoretical/empirical push helped gain necessary adherents for the fledgling approach in both the USA and the UK, but left its implications for treatment less fully explored.

Cluster stage (1967–72): the consolidation of a tradition

At the advent of this stage, fate dealt a tragic hand to the world of personal construct therapy, as George Kelly suffered a fatal heart attack. Having accepted Abraham Maslow's invitation to join the faculty of Brandeis University in 1965, Kelly seemed poised to promote a cross-fertilization of his approach with the humanistic perspectives that were demanding attention in the anti-establishment atmosphere of American universities in the mid-1960s. Moreover, Kelly was fascinated with the emerging cognitive science tradition, avidly reading Neisser's (1967) pioneering work in the area just months before his death (Adams-Webber, 1993, personal communication). Thus, at a time that was especially propitious for the further development of personal construct therapy along both humanistic and cognitive lines, the American wing of the theory group was deprived of its obvious intellectual leader.

In some respects, Kelly's death fostered a more democratic, if less cohesive, social organization of the theory group within the USA. Working at the University of Missouri, Landfield preserved a growing communication network through the development of a clearing house for personal construct research, distributed as an annual newsletter to interested subscribers. Moreover, his ongoing research into psychotherapy process (Landfield, 1971) continued to demonstrate the importance of the interaction of therapist and client constructions in shaping outcome. Straightforward outcome studies comparing fixed-role therapy to rational-emotive therapy (Karst and Trexler, 1970) also were favourable to a personal construct approach. However, in spite of these efforts, the initiative for the future development of PCT as a clinical perspective passed to the active clusters centred in the UK until the mid-1970s.

The cluster stage in sociohistorical perspective

Consistent with Mullins's model, the cluster stage began with a virtual publication explosion from the British PCT cluster at the University of London. Bannister and colleagues continued with their research into schizophrenia, yielding a clinically usable and psychometrically validated repertory grid assessment for thought disorder (Bannister and Fransella, 1967; Bannister et al., 1971) which was widely adopted in the clinic and laboratory alike. Bannister and Mair (1968) also collaborated to create the first methodological sourcebook on repertory grid technique, which, in combination with Slater's (1972) popular computer programmes for analysing repertory grids, consolidated a progressive clinical research paradigm in England and abroad. Fay Fransella, then a faculty member at the University of London, cultivated a many-branched tree of research pursuits, transplanting personal construct therapy into new clinical terrain. Within the domain of speech disorders, Fransella (1968) found that stutterers construed other stutterers in negative terms, but did not construe themselves as conforming to the same stereotype. She also discovered that the 'self when stuttering' carried more implications within the person's construct system than did the 'self when fluent', and that stutterers responding to therapy were those who were able to increase the implicative meaning of the non-stutterer role (Fransella, 1972). These findings lent credence to her earlier interpretation of the symptom as a highly elaborated 'way of life' that is likely to continue until another, equally well elaborated, way of life could be developed (Fransella, 1970). This work was significant in stretching the boundaries of personal construct therapy to a new set of disorders, and emphasized the significance of the maintenance of a problem-saturated identity as a critical theme of therapy.

At the same time, Fransella also pioneered in PCT research on eating disorders. Fransella and Crisp (1970) found that obese women tended to idealize the 'self at normal weight' on their repertory grids. Crisp and Fransella (1972) further observed that the process of change across therapy with anorexic clients could be cyclical, with the clients alternating between periods of tight and loose construing. This result was also found in a study in yet another area explored by Fransella and her colleagues – group psychotherapy (Fransella and Joyston-Bechal, 1971). These results suggested that conceptual reorganization accompanied therapeutic change, and that treatment for a variety of conditions needed to attend to a reconstruction of the client's sense of self.

In Scotland, McPherson's cluster embarked on a programme of schizophrenia research that paralleled Bannister's in London, focusing mainly on the use of 'psychological' constructs by thought-disordered patients. McPherson, Barden and Buckley (1970) found that the infrequent use of psychological constructs was associated with flattening of affect in schizophrenics, but McPherson and Buckley (1970) also found that thought-disordered schizophrenics are less disordered when construing people in objective, physical terms than in psychological terms.

Meanwhile, Anthony Ryle's cluster at Sussex began to produce studies that would spark lines of research still being performed today. Ryle and Breen (1971) demonstrated the diagnostic utility of the repertory grid by blindly differentiating between neurotic patients and normals on the basis of grid scores alone, thus illustrating the value of the grid as a useful clinical tool for the practising psychologist. This cluster also initiated research into marital and family problems. To examine problems of marital dissatisfaction, Ryle and Lunghi (1970) pioneered the construction of a 'dyad grid' (in which the elements were relationships between people rather than individuals). Ryle and Breen (1972) expanded on the use of the dyad grid and compared couples against normative data they had collected using supplied constructs. The significance of this extension of personal construct methods to the couples context has become even more evident in retrospect, as family therapy applications of constructivist ideas grew more frequent during the 1980s.

Early specialty stage (1973–85): the proliferation of a paradigm

By the mid-1970s personal construct theory had attained the status of an identifiable clinical specialty, whose most salient characteristic was its intensive study of the conceptual structure associated with various forms of psychological disorder. Increasingly, however, these studies focused on changes in client construct systems resulting from treatment, which was itself sometimes guided by a constructivist rationale. For example, Bannister and his colleagues continued their research on schizophrenia with the publication of an intriguing but somewhat inconclusive longitudinal study of a *serial validation* hypothesis, the idea that schizophrenics might be helped in psychotherapy to 'tighten' and organize their social construing if given systematic validation for their social predictions (Bannister et al., 1975). Fransella and colleagues similarly continued their prolific work in eating disorders, increasingly shifting their focus toward treatment-related concerns (Button, 1983, 1985a, 1985b; Fransella and Button, 1983; Fransella and Crisp, 1979).

In addition to these extensions of cluster stage research programmes, the early specialty stage also witnessed the proliferation of research into topics previously unexamined by personal construct psychologists, such as agoraphobia. Guidano and Liotti (1983) suggested that agoraphobics did not possess the cognitive skills necessary for dealing with relational crises. O'Sullivan (1984) found that agoraphobic clients utilized fewer constructs having to do with planning interest and ability than did normals. Goldstein and Chambless (1978) connected agoraphobic symptoms with interpersonal difficulties, and Haffner (1977a, 1977b, 1979), focusing on the marriages of agoraphobics, examined the maintenance of phobic symptoms and their relation to a fear of engaging in marital infidelity.

The emergence of an abiding concern with relationship issues proved to be a distinguishing feature of this phase. For example, Childs and Hedges (1980) used grids to examine areas of commonality and divergence in couples' construing. Karst (1980) suggested ways women might overcome problems with 'frigidity', while Bannister and Bott (1973) experimented with different ways to administer grids to couples, including simultaneous administration and having each member of the couple fill out a grid as he or she believed his or her mate would respond. Similarly, Bonarius (1977) and later Kremsdorf (1985) utilized a procedure for joint grid administration in which each partner would alternate in the selection of elements, constructs and ratings. In addition to their diagnostic use in identifying areas of misunderstanding and consensus between partners in the context of marital therapy, these 'exchange grid' formats were suitable for enhancing each member's understanding of the partner's outlook, thereby serving as therapy procedures in their own right.

As was true in other clinical areas, this intensive repertory grid research was soon followed by proposals and procedures for personal construct therapy with couples (e.g. Kremsdorf, 1985; G. Neimeyer and Hudson,

1985; Procter, 1981). For example, Kremsdorf (1985) reported success in extending Kelly's original fixed-role approach to marital therapy, working with both partners together to enact hypothetical identities with each other for a limited time, after which they 'de-roled' and discussed the implications of the experiment for reconstructing their relationship. G. Neimeyer and his colleagues (G. Neimeyer, 1985; G. Neimeyer and R. Neimeyer, 1985) complemented this focus on technique by extending the conceptualization of relational distress, viewing marital discord as a breakdown in the collaboration of two 'personal scientists' in supporting each other's optimal development. In keeping with this focus on restoring constructive collaboration, he used several strategies for facilitating mutual understanding and validation, such as 'laddering', where the more abstract implications of spouses' specific complaints and disagreements are explored in an attempt to identify shared superordinate goals and values.

Procter (1981) further broadened this nascent relational emphasis in PCT by sketching the outlines of a major reinterpretation of Kelly's theory as a form of *family construct psychology*. Rather than focusing on the individual's idiosyncratic system of meanings, Procter posited that these were embedded in a more inclusive system of family constructs that assigned implicit roles to various family members, and which required assessment and intervention in their own right. Subsequent work within this perspective has demonstrated the fecundity of Procter's model in generating conversational strategies for eliciting and modifying those constructive-behavioural cycles through which family members dysfunctionally interpret one another's actions, while unintentionally validating these very interpretations (Feixas, 1992; Fexias et al., 1993; R. Neimeyer, 1993c).

In addition to this burgeoning interest in marital and family therapy, clinical research in the early specialty stage began to focus on other forms of disturbed relationships. Neimeyer and Neimeyer built on Duck's (1973) earlier work in friendship formation by demonstrating that successful relationships were characterized by greater commonality in the structure of partners' construct systems (R. Neimeyer and G. Neimeyer, 1983) and in the application of these constructs to shared acquaintances in their social world (G. Neimeyer and R. Neimeyer, 1981). By extension, they suggested that relationship distress could be seen as reflecting the *absence* of serious commonality at core levels of partners' systems, the *disruption* of such commonality through the maintenance of static views of a dynamic relationship, the *disorganization* of the relationship through a breakdown in the coherence of social construing on the part of one or both partners, or the perpetuation of a *negative* but stable relationship through each partner's use of the other to anchor the contrast poles of central identity constructs (R. Neimeyer and G. Neimeyer, 1985). This conceptualization received some support in a subsequent longitudinal study which demonstrated that deteriorating relationships showed substantially less similarity than developing relationships both before and after an intervention designed to improve group members' mutual understanding, despite the general enhancement of commonality of construing for all participants (G. Neimeyer and R. Neimeyer, 1986).

Following trends in the literature on cognitive therapy (Beck et al., 1979), construct theorists in the early specialty stage also turned their distinctive conceptual and methodological tools to the study of depression. Thus, Marsella and colleagues observed differences in the terms used to construe depression between Western and non-Western cultures (Tamaka-Matsumi and Marsella, 1976; Marsella et al., 1985), and Space and Cromwell (1980) developed a grid measure for negativity in depressive self-construing. As this programme expanded, Space, Dingemans and Cromwell (1983) found that 'mixed self-valence' (ambivalent self-construing which contains large numbers of both positive and negative constructs) was more characteristic of depressives than normals, rather than simply negative self-construing *per se*. In keeping with this finding, R. Neimeyer (1984) postulated that the onset of depression occurs when negative self-constructions are incorporated into the self-schema, yielding a sharp contrast with the previously positive self-schema and thus causing valence inconsistency. R. Neimeyer, Heath and Strauss (1985) later collected data to support this hypothesis in the context of a psychotherapy outcome study designed to test the efficacy of a hybrid personal construct/cognitive therapy intervention. Winter's (1985) study of personal reconstruction in depressives participating in group-analytic therapy further exemplified the interest of construct theorists in constructive changes accompanying effective psychotherapy, regardless of its 'brand name'. In this respect the history of personal construct therapy was quite different than that of other emerging cognitive approaches, such as cognitive therapy, which amassed data on the efficacy of a single preferred model instead of studying change processes common to many varieties of psychotherapy.

The early specialty stage in sociohistorical perspective

By the mid-1970s, PCT had become more distributed in its social structure and more diverse in its application, relative to the highly inbred cluster stage that preceded it. Consistent with the predictions of Mullins's (1973) model, this period witnessed the break-up of the larger British clusters, resulting in a diversification of research programmes as members of successful groups were hired away by other institutions. At a social structural level, the decline of close-knit local clusters during this period was offset by a growing sense of internationality among theory group members. Following Landfield's successful organization of the first International Congress in PCP in the USA in 1976, other conferences followed biannually in the UK, the Netherlands, Canada, Italy, Australia and Spain. Additionally, regional meetings were held in Germany, North America, the Australasian region and Great Britain. The resulting dissemination of PCT concepts and methods fuelled the development of the theory group in a number of regions previously unrepresented in the largely Anglo-American literature, with particularly active networks developing in Australia, Germany and Italy. The widespread availability of methodological handbooks (Fransella and Bannister, 1977), book-length examinations of personal construct therapy (Epting, 1984), and computer programmes for grid administration and analysis (Slater, 1972) helped promote the rapid extension of core therapeutic methods and clinical research in the theory, and made the group less reliant on close apprenticeship to a clinical or methodological mentor.

While the theory group during the early specialty stage was characterized by a general diversification of communication, consolidation was also evident in the models of training in PCT as a therapeutic approach. The most significant development of this kind was Fransella's founding of the Centre for Personal Construct Psychology in London in 1982. Offering a continuous series of courses and workshops in personal construct concepts, methods and therapeutic strategies, the Centre exposed hundreds of mental health practitioners to the implications of Kelly's theory for psychological practice. The formation of other training centres followed in Rome, Dublin, Barcelona and elsewhere, supplementing ongoing university-based training in many countries.

Ironically, in spite of the vast range of clinical applications of PCT during the early specialty stage (see Winter, 1992, for an authoritative review), cross-fertilization of PCT with other therapeutic traditions was relatively uncommon (R. Neimeyer, 1985). While some conceptual exchange between PCT and other perspectives (especially cognitive therapy and family systemic approaches) had begun, most theory group members continued to apply familiar Kellian procedures such as fixed-role therapy to an ever broader range of disorders and populations. As a result of this conceptual conservatism, by the early 1980s the theory group was suffering from 'intellectual isolationism' (R. Neimeyer, 1985), functioning as an archipelago of somewhat insular activity in a sea of alternative approaches.

Late specialty stage (1986–present): the challenge of integration

As the theory group continued to grow in size, internationality and diversity during the 1980s, it also began to contend with converging trends in other psychotherapeutic traditions. In particular, the emergence of a wide variety of cognitive-behavioural approaches (cf. Dryden and Golden, 1987; Kuehlwein and Rosen, 1993) and constructivist variants of family systems work (e.g. Hoffman, 1992) started to erode the distinctiveness of a Kellian perspective, while offering a variety of procedures designed to change the self-schemata, life narratives, or problem-maintaining systems that had long concerned personal construct theorists. By the early 1990s, for example, both Ellis (1993) and Meichenbaum (1993) had reinterpreted their rational-emotive therapy and cognitive behaviour modification, respectively, as constructivist orientations, to the perplexity of some constructivists! Thus, PCT was confronted with a crisis of identity, finding that previously rationalistic or objectivistic therapy traditions had suddenly (at least nominally) 'gone constructivist', enhancing their epistemological and strategic 'family resemblance' to a PCT perspective (R. Neimeyer, 1995).

Reaction within the PCT community to this development was mixed. On one hand, long-time contributors to the theory like Fransella (1988) defended the uniqueness of personal construct therapy and cautioned against its being 'subsumed' by potentially hostile theoretical models. On the other hand, second- and third-generation construct theorists tended to welcome the opportunity for cross-fertilization with other clinical theories sharing a constructivist epistemology. By the mid-1990s personal construct perspectives began to appear routinely alongside narrative (Epston and White, 1995; Gonçalves, 1994), radical constructivist (Efran and Fauber, 1995), social constructionist (McNamee, 1996) and dialectical constructivist (Greenberg and Pascual-Leone, 1995) perspectives in a number of books and journals. The flourishing of such constructivist approaches to psychotherapy (Mahoney, 1995; R. Neimeyer and Mahoney, 1995) represented a congenial shift in the *Zeitgeist* of psychotherapy, but also posed a threat to the distinctiveness of a personal construct perspective.

In general, this confrontation with alternative approaches has enriched the practice of personal construct therapy, if only by prompting construct theorists to mine the ore of their own tradition more carefully. For example, Leitner (1987, 1988, 1995) refined and extended Kelly's preliminary discussion of role relationships, examining the ways in which clients and therapists alike may flee from the potential 'terror' of intimate relationships in an attempt to protect vulnerable core structures from invalidation. Likewise, others have designed distinctive dyadic-interactive formats of group therapy predicated on a personal construct rationale (Landfield, 1979; R. Neimeyer, 1988), which have been applied in a systematic programme of process and outcome research on the treatment of sexual abuse (Alexander et al., 1989; Harter and Neimeyer, 1995; R. Neimeyer et al., 1991). Occasionally this effort to sharpen the implications of Kelly's theory has led to the development of comprehensive treatment programmes for specific conditions, like stuttering, where empirical research has demonstrated the efficacy and novelty of a personal construct approach (Haynow and Levy, 1989). More common than these technical extensions of PCT, however, has been the heuristic use of construct theory to offer a fresh conceptualization of clinical problems that concern therapists of all persuasions, such as client hostility (Pfenninger and Klion, 1996), dependency (Walker, 1993), and the threat of change (Dalton, 1993).

As an alternative to teasing out the implications of a 'pure form' of personal construct therapy or using it as a distinctive conceptual base, some construct theorists have begun to advocate a 'theoretically progressive' integration of various constructivist models (R. Neimeyer, 1988, 1989, 1993b; R. Neimeyer and Feixas, 1990; Winter, 1992). The goal of such an effort is to broaden the therapist's procedural repertoire while, at the same time, preserving the distinctive theoretical and metatheoretical commitments that inform a constructivist approach. From this point of view, the most promising forms of therapy integration would follow from cross-fertilization of different approaches to therapy that share a core understanding of the nature of human beings, the processes of change and so on, while nonetheless offering unique interventions at more concrete levels. This form of careful conceptual analysis of the converging or conflicting epistemologies of different schools of therapy could minimize the risks associated with an 'anything goes' eclecticism, and help yield a more inclusive theory to guide case conceptualization and intervention.

While the eventual integration of personal construct theory with other models of therapy is predicted by most construct theorists,[2] it is not without its dangers. In particular, distinctive features of the theory such as the commitment to the person-as-scientist metaphor, the role of contrast in meaning-making, and the importance of holism in psychological theorizing could be compromised in the hasty blending of therapeutic approaches, producing nominally more 'integrative' theories that are actually less rich than their predecessors.

In summary, as personal construct therapy approaches the next century, it shows remarkable vitality and diversity of application. In addition to continued work in such areas as family therapy (Loos, 1993; G. Neimeyer and R. Neimeyer, 1994), eating disorders, (Button, 1992), client–therapy matching (Winter, 1990), and agoraphobia (Lorenzini and Sassaroli, 1987), PCT has been extended to the treatment of chemical dependency (Klion, 1993), problems of the elderly (Viney, 1993), attention-deficit disorder (Yelich and Salamone, 1994), and trauma (Harter and Neimeyer, 1995; Sewell, 1996). Of equal importance to these topical extensions has been the use of PCT approaches in the exploration of narrative models of psychotherapy (Mair, 1989) and in research on therapy process (Toukmanian, 1992). Thus, as personal construct therapy turns forty years old, it is clear that the history of this approach is still being written.

The late specialty stage in sociohistorical perspective

Ironically, in the context of Mullins's (1973) model, the viable specialty ultimately pays for its success with its life. That is, as it comes to influence the work of others whose professional identities were not forged during 'the good old days' of clusterhood, bands of loyalty and close-knit communication gradually yield to a looser and more eclectic form of communication, publication and clinical practice. Viewed in sociohistorical perspective, the current debate over the purity of Kellian theory and the advisability of its integration with other constructivist perspectives might represent an historical inevitability of late specialty stage development.

This trend toward eventual dissolution and assimilation of the theory group is, in some respects, reinforced in the present technological age, in which intimate apprentice and colleague communication is increasingly supplanted by more anonymous forms of interaction, such as the lively Internet-based discussion groups in which many personal construct theorists are now active participants.[3] However, these less 'committed' forms of communication carry important advantages of their own, allowing for a more democratic freeplay of ideas that may ultimately yield new innovations in clinical research and practice. As personal construct theorists embrace the possibilities afforded by this contemporary communication structure and the continuing tradition of international conferences, they may be coming to participate in a 'global cluster' that transcends national and disciplinary boundaries and offers the prospect of new extensions of constructivism in the clinical context.

In Mullins's (1973) terms, the success of a theory group can be measured by its ability to produce work that is both published and cited, to attract adherents who push back the frontiers of the perspective, and to train and place students who will 'carry the torch' to a new generation of scholars and practitioners. By all of these criteria, personal construct therapy has been a successful tradition, as revealed by previous empirical analyses (R. Neimeyer, 1985; R. Neimeyer et al., 1990). However, until recently, PCT has developed largely outside the mainstream of (American) psychology, forming its own journal (the *International Journal of Personal Construct Psychology*, later broadened to the *Journal of Constructivist Psychology*) and establishing its own training centres, rather than making 'takeover bids' for existing ones. According to Mullins (1973), this pattern of institutionalization is typical of theory groups considered 'revolutionary' by their parent disciplines, which may be a fair description of the attitude of mainstream psychologists to PCT, at least until the last decade. However, the 'radicalism' of a constructivist perspective may be eroding, as non-aligned observers of cognitive therapy predict a continuing epistemic shift away from rationalist assumptions of a knowable reality and towards a constructivist emphasis on the social and personal bases of belief, with all of the ramifications this carries for clinical assessment and psychotherapy (Dobson and Pusch, 1993). To the extent that personal construct theory enters the mainstream, it can be expected to draw the fire of newer 'revolutionary' theory groups, which will attempt to distinguish themselves from constructivism as an increasingly 'respectable' specialty. Already, there are signs that a constructivist position is considered too individualistic and too 'cognitive' to provide a useful guide to therapy by some theorists espousing social constructionist views (Hoffman, 1992). Ultimately, the changing constructions of constructivism are a useful reminder that every psychological theory is, in Kelly's (1955: 31) own terms, 'an eventual candidate for the trash can' as new positions are formulated that subsume previous models while at the same time extending their implications.

Epilogue

Like any living tradition, personal construct therapy has displayed both continuity and discontinuity throughout its relatively brief history. Originating in the solitary work of its founder, George Kelly, in the American Depression of the 1930s, it has matured to become an international specialty in the 1990s. In many respects, it continues to bear the stamp of its origin: Kelly's pioneering spirit, his celebration of human diversity and individuality, and his optimism regarding the possibility of human progress and change still pervade most contemporary personal construct therapy (Mair, 1985). In other respects, however, Kelly might be hard pressed to recognize some of the more creative extensions of his theory, research methodology and clinical procedures, as personal construct therapists have both inspired and taken inspiration from kindred developments in other traditions of thought only vaguely foreshadowed in Kelly's day. As constructivist themes begin to transform many approaches to psychotherapy (R. Neimeyer and Mahoney, 1995), the truest measure of personal construct theory's role in the history of psychotherapy may be its contribution to this trend.

Notes

1. Fransella (1996) has recently offered a penetrating analysis of Kelly's boyhood poverty, his solitary struggle to transcend the limitations of his environment, and their impact on his later theorizing. She also provides her own interpretation of the history of personal construct therapy, one informed by her thirty years of influential work as a social and intellectual leader of the British wing of the theory group. We encourage the reader interested in delving more deeply into the possible readings of personal construct theory's history to consult her work, in part because it provides a counterbalance to our own rendering of the same tradition.

2. To gain a clearer view of the possible future of personal construct theory and therapy as a mature international specialty, we conducted a Delphi poll of leading contributors to the tradition, surveying a panel of fifty-five North American (42 per cent), British (31 per cent), European (21 per cent), and Australasian (6 per cent) construct theorists with an average of nineteen years of experience in the theory. As in a previous poll of theory group members conducted a decade ago (R. Neimeyer et al., 1986), we asked panellists to forecast the probability of a number of developments in the areas of theory and metatheory, methodology, research style and direction, and applications to psychotherapy and counselling. Recording their responses to structured questions on scales of 1 (very unlikely to occur) to 7 (very likely to occur), panellists offered a glimpse of likely developments in personal construct therapy in the next decade. In general, they viewed the approach as unlikely to relinquish the basic metaphor of people as personal scientists (rated 2.1), although they forecast that the theory would continue to evolve in a more social direction (5.2). Like the earlier panel, they confidently predicted that the administration and analysis of repertory grids and related methods for mapping personal meaning systems would boost the popularity of the theory (6.2), although these would in the future be complemented by narrative methods using such procedures as content analysis (5.7). Encouragingly, psychotherapy process and outcome was seen as leading the list of fertile research areas (5.6), particularly in the form of studies tailored to illuminate idiographic processes of change in particular cases (5.2). Finally, panellists forecast that the professional practice of personal construct therapists would continue to become more eclectic (5.3), moving away from established Kellian procedures like fixed-role therapy (4.2) to embrace integration with a variety of other constructivist (5.5), family systemic (5.1), cognitive (4.0), and psychodynamic (4.2) perspectives.

3. Readers interested in exploring these avenues of electronic communication are encouraged to access the World Wide Web page devoted to personal construct theory at http://ksi.cpsc.ucalgary.ca/PCP/.

References

Alexander, P.C., Neimeyer, R.A., Follette, V.M., Moore, M.K. and Harter, S.L. (1989) 'A comparison of group treatments of women sexually abused as children', *Journal of Consulting and Clinical Psychology*, 57: 479–83.

Bannister, D. (1960) 'Conceptual structure in thought-disordered schizophrenics', *Journal of Mental Science*, 106: 1230–49.

Bannister, D. (1963) 'The genesis of schizophrenic thought disorder: a serial invalidation hypothesis', *British Journal of Psychiatry*, 109: 680–6.

Bannister, D. (1965) 'The genesis of schizophrenic thought disorder: re-test of the serial invalidation hypothesis', *British Journal of Psychiatry*, 111: 377–82.

Bannister, D. (1966) 'Psychology as an exercise in paradox', *Bulletin of the British Psychological Society*, 19: 21–6.

Bannister, D. (1977) 'The logic of passion', in D. Bannister (ed.), *New Perspectives in Personal Construct Theory*. London: Academic. pp. 21–38.

Bannister, D. and Bott, M. (1973) 'Evaluating the person', in P. Kline (ed.), *New Approaches in Psychological Measurement*. Chichester: Wiley.

Bannister, D. and Fransella, F. (1966) 'A grid test of schizophrenic thought disorder', *British Journal of Social and Clinical Psychology*, 5: 95–102.

Bannister, D. and Fransella, F. (1967) *A Grid Test of Schizophrenic Thought Disorder: A Standard Clinical Test*. Barnstaple, UK: Psychological Test Publications.

Bannister, D. and Mair, J.M.M. (1968) *The Evaluation of Personal Constructs*. London: Academic Press.

Bannister, D. and Salmon, P. (1966) 'Schizophrenic thought disorder: specific or diffuse?', *British Journal of Medical Psychology*, 39: 215–19.

Bannister, D., Fransella, F. and Agnew, J. (1971) 'Characteristics and validity of the grid test of thought disorder', *British Journal of Social and Clinical Psychology*, 10: 144–51.

Bannister, D., Adams-Webber, J.R., Penn, W.I. and Radley, A.R. (1975) 'Reversing the process of thought disorder: a serial validation experiment', *British Journal of Social and Clinical Psychology*, 14: 169–80.

Beck, A.T., Rush, A.J., Shaw, B.F. and Emery, G. (1979) *Cognitive Therapy of Depression*. New York: Guilford.

Bonarius, J.C.J. (1977) 'The interaction model of communication: through experimental research towards existential relevance', in J.K. Cole and A.W. Landfield (eds), *1976 Nebraska Symposium on Motivation*. Lincoln, NB: University of Nebraska Press.

Button, E.J. (1983) 'Construing the anorexic', in J. Adams-Webber and J.C. Mancuso (eds), *Applications of Personal Construct Theory*. New York: Academic Press.

Button, E. (1985a) 'Eating disorders: a quest for control?', in E. Button (ed.), *Personal Construct Theory and Mental Health*. London: Croom Helm.

Button, E. (1985b) 'Women with weight on their minds', in N. Beail (ed.), *Repertory Grid Technique and Personal Constructs: Applications in Clinical and Educational Settings*. London: Croom Helm.

Button, E. (1992) 'Eating disorders and personal constructs', in R.A. Neimeyer and G.J. Neimeyer (eds), *Advances in Personal Construct Psychology*. Greenwich, CT: JAI Press. pp. 187–216.

Childs, D. and Hedges, R. (1980) 'The analysis of interpersonal perceptions as a repertory grid', *British Journal of Medical Psychology*, 53: 127–36.

Committee on Training in Clinical Psychology (1947) 'Recommended graduate training in clinical psychology', *American Psychologist*, 2: 539–58.

Crisp, A.W. and Fransella, F. (1972) 'Conceptual changes during recovery from anorexia nervosa', *British Journal of Medical Psychology*, 45: 395–405.

Dalton, P. (1993) 'The meaning of choice and the threat of change', in L.M. Leitner and G. Dunnett (eds), *Critical Issues in Personal Construct Psychotherapy*. Malabar, FL: Krieger. pp. 99–116.

Dobson, K. and Pusch, D. (1993) 'Towards a definition of the conceptual and empirical boundaries of cognitive therapy', *Australian Psychologist*, 28: 137–44.

Dryden, W. and Golden, W.L. (1987) *Cognitive-Behavioral Approaches to Psychotherapy*. Cambridge: Hemisphere.

Duck, S.W. (1973) *Personal Relationships and Personal Constructs*. Chichester: Wiley.

Edwards, E.D. (1982) 'Observations of the use and efficacy of changing a patient's concept of his role – a psychotherapeutic device', in R.P. Markley, P.F. Zelhart and T.T. Jackson (eds), *Explorations with Fixed Role Therapy*. Fort Hays, KS: Fort Hays University. pp. 1–49. (Originally published 1943.)

Efran, J.S. and Fauber, R.L. (1995) 'Radical constructivism: questions and answers', in R.A. Neimeyer and M.J. Mahoney (eds), *Constructivism in Psychotherapy*. Washington, DC: American Psychological Association. pp. 275–302.

Ellis, A. (1993) 'Reflections on Rational-Emotive Therapy', *Journal of Consulting and Clinical Psychology*, 61: 199–201.

Epston, D. and White, M. (1995) 'Termination as a rite of passage: questioning strategies for a therapy of inclusion', in R.A. Neimeyer, and M.J. Mahoney (eds), *Constructivism in Psychotherapy*. Washington, DC: American Psychological Association. pp. 339–56.

Epting, F.R. (1984) *Personal Construct Counseling and Psychotherapy*. New York: Wiley.

Feixas, G. (1992) 'Personal construct approaches to family therapy', in R.A. Neimeyer and G.J. Neimeyer (eds), *Advances in Personal Construct Psychology*, (Vol. 2). Greenwich, CT: JAI Press. pp. 217–55.

Feixas, G., Procter, H.G. and Neimeyer, G.J. (1993) 'Convergent lines of assessment: systemic and constructivist contributions', in G.J. Neimeyer (ed.), *Constructivist Assessment*. Newbury Park, CA: Sage Publications. pp. 143–78.

Fransella, F. (1968) 'Self concepts and the stutterer', *British Journal of Psychiatry*, 114: 1531–5.

Fransella, F. (1970) 'Stuttering: not a symptom but a way of life', *British Journal of Communication Disorders*, 5: 22–9.

Fransella, F. (1972) *Personal Change and Reconstruction*. London: Academic Press.

Fransella, F. (1988) 'PCT: still radical thirty years on?', in F. Fransella and L. Thomas (eds), *Experimenting with Personal Construct Psychology*. London: Routledge & Kegan Paul.

Fransella, F. (1996) *George Kelly's Contribution to Psychotherapy*. London: Sage Publications.

Fransella, F. and Bannister, D. (1977) *A Manual for Repertory Grid Technique*. London: Academic Press.

Fransella, F. and Button, E. (1983) 'The "constructing" of self and body size in relation to the maintenance of weight gain in anorexia nervosa', in P.L. Darby (ed.), *Anorexia Nervosa: Recent Developments in Research*. New York: Liss.

Fransella, F. and Crisp, A.H. (1970) 'Conceptual organisation and weight change', *Psychotherapy and Psychosomatics*, 18: 176–85.

Fransella, F. and Crisp, A.H. (1979) 'Comparison of weight concepts in groups of (a) neurotic (b) normal and (c) anorexic females', *British Journal of Psychiatry*, 134: 79–86.

Fransella, F. and Joyston-Bechal, M.P. (1971) 'An investigation of conceptual process and pattern change in a psychotherapy group over one year', *British Journal of Psychiatry*, 119: 199–206.

Goldstein, A.J. and Chambless, D.L. (1978) 'A reanalysis of agoraphobia', *Behavior Therapy*, 9: 47–59.

Gonçalves, O.F. (1994) 'From epistemological truth to existential meaning in cognitive narrative psychotherapy', *Journal of Constructivist Psychology*, 7: 107–18.

Greenberg, L. and Pascual-Leone, J. (1995) 'A dialectical constructivist approach to experiential change', in R.A. Neimeyer and M.J. Mahoney (eds), *Constructivism in Psychotherapy*. Washington, DC: American Psychological Association. pp. 169–91.

Guidano, V.F. and Liotti, G. (1983) *Cognitive Processes and Emotional Disorders*. New York: Guilford.

Haffner, R.J. (1977a) 'The husbands of agoraphobic women: assortative mating or pathogenic interaction?', *British Journal of Psychiatry*, 130: 233–9.

Haffner, R.J. (1977b) 'The husbands of agoraphobic women and their influence on treatment outcome', *British Journal of Psychiatry*, 131: 289–94.

Haffner, R.J. (1979) 'Agoraphobic women married to abnormally jealous men', *British Journal of Medical Psychology*, 52: 99–104.

Harter, S.L. and Neimeyer, R.A. (1995) 'Long term effects of child sexual abuse: toward a constructivist theory of trauma and its treatment', in R.A. Neimeyer and G.J. Neimeyer (eds), *Advances in Personal Construct Theory*. Greenwich, CT: JAI Press.

Haynow, R. and Levy, C. (1989) *Working with Stuttering*. Bicester, UK: Winslow Press.

Hoffman, L. (1992) 'A reflexive stance for family therapy', in S. McNamee and K.J. Gergen (eds), *Therapy as Social Construction*. Newbury Park, CA: Sage Publications. pp. 7–24.

Howard, A.R. and Kelly, G.A. (1954) 'A theoretical approach to psychological movement', *Journal of Abnormal and Social Psychology*, 49: 399–404.

Jackson, T.T., Markley, R.P., Zelhart, P.F. and Guydish, J. (1988) 'Contributions to the history of psychology: XLV. Attitude research: George A. Kelly's use of polar adjectives', *Psychological Reports*, 62: 47–52.

Jones, R.E. (1954) 'Identification in terms of personal constructs'. Unpublished doctoral dissertation, Ohio State University.

Karst, T.O. (1980) 'The relationship between personal construct theory and psychotherapeutic techniques', in A.W. Landfield and L.M. Leitner (eds), *Personal Construct Psychology: Psychotherapy and Personality*. New York: Wiley.

Karst, T.O. and Trexler, L.D. (1970) 'Initial study using fixed role therapy and rational-emotive therapy in treating public speaking anxiety', *Journal of Consulting and Clinical Psychology*, 34: 360–6.

Kelly, G.A. (1955) *The Psychology of Personal Constructs*. New York: Norton.

Klion, R.E. (1993) 'Chemical dependency', in L.M. Leitner and G. Dunnett (eds), *Critical Issues in Personal Construct Therapy*. Malabar, FL: Krieger. pp. 279–302.

Korzybski, A. (1933) *Science and Sanity*. New York: Internatonal Non-Aristotelian Library.

Kremsdorf, R. (1985) 'An extension of fixed-role therapy with a couple', in F. Epting and A.W. Landfield (eds), *Anticipating Personal Construct Psychology*. Lincoln, NB: University of Nebraska Press.

Kuehlwein, K.T. and Rosen, H. (1993) *Cognitive Therapies in Action*. San Francisco: Jossey-Bass.

Landfield, A.W. (1954) 'A movement interpretation of threat', *Journal of Abnormal and Social Psychology*, 49: 529–32.

Landfield, A.W. (1955) 'Self predictive orientation and the movement interpretation of threat', *Journal of Abnormal and Social Psychology*, 51: 434–8.

Landfield, A.W. (1971) *Personal Construct Systems in Psychotherapy*. Chicago: Rand McNally.

Landfield, A.W. (1979) 'Exploring socialization through the Interpersonal Transaction Group', in P. Stringer and D. Bannister (eds), *Constructs of Sociality and Individuality*. London: Academic Press. pp. 133–51.

Landfield, A.W. (1988) 'Personal science and the concept of validation', *International Journal of Personal Construct Psychology*, 1: 237–50.

Landfield, A.W. and Nawas, M.M. (1964) 'Psychotherapeutic improvement as a function of communication and adoption of therapists' values', *Journal of Counseling Psychology*, 11: 336–41.

Leitner, L.M. (1987) 'Crisis of the self: the terror of personal evolution', in R.A. Neimeyer and G.J. Neimeyer (eds), *Personal Construct Therapy Casebook*. New York: Springer.

Leitner, L.M. (1988) 'Terror, risk, and reverence: experiential personal construct psychotherapy', *International Journal of Personal Construct Psychology*, 1: 299–310.

Leitner, L.M. (1995) 'Optimal therapeutic distance', in R.A. Neimeyer and M.J. Mahoney (eds), *Constructivism in Psychotherapy*. Washington, DC: American Psychological Association. pp. 357–70.

Loos, V. (1993) 'Now that I know the techniques, what do I do with the family?', in L. Leitner and G. Dunnett (eds), *Critical Issues in Personal Construct Psychotherapy*. Malabar, FL: Krieger. pp. 239–63.

Lorenzini, R. and Sassaroli, S. (1987) *La paura della paura*. Roma: La Nuova Italia Scientifica.

McNamee, S. (1996) 'The social construction of psychotherapy', in K.T. Kuehlwein and H. Rosen (eds), *Constructing Realities*. San Francisco: Jossey-Bass.

McPherson, F.M. and Buckley, F. (1970) 'Thought-process disorder and personal construct subsystems', *British Journal of Medical Psychology*, 49: 281–90.

McPherson, F.M., Barden, V. and Buckley, F. (1970) 'Use of psychological constructs by affectively flattened schizophrenics', *British Journal of Medical Psychology*, 43: 291–3.

Mahoney, M.J. (ed.) (1995) *Cognitive and Constructive Psychotherapies*. New York: Springer.

Mair, M. (1985) 'The long quest to know', in F. Epting and A.W. Landfield (eds), *Anticipating Personal Construct Psychology*. Lincoln, NB: University of Nebraska Press. pp. 3–14.

Mair, M. (1989) *Between Psychology and Psychotherapy*. London: Routledge.

Marsella, A.J., DeVos, G. and Hsu, F.L.K. (1985) *Culture and Self: Asian and Western Perspectives*. London: Tavistock.

Meichenbaum, D. (1993) 'Changing conceptions of cognitive behavior modification: retrospect and prospect', *Journal of Consulting and Clinical Psychology*, 61: 202–4.

Moreno, J.L. (1937) 'Inter-personal therapy and the psychopathology of interpersonal relations', *Sociometry*, 1: 9–76.

Mullins, N.C. (1973) *Theories and Theory Groups in Contemporary American Sociology*. New York: Harper and Row.

Nawas, M.M. and Landfield, A.W. (1963) 'Improvement in psychotherapy and adoption of the therapist's meaning system', *Psychological Reports*, 13: 97–8.

Neimeyer, G.J. (1985) 'Personal constructs in the counseling of couples', in F.R. Epting and A.W. Landfield (eds), *Anticipating Personal Construct Psychology*. Lincoln, NB: University of Nebraska Press. pp. 201–15.

Neimeyer, G.J. and Hudson J.E. (1985) 'Couples' constructs: personal systems in marital satisfaction', in D. Bannister (ed.), *Issues and Approaches in Personal Construct Theory*. London: Academic Press.

Neimeyer, G.J. and Neimeyer, R.A. (1981) 'Functional similarity and interpersonal attraction', *Journal of Research in Personality*, 15: 427–35.

Neimeyer, G.J. and Neimeyer, R.A. (1985) 'Relational trajectories: a personal construct contribution', *Journal of Social and Personal Relationships*, 2: 325–49.

Neimeyer, G.J. and Neimeyer, R.A. (1986) 'Personal constructs in relationship deterioration: a longitudinal study', *Social Behavior and Personality*, 14: 253–7.

Neimeyer, G.J. and Neimeyer, R.A. (1994) 'Constructivist methods of marital and family therapy : a practical précis', *Journal of Mental Health Counseling*, 16: 85–104.

Neimeyer, R.A. (1984) 'Toward a personal construct conceptualization of depression and suicide', in F.R. Epting and R.A. Neimeyer (eds), *Personal Meanings of Death: Applications of Personal Construct Theory to Clinical Practice*. New York: Hemisphere/McGraw-Hill.

Neimeyer, R.A. (1985) *The Development of Personal Construct Psychology*. Lincoln, NB: University of Nebraska Press.

Neimeyer, R.A. (1987) 'An orientation to personal construct therapy', in R.A. Neimeyer and G.J. Neimeyer (eds), *Personal Construct Therapy Casebook*. New York: Springer. pp. 3–19.

Neimeyer, R.A. (1988) 'Integrative directions in personal construct therapy', *International Journal of Personal Construct Psychology*, 1: 283–97.

Neimeyer, R.A. (1989) 'Constructivist contributions to psychotherapy integration.' Paper presented at the 8th International Congress on Personal Construct Psychology, Assisi, Italy.

Neimeyer, R.A. (1993a) 'Constructivism and the cognitive therapies: some conceptual and strategic contrasts', *Journal of Cognitive Psychotherapy*, 7: 159–71.

Neimeyer, R.A. (1993b) 'Constructivism and the problem of psychotherapy integration', *Journal of Psychotherapy Integration*, 3: 133–57.

Neimeyer, R.A. (1993c) 'Constructivist approaches to the measurement of meaning', in G.J. Neimeyer (ed.), *Constructivist Assessment: A Casebook*. Newbury Park, CA: Sage Publications. pp. 58–103.

Neimeyer, R.A. (1995) 'Constructivist psychotherapies: features, foundations, and future directions', in R.A. Neimeyer and M.J. Mahoney (eds), *Constructivism in Psychotherapy*. Washington, DC: American Psychological Association. pp. 11–38.

Neimeyer, R.A. and Feixas, G. (1990) 'Constructivist contributions to psychotherapy integration', *Journal of Integrative and Eclectic Psychotherapy*, 9: 4–20.

Neimeyer, R.A. and Jackson, T.T. (1996) 'George A. Kelly and the development of personal construct theory', in W.G. Bringmann, R. Lueck, R. Miller and C.E. Early (eds), *A Pictorial History of Psychology*. Carol Stream, IL: Quintessence.

Neimeyer, R.A. and Mahoney, M.J. (eds), (1995) *Constructivism in Psychotherapy*. Washington, DC: American Psychological Association.

Neimeyer, R.A. and Neimeyer, G.J. (1983) 'Structural similarity in the acquaintance process', *Journal of Social and Clinical Psychology*, 1: 146–54.

Neimeyer, R.A. and Neimeyer, G.J. (1985) 'Disturbed relationships: a personal construct view', in E. Button (ed.), *Personal Construct Theory in Mental Health*. London: Croom Helm. pp. 195–223.

Neimeyer, R.A., Heath, A.E. and Strauss, J. (1985) 'Personal reconstruction during group cognitive therapy for depression', in F. Epting and A.W. Landfield (eds), *Anticipating Personal Construct Psychology*. Lincoln, NB: University of Nebraska Press.

Neimeyer, R.A., Davis, K. and Rist, P. (1986) 'The future of personal construct psychology: a Delphi poll', *British Journal of Cognitive Psychotherapy*, 4: 37–44.

Neimeyer, R.A., Baker, K.D. and Neimeyer, G.J. (1990) 'The current status of personal construct theory: some scientometric data', in G.J. Neimeyer and R.A. Neimeyer (eds), *Advances in Personal Construct Psychology*. Greenwich, CT: JAI Press. pp. 3–22.

Neimeyer, R.A., Harter, S. and Alexander, P.C. (1991) 'Group perceptions as predictors of outcome in the treatment of incest survivors', *Psychotherapy Research*, 1: 149–58.

Neisser, U. (1967) *Cognition and Reality*. New York: Appleton-Century-Crofts.

O'Sullivan, B.O. (1984) 'Understanding the experience of agoraphobia.' Unpublished PhD thesis, University of Dublin, Ireland.

Pfenninger, D.T. and Klion, R.E. (1996) 'Re-thinking hostility: is it ever better to fight than switch?', in R.A. Neimeyer and G.J. Neimeyer (eds), *Advances in Personal Construct Psychology*. Greenwich, CT: JAI Press. pp. 271–89.

Procter, H.G. (1981) 'Family construct psychology: an approach to understanding and treating families', in S. Walrond-Skinner (ed.), *Developments in Family Therapy*. London: Routledge & Kegan Paul.

Procter, H.G. (1987) 'Change in the family construct system', in R.A. Neimeyer and G.J. Neimeyer (eds), *Personal Construct Therapy Casebook*. New York: Springer. pp. 153–71.

Raskin, J.D. and Epting, F.R. (1993) 'Personal construct theory and the argument against mental illness', *International Journal of Personal Construct Psychology*, 6: 351–69.

Robinson, A.J. (1982) 'A further validation of role therapy', in R.P. Markley, P.F. Zelhart and T.T. Jackson (eds), *Explorations with Fixed Role Therapy*. Fort Hays, KS: Fort Hays University. pp. 50–90. (Originally published 1943.)

Ryle, A. and Breen, D. (1971) 'The recognition of psychopathology on the repertory grid', *British Journal of Psychiatry*, 119: 317–22.

Ryle, A. and Breen, D. (1972) 'A comparison of adjusted and maladjusted couples using the double dyad grid', *British Journal of Medical Psychology*, 45: 375–82.

Ryle, A. and Lunghi, M. (1970) 'The dyad grid – a modification of repertory grid technique', *British Journal of Psychiatry*, 117: 323–7.

Sechrest, L.B. (1962) 'Stimulus equivalents of the psychotherapist', *Journal of Individual Psychology*, 18: 172–6.

Sewell, K. (1996) 'Constructional risk factors for a post-traumatic stress response following a mass murder', *Journal of Constructivist Psychology*, 9: 97–108.

Slater, P. (1972) 'Notes on INGRID 72'. Unpublished manuscript, Institute of Psychiatry, London.

Space, L.G. and Cromwell, R.L. (1980) 'Personal constructs among depressed patients', *Journal of Nervous and Mental Disease*, 168: 150–8.

Space, L.G., Dingemans, P.M. and Cromwell, R.L. (1983) 'Self-construing and alienation in depressives, schizophrenics, and normals', in J. Adams-Webber and J.C. Mancuso (eds), *Applications of Personal Construct Theory*. Toronto: Academic Press Canada.

Stewart, A.E. and Barry, J.R. (1991) 'Origins of George Kelly's constructivism in the work of Korzybski and Moreno', *International Journal of Personal Construct Psychology*, 4: 121–36.

Tamaka-Matsumi, J. and Marsella, A.J. (1976) 'Cross-cultural variations in the phenomeno-logical experience of depression: word association studies', *Journal of Cross-Cultural Psychology*, 7: 379–96.

Toukmanian, S.G. (1992) 'Studying the client's perceptual processes and their outcomes in psychotherapy', in S.G. Toukmanian and D.L. Rennie (eds), *Psychotherapy Process Research*. Newbury Park, CA: Sage Publications. pp. 77–107.

Tyler, F.B. and Simmons, W.L. (1964) 'Patients' conception of the therapist', *Journal of Clinical Psychology*, 20: 112–33.

Viney, L.L. (1993) *Life Stories: Personal Construct Therapy with the Elderly*. New York: Wiley.

Walker, B.M. (1993) 'Looking for a whole "Mama": personal construct theory and dependency', in L.M. Leitner and G. Dunnett (eds), *Critical Issues in Personal Construct Therapy*. Malabar, FL: Krieger. pp. 61–84.

Winter, D.A. (1985) 'Group therapy with depressives: a personal construct theory perspec-tive', *International Journal of Mental Health*, 13: 67–85.

Winter, D.A. (1990) 'Therapeutic alternatives for psychological disorder', in G.J. Neimeyer and R.A. Neimeyer (eds), *Advances in Personal Construct Psychology*, (Vol. 1). Greenwich, CT: JAI Press.

Winter, D.A. (1992) *Personal Construct Psychology in Clinical Practice*. London: Routledge.

Yelich, G. and Salamone, F.J. (1994) 'Constructivist interpretation of attention-deficit hyperactivity disorder', *Journal of Constructivist Psychology*, 7: 191–212.

Zelhart, P.F., Jackson, T.T. and Markley, R.P. (1982) 'George A. Kelly at Fort Hays', *Fort Hays State University Forum*, 28: 1–2.

7

Developments in Behaviour Therapy

Robert Newell

The nature and scope of behaviour therapy

Modern behaviour therapy consists of a number of strands of therapeutic orientation, all of which are in agreement on basic precepts governing clinical work. These precepts are typically derived from learning theories, especially those concerned with operant and classical conditioning, and, more recently, with social learning theories. Similarly, almost all formulations of behaviour therapy assert that clients' internal motivations are opaque to the therapist and to the client. Such motivations are, therefore, not the subject of examination by the therapist. Indeed, some strict behaviourists deny not only the relevance but the very existence of thoughts, whilst others, most notably radical behaviourists, state that thoughts, whilst they exist, are best considered as subject to precisely the same laws of conditioning as any other behaviours (Jaremko, 1986). Although radical behaviourism *is* concerned with a kind of internal life, it is thus very different from the information-processing accounts of cognition and cognitive therapy. These accounts, and the cognitive and cognitive-behavioural approaches that in part derive from them, are not dealt with in this chapter, which traces the development of only those approaches to therapy derived from learning theory. Cognitive therapy and cognitive behaviour therapy are dealt with in other chapters.

Whilst the extent to which behaviourists deny the relevance or existence of cognitive processes varies, practitioners are generally united by their conviction that the client's behaviour is both the most important element in problem genesis and maintenance and the most appropriate focus for intervention. In this way, behaviour therapists share with behavioural psychologists from non-clinical fields an emphasis on overt behaviour. As well as this emphasis, behaviour therapists have taken from academic psychology an insistence on rigorous evaluation of their interventions and many of the investigation methods used in behavioural psychology. Indeed, in an examination of the meaning of being a behaviour therapist, Thoresen and Coates (1978) note the strong identification of the therapy with scientific principles and methods. They examine five complementary definitions of behaviour therapy: applied learning theory, application of results and methods of experimental behavioural science, experimental study of change processes, controlled experimental studies of the single case, and technical eclecticism. Whilst each of these definitions has excited controversy during the history of behaviour therapy, they all site behaviour therapy clearly within the tradition of empiricism. Thoresen and Coates conclude by suggesting that therapy is best practised and evaluated within this scientific tradition, and characterize the behaviour therapist as one who challenges the non-scientific myths of other therapeutic traditions.

At its best, behaviour therapy is, therefore, 'scientific', in this broad sense of subjecting the therapeutic process to empirical testing. Behaviour therapists seek to engage clients as participants in therapeutic 'experiments', which attempt to establish the relevance of conditioning theories to clients' difficulties. Therapy is also eclectic, drawing on many techniques, challenging of orthodoxy, humanistic (since it seeks to assert the individuality of clients' experiences and difficulties, rather than to ascribe to them mental 'illnesses' which differentiate them from the rest of the population), pragmatic, and driven principally by technique rather than relationship.

Although behaviour therapy is an amalgam of many techniques and approaches, it is possible to describe typical elements of therapy sessions. Assessment is separated from treatment and emphasizes an examination of those particular elements of individuals' experiences and behaviour which contribute to their difficulties, typically through a process of *functional analysis*, which examines conditioning and other learning processes operating in the person's life. The therapist's formulation of the client's difficulties is shared with him, and the client is didactically oriented to the behavioural approach. In treatment, specific techniques may be taught and practised, which principally seek to alter the person's conditioning opportunities, and thus his behaviours.

Problematic behaviours are always the direct focus of treatment, and little discussion of underlying causes will take place. Most behaviour therapists minimize or deny the importance of such assumed causes, or even assert that the very notion of cause and symptom is an inappropriate analogy from medical models of psychological distress. There are both theoretical reasons and empirical support for this contention. Since behavioural theorists argue that the laws of conditioning apply to both adaptive and maladaptive behaviour, there is no logic in describing maladaptive behaviour as a disease-like process. Since we should not describe adaptive behaviours as symptomatic of some underlying pathology, why should we do so with problem behaviours? Empirically, despite early assertions by psychoanalysts, the therapeutic literature does not support the notion of symptom substitution. This construct suggests that any treatment which addresses only symptoms of a complaint will fail, since the underlying cause, if not addressed, will subsequently give rise to further symptoms. However, there have been no adequate accounts of such substitution (Eysenck, 1991), and many of long-term gains and generalized improvements following behavioural interventions. Putative underlying conflicts are, therefore, not addressed by behaviour therapy.

Perhaps the most distinctive aspect of behaviour therapy sessions is the role of the therapist. Whatever techniques are employed or whatever sub-branch of behaviour therapy the therapist espouses, the level of activity by the therapist will be extremely high. Behaviourists are teachers, practical instructors and collaborators with clients, and behaviour therapy is largely a prescriptive treatment, to which the therapist contributes expert knowledge of behavioural theory and techniques, acting as a consultant to the client in much the same way as we would expect of a lawyer or accountant. As a result, the nature of therapy involves the therapist in constant questioning and instruction of the client. In behaviour therapy, the relationship with the client is basic to all interventions, but does not, in itself, constitute an intervention.

The client groups addressed by behavioural interventions are extremely diverse. Unlike traditional verbal psychotherapies, the scope to address different client difficulties is vast. Traditional therapies and counselling have typically concentrated on intelligent, verbally able people with comparatively minor difficulties – the so-called YAVIS (young, attractive, verbal, intelligent, successful) criteria (Eysenck, 1991), and have not strayed far into the territory of severe mental disorder. By contrast, behaviour therapy has, since its inception, concerned itself with the full range of human difficulties, including long-term mental health problems, learning disabilities and consequences of institutional care.

Behavioural accounts of human experience and distress are now often regarded as oversimplifications, and modern cognitive theories appear more attractive to many therapists. However, the simpler learning theory accounts still play a considerable part in treatment. More than this, learning theory is now part of the general folklore of society, and people who have never heard of Pavlov and Skinner, and would possibly be appalled at some of the ideas of these early behaviourists, speak of 'conditioning' and 'reinforcement' in a natural and informal way. Behaviourism has become an accepted part of the way we all look at our daily lives.

Early behavioural approaches

If the language of behaviourism has filtered into our daily discourse, so there are suggestions that the techniques of behaviour therapy have always been part of lay understanding of our difficulties. Although most commentators wish to date the start of formal behaviour therapy to the 1920s, with the works of Watson and Rayner (1920) or later, some writers have sought to demonstrate the existence of informal behaviour therapy throughout history. Whilst it is impossible to state accurately whether tactics employed during biblical or medieval times conformed precisely to schedules of reinforcement or experimental classical conditioning, such accounts provide us with some indication that general precepts of behavioural approaches spring from a folklore tradition of confrontation of anxiety, discrimination of dangerous and safe situations, and appreciation of the importance of reward in mediating behaviour.

Major religious traditions of both East and West contain examples of learning situations congruent with the work of the modern behaviour therapist. De Silva (1984) examines the relationship between behaviour therapy and Buddhist teaching, seeking to demonstrate that the latter may be taken to show that the religious teachers were acting according to the principles of learning and cognitive theory.

From the Christian tradition, Swartz (1988) describes a meditation on hell constructed by Ignatius Loyola (1491–1556), which Swartz describes as similar to covert sensitization, a technique now used by behaviour therapists in the treatment (amongst other things) of undesired sexual behaviours. According to Swartz, the technique is used in such a way as to negatively reinforce abstinence, through removal of the noxious stimulus of meditation on hell. The Loyola example contains many details consistent with modern practice, such as individual tailoring of 'treatment' to the particular abilities of the person meditating and careful monitoring to ensure that the imagery does not lose its potency.

Turn-of-the-century influences

Turning to more modern examples, Kazdin and Pulaski (1977) cite the educational system of Joseph Lancaster in the early nineteenth century as an example of the application of behavioural principles to teaching, whilst, in a clinical example, Miller (1988) describes the work of Robert Brudenell Carter during the mid-nineteenth century as an example of behaviour modification in practice, if not in theory. Carter followed a therapeutic approach which, like behaviour therapy, involved environmental manipulation and the enlistment of family and friends of the client, in order to reduce the attention paid to complaints of illness, whilst rewarding well behaviour. Miller notes that the way in which Carter's treatment for complaints of illness was organized approximates closely to an extinction programme, in which non-reinforced behaviours reduce in frequency.

The clearest example of an early precursor of the work of modern behaviour therapists comes from Prince (1891, 1909), who drew extensively on the work in classical conditioning to create a system of psychotherapeutic intervention based on the principles of association. Freedberg (1973) outlines the contribution not only of Prince, but of a number of other early proponents of techniques we would nowadays recognize as behavioural interventions. He cites such complaints as insomnia, writer's cramp, fear of incontinence, phobias and obsessions. In many cases, the writers describe their clients' difficulties and their own interventions in terms of conditioned reflexes which the therapist attempts to manipulate. From the many examples cited by Freedberg (1973), and even a cursory scan of the titles of psychology journals from the turn of the century, it is clear that a form of therapy making at least informal use of learning principles was a thriving set of treatment interventions well before the famous Watson and Rayner (1920) paper.

The beginnings of formal behaviour therapy: 'Little Albert'

Although not, strictly speaking, therapeutic interventions, the work of Watson and his co-workers during the 1920s, in conditioning and decon-ditioning fear, clearly prefigure formal behaviour therapy. Watson is generally regarded as having been the first to set out what it means to be a behaviourist in psychology, and was well known for his insistence that psychological experiment should avoid the use of mental constructs in accounting for animal or human responses.

In a series of experiments, Watson examined the acquisition of emotional responses in children, using classical conditioning methods. In classical conditioning, an organism's response comes to be elicited by a novel stimulus, rather than one with which it has already been associated. Many people today are aware of the seminal work of Ivan Pavlov (1927), in which he trained dogs to salivate in response to the sound of a bell. This was achieved first by pairing sounding of a bell with presentation of food (an unconditional stimulus for salivation). On subsequent occasions the food was withdrawn, but sounding of the bell repeated. The animals continued to demonstrate the salivation response, which Pavlov referred to as a conditional response to the conditional stimulus of the bell. Later, these stimuli and responses came to be called conditioned stimuli and responses in popular conversation, and are still so described today. Pavlov noticed numerous associated phenomena during the training sessions, including generalization (where the animal responds to bells at frequencies other than that to which it has been trained), discrimination (where the animal discriminates, often to a very fine degree, between tones which have been followed by presentation of food and those which have not, and exhibits salivation only in response to the former) and, perhaps most importantly, extinction, in which the animal's conditional responses gradually wane following repeated presentation of the conditional stimulus (the bell), without further presentation of the unconditional stimulus of food.

Watson's paper (Watson and Rayner, 1920) describing the acquisition of fear of a white rat in a one-year-old child (Little Albert) is now regarded as a turning point both in behaviour therapy (whose commencement it is said to mark) and in psychotherapy more generally, since it was an early demon-stration that neurotic complaints might be acquired by learning, and, therefore, was the beginning of the first serious therapeutic rival to psychoanalysis. Fear was conditioned by pairing presentation of the rat with a loud noise. The fear response generalized to other similar objects, such as a white rabbit and a Santa Claus mask. In some senses, the work of Watson's colleague Mary Cover Jones (e.g. Jones, 1924) is even more relevant to

modern behaviourism. Just as the basic conditioning paradigms for acquisition and maintenance of fear can be clearly seen in the Watson and Rayner
experiment, so Jones's work laid down the basic procedures for treatment of
phobias and also investigated both effective and ineffective intervention
strategies (Jones, 1924). Of the ineffective tactics, two are especially worthy
of note. Avoidance of the feared object did not cause fear reduction,
something nowadays quite familiar both to behaviour therapists and their
clients. Second, repeated exposure did not lead to diminution of fear. At
first glance this is surprising, given the current popularity of the exposure
therapies, which work on precisely this principle. However, we cannot know
the precise circumstances in which exposure was offered in these early
experiments. Two successful methods led directly to treatments which
became mainstays of clinical behaviour therapy. The first, direct conditioning, involved the use of a competing response to anxiety to promote
extinction of the fear response, and so anticipated Wolpe's 'reciprocal
inhibition', whilst social imitation clearly prefigures Bandura's modelling
techniques and social learning theory. Jones also described the use of a
hierarchical approach to confronting the feared stimulus, again anticipating
the work of Wolpe.

B.F. Skinner and operant conditioning

During the early years of the twentieth century, Edward Thorndyke
formulated the well-known 'law of effect'. He postulated a form of learning
based on the strengthening and weakening of connections between situations and responses made to them. The law of effect states that responses
that have consequences which are satisfactory to the animal are likely to
have their connections to the situation in which they were made strengthened, and therefore are more likely to be made again in similar situations
(Thorndyke, 1931). By contrast, those responses which have unsatisfactory
consequences are likely to decrease in frequency. Skinner's early work
attempted to clarify the distinction between the work of Thorndyke, upon
whose law of effect he drew heavily, and that of Pavlov. However, the
majority of his experimental work involved investigation of the nature of
operant conditioning, whose principles he refined from Thorndyke's law of
effect and systematized into a coherent account of how new behaviours are
acquired.

Operant conditioning led to arguably the most significant contribution to
therapy of the behavioural approaches. This highly flexible type of learning
facilitates the acquisition of new behaviours, as well as changing or
suppressing existing responses, essentially through the systematized application of rewards and punishments. In operant conditioning, positive and
negative reinforcement both serve to increase the frequency of behaviours.
Positive reinforcement involves the application of a pleasant stimulus
following a desired response by the subject, whilst negative reinforcement is

the withdrawal of some noxious stimulus in response to such a desired behaviour. Two chief variants on reinforcement involve the use of differing schedules of reinforcement to elicit and maintain behaviour (fixed-interval schedules are best at initiating new behaviours, whilst intermittent schedules maintain them most effectively once established), and the use of reinforcement for successive approximations to an ultimately desired behaviour. In this procedure, also known as shaping, complex new behaviours may be 'shaped up' by closely observing chance behaviours which already exist and differentially reinforcing those which make slight approximations to the desired response. As only these behaviours are reinforced, they soon increase in frequency, which allows increased opportunities for reinforcement of further approximation to eventual target behaviours. Although many of its elements had been developed by earlier researchers, the systematic investigation of operant conditioning and suggestions regarding its application to therapy are generally ascribed to B.F. Skinner.

Although Skinner's work was principally in animal laboratories, he wrote extensively about the application of operant conditioning principles to human behaviour, including the alleviation of human distress and the construction of a society based on operant principles (Skinner, 1948, 1953, 1971). During the 1950s, he also undertook experimental studies using human participants, most notably training responses in psychotic patients and non-clinical participants as part of a project for the Office of Naval Research (Lindsley, 1960). Although the tasks involved were simple responses which were in themselves therapeutically trivial, they demonstrated the applicability of learning techniques based on animal studies to human learning, and laid the foundation for much of the early clinical work which was to follow. The first recorded use of the term 'behaviour therapy' dates from the work of Skinner and his co-workers at this time (Lindsley et al., 1953). The influence of this work, coupled with the great emerging need for psychotherapeutic intervention in the context of the social and psychological changes following the war years, contributed greatly to the rising importance of behaviourism during the 1950s in the USA. Similarly, Glass and Arnkoff (1992) have noted that the rise in dissatisfaction with traditional models of psychopathology, in terms of both theoretical validity and practical effectiveness, created a fertile ground for the methodologically exacting and therapeutically effective profile of a behaviour therapy based on operant conditioning.

Although operant conditioning made less of a contribution to behaviour therapy in Britain, it had substantial impact in the USA, particularly in the fields of child psychology, work with people with learning disabilities and rehabilitation of institutionalized psychiatric patients. In general terms, operant work with these three groups of clients was essentially similar and involved the encouragement of desired behaviours (washing, shaving, social interaction) through the use of rewards and discouragement of unwanted behaviours (aggressive acts, temper tantrums) either through punishment (ignoring the behaviour, withdrawal of a privilege) or the differential reinforcement of activities incompatible with the unwanted behaviours.

In work with children, operant conditioning has been used both to address specific childhood difficulties, such as temper tantrums (Carlson et al., 1968), and to aid in organizing general classroom regimes, for example in the management of disruptive children. One particularly influential researcher in the field, Patterson (1971), carried out extensive work in behaviour modification with children, moving from single case reports to wide-ranging interventions covering whole institutions. Apart from its use with clinical populations, the use of operant techniques has broadened to provide in-structional methods, such as programmed learning, for the imparting of new skills to children not exhibiting behavioural problems, and to dealing with problematic behaviours of all kinds within mainstream educational settings.

The application of rewards (or reinforcers) to elicit or increase desired behaviours was for many years a dominant theoretical framework for much of the teaching endeavour. Although now a relatively minor part of formal teaching technique in mainstream education, where more 'humanistic' ap-proaches are in vogue, behavioural principles still underlie many of the tactics employed in schools, particularly in dealing with disruptive be-haviour, whilst behavioural treatments for child behaviour problems both retain clinical supporters (Herbert, 1987), and have passed into the more general sphere of lay knowledge through the publication of self-help books for parents.

In the field of learning disability, no set of interventions has attracted more interest or more debate than behaviour modification. The debate has been caused chiefly by worries about ethics which have occupied both behaviour therapists and their critics for many years, whilst the interest resulted both from the growing awareness of the effectiveness of be-havioural techniques in learning disability and a more general change in perception on the part of both professionals and carers towards a belief that even severely impaired people are educable. As with much of the work on operant conditioning, the early literature came from the USA. Case studies and single case experiments formed the bulk of the early literature during the 1960s. By the beginning of the next decade, group studies had begun to accumulate (see Yule and Carr, 1987 for a comprehensive account of the status of behaviour therapy with learning disabilities), and a number of key texts had been published (e.g. Gardner, 1971). Apart from the important message of hope regarding the teachability of people with learning disabili-ties, the other important contribution was the training of non-psychologists and non-clinicians in the treatment methods used (Yule, 1975). By the mid-1970s, behaviour therapy was the mainstay of education of people with learning disabilities. Although the *term* behaviour therapy is currently somewhat unfashionable in learning disability circles, where approaches such as 'gentle teaching' (McGee, 1990) have attracted considerable inter-est, behavioural methods remain at the heart of such teaching today. In remedial education programmes and education of people with learning disabilities, behavioural principles continue to exert a major influence, and make a considerable contribution to the quality of life of these individuals.

In institutional settings, behaviours associated with years of incarceration and dependent roles have proved a major obstacle to reintegration of inmates into the community, whilst also being a source of difficulty to staff who attempt to manage such facilities. Perhaps most importantly, the small range of activities exhibited by 'institutionalized' individuals represents a great impoverishment of their quality of life. Whilst issues surrounding institutionalization and reintegration into the community certainly remain today, the problem was far more widespread during the 1950s and 1960s, when in-patient populations, both in the USA and Britain, were far larger, since effective drug treatments for major psychiatric illnesses were in their infancy. In this context, the introduction of operant regimes to encourage self-care and interactive skills, and to decrease undesirable institutional behaviours, such as stereotypical behaviours, swearing, 'crazy talk' and inappropriate eating behaviours, was a great source of hope for staff, and by extension, the patients with whom they worked. The work of Ayllon is widely cited (e.g. Kazdin, 1978; Glass and Arnkoff, 1992) as being of the utmost importance to the development of these operant regimes. At the heart of Ayllon's work was the use of nurses to effect the changes in patient behaviour required. In an early report (Ayllon and Michael, 1959) several case examples were given, including the extinguishing of violent behaviour in one patient through the use of reinforcement contingent upon violence-free periods of time. Ayllon expanded the compass of his work by arranging for entire wards to be run along operant lines, establishing new and appropriate behaviours amongst greatly disadvantaged, often psychotic, clients. Once again, the primary therapists in these regimes were ward nurses and attendants. The systems operated through the awarding of contingent reinforcement, in the form of tokens, for appropriate behaviours (Ayllon and Azrin, 1965). The use of tokens was important, since it allowed immediate reinforcement of the desired behaviours and accurate monitoring of the use of reinforcement by staff. The tokens were exchangeable for desired items or activities. Some of these items were very basic indeed (such as access to one's own chair), but reliably led to improvements in client behaviour and the acquisition of new, socially desirable responses. There was a great initial enthusiasm for so-called 'token economy' wards, where seriously socially disabled patients learned to perform basic personal care and communication skills. The allegedly mechanistic approach of token economy approaches combined with doubts over its eventual effectiveness to result in its gradual disappearance from general use in the UK, but the general use of operant principles remains a mainstay of such retraining approaches.

Although there were ethical debates about the appropriateness of operant procedures, often fuelled by lack of knowledge about the actual workings of such interventions (Rapp, 1984), their effectiveness offered an alternative at a time when little in the way of active treatment was available, particularly to people with learning disabilities and individuals suffering the effects of long-term incarceration in mental institutions. This ability to offer therapy to some of the most disadvantaged groups in mental health care provision, at a time when their needs were otherwise only addressed by medication and custodial care, was a great advantage of operant interventions, as was the use of non-specialist therapists such as nurses, a move which paved the way for the broadening of the use of behaviour therapy by many disciplines other than psychologists and psychiatrists.

Apart from his many theoretical insights and the lasting practical contribution made to behaviour therapy by the introduction of operant conditioning into the clinical arena, Skinner's work played a major role in giving behaviour therapy both a system of assessment and a distinctive clinical research method. Applied behavioural analysis (the systematic application of behavioural principles to the alleviation of human distress) and single case experimental design (its associated experimental method), whilst not solely the contributions of Skinner, are closely associated with his work and his emphasis on establishing laws of human behaviour (Kazdin, 1976). These methods have been mainstays of behaviour therapy almost since its inception, and continue to guide much clinical and experimental work in the field.

Although considerable interest in operant conditioning as a therapeutic intervention remains, it is now unusual to see it used as a sole approach to treatment. By the time conditioning theory had been developed into a system of treatment, it was already a comparatively old theory of human and animal behaviour, having been superseded as early as the 1960s by accounts which emphasized the importance of mediating processes in controlling human interaction with the environment. Amongst many psychologists, behaviour therapy was often regarded as an anachronism, even at the height of its therapeutic success. A further contributing factor to the demise of the operant approach to therapy was the appearance of divisions within behaviour therapy, between those who sought to retain a comparatively 'pure' therapy based on conditioning principles and those who sought rapprochement with other therapies such as psychoanalysis and humanistic therapies. Even amongst theoretical adherents to conditioning theory, it was noted that the conditioning regimes used in treatment often bore little resemblance to the reinforcement schedules used in the animal studies upon which they were supposedly based.

Perhaps most tellingly of all, the social climate changed rapidly during the 1960s and 1970s, in both America and the UK. The works of writers like Szasz (1970) and Laing (1967) emphasized, amongst other things, the worth and meaning of mental distress, whilst Rogers's (1951) humanistic approach gained greatly in popularity. It may be that a behaviour therapy which appeared not to emphasize meaning, thought and personal agency was too unpopular in this climate to continue to attract support, especially when there was division amongst its own adherents.

The contribution of B.F. Skinner, not only to behaviour therapy but to psychology as a whole, cannot be overestimated. Skinner recognized the wide applicability of behaviourism as a force in the prediction and mediation of human behaviour, and wrote influentially on a broad range of topics, including, for example, behavioural accounts of the process of analytical psychotherapy (1953) and of the acquisition of language (1957). Although his work has attracted continuing controversy, principally from those who decried the mechanism of behaviourism and behaviour therapy, he was widely recognized as a humanitarian, who cared passionately about individuals and society. He was a focus for research and teaching for most of his life, and is apparently remembered fondly by many students and collaborators (Cullen and Cole, 1991). Although unwell during the last years of his life, his influence remained extensive amongst behaviour therapists.

Joseph Wolpe and reciprocal inhibition

Important as these experimental demonstrations and early clinical interventions were, most commentators (e.g. Kazdin, 1978) credit the South African, Joseph Wolpe, with having developed the first credible alternative to traditional verbal psychotherapy, through his description and clinical exploration of the concept of reciprocal inhibition to deal with psychological disorders, particularly those based upon anxiety. Originally trained in psychoanalysis, Wolpe became increasingly disillusioned, during the 1940s, with the apparent inability of this system to affect the problems of clients, and sought an alternative system of practical benefit. Following contact with and influence from South African and American experimental psychologists, Wolpe began experimental work with animals, inducing fear in cats. As part of his observations, he noted that feeding behaviour was inhibited when the animals made the fear response induced experimentally. He hypothesized that an opposite inhibition, of anxiety by feeding, might also apply, and might have consequences for the treatment of neurotic complaints. These mutually exclusive behaviours he referred to as reciprocal inhibition (Wolpe, 1952). In order to extinguish the cats' experimentally created fears, Wolpe began by offering food in a setting which bore scant similarity to the cage in which the fear had been acquired. He then subsequently offered food in settings which bore ever closer approximations to the acquisition cage, proceeding to each successive setting once the animal showed no fear. Finally, the animal could tolerate the acquisition cage without showing anxiety.

Wolpe's key argument (1958), is that anxiety is a learned phenomenon, resulting primarily from the classical conditioning pairing of some object or situation with the onset of unpleasant bodily sensations (such as pain), which then comes to be associated with that object on future occasions and evokes the fear response. Thus, the role of reciprocal inhibition in successful treatment, according to Wolpe, is that it enables the client to enter the feared situation without experiencing the unpleasant sensations of anxiety. In consequence, the conditional stimulus (the feared object) can be presented without the unconditional stimulus of the bodily sensations, allowing extinction of the conditional anxiety response to the object to be extinguished.

Wolpe systematically extended his animal work, during the 1950s, to address the difficulties of human clients, typically using relaxation or assertive behaviour (but occasionally sexual activity) as the response said to be reciprocally inhibiting with anxiety. Although beginning his work using *in vivo* procedures, he found these often to be practically difficult, and experimented with the use of covert procedures, principally involving the use of a graded hierarchy of fearful imagery, which the client practised whilst in a state of relaxation, moving through the hierarchy from least to most feared situations once each step in the hierarchy could be visualized without anxiety. The client then confronted the feared situations in life. Wolpe formulated the treatment of many different problems in terms of reciprocal inhibition, and reported the successful treatment of a broad range of psychological disorders, including specific phobias, agoraphobia and social phobias, illness fears, sexual problems and unwanted habits. In 1958 Wolpe published *Psychotherapy by Reciprocal Inhibition*, a text which was to have great influence on clinical behaviour therapy.

Kazdin (1978) notes that much of the work of Wolpe was not innovative. For example, his theoretical work was very closely linked to that of earlier learning theorists such as Pavlov, Watson and Hull, while his practical procedures owed a great deal both to the 'Little Albert' experiments and to the animal work of Masserman (1943). Kazdin sees Wolpe's distinctive contribution to behaviour therapy as stemming from three elements of his work. His therapeutic system was grounded in 'hard' science, drawing on experimental psychology and physiology; he applied his findings from the laboratory to clinical populations; he made testable claims about his methods, which stimulated research.

To these contributions, perhaps a fourth important consequence of Wolpe's work should be added. During the 1950s and 1960s Wolpe became a focus for training, experimentation and treatment using behaviour therapy. Both in South Africa and, later, in the USA, Wolpe was at the centre of groups of clinicians who worked with and learned from him, often going on to make highly significant contributions to the development of behaviour therapy. Most notable of Wolpe's students and collaborators were S.J. Rachman and A.A. Lazarus, who were influential in spreading behavioural treatments to the UK (later Canada) and the USA respectively. Rachman worked for some years in London with Eysenck's group and jointly founded with him the first journal to be devoted exclusively to clinical applications of behaviour therapy – *Behaviour Research and Therapy*. Lazarus has made many contributions and extensions to behaviour therapy over the years, initially extending systematic desensitization to use with children and in groups. He has moved some distance from formal behaviour therapy, practising a system of therapy – multimodal therapy (Lazarus, 1973) – based on a broad cognitive-behavioural approach to client difficulties, but remains a highly influential figure in the field of psychotherapy.

Reciprocal inhibition in its strict sense, involving imaginal exposure to feared stimuli in a hierarchical way while practising relaxation, is rarely used. By the early 1970s it had become apparent that systematic desensitiz-ation, a time-consuming intervention involving laborious construction of hierarchies and training in relaxation, was by no means the only way of addressing anxiety disorders. In particular, flooding (e.g. Marks, 1972) and its variants provided a rapid alternative to desensitization. As well as offering a briefer, more cost-effective therapy, such treatments threw doubt on the necessity for conceptualizing therapeutic gains in terms of the classical conditioning model proposed by reciprocal inhibition, and empiri-cal approaches to treatment, which laid little emphasis on particular learning theories, were gaining in influence, especially in the UK. Systematic desensitization was also subject to criticism from the newly emerging cognitive approaches to therapy. Wolpe has become a critic of many recent developments in behaviour therapy (Wolpe, 1989), most notably 'exposure' therapy and cognitive therapy, upholding the theoretical and clinical claims of reciprocal inhibition in the face of a rapid decline in its use.

H.J. Eysenck and the Maudsley group

Hans Eysenck remains one of the most eminent psychological researchers of the century, having made distinctive contributions to personality theory, to the dismantling of psychoanalysis and psychotherapy as interventions in mental health care, and, most particularly, as a leading proponent of and contributor to the development of behaviour therapy. It is in this last capacity that we shall consider him in most detail, but Eysenck's critique of psychoanalysis is also relevant, since opposition to analysis and its associ-ated psychotherapies was a feature of experimental psychology and of early behaviour therapy which has continued to a marked extent to the present day. Eysenck originally asserted (1952), following a review of the outcome literature on psychoanalysis, that untreated clients improved at a similar rate to those who had had the benefit of analysis. Following this initial attack on analysis, Eysenck has continued to be a trenchant critic of traditional verbal psychotherapy (e.g. Eysenck and Wilson, 1973), while advocating therapy derived from experimental psychology as an effective alternative.

During the 1950s there had been considerable expansion in the numbers of psychologists trained, many of whom had moved into the new profession of clinical psychology. The clinical psychologist's work at this time principally involved the administration of various forms of psychometric test and the preparation of reports based upon them. This had led to some frustration, since treatment remained firmly under the control of psychiatrists. Although there were small numbers of lay psychotherapists, they were, like those psychiatrists who espoused psychotherapeutic rather than physical methods of treatment, trained in the psychoanalytical tradition, and usually worked under the direction of psychiatrists. At the Institute of Psychiatry (a constituent college of the University of London), Eysenck gathered a group of psychologists and students who were both critical of analytical techniques and physical treatments and keen to enter the field of therapy, using the techniques, assessment methods and evaluation strategies in which they had been trained as academic psychologists. Although Eysenck did not himself see patients, his influence on the group, as theoretician and teacher, was enormous. The group stressed the importance of learning principles in mediating client distress, and rejected the importance of medical models of psychiatric care involving such notions as symptoms, pathology and diagnosis. Fishman and Franks (1992) describe the growth of behaviour therapy at the Institute of Psychiatry and its associated hospital, the Maudsley Hospital, as a time of great excitement.

Certainly, considerable influence centred around the Institute, and the first case reports based on learning theory approaches to therapy began to be published by members of the Institute/Maudsley group. Franks (1987), in a reminiscence of these early days, notes that the group around Eysenck saw themselves as working within the conditioning tradition established by Pavlov and later by Hull and others, and much of the writing of the time draws much more on classical rather than operant conditioning. However, Franks also notes that the tone of the research and clinical work was characterized more by empirical investigation than by adherence to any specific theoretical ideology. Yates, another member of the Institute/ Maudsley group of the time, goes further, asserting that the behaviour therapy then being developed owed more to the use of the single case experimental study of clients than to learning theory, and more to the personal influence of Shapiro (a prominent exponent of single case experimental methods – see, for example Shapiro, 1961) than to Eysenck (Yates, 1981). Whilst the influence of Shapiro on the development of behaviour therapy at the Institute/Maudsley is widely acknowledged, Yates's assertion is not generally accepted, and Wilson (1978) notes that Eysenck's assertion that the many behavioural techniques reflected a common set of underlying principles based on learning theory was, by 1968 (when the AABT changed its name from the Association for the Advancement of the Behaviour Therapies to the Association for the Advancement of Behaviour Therapy: Franks, 1987), generally accepted. By this time, Eysenck (1960) had also published an important textbook on abnormal psychology, based on behavioural principles and an influential volume of case studies (Eysenck, 1964), and had co-founded *Behaviour Research and Therapy*.

Although Yates's account of the beginnings of behaviour therapy has not found broad acceptance, the pragmatic approach to behavioural inter-vention, which emphasizes empirical investigation of treatment techniques regardless of background in learning theory, has enjoyed considerable support. Perhaps best known amongst these pragmatic behaviourists is Isaac Marks, a Maudsley psychiatrist whose early experiments with flooding (1972) led him to become chief amongst the proponents of 'exposure' treatment. According to Marks (1987), the complicated treatment hierar-chies and relaxation exercises associated with reciprocal inhibition were not necessary to induce therapeutic improvement in phobics and other sufferers from anxiety-based problems. Instead, clients were simply encouraged to stay in the feared situations for sufficiently long for the anxiety to subside, being exposed to increasingly difficult situations at as fast a rate as they could tolerate.

Whilst exposure therapy has been subjected to considerable criticism, particularly from Wolpe, who characterizes it as lacking in any theoretical content, there is now a great deal of empirical work which supports its effectiveness. Moreover, exposure therapy does have theoretical roots, in its use of the concepts of habituation, and extinction of negative reinforce-ment. Habituation is generally described as the most basic process of learning, and is reliably demonstrated in humans and across the other species. The process refers to the tendency of organisms reliably to cease to respond to a stimulus which is repeatedly or continuously presented to them (Hinde, 1966). For example, our tendency to orient to loud noises when we first hear them, but to stop doing so (perhaps even continuing with complex tasks requiring considerable concentration) when the noise continues, is an example of habituation. Likewise, in a more primitive animal, a snail will respond by withdrawing its tentacles on initial stimulation, but will cease to do so on further occurrences (Humphrey, 1933). This phenomenon has been exploited in treatment situations, by helping people to *habituate* to anxiety through staying in the situations which cause fear either sufficiently long or sufficiently often for the fear response to cease to be elicited by the situation. Marks and others regarded habituation as the mechanism underlying the effectiveness of flooding and 'exposure', along with extinction of the negatively reinforcing consequences of avoidance and escape. In the anxiety disorders, the phobic, when confronted by the feared object, leaves the feared situation quickly, in a state of high arousal. The resultant situation of safety leads to rapid diminution of fear. Since the physical feelings of fear are unpleasant, escape is negatively reinforced, and thus is likely to increase in frequency in future. Treatment, through encouraging confrontation and habituation, aims to break the contingency chains between confrontation and punishment and escape and reward. Exposure therapy continues to be practised widely today, but is often now integrated into the context of broader cognitive-behavioural approaches.

For over twenty years, the Maudsley group and its successors formed perhaps the most important focus for British behaviour therapy. Amongst its achievements are the general introduction of behaviour therapy to the

UK, the introduction of many new interventions, including, perhaps most notably, 'exposure' therapy, maintenance of high standards of outcome evaluation and the education of a whole generation of behaviour therapists, from a wide range of disciplines.

Bandura and social learning

The work of Albert Bandura stands at one of the boundaries between behaviour therapy and cognitive therapy. His social learning theory (Bandura, 1977) and its associated therapeutic intervention of modelling are clearly based on the standard behavioural notion of operant conditioning, and involve an increase in behaviour by a human or animal that has seen that behaviour rewarded in another individual. However, social learning implied a great deal of cognitive processing by the client. Unlike strict behaviourists, Bandura not only acknowledges the existence of such processes, but sees them as interacting with the external environment in a reciprocal way, shaping events as well as being shaped by them. Since the late 1960s and early 1970s, Bandura has developed treatment principles based on social learning. These have chiefly involved the demonstration of either novel behaviours (such as particular social skills) or desired behaviours (such as approach to a feared object) by the therapist or a surrogate, followed by reinforcement of that behaviour. Apart from such real-life modelling, desired behaviours may be demonstrated cognitively or symbolically. Similarly, the client may be encouraged to self-monitor, self-model and self-reinforce (Bandura, 1986). This use of imagery and other internal tactics serves to indicate how far Bandura has moved from traditional behaviour therapy, and his treatment methods, which consider internal processing in complex ways, may more properly be considered as part of the developing tradition of cognitive therapy. However, behaviour therapists have made use of his approaches as part of their therapeutic interventions for many years, both to enhance other behavioural approaches and as interventions in their own right. Nevertheless, Bandura's work was of considerable theoretical importance. The acknowledgement of the principle of vicarious learning was in some respects a turning point for behavioural theories and behaviour therapy, since it is extremely difficult to reconcile the phenomenon of learning through observation with a view of experience which lacks any internal processing of incoming information.

Current status of behaviour therapy

The influence of behaviour therapy can hardly be overestimated. Behaviour therapy is a comprehensive set of interventions which has expanded the availability of psychotherapeutic treatments dramatically. Previously, verbal treatments had been offered only by doctors and a few others trained in the esoteric discipline of psychoanalysis. Following the introduction of behaviour therapy, the range of professionals offering therapy increased, and insights from behaviourism were also introduced through teaching programmes, publications and the self-help movement. Behaviour therapy is now practised not only by psychologists and psychiatrists, but by nurses, teachers, counsellors and social workers, as well as informally by members of the public in self-help contexts. Furthermore, the range of applicability of psychotherapy has widened. Rather than being the perquisite of financially secure, highly verbal individuals, with comparatively minor psychological difficulties, behaviour therapy is available with far less regard to social status, and is adaptable enough to address the difficulties of a wide range of client disorders, including those for which intervention would previously have been regarded as almost unthinkable, and certainly unworkable.

As well as this increase in applicability and availability, the main direct contributions of behaviour therapy have been a greater interest in evaluation of treatment outcome and the establishment of a series of therapeutic interventions of rigorously established effectiveness. By 1980, a major review of outcome studies (Rachman and Wilson, 1980) demonstrated the superiority of behavioural interventions over other therapeutic approaches. Although conducted by two eminent behaviourists, the review is extremely thorough, and examines the findings of earlier studies and earlier reviews with considerable critical rigour. Moreover, many of Rachman and Wilson's findings have found support from other writers, including those from disciplines other than behaviour therapy, and much endeavour is now directed by these disciplines at demonstrating the effectiveness of their own interventions.

There remain, however, many misconceptions about the nature of behaviour therapy (Kazdin, 1979; Wilson, 1978). Chief amongst these has been the notion that behaviour therapy is unethical and dehumanizing. The notion of behaviour therapy as dehumanizing derives, in part, from its origins in the study of animal behaviour. However, Wolpe (1978) advances a strong defence of the humanity of behaviour therapy, noting its emphasis on individual experiences, concerns and suffering and pointing out that it is mistaken to assume that drawing on work with animals means behaviourists regard their clients as animals. Clearly, we should not say the same of physicians whose drug treatments had a similar basis in animal research. Wolpe also notes the individual nature of behavioural interventions, which are tailored to client needs following rigorous assessment. Regarding ethics, Rapp (1984) notes that behaviour therapy has always been considerably concerned with the ethical implications of its interventions, and outlines a number of issues which led to doubts amongst the public and the profession, including increased publicity and the apparently great effectiveness of the interventions. He describes a number of ethical dilemmas associated with behaviour therapy, but concludes that they are, in fact, common to most interventions, and that behaviour therapy is not alone in facing such ethical issues.

Kazdin (1979) describes other misconceptions. Amongst other things, behaviour therapy is often characterized as being derived entirely from theories of experimental psychology, unconcerned with the therapeutic relationship, novel, and focused only on overt behaviour. In each of these areas, Kazdin demonstrates how a fuller reading of the behaviour therapy literature demonstrates the weakness of these notions. Experimentally derived theories often equate only loosely with what happens during improvement as a result of behaviour therapy, while the therapeutic relationship has been regarded as important by many notable clinicians (e.g. Wolpe, 1958). We noted earlier that behaviour therapy has many historical precursors, and that covert experiences have been examined by behaviourism since its beginnings. Indeed, Wolpe's systematic desensitization is itself a covert procedure, involving mental imagery.

From the above account, it might be concluded that behaviour therapy has had considerable impact upon both clinical practice and client difficulties. Indeed, despite much criticism, generally from those seeking to defend other therapeutic orientations, behaviour therapy has proved remarkably resilient as an account of the acquisition, maintenance and treatment of human distress. However, the early forms of behaviour therapy described here contain a number of significant weaknesses (Newell and Dryden, 1991). It has been argued that behaviour therapy is by no means always successful, even in those client difficulties for which it is regarded as the treatment of choice; that behaviour therapy is overly focused on observable behaviour, whilst such behaviour is not always present in client difficulties, and is insufficiently powerful to explain complex difficulties. Finally, behaviour therapy pays too little attention to issues of client compliance. Whilst none of these objections to behaviour therapy is new, and indeed they have been dealt with by Kazdin (1979), they contributed to a desire to extend the range of behavioural approaches, both in terms of the way they are practised and the client difficulties that behaviour therapy addresses.

Similarly, Hawton et al. (1987) note that the preoccupation with proving the validity of behaviour therapy as a therapeutic approach had faded by the mid-1970s, when numerous important trials had already been published. Instead, behaviour therapists turned to an examination of how behaviour therapy could be improved and broadened, often finding purely behavioural accounts inadequate explanations for poor client compliance or for the maintenance of complaints such as depression, which seemed to show little observable behaviour. Many behaviourists embraced the newly emerging cognitive therapies, incorporated them into their practice, and were influential in the creation of the cognitive-behavioural approaches which sought to combine learning theory approaches, the clinical methods of Beck (1976) and Ellis (1962) and therapeutic approaches derived from modern cognitive psychology. Purely behavioural techniques are still practised as part of the cognitive-behavioural therapies and the recent writings of Wolpe (1989) and Eysenck (1994) in particular indicate that adherence to a therapy based chiefly on learning theory principles and the examination of overt behaviour is by no means over, but history may view the key contribution of behaviour therapy not as these techniques but as its role as a critical precursor to the emergence of cognitive-behaviour therapy.

References

Ayllon, T. and Azrin, N.H. (1965) 'The measurement and reinforcement of behavior of psychotics', *Journal of the Experimental Analysis of Behavior*, 8: 357–83.
Ayllon, T. and Michael, J. (1959) 'The psychiatric nurse as a behavioral engineer', *Journal of the Experimental Analysis of Behavior*, 2: 323–34.
Bandura, A. (1977) *Social Learning Theory*. Englewood Cliffs, NJ: Prentice-Hall.
Bandura, A. (1986) *Social Foundations of Thought and Action: A Social Cognitive Theory*. Englewood Cliffs, NJ: Prentice-Hall.
Beck, A.T. (1976) *Cognitive Therapy and the Emotional Disorders*. New York: International Universities Press.
Carlson, C.S., Arnold, C.R., Becker, W.C. and Madsen, C.H. (1968) 'The elimination of tantrum behaviour in a child in an elementary classroom', *Behaviour Research and Therapy*, 6: 117–19.
Cullen, C. and Cole, C. (1991) 'Obituary: B.F. Skinner', *Behavioural Psychotherapy*, 19(1): 137–40.
De Silva, P. (1984) 'Buddhism and behaviour modification', *Behaviour Research and Therapy*, 22(6): 661–78.
Ellis, A. (1962) *Reason and Emotion in Psychotherapy*. New York: Lyle Stuart.
Eysenck, H.J. (1952) 'The effects of psychotherapy: an evaluation', *Journal of Consulting Psychology*, 16: 319–24.
Eysenck, H.J. (ed.) (1960) *Handbook of Abnormal Psychology: An Experimental Approach*. London: Pitman.
Eysenck, H.J. (ed.) (1964) *Experiments in Behaviour Therapy*. Oxford: Pergamon.
Eysenck, H.J. (1991) *Decline and Fall of the Freudian Empire*. Harmondsworth: Penguin.
Eysenck, H.J. (1994) 'The outcome problem in psychotherapy: what have we learned?', *Behaviour Research and Therapy*, 32(5): 477–95.
Eysenck, H.J. and Wilson, G.T. (1973) *The Experimental Study of Freudian Theories*. London: Methuen.
Fishman, D.B. and Franks, C.M. (1992) 'Evolution and differentiation within behavior therapy: a theoretical and epistemological review', in D.K. Freedheim (ed.), *History of Psychotherapy: A Century of Change*. Washington, DC: American Psychological Association.
Franks, C.M. (1987) 'Behavior therapy and AABT: personal recollections, conceptions and misconceptions', *The Behavior Therapist*, 10(8): 171–4.
Freedberg, E.J. (1973) 'Behaviour therapy: a comparison between early (1890–1920) and contemporary techniques', *The Canadian Psychologist*, 14(3): 225–40.
Gardner, W.I. (1971) *Behavior Modification in Mental Retardation*. Chicago: Aldine Atherton.
Glass, C.R. and Arnkoff, D.B. (1992) 'Behavior therapy', in D.K. Freedheim (ed.), *History of Psychotherapy: A Century of Change*. Washington, DC: American Psychological Association.
Hawton, K., Salkovskis, P.M., Kirk, J. and Clark, D.M. (1987) 'The development and principles of cognitive-behavioural treatments', in K. Hawton, P.M. Salkovskis, J. Kirk and D.M. Clark (eds), *Cognitive Behaviour Therapy for Psychiatric Problems*. Oxford: Oxford University Press.
Herbert, M. (1987) *Behavioural Treatment of Problem Children: A Practice Manual*. London: Academic Press.
Hinde, R.A. (1966) *Animal Behaviour: A Synthesis of Ethology and Comparative Psychology*. New York: McGraw-Hill.

Humphrey, G. (1933) *The Nature of Learning*. New York: Kegan Paul.

Jaremko, M.E. (1986) 'Cognitive-behaviour modification: the shaping of rule-governed behaviour', in W. Dryden and R. Rentoul (eds), *Adult Clinical Problems: A Cognitive-Behavioural Approach*. London: Routledge.

Jones, M.C. (1924) 'The elimination of children's fears', *Journal of Experimental Psychology*, 7: 382–90.

Kazdin, A.E. (1976) 'Statistical analyses for single-case experimental designs', in M. Hersen and D.H. Barlow (eds), *Single Case Experimental Designs*. New York: Pergamon.

Kazdin, A.E. (1978) *History of Behavior Modification: Experimental Foundations and Contemporary Research*. Baltimore, MD: University Park Press.

Kazdin, A.E. (1979) 'Fictions, factions and functions of behaviour therapy', *Behaviour Therapy*, 10: 629–54.

Kazdin, A.E. and Pulaski, J.L. (1977) 'Joseph Lancaster and behavior modification in education', *Journal of the History of the Behavioral Sciences*, 13: 261–6.

Laing, R.D. (1967) *The Politics of Experience and The Bird of Paradise*. Harmondsworth: Penguin.

Lazarus, A.A. (1958) 'New methods in psychotherapy: a case study', *South African Medical Journal*, 32: 660–4.

Lazarus, A.A. (1973) 'Multimodal behavior therapy: treating the BASIC ID', *Journal of Nervous and Mental Diseases*, 156(6): 404–11.

Lindsley, O.R. (1960) 'Characteristics of the behaviour of chronic psychotics as revealed by free-operant conditioning methods', *Diseases of the Nervous System*, 21: 66–78.

Lindsley, O.R., Skinner, B.F. and Solomon, H.C. (1953) *Studies in Behavior Therapy (Status Report I)*. Waltham, MA: Metropolitan State Hospital. (Cited in A.E. Kazdin (1978) *History of Behavior Modification: Experimental Foundations and Contemporary Research*. Baltimore, MD: University Park Press).

McGee, J. (1990) 'Gentle teaching: the basic tenet', *Nursing Times*, 86(32): 68–72.

Marks, I.M. (1972) 'Flooding (implosion) and allied treatments', in W.S. Agras (ed.), *Behavior Modification: Principles and Clinical Applications*. Boston, MA: Little Brown.

Marks, I.M. (1987) *Fears, Phobias and Rituals*. Oxford: Oxford University Press.

Masserman, J.H. (1943) *Behavior and Neurosis: An Experimental Psycho-Analytic Approach to Psychobiologic Principles*. Chicago: University of Chicago Press.

Miller, E. (1988) 'Behaviour modification mid 19th century style: Robert Brudenell Carter and the treatment of hysteria', *British Journal of Clinical Psychology*, 27: 297–301.

Newell, R.J. and Dryden, W. (1991) 'Clinical problems: an introduction to the cognitive behavioural approach', in W. Dryden and R. Rentoul (eds), *Adult Clinical Problems: A Cognitive-Behavioural Approach*. London: Routledge.

Patterson, G.R. (1971) 'Behavioral intervention procedures in the classroom and in the home', in A.E. Bergin and S.L. Garfield (eds), *Handbook of Psychotherapy and Behavior Change: An Empirical Analysis*. New York: Wiley.

Pavlov, I. (1927) *Conditioned Reflexes: An Investigation of the Physiological Activity of the Cerebral Cortex*. London: Oxford University Press.

Prince, M. (1891) 'Association neuroses. A study of the pathology of hysterical joint affections, neurasthenia and allied forms of neuromimesis', *Journal of Nervous and Mental Disease*, 18: 275–82.

Prince, M. (1909) 'The psychological principles and field of psychotherapy', *Journal of Abnormal Psychology*, 4: 72–98.

Rachman, S.J. and Wilson, G.T. (1980) *The Effects of Psychological Therapy*. Oxford: Pergamon.

Rapp, M.S. (1984) 'Ethics in behaviour therapy: historical aspects and current status', *Canadian Journal of Psychiatry*, 29(7): 547–50.

Rogers, C. (1951) *Client-centered Therapy*. Boston, MA: Houghton-Mifflin.

Shapiro, M.B. (1961) 'The single case in fundamental psychological research', *British Journal of Medical Psychology*, 34: 255–62.

Skinner, B.F. (1948) *Walden Two*. New York: Macmillan.

Skinner, B.F. (1953) *Science and Human Behavior*. New York: Macmillan.

Skinner, B.F. (1957) *Verbal Behavior*. New York: Appleton Century Crofts.

Skinner, B.F. (1971) *Beyond Freedom and Dignity*. New York: Knopf.

Swartz, P. (1988) 'Contributions to the history of psychology XLVII. Ignatius Loyola and behavior therapy', *Perceptual and Motor Skills*, 66: 617–18.

Szasz, T. (1970) *Ideology and Insanity*. New York: Doubleday.

Thoresen, C.E. and Coates, T.J. (1978) 'What does it mean to be a behavior therapist?', *Counseling Psychologist*, 7(3): 3–21.

Thorndyke, E.L. (1931) *Human Learning*. New York: Century.

Watson, J.B. and Rayner, R. (1920) 'Conditioned emotional reactions', *Journal of Experimental Psychology*, 3: 1–14.

Wilson, G.T. (1978) 'On the much discussed nature of the term "behavior therapy"', *Behavior Therapy*, 8: 89–98.

Wolpe, J. (1952) 'Objective psychotherapy of the neuroses', *South African Medical Journal*, 26: 825–9.

Wolpe, J. (1958) *Psychotherapy by Reciprocal Inhibition*. Stanford, CA: Stanford University Press.

Wolpe, J. (1978) 'The humanity of behavior therapy', *Journal of Behavior Therapy & Experimental Psychiatry*, 9: 205–9.

Wolpe, J. (1989) 'The derailment of behavior therapy: a tale of conceptual misdirection', *Scandinavian Journal of Behavior Therapy*, 18: 1–19.

Yates, A.J. (1981) 'Behaviour therapy – past, present, future – imperfect?', *Clinical Psychology Review*, 1: 269–91.

Yule, W. (1975) 'Teaching psychological principles to non-psychologists: training parents in child management', *Journal of the Association of Educational Psychologists*, 10(3): 5–16.

Yule, W. and Carr, J. (1987) *Behaviour Modification for People with Mental Handicaps*. London: Chapman & Hall.

8

Developments in Cognitive Therapy: 1960–95

Marjorie E. Weishaar

Cognitive therapy is a form of psychotherapy which focuses on how an individual perceives, interprets and assigns meanings to experiences. It is based on an information-processing model which posits that during psychological distress a person's thinking becomes more rigid and distorted, judgements become overgeneralized and absolute, and the person's basic beliefs about the self and the world become fixed. Cognitive therapy is an active, structured, time-limited form of therapy. It is a collaborative process of examining and empirically testing clients' maladaptive beliefs and finding alternative, more productive ways of responding. Clients' beliefs are treated as hypotheses to be tested through verbal examination and behavioural experiments. The goals of therapy are (1) to teach the patient how to correct biased cognitive processing; and (2) to alter the dysfunctional beliefs which predispose the patient to distort experience (Beck et al., 1979b).

Cognitive therapy is derived from research findings on depressed patients. American psychiatrist Aaron T. Beck of the University of Pennsylvania observed that psychological distress frequently stems from specific, habitual errors in thinking (Beck, 1972). During episodes of depression, Beck found, individuals process information differently. Errors in logic proliferate and the ability to self-correct misperceptions and misinterpretations is impaired. Among depressed patients, thinking is negatively biased so that negative information about oneself and one's life is freely admitted while more positive or neutral self-referent information is screened out of awareness. In addition, the negative thoughts which preoccupy the person are idiosyncratic and reflect the person's underlying beliefs about the self and how the world operates. Thus, the contents of dreams, images and thoughts do not reflect classic psychoanalytic themes, but previous life experiences and the conclusions derived from them. Moreover, certain types of dysfunctional assumptions may predispose someone to depression, anxiety or other disorders.

Since Beck's early research in the 1960s, cognitive therapy has found empirical support for aspects of its theory and for its application to a wide range of clinical diagnoses, non-clinical problems, and patient populations. This chapter will trace the history of Beck's work and the growth of cognitive therapy to its current standing as an influential and efficacious form of psychotherapy.

The 1960s: initial formulations

Aaron Beck was trained in psychoanalysis, but found it lacking in scientific rigour and unrewarding in practice. Upon completing his psychoanalytic training in 1958, Beck took a position as an Associate Professor of Psychiatry at the University of Pennsylvania. In 1959 he received a grant to study the dreams of depressed patients. He was expecting to validate Freud's theory of depression by investigating the dreams and 'stream of consciousness' reports of the patients. However, instead of finding evidence of retroflected anger and hostility, he found that the dreams of depressed patients contained themes of loss, deprivation and defeat.

Concurrently, Beck was treating out-patients in his private practice. During his clinical interviews he began to notice that in addition to stream of consciousness reports, patients had a parallel set of thoughts which they kept to themselves. While free-associating in a session, a patient began criticizing Beck angrily. Beck asked him what he was feeling. 'I feel guilty,' said the patient, for while he was yelling at Beck, he was simultaneously having self-critical thoughts, such as 'I shouldn't have said that. I'm wrong to criticize him. I'm bad. He won't like me' (Diffily, 1991). Instead of the patient's anger leading directly to guilt feelings, the secondary train of thought acted as an intermediary between the outward emotion and the guilt feelings.

Beck had tapped another level of consciousness, analogous to Freud's level, the 'preconscious'. This level of consciousness reflects what people say to themselves, not necessarily what they say to others. Following Beck's initial observations, he discovered that Albert Ellis reported similar observations and called these thoughts 'self-statements' (Ellis, 1962).

Beck labelled this internal monologue 'automatic thoughts' since the thoughts appeared rapidly as if by reflex. Automatic thoughts are plausible to the individual and go unchallenged. They provide running commentary on a person's experience. In the case of depressed persons, automatic thoughts are negatively biased. Beck theorized that in depression, there is a negative *cognitive shift* so that positive information is screened out, but negative information is allowed to influence further thinking. Beck also observed a number of logical errors in depressive thinking which he termed *cognitive distortions*. Among the cognitive distortions are (1) dichotomous or all-or-nothing thinking; (2) selective abstraction (attending to only a portion of relevant information); (3) arbitrary inference (jumping to unwarranted conclusions); (4) minimization and maximization (errors of exaggeration); (5) overgeneralization; and (6) personalization (misattributing causality entirely to oneself and ignoring other factors).

Finally, Beck found that the content of automatic thoughts is idiosyncratic to the individual rather than reflective of classic psychoanalytic themes. He proposed that the meanings people assign to upsetting events constitute a network of beliefs, assumptions and rules which are connected to memories and learning experiences (Beck, 1964, 1972). He proposed that such beliefs exist in cognitive structures called *schemas*. Depressogenic schemas, for example, may be latent until a life event related to self-worth, deprivation, defeat or loss triggers a schema, at which time the person experiences strong emotion and is flooded by automatic thoughts reflecting schema content. Thus, certain types of schema content, specifically dysfunctional beliefs and assumptions, pose a *cognitive vulnerability* to depression.

Beck describes the early 1960s as the most important time for him professionally.

> I started to re-examine psychoanalytic theory and was doing research. The whole thing seemed to cave in. Then Cognitive Therapy started to come up. Within a couple of years, I really laid the framework for everything that's happened since then. There's nothing that I've been associated with since 1963 the seeds of which were not in the 1962 to 1964 articles. That was the critical period. (Weishaar, 1993: 21)

In 1963, Beck published 'Thinking and depression: I. Idiosyncratic content and cognitive distortions', and in 1964 he followed with 'Thinking and depression: II. Theory and therapy'. In addition to these seminal articles, Beck and his associates published a scale for measuring depressive symptomology, the Beck Depression Inventory (BDI, Beck et al., 1961). This twenty-one-item, self-report assessment scale has since been used in hundreds of outcome studies and in a wide range of clinical settings from psychiatric hospitals to general medical and mental health practices. An important aspect of the BDI is that it enquires about cognitive as well as vegetative symptoms of depression, including hopelessness about the future. Research on suicide, for example, has found cognitive factors to be more reflective of suicide risk than are vegetative signs (Beck et al., 1973a).

Beck continued his research and teaching of psychiatry residents and became an Associate Professor of Psychiatry in 1967. As he was developing his theory of psychopathology, he was influenced by the phenomenological approach of the Greek Stoic philosophers, Kant's (1798) emphasis on subjective experience, and Freud's concept of the hierarchical structure of cognitions into primary and secondary processes as well as by the more contemporary expressions of phenomenology by Alfred Adler (1936), Alexander (1950), Horney (1950) and Sullivan (1953). He was also greatly influenced by George Kelly (1955), whose work provided terminology for Beck's work and validation for a non-motivational theory of psycho-pathology. Cognitive theories of emotion posited by Magda Arnold (1960) and Richard Lazarus (1966) also influenced the development of cognitive therapy.

During this period when Beck was building his theory, he got only a one-year renewal on his depression grant and, consequently, lost his office on campus. He decided to work at home and wrote his formulation of depression, published initially as *Depression: Clinical, Experimental and Theoretical Aspects* and later as *Depression: Causes and Treatment* (Beck, 1970a). Beck believes he was mildly depressed while writing the book and found the endeavour therapeutic. His ability to examine his own symptoms of depression and anxiety has contributed to the formulations of his theory.

Depression: Causes and Treatment (Beck, 1972) is a treatise on depression, covering symptoms, research findings, alternative theories of depression and the cognitive model. In this book Beck introduces the three main concepts of the cognitive model of depression: (1) the cognitive triad; (2) schemas; and (3) cognitive errors (faulty information processing).

The *cognitive triad* is the term used to characterize the depressed person's negative view of the self, the world and the future. According to cognitive therapy, depressed individuals see themselves as worthless and as failures. This leads to lethargy and lack of motivation, which prevents the person from taking action that might dispute this self-image. Lack of activity is then interpreted as further evidence of incompetence and failure. In addition, the depressive world-view is a harsh and punishing one. There are too many perceived barriers between the depressed person and his or her goals. Moreover, the future is predicted to be unremittingly dismal. Such negative expectations lead to hopelessness.

Beck acknowledges his debts to Piaget (1926), Kelly (1955) and others in the development of his schema concept. In cognitive therapy, schemas are cognitive

> structures for screening, coding, and evaluating the stimuli that impinge on the organism. . . . The notion of schemas is used to account for the repetitive themes in free associations, daydreams, ruminations and dreams, as well as in the immediate reactions to environmental events. . . . An individual who, for example, has the notion that everybody hates him will tend to interpret other people's reactions on the basis of this premise. Schemas such as these are involved in the inaccuracies, misinterpretations, and distortions associated with all kinds of psychopathology. (Beck, 1972: 283)

Faulty information processing is characterized by a shift from higher-order or secondary process thinking to lower-order or primary process thinking. Higher-order thinking utilizes judgement, weighs evidence, and considers alternative explanations. Primary process thinking is rapid and does not involve logic. Cognitive therapy aims not only to modify the content of dysfunctional beliefs but to teach the patient how to return to higher-order thinking.

Depression: Causes and Treatment (Beck, 1972) outlines seven steps in cognitive therapy: (1) pinpoint depressive cognitions; (2) identify their idiosyncratic content; (3) recognize the characteristics of these cognitions (e.g. lower-order or primary process, automatic, involuntary, and plausible); (4) distinguish 'ideas' from 'facts'; (5) check one's conclusions by re-examining the evidence; (6) respond to depressive cognitions by stating the reasons why they are erroneous; and (7) identify the cognitive distortions operating.

Two other points raised in this early book are worth noting. One is the relationship between cognition and emotion. Cognitive therapy has been misunderstood to purport that thoughts cause emotion. In this book, Beck states that cognition and emotion are probably in a mutually reinforcing system of circular feedback. In addition, 'affective reactions may facilitate the activity of idiosyncratic schemas' (Beck, 1972: 290). Specifically in relation to depression, Beck states that the activation of schemas is the mechanism by which depression develops, not the cause. The cause may be any combination of genetic, biological, environmental and personality factors. Once depression is set in motion, however, cognitive processes maintain and exacerbate it. Beck acknowledged later (Beck, 1991a) that in a 'reactive depression' the interaction of personality and stressful life events, in the presence of other factors, may play a causal role.

The other point worth noting is that while this book is about depression, Beck begins to generalize about the cognitive model and how thought content is congruent with various mood states. He writes:

> When thoughts associated with depressive affects were identified, they were generally found to contain the type of conceptual distortions or errors already described, as well as the typical depressive theme content. Similarly, when the affect was anxiety, anger, or elation, the associated cognitions had a content congruent with these feelings. (Beck, 1972: 237–8)

This finding helped establish Beck's *content-specificity hypothesis*, which proposes that each disorder has identifiable cognitions specific to it. The content-specificity hypothesis would be empirically validated in a number of studies in the 1980s.

Throughout the 1960s Beck's closest associates were psychologists. At the University of Pennsylvania, psychologists Marvin Hurvich and Seymour Feshbach taught him skills in research methodology and were valued critics. Outside of the university, Beck also found colleagues. In 1963, Albert Ellis, founder of rational emotive behaviour therapy (REBT: Ellis, 1962), read Beck's articles on thinking and depression in the Archives of General Psychiatry and, recognizing the overlap in their formulations, sent Beck reprints of his work. Beck credits Ellis with being first to promote the notion that assumptions and beliefs are much more accessible to patients than psychoanalysts believed. Beck also admired Ellis's focus on here-and-now problem-solving.

During the late 1960s Beck also shared ideas with psychologist Gerald Davison at the University of New York at Stony Brook, a bastion of behaviourism. Behaviour therapy in the United States was starting to change and the so-called 'cognitive revolution' in psychology was beginning.

The 1970s: establishment of cognitive therapy

Cognitive therapy established itself as a viable and efficacious form of psychotherapy in the 1970s. Several key events that occurred during the decade contributed to the recognition of Beck's model. They are the cognitive revolution in psychology, the publication of the first outcome study demonstrating the effectiveness of cognitive therapy in treating unipolar depression, the generalization of the model to other disorders such as anxiety, and the publication of two of Beck's best-known books, *Cognitive Therapy and the Emotional Disorders* (Beck, 1976) and *Cognitive Therapy of Depression* (Beck et al., 1979b).

The cognitive revolution

In 1970 Beck published 'Cognitive therapy: nature and relation to behavior therapy' (Beck, 1970) and thus entered the continuing debate on the respective roles of cognitions and behaviour in therapeutic change. Radical behaviourists argued against the emergence of all cognitive therapies from two points of view: (1) cognitions could only be speculated about and not demonstrated, so they were not within the realm of behaviourism (Skinner, 1977); or (2) thoughts are a form of behaviour and thus already explained by conditioning models (Wolpe, 1976). The cognitive revolution occurred as those emphasizing the mediational role of cognition in human experience pushed for its theoretical and clinical recognition. As a consequence of much debate as well as empirical research, there occurred a paradigm shift within behaviour therapy from primarily operant models to an information-processing one. As with other revolutions, the cognitive revolution was accompanied by political fallout and many theoretical debates persist concerning the nature of cognition and its importance in behaviour change.

As a psychiatrist, Beck was initially an outsider to this revolution in psychology. Yet his theoretical and therapeutic interests coincided with the work of psychologists Albert Ellis, Michael Mahoney, Marvin Goldfried, Arnold Lazarus, Donald Meichenbaum, Albert Bandura, and others. Just as Beck's work grew out of his dissatisfaction with psychoanalysis, behaviourists were also confronting limitations in conditioning models. Cognitive therapies offered a return to the patient's inner world along with empirically based interventions.

Beck's research provided credibility to the cognitive movement in psychology, for it was based on clinical populations, not college student volunteers. In turn, Beck's work received a greater positive response from psychology than from psychiatry. Beck explains: 'psychology, because it has such a powerful academic base, is far more influenced by the empirical data than psychiatry is' (Weishaar, 1993: 29). Beck moved into what was becoming mainstream psychology at a time when mainstream psychiatry was moving toward its present emphasis on drug therapies (Diffily, 1991).

At the time of its inception, cognitive therapy was considered one of the three leading cognitive therapies (Mahoney and Arnkoff, 1978; Meyers and Craighead, 1984). Rational-emotive therapy (later Rational emotive be-haviour therapy), founded by Albert Ellis, and cognitive behaviour modification, originated by Donald Meichenbaum (1977), were the others.

During the 1970s Beck's thinking was also influenced by the works of Mahoney (1974), Goldfried and Davison (1976), A. Lazarus (1976), and Bandura (1977). Beck's cognitive colleagues invited him to participate in the annual conference of the Association for the Advancement of Behavior Therapy (AABT) in 1973 and he has been active since. The growing professional closeness among Beck, Mahoney, Goldfried and Meichenbaum led them to publish a new journal, *Cognitive Therapy and Research*, which was founded during great political unrest in AABT and served the purpose of disseminating research on cognitive therapies.

Outcome research

In the early 1970s Beck became a full Professor of Psychiatry and integrated training his students with research and clinical service. He assembled a remarkable cohort of students from psychiatry and psychology and trained them in cognitive therapy for depressed patients. By 1973 Beck and his students Maria Kovacs, John Rush, Brian Shaw, Steven Hollon and Gary Emery had written a clinician's manual based on what they did with patients in an outcome study comparing cognitive therapy with the standard treatment, antidepressant medication plus brief supportive therapy. That outcome study demonstrated the efficacy of cognitive therapy and appeared in the first issue of *Cognitive Therapy and Research* (Rush et al., 1977). Not only was cognitive therapy found to be superior in the treatment of unipolar depression, but there was less attrition among those receiving cognitive therapy. A follow-up study supported the initial results substantiating cognitive therapy's effectiveness (Kovacs et al., 1981). These studies paved the way for future research and suggested that cognitive therapy was a promising psychotherapy.

As a natural outgrowth of his depression studies, Beck began longitudinal research on suicide risk assessment and prediction. He helped develop the classification of suicidal behaviours for the National Institute of Mental Health Center for Studies of Suicide Prevention (Beck et al., 1973b). He also devised assessment scales to aid suicide prediction: the Suicide Intent Scale (Beck et al., 1974b) which assesses the severity of a person's wish to die at the time of a recent suicide attempt, the Scale for Suicide Ideation (Beck et al., 1979a) which measures the degree to which someone is currently thinking about suicide, and the Hopelessness Scale (Beck et al., 1974c) which assesses the person's negative view of the future. Research by Beck and others found that hopelessness is more strongly related to suicide intent than is depression *per se* (Beck et al., 1975, 1976; Bedrosian and Beck, 1979; Dyer and Kreitman, 1984; Goldney, 1979; Minkoff et al., 1973; Petrie and Chamberlain, 1983; Weissman et al., 1979; Wetzel, 1976).

The results of Beck's prospective studies were arrived at a decade later and confirmed that hopelessness is a key psychological variable in suicide. For both depressed in-patients (Beck et al., 1985b) and out-patients (Beck et al., 1990b), a score of nine or more on the Beck Hopelessness Scale predicted eventual suicide in more than 90 per cent of suicide completers. The Beck Hopelessness Scale yields a relatively high false positive rate and is, therefore, used with other tools such as the Beck Self-Concept Test (Beck et al., 1990c) in research. Its clinical utility remains powerful.

An additional scale, the Dysfunctional Attitude Scale, was developed in the 1970s (Weissman and Beck, 1978) to identify the strength and content of people's underlying beliefs and assumptions. The Dysfunctional Attitude Scale has been used in many studies as a measure of cognitive vulnerability to depression.

Application of the model to anxiety

Cognitive therapy expanded its clinical focus in the 1970s to include research on anxiety disorders. Beck and his associates found evidence to contradict the notion of 'free-floating anxiety', for they determined that anxiety is accompanied by specific, identifiable thoughts and images (Beck et al., 1974a). The systematic study of anxious cognitions was continued in the 1980s. In addition, this study helped establish intrusive visual imagery as an important cognitive component in anxiety.

Major publications in the 1970s

In 1976 Beck published *Cognitive Therapy and the Emotional Disorders* which presents the cognitive model as applied to many clinical problems and diagnoses. In *Cognitive Therapy and the Emotional Disorders*, Beck describes cognitive biases apparent in disorders, such as the positive bias in mania or the heightened sense of vulnerability in anxiety as well as the negative bias in depression. Beck proposes that each psychological disorder has its own specific cognitive conceptualization or *cognitive profile*. This notion that each disorder has its own general cognitive content is called the *specificity hypothesis*. It was later substantiated by empirical research which found that types of cognition were unique to each disorder (Beck et al., 1986, 1987; Greenberg and Beck, 1989).

A second hypothesis presented in *Cognitive Therapy and the Emotional Disorders* is the *continuity hypothesis* which posits that psychopathological syndromes represent exaggerated forms of normal emotions. They are extreme expressions of normal adaptive processes. This view emphasizes the evolutionary roots of various syndromes and also helps explain the more subtle biases apparent in the psychology of everyday life. For example, the overconcern about physical danger apparent in phobias points to similar sources of anxiety in the psychology of normal people.

Cognitive Therapy and the Emotional Disorders describes the principles of cognitive therapy as a combination of the 'intellectual approach' and the 'experimental approach'. The intellectual approach refers to identifying misconceptions, testing their validity and substituting more appropriate concepts. The experimental approach is similar to Alexander's (1950) 'corrective emotional experience', for it exposes the patient to experiences which contradict his or her misconceptions. Thus, Beck is advocating both verbal procedures and behavioural experiments to promote cognitive change. He identifies the techniques of Socratic dialogue, correctly labelling situations and beliefs to test, setting up hypotheses, considering alternatives, and using cognitive rehearsal to prepare for situations. He also describes behavioural techniques such as Graded Task Assignment to overcome the inertia of depression.

For Beck, the nature of the therapeutic relationship is best described by Kelly (1955), who viewed it as two scientists collaborating. Following Rogers (1951) and Truax (1963), Beck states that the necessary qualities of a (cognitive) therapist are genuine warmth, acceptance, and accurate empathy. Much of what Beck was to develop in theoretical refinements or pursue in his research first appears in this book.

Towards the end of the decade, Beck published perhaps his most famous book. By elaborating the treatment manual used in the 1977 depression study (Rush et al., 1977), Beck and some of his students wrote *Cognitive Therapy of Depression* (Beck et al., 1979b). This text further describes the principles of cognitive therapy in the treatment of unipolar depression: collaborative empiricism, Socratic questioning, and guided discovery. Collaborative empiricism is the process by which the therapist and patient, working together, frame the patient's assumptions as hypotheses to be tested and then examine them logically and through behavioural experiments. The patient arrives at new conclusions as a consequence of confronting and incorporating new evidence. Socratic questioning refers to the manner in which cognitive therapists use questions to understand the patient's beliefs and then open them to include other possible alternatives. Questions are used to (1) clarify or define problems; (2) assist in the identification of thoughts, pictorial images or assumptions; (3) examine the meanings of events for the client; and (4) assess the consequences of specific thoughts and behaviours (Beck and Young, 1985). Guided discovery is the investigative process by which clients 'discover' their own errors in logic or misperceptions as opposed to the therapist persuading them to adopt a particular point of view (Beck and Young, 1985). Guided discovery has also come to mean the identification of themes operating in the patient's present thoughts and their connections to past experiences (Beck and Weishaar, 1989).

Cognitive Therapy of Depression specifies not only the qualities of a good therapist, but the specific skills necessary for cognitive therapists. This checklist, the Cognitive Therapy Rating Scale (Young and Beck, 1980), has since been used in outcome studies to assure adherence and competence of cognitive therapists.

The book also presents a wealth of cognitive and behavioural intervention techniques which serve the following operations: (1) to monitor negative, automatic thoughts; (2) to recognize the connections between cognition, affect and behaviour; (3) to examine evidence for and against distorted automatic thoughts; (4) to substitute more reality-oriented interpretations for biased cognitions; and (5) to learn to identify dysfunctional beliefs which predispose one to distort experiences (Beck et al., 1979b: 4).

Of note is the inclusion of a chapter on group cognitive therapy for depressed patients. Depressed patients, it had been assumed, were too difficult to treat in a group format. However, Hollon and Shaw conducted group therapy with patients too depressed for the 1977 study. Their methods, included in *Cognitive Therapy of Depression*, offer the first application of cognitive therapy for groups.

The structure of cognitive therapy with its format, homework assignments and procedural guidelines contrasted with non-directive therapies. Some criticized cognitive therapy based on their reading of *Cognitive Therapy of Depression* and claimed it was technique oriented, avoidant or neglectful of emotion, and too simplistic with its emphasis on here-and-now problem-solving. On the other hand, the book provided a wellspring for therapists thirsty for strategies and patients desperate for concrete help. It also reformulated the theory of depression and presented a coherent therapy.

In 1979 the American Psychiatric Association awarded Aaron Beck the Foundation Fund Prize for Research in Psychiatry for his research on depression and the development of cognitive therapy.

The 1980s: the growth of cognitive therapy

During the 1980s a number of empirical studies were conducted at various sites to investigate the efficacy and theoretical soundness of cognitive therapy for depression. Meanwhile, Beck's research on anxiety disorders and panic increased. The influence of evolutionary theory on Beck's conceptualizations of psychological disorders became more apparent in his book *Anxiety Disorders and Phobias*, co-written with Gary Emery and Ruth Greenberg (Beck et al., 1985a). Cognitive therapy expanded to other disorders as well, with Beck's students and associates publishing a number of texts and Beck himself writing a book on couples therapy which is intended for both professionals and clients (Beck, 1988).

The 1980s is also the decade when Beck's model of depression began to be criticized for focusing exclusively on cognition in the aetiology of depression. Other theorists cited developmental, interpersonal and environmental factors in the onset and maintenance of depression. In addition, constructivism, a philosophy which fostered the development of several new cognitive therapies, posed challenges to cognitive therapy. Specifically, the theoretical and philosophical challenges to Beck's model concerned the extent to which it was a comprehensive model to explain all types of depression and whether it assumed that depression is caused by faulty reasoning. As a consequence of these criticisms and challenges,

Beck reformulated his theory of depression and adapted cognitive therapy to work with more chronic and difficult patients.

Research: cognitive theory and treatment outcome studies

The cognitive model of depression was the focus of much research in the 1980s. The model specifies three concepts: (1) the cognitive triad; (2) schemas; and (3) cognitive errors (Beck, 1972; Beck et al., 1979b). Empirical studies of cognitive theory are supportive of the postulates of increased negative cognitions about the self, increased hopelessness, and themes of loss in depression. These results are summarized by Haaga, Dyck and Ernst (1991). Dobson (1989) conducted a meta-analysis of twenty-seven systematic studies using thirty-four comparisons of cognitive therapy with either some form of treatment or a wait-list control. He found cognitive therapy to be superior to other treatments, including behaviour therapy and psychodynamic psychotherapy as well as to the controls. In addition, studies from various centres compared cognitive therapy with antidepressant medication. Cognitive therapy was found to be superior or equally efficacious to medication (Dobson, 1989; Haaga et al., 1991). Cognitive therapy seems to have an especially beneficial effect over time. Follow-up studies, observing patients for three months to two years after treatment, indicate that cognitive therapy has greater long-term effects than drug therapy (Blackburn et al., 1986; Evans et al., 1992; Kovacs et al., 1981; Simons et al., 1986).

The best-known outcome study compared cognitive therapy and another short-term therapy, interpersonal psychotherapy, to antidepressant medication. This multi-site study was conducted in the United States by the National Institute of Mental Health. At the time of termination of treatment, both psychological treatments were as effective as medication for moderately depressed subjects. In the case of severely depressed subjects, medication and interpersonal psychotherapy were significantly more effective than the placebo condition, but cognitive therapy was not (Elkin et al., 1989). However, long-term follow-up results indicate that patients receiving cognitive therapy, including those severely depressed, had the lowest relapse rates at the one-year point (Shea et al., 1992). These findings suggest that cognitive therapy may have a prophylactic effect against future depressions.

In summary, the outcome research of the 1980s found that cognitive therapy alone is comparable to tricyclic antidepressant medication in terms of acute symptom reduction and that the combination of the two may be superior to either one alone (Hollon and Najavits, 1988). Of special significance is the evidence of greater sustained improvement over time with cognitive therapy.

Expanded applications

In 1980, one of Beck's students, David Burns, published a self-help version of cognitive therapy. *Feeling Good* explains how thoughts and beliefs affect mood and behaviour. It teaches readers how to use basic skills employed in cognitive therapy such as examining evidence that supports one's view vs. evidence that contradicts one's view, how to challenge automatic thoughts by identifying cognitive distortions, and how to overcome inertia. *Feeling Good* did much to popularize cognitive therapy. Later, Burns published a self-help manual, *The Feeling Good Handbook* (Burns, 1989). He also wrote a self-help book on interpersonal relationships, *Intimate Connections* (Burns, 1985). In addition, Gary Emery published the self-help volume, *Own Your Own Life* (Emery, 1984).

Others also extended the cognitive model to different populations and clinical problems. In 1981, Gary Emery, Steven Hollon and Richard Bedrosian edited *New Directions in Cognitive Therapy*. In this book, applications of cognitive therapy range from working with the elderly to therapy with children, from dealing with loneliness to sexual dysfunction. In her chapter, Arnkoff (1981) advises and encourages therapists to be flexible and creative in their use of cognitive therapy strategies. This message again contradicts the misperception that cognitive therapy is technique oriented and reiterates the point that it is not easy to do this type of therapy well.

In 1983 Arthur Freeman edited *Cognitive Therapy with Couples and Groups*, thereby extending the cognitive model to a new format. The model for group supervision of cognitive therapists which appears in this book was the first of its kind (Childress and Burns, 1983).

For clinicians, Carlo Perris published *Cognitive Therapy with Schizophrenic Patients* (1989), which demonstrates the utility of the approach, in conjunction with medication, with a population previously considered too ill for cognitive therapy.

In addition, the works of leading cognitive therapists worldwide were combined in a handbook for clinicians, *Comprehensive Handbook of Cognitive Therapy* (Freeman et al., 1989).

At the same time, empirical research supported the use of cognitive therapy in such diverse areas as eating disorders (Garner and Bemis, 1982), heroin addiction (Woody et al., 1984), schizophrenia (Perris, 1989), panic attacks (Sokol et al., 1989a, 1989b), and in-patient depression (Miller et al., 1989a, 1989b). A study by Persons, Burns and Perloff (1988) found that, contrary to popular belief, cognitive therapy is effective for patients of different levels of education, income and backgrounds, and not just well-educated, psychologically minded clients.

Beck also extended the cognitive model to couples therapy in *Love Is Never Enough* (Beck, 1988). Here Beck lists five additional cognitive distortions apparent in distressed relationships: (1) *tunnel vision* in which the person perceives only what fits his or her state of mind; (2) *biased explanations* or negative attributions about one's partner; (3) *negative labelling* or name calling; (4) *mind reading*, which is the assumption that one knows what one's partner is thinking and/or that the partner should be able to intuit what one is thinking; and (5) *subjective reasoning* or the belief that if one feels an emotion strongly enough, then it must be justified.

Anxiety disorders

A major focus for Beck in the 1980s was the development of a theory of anxiety disorders. In 1985 he published *Anxiety Disorders and Phobias*, co-authored with Emery and Greenberg (Beck et al., 1985a). It describes how the cognitive bias in anxiety blocks accurate perceptions and interpretations of threatening situations so that one over-reacts to cues of danger. Cognitive distortions contribute to an exaggerated sense of threat, which results in increased physiological arousal and the behavioural responses of fight, flight or freeze. Beck uses Richard Lazarus's distinction between primary and secondary appraisal (Lazarus, 1966). A person initially makes a 'primary appraisal' of the degree of threat involved in a situation, and then makes a 'secondary appraisal' of the available resources to counter the stressors. According to the cognitive model of anxiety, the person is likely to overestimate threat (both the likelihood of its occurring and its severity of harm) and underestimate his or her coping resources (Beck et al., 1985a). Cognitive therapy for generalized anxiety disorder, for example, emphasizes the reappraisal of risk in a particular situation and one's resources for dealing with the threat.

Beck's theory of anxiety disorders and phobias uses an evolutionary model to explain the adaptive value of the cognitive shift and physiological arousal accompanying anxiety reactions. Human beings possess primate physiology, but are responsive to psychosocial cues as well as to environmental dangers. We are biologically programmed to respond to threat, whatever its source. In terms of survival, it is more adaptive to be sensitive to cues of danger than to be unresponsive and run the risk of serious harm or injury. Thus, in anxiety, judgements tend to be over-inclusive and not finely discriminating.

Cognition is involved not only in our assessment of risk, but in our interpretations of our own physiological responses. At times of great arousal, we may misinterpret our physiology in catastrophic ways. This is evident in the case of panic, for increased physiological activity is interpreted as a sign of internal disaster. Treatment for panic disorder entails the testing of the patient's catastrophic misinterpretations of bodily or mental sensations (Clark, 1986).

To aid his research on anxiety, Beck developed the Beck Anxiety Inventory (Beck et al., 1988).

Reformulations of the theory of depression

Beck has made two important theoretical contributions in the 1990s. One is his research on personality variables and depression, and the other the reformulation of his theory of depression. The growing interest in Bowlby's (1977) work on attachment and loss prompted Beck and his associates to conduct research on personality as a vulnerability to depression. Bowlby hypothesized that the disruption of social bonding was essential to depression. Beck found this true for only one 'type' of personality, which he termed 'sociotropic'. Among the depressed patients he studied, sociotropic individuals valued closeness and became depressed following the loss of a relationship, a rejection, or an experience of social deprivation. In contrast to this group was another 'type' of individual which Beck labelled 'autonomous'. Autonomous individuals valued independence and mobility and were likely to become depressed when their quests for achievement and mobility were thwarted, when they failed to reach a goal, or when they were forced to conform (Beck, 1983). These two pure types represent opposite ends of a dimension which is operationalized in the Sociotropy–Autonomy Scale (Beck et al., 1983). In addition, the same interaction of personality type and adverse experience was found in anxiety as in depression. In anxiety disorders, however, the congruent stressors are the threat of abandonment or failure rather than the actual occurrence of the event (Beck, 1991a).

The distinction between autonomous and sociotropic personality modes allowed for further research into the interaction of personality and life events in the development of depression. Results to date have been inconclusive. For example, Hammen, Ellicott and Gitlin (1989) found a relationship between type of stressor and type of personality only for the highly autonomous patients. In contrast, Segal, Shaw and Vella (1989) found such a relationship only among sociotropic patients who relapsed.

A second consideration in the reformulation of Beck's model was the criticism that his theory wrongly assumed that all depressive thinking was illogical or irrational. It had been reported in the literature that depressed individuals viewed negative feedback realistically (Alloy and Abramson, 1979) and that non-depressed subjects were too optimistic in reaction to feedback (Coyne and Gotlib, 1983). This was termed 'depressive realism'. In addition, in their review of empirical studies of cognitive therapy, Haaga et al. (1991) found evidence of a negative bias in the judgements of depressed persons, but no evidence that they always distort reality.

Beck clarified his description of cognitive processing in depression to emphasize this negative bias or 'cognitive set' and to de-emphasize whether depressed cognitions are rational or irrational. He states that depressed thinking is characterized by the following: (1) a predominant emphasis on the negative aspects of life events; (2) self-attribution for problems across all situations; (3) devaluation of one's self-worth as a consequence of attributing responsibility to oneself; (4) overgeneralization of errors or deficiencies to the past, present and future; and (5) a 'blind alley' view of problem-solving which prevents the generation of alternative solutions (Beck, 1987: 12).

Beck does not stress the irrationality of maladaptive thoughts, for at one time in the person's life, these beliefs made sense. Dysfunctional beliefs contribute to psychological distress because they interfere with normal cognitive processing, not because they are irrational (Beck and Weishaar, 1989).

Cognitive therapy proposes that non-depressed individuals have a greater capacity to self-correct initial appraisals, not that their thinking is free of bias and distortions (Beck and Weishaar, 1989). The negative bias in thinking apparent in depression is most likely to occur when data are not immediately present, are not concrete, are ambiguous, and are relevant to self-evaluation (Riskind, 1983).

In response to findings suggesting a positive bias in non-depressed thinking, Beck proposed the following sequence: (1) the non-depressed cognitive organization has a positive bias; (2) as it shifts towards depression, the positive bias is neutralized; (3) as depression develops, a negative bias occurs; (4) in bipolar cases there is a swing into an exaggerated positive bias as the manic phase develops (Beck, 1991a: 372).

A final criticism of Beck's theory of depression was that it ignored the roles of life events (Krantz, 1985) and interpersonal interactions (Coyne and Gotlib, 1983) in the onset and maintenance of depression. Beck responded to these criticisms by reformulating his theory of depression into six separable but overlapping models: cross-sectional, structural, stressor-vulnerability, reciprocal interaction, psychobiological, and evolutionary. These models are descriptive, explanatory or aetiological.

The stressor-vulnerability model is the closest to his original theory in which schemas pose a cognitive vulnerability which is expressed when triggered by a personally relevant life event. Beck's delineation of the sociotropic and autonomous personality modes suggests that certain types of life event are likely to activate depression among individuals holding certain types of core belief.

The reciprocal interaction model addresses the interpersonal dynamics contributing to depression. For example, difficult interactions between a patient and spouse reflect mutually reinforcing interactions of beliefs held by those individuals. According to Beck, the reciprocal interaction model is more applicable to the maintenance of depression than to its onset.

For his research on depression and the formulation of cognitive therapy, Beck received the Distinguished Scientific Award for the Application of Psychology from the American Psychological Association in 1989.

The 1990s: current status and future directions

In the 1990s, applications of the cognitive model have proliferated, some empirically driven (e.g. Baucom et al., 1990) and others theoretically based (e.g. Young and Lindemann, 1992).

Perhaps the most important shift in cognitive therapy in the 1990s occurred in its approach to personality disorders. Extension of the cognitive model to the area of personality disorders necessitated changes in how cognitive therapy is conducted and also prompted Beck to focus on the theoretical and therapeutic issues that were confronting the field of cognitive psychotherapy in general. These issues or influences were findings in cognitive and developmental psychology, research on emotion, and a renewed interest in the therapeutic relationship as a vital factor in therapy. As a consequence of these influences, newer cognitive therapies were developed. One, called schema-focused cognitive therapy (Young 1990), is derived from Beck's cognitive therapy yet contrasts with it in specific ways.

In addition to new emphases in the theory and practice of cognitive therapy, there have been contributions to the future of psychotherapy and the movement toward psychotherapy integration. Beck proposes a central role for cognitive therapy in the integration movement.

Further applications in the 1990s

The 1990s have witnessed an outpouring of books written by cognitive therapists for both clinicians and clients. In addition to Beck's work on personality disorders (Beck et al., 1990a), there are books for clinicians on borderline personality disorder (Layden et al., 1993), distressed relationships (Baucom and Epstein, 1990; Dattilio and Padesky, 1990), substance abuse (Beck et al., 1993), and in-patients (Wright et al., 1993). Judith Beck authored a contemporary text for clinicians, *Cognitive Therapy: Basics and Beyond* (Beck, 1995).

A number of handbooks and casebooks have been published on a range of clinical problems (Dattilio and Freeman, 1994; Freeman and Dattilio, 1992; Freeman et al., 1990), and self-help books, including *Reinventing Your Life* (Young and Klosko, 1993) and *Mind over Mood* (Greenberger and Padesky, 1995).

Trends in theory

As cognitive therapy was becoming more familiar to the public and numerous empirical studies demonstrated its effectiveness in treating depression and anxiety, challenges to cognitive theory and practice necessitated some modifications of the traditional, short-term approach.

In the 1990s there were calls for cognitive therapies to acknowledge and explore the importance of interpersonal interactions and schemas in psychological distress; view emotion as a source of information about oneself and one's environment; and use more historical and developmental conceptualizations. The works of Liotti and of Safran and his associates, for example, emphasize interpersonal processes and the importance of emotion in psychotherapy (Greenberg and Safran, 1987; Liotti, 1991; Muran and Safran, 1993; Safran and Segal, 1990). Others, such as Guidano (1987), Goncalves and Ivey (1993) and Rosen (1993), focus on developmental theory.

In clinical practice, these trends have shifted attention to early life experiences, experiential and emotive techniques to gain access to emotions and the core beliefs connected to them, and a greater focus on how individuals maintain beliefs in the face of contradictory evidence. Concepts such as resistance (Mahoney, 1993), cognitive avoidance (Young, 1990), and defensive information processing (Beck et al., 1990a) have a place in cognitive therapies, but not as they are used in psychoanalysis. These newly defined concepts owe more to cognitive science than to traditional psychotherapy. For example, Beck's conceptualization of automatic thoughts as not being volitional, being difficult to inhibit and being fast fits the definition of unconscious processes as they are defined in cognitive psychology (Power, 1987).

Cognitive therapy of personality disorders

In 1990 Beck and his associates turned their attention to personality disorders and published cognitive therapy's theoretical and clinical perspectives in *Cognitive Therapy of Personality Disorders* (Beck et al., 1990a). In working with personality disorders, cognitive therapy becomes longer term, focuses more on the therapeutic relationship, and pays greater attention to early learning experiences in order to understand the origins of schemas. Theoretical emphasis is placed on the schema concept as 'the fundamental unit of personality' (Beck et al., 1990a: 22). The authors state:

> The typical maladaptive schemas in personality disorders are evoked across many or even most situations, have a compulsive quality, and are less easy to control or modify than are their counterparts in other people. . . . In sum, relative to other people, their dysfunctional attitudes and behaviors are overgeneralized, inflexible, imperative, and resistant to change. (Beck et al., 1990a: 29)

Following the *continuity hypothesis*, the types of attitudes and beliefs apparent in personality disorders are exaggerated forms of beliefs held by persons who do not have personality disorders. As in normal individuals, there are relationships between beliefs, emotions and behaviours. Each personality disorder is characterized by a set of beliefs, attitudes, affects and behaviours, forming a *cognitive profile* for that disorder. For example, a core belief of the dependent personality is, 'I am helpless' and the corresponding behaviour is towards attachment. The beliefs at the core of personality disorders originate as a consequence of the interaction of the individual's genetic predisposition with exposure to undesirable influences from other people and specific traumatic events.

As with anxiety (Beck et al., 1985a) and depression (Beck, 1987), Beck uses evolutionary theory to explain the existence of personality disorders. The cognitive model proposes that prototypes of our personality patterns could have been 'strategies' which influenced survival and reproductive success during hominid evolution. Present-day personality disorders may be viewed as exaggerated expressions of those primitive strategies.

Clinical changes in working with personality disorders are made to accommodate the difficulties in establishing a collaborative therapeutic relationship. Beck et al. (1990a) list nineteen obstacles that can inhibit collaborative empiricism. They include such problems as 'The patient may lack the skill to be collaborative' and 'Patients' rigidity may foil compliance'.

Changes in therapy include greater attention to the activation of schemas within the therapy session and to childhood memories which aid in the conceptualization of the origins and current functioning of schemas. Because the client's beliefs are so rigidly maintained, the standard cognitive techniques of logical examination and behavioural experiments may not be sufficient for change. Cognitive therapy for personality disorders therefore makes greater use of role play, imagery, and re-experiencing childhood events to elicit schemas and respond to them in more adaptive ways.

Jeffrey Young, who was trained by Beck, has developed a cognitive approach to working with personality disorders which he calls schema-focused cognitive therapy (Young, 1990). Young centres his approach on the content and defensive processes of early maladaptive schemas (EMS) which are broad themes about oneself and one's relationships with others. They are usually established early in life, are self-perpetuating, unconditional, and resistant to change. They are tied to affect and are capable of driving self-defeating behaviours. Young and Lindemann (1992) propose sixteen EMS grouped in six domains: instability and disconnection, impaired autonomy, undesirability, restricted self-expression, restricted gratification, and impaired limits. One theoretical difference from Beck's model is that Young defines schemas by their content. Beck says they are structures, the content of which is idiosyncratic.

Young also emphasizes the volitional and unconscious manoeuvres used to keep maladaptive schemas intact. He identifies three processes: schema maintenance, schema avoidance, and schema compensation. Schemas are maintained by cognitive distortions and behaviours that allow the schemas to be believable and feel familiar. Schema avoidance, whether cognitive, affective or behavioural, keeps the person from experiencing the pain which occurs when a schema is triggered. In other words, the person might avoid situations in which a schema is likely to be triggered, not think about what is bothering them, or shut themselves off from experiencing emotion. Schema compensation occurs when one acts contrary to a schema. This tends to be short-lived since the person is unprepared to deal with the consequences. For example, if someone has been subjugated, acting in an aggressive manner without any preparation is unlikely to meet a positive response and the person could feel subjugated further. Thus, the strategy backfires and the schema is reinforced.

As with Beck's model, schema-focused cognitive therapy uses emotive, interpersonal, cognitive and behavioural techniques to identify and change schemas. However, in contrast to Beck's approach (Beck et al., 1990a; Pretzer and Fleming, 1989), emotive and interpersonal techniques precede cognitive and behavioural ones in order to make schemas more accessible and fluid.

The future of psychotherapy

In less than thirty years, cognitive therapy research has developed a model of depression and a corresponding therapy, tested the therapy's efficacy, applied the model to diverse problems and populations, and is now returning to consider the viability of the theory.

Shaw and Segal (1988) recommend three research areas for the future of cognitive therapy: (1) the viability of the model, including variables which would increase its explanatory and predictive capacities; (2) the ways in which cognitive and personality variables interact with stressful life events in the aetiology of depression; and (3) the identification of those at risk of relapse.

For psychotherapy theory and practice in general, Beck and Haaga (1992) predict five trends: (1) psychotherapy will confront the issues of specificity versus non-specificity in terms of the characteristics of well-being and of psychopathology; (2) psychotherapy will respond to continued pressure for research and accountability; (3) psychotherapy will make further connections with basic psychological science; (4) delivery systems for psychotherapeutic knowledge will become more diverse; and (5) different systems of psychotherapy will continue to influence one another.

For cognitive therapy, these trends suggest further research on its newer applications as well as refinements of the model to explain and predict psychological distress. Beck's use of ethology and evolutionary theory will continue to inform his thinking. Research in cognitive and social psychology will aid cognitive therapy in understanding how people generate and modify affect-laden beliefs (Hollon and Garber, 1990; Power, 1987). Self-help groups and the bibliotherapy offered by manuals such as *Mind over Mood* (Greenberger and Padesky, 1995) will help clients who cannot participate in extended therapy or who want to maintain gains once therapy ends. Finally, cognitive therapy will continue to play an active role in the movement towards psychotherapy integration.

Psychotherapy integration

The movement for psychotherapy integration, begun in the 1970s, reflects a growing interest in eclectic and integrative therapy based on common principles and elements from different orientations. Paul Wachtel (1977) and Marvin Goldfried (1980) are credited as founders of the modern integrationist movement which arose from (1) a general dissatisfaction with the clinical limitations of various schools; (2) the failure of any single school to dominate the outcome research for all disorders; and (3) the need for accountability and responsiveness to third-party insurance payers in the United States (Arnkoff and Glass, 1992).

Just as cognitive therapy is influenced by other orientations, it offers contributions to psychotherapy integration. Beck and Haaga (1992) identify three such contributions: (1) any model of psychopathology and psychotherapy will have to consider the role of cognitive processing; (2) cognitive therapy's use of a range of therapeutic strategies demonstrates how techniques can be integrated; and (3) the nature of the therapeutic relationship should be collaborative.

Alford and Norcross (1991) see cognitive therapy as having integrative components, for they see cognition as a bridge between diverse orientations. In addition, cognitive therapy emphasizes a common factors approach and is theoretically integrative in an historical sense. Moreover, it maintains a collaborative, not confrontational, stance towards other contemporary models.

Beck believes that cognitive therapy can serve as *the* integrative therapy because of its explanatory power, its blend of techniques, and its cohesive theory (Beck, 1991b). Its viability as a theory and a therapy will continue to be tested. Its longevity will be determined by how well cognitive therapy continues to meet these tests.

References

Adler, A. (1936) 'The neurotic's picture of the world', *International Journal of Individual Psychology*, 2: 3–10.

Alexander, F. (1950) *Psychosomatic Medicine: Its Principles and Applications*. New York: Norton.

Alford, B.A. and Norcross, J.C. (1991) 'Cognitive therapy as integrative therapy', *Journal of Psychotherapy Integration*, 1: 175–90.

Alloy, L.B. and Abramson, L.Y. (1979) 'Judgment of contingency in depressed and non-depressed students: sadder but wiser?', *Journal of Experimental Psychology: General*, 108: 441–85.

Arnkoff, D.B. (1981) 'Flexibility in practicing cognitive therapy', in G. Emery, S.D. Hollon and R.C. Bedrosian (eds), *New Directions in Cognitive Therapy*. New York: Guilford Press. pp. 203–23.

Arnkoff, D.B. and Glass, C.R. (1992) 'Cognitive therapy and psychotherapy integration', in D.K. Freedheim (ed.), *History of Psychotherapy: A Century of Change*. Washington, DC: American Psychological Association. pp. 657–94.

Arnold, M. (1960) *Emotion and Personality*, Vol. 1. New York: Columbia University Press.

Bandura, A. (1977) *Social Learning Theory*. Englewood Cliffs, NJ: Prentice-Hall.

Baucom, D. and Epstein, N. (1990) *Cognitive-Behavioral Marital Therapy*. New York: Bruner/Mazel.

Baucom, D.H., Sayers, S.L. and Sher, T.G. (1990) 'Supplementing behavioral marital therapy with cognitive restructuring and emotional expressiveness training: an outcome investigation', *Journal of Consulting and Clinical Psychology*, 58: 636–45.

Beck, A.T. (1963) 'Thinking and depression: I. Idiosyncratic content and cognitive distortions', *Archives of General Psychiatry*, 9: 324–33.

Beck, A.T. (1964) 'Thinking and depression: II. Theory and therapy', *Archives of General Psychiatry*, 10: 561–71.

Beck, A.T. (1970) 'Cognitive therapy: nature and relation to behavior therapy', *Behavior Therapy*, 1: 184–200.

Beck, A.T. (1972) *Depression: Causes and Treatment*. Philadelphia: University of Pennsylvania Press.

Beck, A.T. (1976) *Cognitive Therapy and the Emotional Disorders*. New York: New American Library.

Beck, A.T. (1983) 'Cognitive therapy of depression: new perspectives', in P.J. Clayton and J.E. Barnett (eds), *Treatment of Depression: Old Controversies and New Approaches*. New York: Raven Press. pp. 265–84.

Beck, A.T. (1987) 'Cognitive models of depression', *Journal of Cognitive Psychotherapy. An International Quarterly*, 1(1): 5–37.

Beck, A.T. (1988) *Love is Never Enough*. New York: Harper & Row.

Beck, A.T. (1991a) 'Cognitive therapy: a 30 year retrospective', *American Psychologist*, 46(4): 368–75.

Beck, A.T. (1991b) 'Cognitive therapy as the integrative therapy: comment on Alford and Norcross', *Journal of Psychotherapy Integration*, 1: 191–8.

Beck, A.T. and Haaga, D. (1992) 'The future of cognitive therapy', *Psychotherapy*, 29(1): 34–8.

Beck, A.T. and Weishaar, M.E. (1989) 'Cognitive therapy', in R.J. Corsini and D. Wedding (eds), *Current Psychotherapies*. Itasca, IL: F.E. Peacock. pp. 285–320.

Beck, A.T. and Young, J.E. (1985) 'Depression', in D.H. Barlow (ed.), *Clinical Handbook of Psychological Disorders*. New York: Guilford Press. pp. 206–44.

Beck, A.T., Lester, D. and Albert, N. (1973a) 'Suicidal wishes and symptoms of depression', *Psychological Reports*, 33: 770.

Beck, A.T., Davis, J.H., Frederick, C.J., Perlin, S., Pokorny, A.D., Schulman, R.E., Seiden, R.H. and Wittlin, B.J. (1973b) 'Classification and nomenclature', in H.C.P. Resnik and B.C. Hathorne (eds), *Suicide Prevention in the Seventies* (DHEW Publication HSM 72–9054 pp. 7–12). Washington, DC: US Government Printing Office.

Beck, A.T., Laude, R. and Bohnert, M. (1974a) 'Ideation components of anxiety neurosis', *Archives of General Psychiatry*, 31: 456–9.

Beck, A.T., Schuyler, D. and Herman, I. (1974b) 'Development of suicidal intent scales', in A.T. Beck, H.C.P. Resnik and D.J. Lettieri (eds), *The Prediction of Suicide*. Bowie, MD: Charles Press. pp. 45–56.

Beck, A.T., Ward, C.H., Mendelson, M., Mock, J. and Erbaugh, J. (1961) 'An inventory for measuring depression', *Archives of General Psychiatry*, 4: 561–71.

Beck, A.T., Weissman, A., Lester, D. and Trexler, L. (1974c) 'The measurement of pessimism: the hopelessness scale', *Journal of Consulting and Clinical Psychology*, 42: 861–5.

Beck, A.T., Kovacs, M. and Weissman, A. (1975) 'Hopelessness and suicidal behavior: an overview', *Journal of the American Medical Association*, 234(11): 1146–9.

Beck, A.T., Weissman, A. and Kovacs, M. (1976) 'Alcoholism, hopelessness and suicidal behavior', *Journal of Studies of Alcohol*, 37(1): 66–77.

Beck, A.T., Kovacs, M. and Weissman, A. (1979a) 'Assessment of suicidal intention: the scale for suicide ideation', *Journal of Consulting and Clinical Psychology*, 47(2): 343–52.

Beck, A.T., Rush, A.J., Shaw, B.F. and Emery, G. (1979b) *Cognitive Therapy of Depression*. New York: Guilford Press.

Beck, A.T., Epstein, N. and Harrison, R. (1983) 'Cognition, attitudes and personality dimensions in depression', *British Journal of Cognitive Psychotherapy*, 1: 1–16.

Beck, A.T., Emery, G. with Greenberg, R.L. (1985a) *Anxiety Disorders and Phobias: A Cognitive Perspective*. New York: Basic Books.

Beck, A.T., Steer, R.A., Kovacs, M. and Garrison, B. (1985b) 'Hopelessness and eventual suicide: a ten-year prospective study of patients hospitalized with suicidal ideation', *American Journal of Psychiatry*, 142(5): 559–63.

Beck, A.T., Riskind, J.H., Brown, G. and Sherrod, A. (1986) 'A comparison of likelihood estimates for imagined positive and negative outcomes in anxiety and depression'. Paper presented at the annual meeting of the Society for Psychotherapy Research, Wellesley, MA, June.

Beck, A.T., Brown, G., Steer, R.A., Eidelson, J.I. and Riskind, J.H. (1987) 'Differentiating anxiety and depression: a test of the cognitive content-specificity hypothesis', *Journal of Abnormal Psychology*, 96: 179–83.

Beck, A.T., Epstein, N., Brown, G. and Steer, R.A. (1988) 'An inventory for measuring clinical anxiety: psychometric properties', *Journal of Consulting and Clinical Psychology*, 56(6): 893–7.

Beck, A.T., Freeman, A. and Associates (1990a) *Cognitive Therapy of Personality Disorders*. New York: Guilford Press.

Beck, A.T., Brown, G., Berchick, R.J., Stewart, B.L. and Steer, R.A. (1990b) 'Relationship between hopelessness and ultimate suicide: a replication with psychiatric outpatients', *American Journal of Psychiatry*, 147(2): 190–5.

Beck, A.T., Steer, R.A., Epstein, N. and Brown, G. (1990c) 'The Beck Self-Concept Test', *Psychological Assessment: A Journal of Consulting and Clinical Psychology*, 2(2): 191–7.

Beck, A.T., Wright, F.D., Newman, C.F. and Liese, B.S. (1993) *Cognitive Therapy of Substance Abuse*. New York: Guilford Press.

Beck, J.S. (1995) *Cognitive Therapy: Basics and Beyond*. New York: Guilford Press.

Bedrosian, R.C. and Beck, A.T. (1979) 'Cognitive aspects of suicidal behavior', *Suicide and Life Threatening Behavior*, 9(2): 87–96.

Blackburn, I.M., Eunson, K.M. and Bishop, S. (1986) 'A two-year naturalistic follow-up of depressed patients treated with cognitive therapy, pharmacotherapy and a combination of both', *Journal of Affective Disorders*, 10: 67–75.

Bowlby, J. (1977) 'The making and breaking of affectional bonds', *British Journal of Psychiatry*, 130: 201–10.

Burns, D. (1980) *Feeling Good: The New Mood Therapy*. New York: New American Library.

Burns, D. (1985) *Intimate Connections*. New York: William Morrow.

Burns, D. (1989) *The Feeling Good Handbook: Using New Mood Therapy in Everyday Life*. New York: William Morrow.

Childress, A.R. and Burns, D. (1983) 'The group supervision model in cognitive therapy training', in A. Freeman (ed.), *Cognitive Therapy of Couples and Groups*. New York: Plenum. pp. 323–35.

Clark, D.M. (1986) 'A cognitive approach to panic', *Behaviour Research and Therapy*, 24: 461–70.

Coyne, J.L. and Gotlib, I.H. (1983) 'The role of cognition in depression: a critical appraisal', *Psychological Bulletin*, 94: 472–505.

Dattilio, F.M. and Freeman, A. (eds) (1994) *Cognitive-Behavioral Strategies in Crisis Intervention*. New York: Guilford Press.

Dattilio, F.M. and Padesky, C.A. (1990) *Cognitive Therapy with Couples*. Sarasota, FL: Professional Resource Exchange.

Diffily, A. (1991) 'Father and child: Tim Beck and his uncommon common sense', *Penn Medicine*, 4: 20–7.

Dobson, K.S. (1989) 'A meta-analysis of the efficacy of cognitive therapy for depression', *Journal of Consulting and Clinical Psychology*, 57(3): 414–19.

Dyer, J.A.T. and Kreitman, N. (1984) 'Hopelessness, depression and suicidal intent in parasuicide', *British Journal of Psychiatry*, 144: 127–33.

Elkin, I., Shea, M.T., Watkins, J.T., Imber, S., Sotsky, S.M., Collins, J.F., Glass, D.R., Pilkonis, P.A., Leber, W.R., Docherty, J.P., Fiester, S.J. and Parloff, M.B. (1989) 'National Institute of Mental Health Treatment of Depression Collaborative Research Program: general effectiveness of treatments', *Archives of General Psychiatry*, 46: 971–83.

Ellis, A. (1962) *Reason and Emotion in Psychotherapy*. Seacaucus, NJ: Lyle Stuart.

Emery, G. (1984) *Own Your Own Life*. New York: Signet.

Emery, G., Hollon, S, and Bedrosian, R. (eds) (1981) *New Directions in Cognitive Therapy*. New York: Guilford Press.

Evans, M.D., Hollon, S.D., DeRubeis, R.J., Piasecki, J.M., Grove, W.M., Garvey, M.J. and Tuason, V.B. (1992) 'Differential relapse following cognitive therapy and pharmacotherapy for depression', *Archives of General Psychiatry*, 49: 802–8.

Freeman, A. (ed.) (1983) *Cognitive Therapy with Couples and Groups*. New York: Plenum Press.

Freeman, A. and Dattilio, F.M. (eds) (1992) *Comprehensive Casebook of Cognitive Therapy*. New York: Plenum Press.

Freeman, A., Simon, K.M., Beutler, L.E. and Arkowitz, H. (eds) (1989) *Comprehensive Handbook of Cognitive Therapy*. New York: Plenum Press.

Freeman, A., Pretzer, J., Fleming, B. and Simon, K. (1990) *Clinical Applications of Cognitive Therapy*. New York: Plenum Press.

Garner, D.M. and Bemis, K.M. (1982) 'A cognitive-behavioral approach to anorexia nervosa', *Cognitive Therapy and Research*, 6: 123–50.

Goldfried, M.R. (1980) 'Toward the delineation of therapeutic change principles', *American Psychologist*, 35(11): 991–9.

Goldfried, M.R. and Davison, G.C. (1976) *Clinical Behavior Therapy*. New York: Holt, Rinehart & Winston.

Goldney, R.D. (1979) 'Attempted suicide: correlates of lethality'. Unpublished doctoral dissertation, University of Adelaide, Australia.

Goncalves, O.F. and Ivey, A.E. (1993) 'Developmental therapy: clinical applications', in K.T. Kuehlwein and H. Rosen (eds), *Cognitive Therapies in Action: Evolving Innovative Practices*. San Francisco: Jossey-Bass. pp. 326–52.

Greenberg, M.S. and Beck, A.T. (1989) 'Depression versus anxiety: a test of the content specificity hypothesis', *Journal of Abnormal Psychology*, 98: 9–13.

Greenberg, L.S. and Safran, J.D. (1987) *Emotion in Psychotherapy*. New York: Guilford Press.

Greenberger, D. and Padesky, C.A. (1995) *Mind over Mood*. New York: Guilford Press.

Guidano, V.F. (1987) *Complexity of the Self: A Developmental Approach to Psychopathology and Therapy*. New York: Guilford Press.

Haaga, D.A.F., Dyck, M.J. and Ernst, D. (1991) 'Empirical status of cognitive theory of depression', *Psychological Bulletin*, 110(2): 215–36.

Hammen, C., Ellicott, A. and Gitlin, M. (1989) 'Vulnerability to specific life events and prediction of course of disorder in unipolar depressed patients', *Canadian Journal of Behavioural Science*, 21: 377–88.

Hollon, S.D. and Garber, J. (1990) 'Cognitive therapy for depression: a social cognitive perspective', *Personality and Social Psychology Bulletin*, 16(1): 58–73.

Hollon, S.D. and Najavits, L. (1988) 'Review of empirical studies on cognitive therapy', in A.J. Frances and R.E. Hales (eds), *Review of Psychiatry*, Vol. 7. Washington, DC: American Psychiatric Press. pp. 643–66.

Horney, K. (1950) *Neurosis and Human Growth: The Struggle toward Self-Realization*. New York: Norton.

Kant, I. (1798) *The Classification of Mental Disorders*. Königsberg, Germany: Nicolovius.

Kelly, G. (1955) *The Psychology of Personal Constructs*, 2 vols. New York: Norton.

Kovacs, M., Rush, A.J., Beck, A.T. and Hollon, S.D. (1981) 'Depressed outpatients treated with cognitive therapy or pharmacotherapy: a one-year follow-up', *Archives of General Psychiatry*, 38: 33–9.

Krantz, S.E. (1985) 'When depressive cognitions reflect negative realities', *Cognitive Therapy and Research*, 9(6): 595–610.

Layden, M.A., Newman, C.F., Freeman A. and Morse, S.B. (1993) *Cognitive Therapy of Borderline Personality Disorder*. Boston, MA: Allyn & Bacon.

Lazarus, A.A. (1976) *Multi-Modal Behavior Therapy*. New York: Springer.

Lazarus, R.S. (1966) *Psychological Stress and the Coping Process*. New York: McGraw-Hill.

Liotti, G. (1991) 'Patterns of attachments and the assessment of interpersonal schemata: understanding and changing difficult patient–therapist relationships in cognitive psychotherapy', *Journal of Cognitive Psychotherapy: An International Quarterly*, 5(2): 105–14.

Mahoney, M.J. (1974) *Cognition and Behavior Modification*. Cambridge, MA: Ballinger.

Mahoney, M.J. (1993) 'Introduction to special section: theoretical developments in the cognitive psychotherapies', *Journal of Consulting and Clinical Psychology*, 61(2): 187–93.

Mahoney, M.J. and Arnkoff, D.B. (1978) 'Cognitive and self-control therapies', in S.L. Garfield and A.E. Bergin (eds), *Handbook of Psychotherapy and Behavior Change: An Empirical Analysis*. New York: John Wiley and Sons. pp. 689–722.

Meichenbaum, D. (1977) *Cognitive Behavior Modification*. New York: Plenum.

Meyers, A.W. and Craighead, W.E. (1984) 'Cognitive behavior therapy with children: a historical, conceptual and organizational overview', in A.W. Meyers and W.E. Craighead (eds), *Cognitive Behavior Therapy with Children*. New York: Plenum. pp. 1–17.

Miller, I.W., Norman, W.H. and Keitner, G.I. (1989a) 'Cognitive-behavioral treatment of depressed inpatients: six and twelve-month follow-up', *American Journal of Psychiatry*, 146: 1274–9.

Miller, I.W., Norman, W.H., Keitner, G.I., Bishop, S.B. and Dow, M.G. (1989b) 'Cognitive-behavioral treatment of depressed inpatients', *Behavior Therapy*, 20(1): 25–47.

Minkoff, K., Bergman, E., Beck, A.T. and Beck, R. (1973) 'Hopelessness, depression and attempted suicide', *American Journal of Psychiatry*, 130: 455–9.

Muran, J.C. and Safran, J.D. (1993) 'Emotional and interpersonal considerations in cognitive therapy', in K.T. Kuehlwein and H. Rosen (eds), *Cognitive Therapies in Action: Evolving Innovative Practice*. San Francisco: Jossey-Bass. pp. 185–212.

Perris, C. (1989) *Cognitive Therapy with Schizophrenic Patients*. New York: Guilford Press.

Persons, J.B., Burns, D.D. and Perloff, J.M. (1988) 'Predictors of dropout and outcome in cognitive therapy for depression in a private practice setting', *Cognitive Therapy and Research*, 12: 557–75.

Petrie, K. and Chamberlain, K. (1983) 'Hopelessness and social desirability as moderator variables in predicting suicidal behavior', *Journal of Consulting and Clinical Psychology*, 51: 485–7.

Piaget, J. (1926) *The Language and Thought of the Child*. New York: Harcourt, Brace.

Power, M.J. (1987) 'Cognitive theories of depression', in H.J. Eysenck and I. Martin (eds), *Theoretical Foundation of Behavior Therapy*. New York: Plenum Press. pp. 235–55.

Pretzer, J.L. and Fleming, B. (1989) 'Cognitive-behavioral treatment of personality disorders', *The Behavior Therapist*, 12: 105–9.

Riskind, J.H. (1983) 'Misconceptions of the cognitive model of depression'. Paper presented at the 91st Annual Convention of the American Psychological Association, Anaheim, CA, August.

Rogers, C.R. (1951) *Client-Centered Therapy: Its Current Practice, Implications, and Theory*. Boston, MA: Houghton Mifflin.

Rosen, H. (1993) 'Developing themes in the field of cognitive therapy', in K.T. Kuehlwein and H. Rosen (eds), *Cognitive Therapies in Action: Evolving Innovative Practice*. San Francisco: Jossey-Bass. pp. 403–34.

Rush, A.J., Beck, A.T., Kovacs, M. and Hollon, S.D. (1977) 'Comparative efficacy of cognitive therapy and pharmacotherapy in the treatment of depressed outpatients', *Cognitive Therapy and Research*, 1: 17–37.

Safran, J.D. and Segal, Z.V. (1990) *Interpersonal Process in Cognitive Therapy*. New York: Basic Books.

Segal, Z.V., Shaw, B.F. and Vella, D.D. (1989) 'Life stress and depression: a test of the congruency hypothesis for life event content and depressive subtype', *Canadian Journal of Behavioural Science*, 21: 389–400.

Shaw, B.F. and Segal, Z.V. (1988) 'Introduction to cognitive theory and therapy', in A.J. Frances and R.E. Hales (eds), *Review of Psychiatry*, Vol. 7. Washington, DC: American Psychiatric Press. pp. 538–53.

Shea, M.T., Elkin, I., Imber, S.D., Sotsky, S.M., Watkins, J.T., Collins, J.F., Pilkonis, P.A., Beckham, E., Glass, D.R., Dolan, R.T. and Parloff, M.B. (1992) 'Course of depressive symptoms over follow-up: findings from the National Institute of Mental Health treatment of depression collaborative research program', *Archives of General Psychiatry*, 49: 782–7.

Simons, A.D., Murphy, G.E., Levine, J.E. and Wetzel, R.D. (1986) 'Cognitive therapy and pharmacotherapy for depression: sustained improvement over one year', *Archives of General Psychiatry*, 43: 43–9.

Skinner, B.F. (1977) 'Why I am not a cognitive psychologist', *Behaviorism*, 5: 1–10.

Sokol, L., Beck, A.T. and Clark, D.A. (1989a) 'A controlled treatment trial of cognitive therapy for panic disorder'. Paper presented at the World Congress of Cognitive Therapy. Oxford, June.

Sokol, L., Beck, A.T., Greenberg, R.L., Berchick, R.J. and Wright, E.D. (1989b) 'Cognitive therapy of panic disorder: a non-pharmacological alternative', *Journal of Nervous and Mental Diseases*, 177: 711–16.

Sullivan, M.S. (1953) *The Interpersonal Theory of Psychiatry*. New York: Norton.

Truax, C.B. (1963) 'Effective ingredients in psychotherapy: an approach to unraveling the patient–therapist interaction', *Journal of Counseling Psychology*, 10: 256–63.

Wachtel, P.L. (1977) *Psychoanalysis and Behavior Therapy: Toward an Integration*. New York: Basic Books.

Weishaar, M.E. (1993) *Aaron T. Beck*. London: Sage Publications.

Weissman, A. and Beck, A.T. (1978) 'Development and validation of the Dysfunctional Attitude Scale'. Paper presented at the Annual Convention of the Association for Advancement of Behavior Therapy, Chicago.

Weissman, A., Beck, A.T. and Kovacs, M.(1979) 'Drug abuse, hopelessness, and suicidal behavior', *International Journal of the Addictions*, 14: 451–64.

Wetzel, R.D. (1976) 'Hopelessness, depression and suicide intent', *Archives of General Psychiatry*, 33: 1069–73.

Wolpe, J. (1976) 'Behavior therapy and its malcontents: II. Multimodal eclecticism, cognitive exclusivism and "exposure" empiricism', *Journal of Behavior Therapy and Experimental Psychiatry*, 7: 109–16.

Woody, G.E., McLellan, A.T., Luborsky, L., O'Brien, C.P., Blaine, J., Fox, S., Herman, I. and Beck, A.T. (1984) 'Severity of psychiatric symptoms as a predictor of benefits from psychotherapy: the Veterans Administration–Penn Study', *American Journal of Psychiatry*, 141: 1172–7.

Wright, J.H., Thase, M.E., Beck, A.T. and Ludgate, J.W. (eds) (1993) *Cognitive Therapy with Inpatients: Developing a Cognitive Milieu*. New York: Guilford Press.

Young, J.E. (1990) *Cognitive Therapy for Personality Disorders: A Schema-Focused Approach*. Sarasota, FL: Professional Resource Exchange.

Young, J. and Beck, A.T. (1980) 'Cognitive Therapy Rating Scale: Rating Manual'. Unpublished manuscript, Center for Cognitive Therapy, Philadelphia.

Young, J. and Klosko, J.S. (1993) *Reinventing Your Life: Smart Moves for Escaping Negative Life Patterns*. New York: Dutton.

Young, J.E. and Lindemann, M.D. (1992) 'An integrative schema-focused model for personality disorders', *Journal of Cognitive Psychotherapy: An International Quarterly*, 6(1): 11–23.

9

Trends in Rational Emotive Behaviour Therapy: 1955–95

Michael Neenan and Windy Dryden

Rational emotive behaviour therapy (REBT) is a system of psychotherapy which teaches individuals how their belief systems largely determine their emotional and behavioural reactions to life events (Ellis and Bernard, 1985). More specifically, it is rigid, unrealistic, and absolute beliefs couched in the form of musts, shoulds, have to's, got to's, oughts, which lie at the core of emotional and behavioural disturbance, e.g. the depression-inducing belief, 'I must have the love of my partner otherwise I will be worthless'. Such beliefs are targeted for challenge and change through a variety of multimodal methods (cognitive, emotive, behavioural and imaginal) in order to develop a rational philosophy of living based on preferences and desires. REBT hypothesizes that a preferential belief system is more likely to produce emotional stability and constructive behaviour that will aid goal attainment than a belief system based on dogmatic demands.

Albert Ellis, an American clinical psychologist, originally practised as a liberal psychoanalyst but became increasingly disillusioned with what he regarded as the inefficiency and ineffectiveness of this discipline in tackling emotional disturbance, as well as with his own inability to make its tenets more scientifically based. After experimenting with different therapeutic methods, he launched REBT in 1955 as a mixture of philosophical insight and behaviour therapy. This chapter examines some of the trends that have shaped the development of REBT over the last forty years.

Rational therapy: 1955–61

REBT was originally called rational therapy (RT) to emphasize its use of reason and the intellect in combating emotional distress. (Ellis later came to regret the use of the term 'rational' because it suggested to people that he was advocating cognition to the exclusion of affect.) As the originator of the first of the cognitive or cognitive-behaviour therapies (Ellis, 1994a), Ellis went back to a first-century Stoic philosopher, Epictetus, to provide the major underpinning of his new approach: 'People are disturbed not by things, but by the views which they take of them.' Such an outlook clearly placed primary responsibility on individuals for their emotional disturbance rather than on early childhood influences (psychoanalysis) or environmental conditioning (behaviourism). Ellis developed an active-directive, confrontational style in attacking the illogical and unrealistic aspects of clients' belief systems and therefore eschewed the passive, non-directive approaches of psychoanalysis and Carl Rogers's client-centred therapy.

Clients were urged to adopt a scientific approach to tackling their problems by being open-minded and flexible in searching for evidence to confirm or disconfirm their beliefs; also to treat their beliefs as hypotheses about reality rather than as grounded in fact. Ellis (1958a) distinguished between two types of belief: irrational ones were usually rigid, disturbance-producing, and goal-blocking; rational ones were more likely to be adaptable, disturbance-reducing, and goal-oriented. At this stage of REBT's development, Ellis did not 'fully realize that neurotic beliefs include explicit or implicit absolutist musts or demands' (1994a: 17) and therefore advanced eleven irrational ideas (e.g. the idea that it is awful and catastrophic when things are not the way one would very much like them to be) as the major source of neurosis. In the 1970s, these ideas would be subsumed within three musturbatory (musts) categories. As well as bifurcating beliefs into rational and irrational, Ellis (1958a) also divided emotions into disturbed or self-defeating (e.g. anger, depression) and non-disturbed or self-helping (annoyance, sadness) states. Emotions were designated in this fashion if they, respectively, blocked or aided people's goal-seeking behaviour. The use of reason for personal problem-solving was not meant, as some critics believed, to remove all human emotions because 'many kinds of negative emotions [e.g. sorrow, regret] are perfectly legitimate reactions to deprivation and frustration' (Ellis et al., 1960: 16). REBT never encouraged or encourages clients to feel passive, apathetic or emotionless in the face of adverse life events. In *Reason and Emotion in Psychotherapy* (1962), Ellis began to describe affective states as appropriate or inappropriate negative emotions. For over thirty years, Ellis adhered to this appropriate vs. inappropriate division before adopting in 1994 Dryden's (1990) taxonomy of unhealthy and healthy negative emotions.

Ellis (1958a; Ellis et al., 1960) offered to his clients a relatively simple model of the development and maintenance of emotional disturbance, ABC: A represents the activating event which is mediated by irrational beliefs at B which, in turn, largely create emotional and behavioural consequences at C. (In the early 1970s, D for disputing in order to create a new and effective philosophy at E would be added to the ABCs.) As humans have the ability to think about their thinking, the model also demonstrates how they frequently develop secondary and/or tertiary emotional disturbances about their primary ones (e.g. anxiety about becoming depressed; ashamed of feeling anxious about being anxious) and thereby block or make it more difficult for themselves to work on these primary issues. In 1962 Ellis stressed the importance of routinely searching for these second- and third-order problems during assessment but stressed it even more later (Ellis, 1994a).

From the outset, REBT emphasized its humanistic and existential aspects, which included placing rationality in the service of achieving human happiness; favouring long-range rather than short-range hedonism to achieve a healthy balance between the pleasures of the moment and realizing long-term goals; stressing that humans have considerable, but not total, free will and choice in determining how they live their lives; assuming that humans are neither superhuman nor subhuman but fallible and can choose to accept themselves as worthwhile simply because they exist and not because of any external achievements. However, this concept of self-acceptance was still a measurement of sorts (e.g. an individual can say she is worthless because she is alive) and therefore conditional. Ellis (1971, 1973a) would later remove this pitfall and emphasize unconditional self-acceptance.

During this period, Ellis was still prone to accept the psychoanalytic view that an individual's fallacious and disturbance-creating ideas were instilled by his parents and the wider society and he then kept reindoctrinating himself with them. Even though he emphasized humans' biological pre-disposition to crooked thinking, Ellis did not fully develop this viewpoint until later decades when he hypothesized that our innate ability to disturb ourselves about familial and societal ideas is the real culprit rather than the ideas themselves (Ellis, 1976a, 1978a). In subsequent years REBT would largely concentrate on the perpetuation rather than the acquisition of emotional disturbance.

From the inception of REBT, Ellis sought to tackle a wide range of emotional disorders and offer his new therapeutic approach to the general public (as opposed to Beck's cognitive therapy, founded in the early 1960s, which initially focused on depression within a clinical setting). Some of his early titles aimed at a public audience include *How to Live with a Neurotic* (1957) and (with Robert Harper) *A Guide to Rational Living in an Irrational World* (1961). In 1959 Ellis founded the Institute for Rational Living (located in his own apartment), 'dedicated to treating and educating the public in Rational Therapy' (Wiener, 1988: 96). As well as originating and promulgating REBT, Ellis continued his career as a pioneering and outspoken sex therapist whose books on this subject, from the mid-1950s onwards, contained REBT principles and practices; these include *Sex without Guilt* (1958b) and *The Art and Science of Love* (1960). This aspect of Ellis's work diminished in the early 1980s.

Some critics of this new therapeutic approach accused it of ignoring emotions and behaviour as vehicles for constructive change in its 'narrow' concerns with only thought processes; others saw it as a form of rationalism (the philosophical view that knowledge of the world is obtained through reason alone). Both groups of critics were mistaken because REBT 'always had very strong evocative-emotive and behavioral components and from the start favored activity-oriented, therapeutic homework assignments, in vivo desensitization, and skill training' (Ellis and Bernard, 1985: 2). In order to try and avoid this confusion and convey more accurately his therapeutic method, Ellis in 1961 changed rational therapy's name to rational-emotive therapy (RET) because 'the term implies, as the theory of rational-emotive psychotherapy holds, that human thinking and emotions are, in some of their essences, the same thing, and that by changing the former one does change the latter' (Ellis, 1962: 122).

Rational-emotive therapy: 1961–93

The year 1962 was a milestone in REBT's development, with the publication of *Reason and Emotion in Psychotherapy* which pulled together and revised Ellis's earlier articles on REBT. This synthesis 'represented his first attempt to present his ideas on therapy in a systematic and comprehensive form, and can be considered an early classic with respect to modern cognitive-behavioural therapy' (Yankura and Dryden, 1994: 14). This book remains the main text for REBT practitioners (Ellis, 1994a) and, along with other REBT literature, 'led to the "cognitive revolution" in modern psycho-therapy, which followed about ten years after I started teaching REBT in 1955' (Ellis, 1994a: xiii). *Reason and Emotion in Psychotherapy* also set down three major insights into human disturbance which ever since have provided clients with a concise account of REBT and act as a lifelong guide to emotional problem-solving. These insights are: (1) emotional disturbance is largely created by irrational ideas: we mainly feel the way we think; (2) we remain disturbed in the present because we continually reindoctrinate ourselves with these ideas; (3) the only enduring way to overcome our problems is through persistent hard work and practice – to think, feel and act against our irrational ideas. These insights were later augmented by other ways humans perpetuate their psychological problems, e.g. the process of change is too hard to undertake (low frustration tolerance); secondary emotional problems (e.g. shame) block individuals from tackling their primary ones (e.g. anxiety); individuals predict failure before carrying out a goal-directed task (self-fulfilling prophecy).

While REBT was gathering more adherents, both professional and public, Ellis continued to refine its theory and practice. An early paper on the differences between intellectual and emotional insight showed that understanding of one's problems is usually insufficient to effect deep-rooted change unless accompanied by vigorous and sustained action against one's irrational ideas; in this way, one can both think and feel the efficacy of newly acquired rational beliefs (Ellis, 1963a). In the same year, Ellis used the medium of film to demonstrate REBT by appearing in *Gloria*. Along with Carl Rogers and Fritz Perls, he sought to provide therapeutic help for the eponymous client. *Gloria* has generally not provided good publicity for REBT because of Ellis's 'aggressive' and overly intellectual style in the film. Later films demonstrate Ellis's much more relaxed therapeutic style and the use of a multimodal approach to tackling emotional problems; these films are a more accurate depiction of REBT in practice (Bernard, 1986). Ellis later judged *Gloria* as 'the worst session of recorded psychotherapy I ever had' (Palmer and Ellis, 1993: 173). However, some counselling trainees and professionals still judge Ellis and REBT by what occurred over thirty years ago.

In 1965 Ellis moved the Institute out of his apartment and into a six-storey building in Manhattan. The building was now called the Institute for RET and has remained so ever since, despite RET's conversion to REBT in 1993. The Institute offers training programmes for mental health professionals, and workshops and courses for the general public including a Friday night workshop entitled 'Problems of Daily Living' (see Dryden and Backx, 1987). This workshop asks for volunteers from the audience to come on to the stage to discuss their problems with Ellis while the rest of the audience can absorb from this session REBT principles and practices to tackle their own problems. At the end of the session questions and discussion are invited from the audience. Such workshops underscored Ellis's belief that REBT was primarily a psychoeducational approach rather than a merely therapeutic one. Because of 'the ubiquity of emotional disturbance' (Ellis, 1980a: 10), Ellis hypothesizes that a 'public education policy of disseminating some of the main elements of RE[B]T to the general populace would effect a great deal of prophylaxis and treatment of emotional ills' (Ellis, 1980a: 11). Indeed, Ellis has frequently suggested that the 'psycho-educational aspects of RE[B]T are more likely to be important in the future than the psychotherapeutic aspects. It [REBT] had better encourage public education and public acceptance of its principles and practices' (quoted in Bernard, 1986: 271).

In 1966 REBT set up its own journal, which was called *Rational Living* until 1983, when it changed its name to the *Journal of Rational-Emotive Therapy*; in 1988 it became the *Journal of Rational-Emotive and Cognitive Behavior Therapy*. The journal 'seeks to provide a forum to stimulate research and discussion into the development and promulgation of Rational-Emotive Therapy (RET) and other forms of cognitive-behavioral therapy' (from the journal's statement of intent). Published by the Institute until 1984, in the following year it was taken over by Human Sciences Press but remains sponsored by the Institute for RET.

As well as seeking to educate emotionally the general public, Ellis (Ellis and Blum, 1967) also turned his attention to the workplace and advocated rational training as a method of helping 'people function more effectively in their work by actively teaching them certain basic principles of interpersonal relations which promote better self-understanding as well as increase insight into others'. The aim of rational training is to facilitate the development of more productive relations between management and labour. In the early 1970s, Ellis wrote a book for business executives, *Executive Leadership*, to show them how to deal effectively 'with the inanities and insanities of the organizational world' (1972a: 15) and to discover how they sabotaged their potential effectiveness. Eventually the Institute for RET established its own corporate affairs division to introduce the concepts of REBT into management training as well as, more ambitiously, to influence corporate cultures. REBT – when used in industry it is commonly called rational effectiveness training – focuses 'always on the relation of self-defeating beliefs to low productivity, not on irrationality and emotional consequences' (DiMattia, 1991: 309). Using the word 'therapy' in training programmes usually deters more potential applicants than it attracts.

REBT has always been eager to increase its stock of therapeutic techniques to help clients undermine and remove their often tenaciously held self-defeating beliefs. While others still saw REBT as mainly a cognitive approach, Ellis, before and after 1962, was busily introducing emotive-evocative methods into his practice: these included imagery (Maultsby and Ellis, 1974), role-playing, forceful coping statements, forceful disputing, humour, unconditional acceptance of clients as fallible human beings but not always of their behaviour (Ellis, 1965, 1973a), and his famous shame-attacking exercises (Ellis, 1969). These exercises encourage clients to act in a 'shameful' way (e.g. walking backwards down the street) in order to attract public ridicule or disapproval while at the same time learning to accept themselves for acting in such a manner. Behavioural methods added to REBT's armamentarium include exposure, *in vivo* desensitization (rapid rather than gradual), rewards and penalties, skill training, and assertiveness training. REBT was developing into a truly multimodal approach to constructive change, in contrast to Ellis's declaration in *Reason and Emotion in Psychotherapy* that 'this book will one-sidedly emphasize the rational techniques, while admitting the possible efficacy of other legitimate means of affecting disordered human emotions' (1962: 41).

REBT was increasing not only its range of techniques but also its therapeutic application. Influenced 'by the experiential and encounter movements of Will Schutz, Fritz Perls, and others', Ellis, in the late 1960s, 'incorporated some of their methods in individual and group sessions of REBT and, especially, in one- or two-day rational encounter marathons' (Ellis, 1994a: 48). The aim of the marathon is twofold: 'first, to provide maximum encountering experiences for all the group members; and second, to include a good measure of cognitive and action-oriented group psychotherapy that is designed not only to help the participants feel better but also to get better' (Ellis and Dryden, 1987: 180). The length of the marathon was eventually reduced from two days to a single day of fourteen hours, as any longer did not produce any discernible benefits.

The 1970s

In *Reason and Emotion in Psychotherapy* Ellis (1962) suggested that helping the parents of a disturbed child to become rational and problem focused was usually the best way to help the child. However, by the late 1960s he had become more optimistic about directly helping children to overcome their problems, and in 1970 he launched an ambitious project in emotional education and preventive psychotherapy, the Living School. This private school was located at the Institute for RET in New York and designed to teach ordinary schoolchildren the basic principles and practices of REBT alongside their normal academic curriculum. Such an emotional education programme, it was hypothesized, would help the children: 'if they work within this program for several years, they will have a significantly lesser chance of developing mild or severe personality maladjustment than they might otherwise commonly develop' (Ellis, 1973b). The school's teachers were supervised by REBT therapists. The experiment lasted only five years due to a high turnover rate as parents sent their children to bigger and better equipped schools – the Living School wanted to monitor the progress of the children from the first grade (6 years old) to the eighth. Such a turnover rate interfered with the long-term follow-up studies (also there was no control group to compare the children with), so the school was closed in 1975. REBT educational materials such as Ann Vernon's (1989) *Thinking, Feeling, Behaving* are used in more traditional American schools and there is nowadays a greater emphasis within REBT on working with children and adolescents in general (DiGiuseppe, 1977; Knaus, 1977; Knaus and Haberstroh, 1993).

REBT had always sought to teach clients self-acceptance rather than self-esteem, as the latter concept placed intrinsic worth on external achievement. However, as we noted previously in this chapter, Ellis's earlier formulation of self-acceptance still contained an element of self-measurement. This was finally eliminated when Ellis (1971, 1973a) advocated that clients should strive for unconditional self-acceptance, i.e. they should refuse to rate themselves in any way whatsoever, but only rate their specific traits, actions and performances. This kind of rating helps individuals to decide if particular traits or deeds aid or interfere with their goal-seeking behaviour. Unconditional self-acceptance became the 'elegant' solution (Ellis, 1976b) to the problem of self-worth as Ellis advises individuals to 'abolish most of what we normally call your human ego and retain those parts of it which you can empirically verify and fairly accurately define' (1976b: 6). The 'inelegant' solution to self-rating (if individuals were unable to achieve the elegant one) was to choose to rate themselves as good or worthwhile simply because they were human and alive. The elegant solution to human emotional disturbance remains one of the most difficult concepts for clients not only to understand but also to internalize.

REBT has long argued that its aim in therapy is not merely the removal of clients' presenting symptoms, but to effect a deep-seated change in their basic philosophies of living (Ellis, 1963b). To this end, REBT teaches clients not only how to feel better through amelioration of disturbed emotional states (e.g. depression, guilt) but also how to get better by identifying and removing the core disturbance-creating beliefs (Ellis, 1972b). Feeling better usually produces a palliative and short-term solution to clients' problems, while getting better frequently brings about a philosophical and enduring one. As we shall see later, therapies which only emphasize feeling better can be considered inefficient and potentially harmful.

Ellis (1973c) stresses that the REBT therapist is primarily a teacher who shows clients the ABCDE model of the acquisition, maintenance and eventual remediation of emotional disturbance. Such a process puts the therapist in the role of an authoritative (but not authoritarian) teacher, though some REBT therapists might demur at the thought of teachers making 'a forthright, unequivocal attack on his [client's] general and specific irrational ideas and to try to induce him to adopt more rational views' (Ellis, 1962: 94) and prefer an approach more subtle and less forceful than full-frontal assault. Though Ellis (1962, 1977a) argues that a vigorous and challenging active-directive approach to therapy rather than a passive, non-directive one is more likely to help clients overcome their problems, REBT therapists generally adopt an approach that suits their preferences and personality styles.

A notable addition in the 1970s to REBT's emotive-evocative methods was rational-emotive imagery (Maultsby and Ellis, 1974) which Ellis adapted from Maultsby. In Ellis's version, a client is asked, for example, to imagine vividly being rejected by his girlfriend and to let himself experience what he spontaneously feels (such as anger) and then really implode that emotion. Without changing any details of the imagined rejection, the client is then asked to feel only displeased at what is happening rather than angry about the rejection. When asked by the therapist how he accomplished this, the client ideally responds that he modified his disturbance-producing cognitions. Rational-emotive imagery 'can serve as an in-session demonstration to clients that they can exert control over their feelings, and that focusing on changing some aspect of their thinking represents the most effective and efficient way of doing so' (Yankura and Dryden, 1990: 16). This technique is frequently given to clients as a homework task.

One of the major philosophical influences on the development of REBT was the work of the general semanticists (e.g. Korzybski, 1993). They considered the important ways in which language influences thought, which, in turn, affects emotions. The imprecise or careless use of language can lead to overgeneralization, as when individuals equate themselves with an action, trait or event: e.g. 'I am a failure because I failed my driving test.' Known in general semantics as 'the is of identity', this form of linguistic inaccuracy would be changed by omitting the verb 'to be' and the preferred mode of expression might be 'It is true that I failed my driving test but this fact does not make me a failure as a person.' The written form of this semantic position is called e-prime and during the 1970s Ellis wrote four books in this style (e.g. *Anger – How to Live With and Without It*, 1977a). According to Wessler and Wessler, 'while this practice underscored his position against global evaluations of anything, especially of the self, it proved to be an awkward mode of writing, and he later abandoned the practice. Although e-prime is a cumbersome mode of writing, and nearly impossible to speak, the basic notion remains an important feature of RE[B]T' (1980: 249).

Ellis originally created REBT on the basis of logical positivism, 'a modern view of science which was prevalent in the US and Europe in the 1950s' (Ellis, 1994a: 405). This doctrine argued that any statement or proposition would be excluded as meaningless if it was not directly verifiable: for example, it would be impossible to prove conclusively an individual's universal claim that 'I'm always going to be rejected in life.' Though REBT has always attempted to be scientifically minded in constructing its theories and monitoring its practice, Ellis eventually came to the conclusion 'that scientific statements are not empirically confirmable' (quoted in Jacobs, 1989: 184) and therefore abandoned logical positivism. Since 1976, 'it [REBT] is close to Popper's (1962, 1985) critical realism . . . which focuses on critically assessing theories and trying to learn by falsifying them rather than on striving for their "truth" or "validity"' (Ellis, 1993a: 10). In the above example, it only takes one instance where the individual is not rejected to falsify her claim and thus allow the therapist to start 'chipping away' at her irrational beliefs. The principle of falsifiability is also applied to her rational beliefs (wishes and desires): these are seen as self-helping and goal-oriented until the time experience and evidence suggest the opposite.

From the inception of REBT, Ellis has argued that human beings have a biologically rooted propensity towards crooked thinking and emotional disturbance (though in REBT's early phase, Ellis emphasized a largely environmentally based view of disturbance). This theory of biological predisposition to irrationality set REBT apart, then and now, from other major psychotherapeutic approaches which usually stress environmental conditioning or social learning theories. Accumulated clinical experience, among other factors, reinforced Ellis's biological view of disturbance and in a 1976 paper he presented evidence to support his hypothesis. This evidence includes the following: virtually all humans subscribe, at some time or another, to a greater or lesser degree, to some form of irrational thinking, e.g. the belief that people cannot be happy without love; no society or culture which has ever been studied is devoid of irrational beliefs; many of the self-defeating ideas that individuals hold run counter to the self-helping teachings of parents, peers, the mass media, etc., e.g. parents may teach their children to work hard to get ahead in life but instead of heeding this advice, some choose to pursue a downward path of apathy and idleness; just because individuals acknowledge that they adhere to dysfunctional beliefs and behaviours does not necessarily mean they will relinquish them, e.g. 'I know it is silly to think you can be a perfect human being but why not?'; people revert to self-destructive patterns of behaviour after working hard to give them up, e.g. alcoholism. Ellis also hypothesized that we have a second biologically based tendency to think rationally and therefore are able to examine our irrational ideas in order to counteract their influence on our lives.

Another important development in REBT that was not clearly seen and articulated until the 1970s was the centrality of the musts in emotional disturbance. Ellis (1994a) realized from the start of REBT that underneath clients' irrational ideas lay rigid musts and shoulds, e.g. 'If I don't do well at this task, as I absolutely must do, then I'm a complete failure', that seemed to create and maintain these irrational ideas. But, he says, he only saw this 'musturbatory' influence faintly and incompletely. When he compared REBT with Beck's cognitive therapy and its emphasis on automatic thoughts (distorted negative inferences) and illogical thinking but which accorded no particular significance to musts in mainly creating emotional disturbance, 'I [Ellis] clearly (and strongly) began to realize the primacy of people's Jehovian musts and saw how they usually underlay their other dysfunctional beliefs' (1994a: xvii).

Ellis (1977b) eventually collapsed his ten or so major irrational beliefs into three basic musturbatory categories: demands on self – 'I must . . .'; demands on others – 'You must . . .'; demands on the world/life conditions – 'Life conditions must . . .'. Ellis suggests that what 'we normally call "emotional disturbance", "neurosis", or "mental illness", then, largely consists of demandingness – or what I now refer to as musturbation' (1977b: 27). From these basic musts flow three major derivatives (though these were not seen as logical deductions from the musts until the 1980s): awfulizing – seeing events as worse than they could conceivably be; I can't-stand-it-itis (low frustration tolerance) – the perceived inability to tolerate discomfort in life; damnation – labelling oneself or others as worthless, useless, inadequate, etc. on the basis of failures and rejections in life. Derivatives play an important role in contributing to self-defeating emotions and behaviours, but REBT generally regards them as secondary and musts as primary in the creation of emotional disturbance.

In order for people to achieve a profound philosophical change in their lives (surrendering musturbatory thinking and replacing it with a preferential outlook), Ellis (1977b) advocates the logico-empirical method of scientific debate in challenging irrational beliefs and identifies several important steps in this. First, detecting – this refers to discovering one's disturbance-producing ideas, mainly in the form of rigid musts and shoulds; as Ellis's franglais has it: '*cherchez* [look for] *les* "musts", *cherchez les* "shoulds"'. Second, debating – this requires individuals to challenge their detected musts and shoulds to determine if they are logical, realistic and pragmatic (helpful) and discard them if they are not. Third, discriminating – this consists of distinguishing between irrational beliefs with their self-defeating consequences and rational beliefs with their self-helping nature. Fourth, defining – this refers to semantic precision in the use of language and the avoidance of disturbance-generating overgeneralizations. For example, 'Because I failed to get this job, I'll never get another one' is more accurately translated as, 'It is a fact that I didn't get this job but this certainly does not mean that I will never get another one.' Ellis (1979a) later devised a formal method of challenging self-defeating ideas known as DIBS (Disputing

Irrational Beliefs) which uses forms to guide clients through the ABCDE model of emotional disturbance and its amelioration.

One of the major causes of human disturbance, Ellis (1977c) hypothesizes, is individuals taking themselves and their ideas too seriously. An important means of undermining clients' irrational thinking is by poking fun at it (but not at the clients themselves). Humorous techniques include puns, witticisms, irony, slogans, reduction to absurdity of dysfunctional ideas, and paradoxical intention. Humour in therapy can help clients to, among other things, 'lighten the load' while still absorbing rational concepts; become more objective observers of how they disturb themselves and less liable to keep on repeating this process; build rapport with the therapist and thereby construct a productive working alliance. When humour is used it should be guided by a clinical rationale, not used for the purpose of the therapist's enjoyment. Humour should be omitted from therapy if the client objects to it. One of Ellis's (1977d) most famous comical interventions is his rational humorous songs. These are popular songs with lyrics rewritten in order to impart a self-helping philosophy of living or to attack a self-defeating one, e.g. 'Perfect Rationality' set to the tune of Luigi Denza's 'Finiculi Finicula'. The songs, like advertising jingles, are designed 'to repetitively go around and around in your patients' heads . . . and thereby to have their messages sink in and influence the person who sings them aloud or internally "hears" them' (Ellis and Abrahms, 1978: 147). The songs Ellis has rewritten are of a certain vintage, and REBT therapists may need to use modern songs for their younger clients.

Ellis (1962, 1973b) has long argued that a forceful and confrontational approach to therapy is usually the best means of promoting constructive change; the assumption in REBT is that those of its practitioners who have certain characteristics will produce better client outcomes than REBT therapists who lack them. Ellis (1978b) suggests what some of these characteristics might be, including: the ability to work comfortably within a structured (but not inflexible) format; having a philosophical bent towards disputation and being scientifically minded in analysing the evidence for and against clients' beliefs; working generally in a strong active-directive manner in helping clients to tackle their problems; not needing the love or approval of clients, and fearing neither therapeutic failure nor taking calculated risks if impasses in therapy occur; working comfortably within a multimodal approach to therapy and not adhering rigidly to any one modality. Despite Ellis's preferred therapeutic approach, some REBT practitioners may lack some of the above characteristics or may modify REBT to suit their own personality traits, so 'whether such modification of the preferred practice of RE[B]T is effective is a question awaiting empirical enquiry' (Ellis and Dryden, 1987: 32).

While REBT has always implied a theory of personality originating from its theory of personality disturbance and change (Ellis, 1962, 1977e), it was not until the late 1970s that Ellis (1978a) explicitly offered one. First, he suggests how crooked thinking impairs many personality theories, e.g. environmental prejudices – because an individual has learned to behave badly she is not responsible for continuing to act badly, or environmental conditions have to change before she can; overemphasis on dramatic incidents from the past – the belief that a past trauma (e.g. sexual abuse) accounts completely for an individual's present self-defeating behaviour rather than other additional factors. REBT's theory of personality formation rests largely on how individuals appraise themselves, others and the world and 'hypothesizes that probably 80% of the variance of human behaviour rests on biological bases and about 20% on environmental training' (1978a: 41). For example, we usually accept and follow familial and societal standards, but because of our innate ability to disturb ourselves we may transmute these standards into dogmatic musts and shoulds that eventually prove more self-defeating than self-helping: e.g. cultural encouragement that being slim equates with confidence and sexual success is converted into a demand that one must be thin to be happy, which then leads to the development of anorexia nervosa. REBT's 'emphasis on the importance of the biological bases of human behavior attempts to balance the environmentalist position, which has dominated personality and therapy theory for the last half century' (1978a: 43).

From the outset of REBT, Ellis emphasized the centrality of ego disturbance in clients' problems, i.e. damning themselves on the basis of their failures and rejections in life. Through clinical observation he developed another equally important theory of disturbance: discomfort anxiety or low frustration tolerance (Ellis, 1979b, 1980b): the worry that individuals experience when anticipating pain or unpleasantness and therefore demand that this discomfort must not occur. Discomfort anxiety was eventually absorbed into a broader category called 'discomfort disturbance' when it was realized that other disturbed emotional states had low frustration tolerance aspects, e.g. discomfort depression (Dryden, 1987) and discomfort anger (Dryden, 1994). Ego and discomfort disturbance are discrete entities but frequently interact, as when an individual damns herself as a failure because she is unable to tolerate difficult working conditions. Ellis asserts that ego and discomfort disturbance are the 'two main sources of just about all neurosis' (quoted in Dryden, 1991: 28).

Clients can become so habituated to irrational ideas that they cling tenaciously to them while acknowledging how counterproductive they are, e.g. a client who believes 'I must be liked otherwise I'm no good' always tries to please everyone even though he remains friendless. In order to tackle this problem, Ellis (1979c) advises therapists to teach their clients how to combat their self-defeating ideas through the use of force and energy. Such an attack can be launched on a multimodal front: cognitive (powerful disputation), emotive (shame-attacking exercises), behavioural (flooding), imaginal (rational-emotive imagery). Clients who only challenge their dysfunctional beliefs in a milk-and-water fashion rather than in a vigorous way run the considerable risk of being marooned at the level of intellectual insight (rational beliefs lightly and intermittently held) instead of reaching emotional insight (rational beliefs deeply and consistently held).

The 1980s

The year 1980 produced a clutch of excellent and influential REBT texts aimed at trainee and experienced REBT practitioners (most of the REBT books up to that point had been directed at a non-professional audience). These works include *The Principles and Practice of Rational-Emotive Therapy* (Wessler and Wessler, 1980), *Rational-Emotive Therapy: A Skills-Based Approach* (Grieger and Boyd, 1980), *A Practitioner's Guide to Rational-Emotive Therapy* (Walen et al., 1980) and *Brief Counseling with RET* (Hauck, 1980). The Wesslers introduced an expanded ABC model called the emotional episode which is broken down into eight steps. Part of the activating event (A) includes inferences people make about As and these inferences can be linked. However, it is appraisals (rigid or flexible) at B of these inferences that actually determine people's emotional and behavioural reactions at C. Grieger and Boyd, echoing Ellis (1979c), largely eschewed traditional clinical assessment procedures (such as extensive history-taking and projective tests e.g. Rorschach) in favour of understanding clients' presenting problems within the ABC framework. Such a process can take, 'depending upon the therapist's expertise and the complexity of the client's problems . . . from ten minutes to several sessions' (Grieger and Boyd, 1980: 52). Walen et al. provided the first manual for the therapist-in-training as 'leading a client successfully through the RE[B]T maze often sounds a lot easier than it actually is' (1980: xiii). Hauck presented the best rational arguments to deploy against clients' irrational ideas, 'which are so reasonable, so irrefutably right, that an opposing idea cannot exist once the rational one has been grasped' (1980: 117). These books also demonstrated a broadening REBT authorship rather than the narrow focus on Ellis as largely the sole exponent of REBT.

As a pioneering form of cognitive-behaviour therapy (CBT) and one of the most influential within the field – Mahoney (1987) lists seventeen current cognitive therapies – Ellis (1980c) details the differences between REBT and other CBT approaches. These differences include: seeking enduring and profound philosophical change (uprooting musturbatory thinking) rather than mere symptom removal through inferential change, thereby leaving disturbance-producing ideas intact; stressing unconditional self-acceptance and avoiding conditional self-esteem; according low frustration tolerance a central rather than a relatively peripheral role in the creation of emotional disturbance; discriminating keenly between self-defeating (e.g. anxiety) and self-helping (concern, the healthy alternative) emotions which are, along with their cognitive correlates, located on separate continua rather than along a single continuum; standing alone among other CBT approaches in emphasizing the biologically rooted nature of human irrationality and the consequent need to fight against it with force and energy. While agreeing with most of these differences, the authors would like to stress that Beck's cognitive therapy also strives for enduring and fundamental attitudinal change.

Because of Ellis's profound disenchantment with what he regarded as psychoanalysis's inefficiency and ineffectiveness, he left the fold and eventually founded REBT. In striving for efficiency in therapy, REBT seeks to identify, challenge and change as rapidly as possible clients' disturbance-creating ideas in order to, ideally, effect profound philosophical change in their lives. Ellis (1980d) lists what he considers are the characteristics of efficient therapy. *Brevity* – achieving constructive change within a relatively short timescale. *Depth-centredness* – focusing on the deeply rooted causes of clients' presenting problems as well as increasing their understanding of how they disturb themselves; in REBT, this would be core musturbatory ideologies they adhere to. *Pervasiveness* – dealing not only with clients' presenting symptoms but also with other problem areas in their lives; in this sense, REBT equips them with a lifelong therapeutic approach. *Extensiveness* – helping clients through 'intensive' therapy to reduce their emotional distress and through 'extensive' therapy to maximize their potential for a happier and more fulfilling life. *Thoroughgoingness* – selecting multimodal methods (cognitive, emotive, behavioural and imaginal) to help therapists achieve better client outcomes. *Maintenance of therapeutic progress* – helping clients to achieve symptom removal and enduring constructive change after formal therapy has ended. *Prevention* – showing clients how they disturb themselves and how to tackle it in order to achieve emotional stability in facing future problems. Homework tasks are an important feature of efficiency as they encourage clients to gain both competence and confidence in facing their problems outside of therapy sessions and decrease the likelihood of clients becoming dependent on the therapist; homework also provides the bridge between intellectual and emotional insight into their problems. Ellis's zest for efficiency in psychotherapy may derive from his somewhat humorous claim that 'I have a gene for efficiency' (1993a: 12).

As well as expounding on the characteristics of efficient therapy, Ellis (1982) describes therapeutic methods which he considers to be inefficient, unhelpful or iatrogenic (symptoms induced or exacerbated inadvertently by the therapist or his/her treatment). Such methods include the following: giving excessive warmth and approval to clients may reinforce their dire needs for these things and increase their dependence on the therapist; allowing clients to talk incessantly about their feelings instead of encouraging them to examine the ideas largely creating these feelings; expressing suppressed emotions (e.g. anger) often in dramatic ways to achieve catharsis, which may provide respite from but not removal of these emotions as the disturbance-creating ideas are strengthened through frequent catharsis; employing gradual desensitization techniques rather than implosive ones can reinforce clients' low frustration tolerance of feared objects or situations; putting the locus of control for change on to an external force or higher power (e.g. Alcoholics Anonymous) rather than within the individual. Such methods distract, interfere with or prevent clients from becoming their own self-therapist; this role usually enables them to achieve effective results from present and future problem-solving.

Like any other therapeutic approach, REBT has its share of failures with clients. Ellis (1983) lists the characteristics of clients who failed in REBT (even though some of them initially appeared good candidates for therapy) including clients who were: highly disturbed and therefore unable or unwilling to show any persistence in disputing their irrational beliefs; angry, rebellious, or resistant to what was required of them (e.g. taking responsibility for their emotional problems) and generally avoiding the hard and uncomfortable work involved in the change process. Failures in REBT also result from therapist errors, actions or characteristics such as lack of force and energy in encouraging clients to surrender their musturbatory thinking; getting quickly discouraged or impatient with difficult clients because of their own low frustration tolerance beliefs; focusing too heavily on REBT's cognitive aspects and thereby neglecting its multimodal approach to facilitate optimum change. Ellis suggests that more research needs to be undertaken in the area of REBT failures so that its efficacy and efficiency can be significantly improved.

REBT's group therapy activities were expanded in 1984 with the creation of day-long rational-emotive training intensives. These draw on the est (Erhard Seminars Training) movement and other intensive group procedures, 'but throwing out the cultish and mystical procedures that they often include' (Ellis, 1994a: 49), and frequently attract over 200 participants. Group members receive cognitive lectures and undertake experiential and behavioural tasks. As preliminary research findings 'on several hundred participants indicate, [these methods] can produce favorable results in a single eight-hour large-scale intensive' (Ellis and Dryden, 1987: 155).

Though Ellis had vast clinical experience of resistance in therapy, it was not until the 1980s that he 'trained his sights' on the subject in his writings and suggested that 'overcoming clients' resistance to therapeutic change is in some ways the most important problem of psychotherapy' (1985a: 1). Ellis distinguishes between healthy and pathological forms of resistance. An example of the former is a client who refuses to accept the therapist's rigid insistence that her present depression is caused by her parents' divorce. The latter include fear of discomfort – that change is too hard and uncomfortable to endure; fear of disclosure and shame – that by revealing shameful thoughts and deeds clients will be condemned by their therapist; fear of success – actually, fear of subsequent failure after initial therapeutic success. Ellis also examines therapists' resistance which can impede progress if they subscribe to certain irrational beliefs, e.g. 'I have to be successful with all my clients practically all the time'; 'I have to be greatly respected and loved by all my clients'. If therapeutic movement rather than impasse is to occur, Ellis urges both clients and therapists to use force and energy in challenging and changing their resistance-creating beliefs.

REBT asserts that a philosophy based on preferences (including wishes, wants, desires, hopes) will usually lead to psychological health because these beliefs are adaptable, will minimize emotional disturbance and aid goal attainment. Over the previous decades Ellis had been establishing and increasing the criteria underpinning psychological health (or, rather, his version of it) until he reached thirteen (Ellis and Bernard, 1985). The thirteen criteria are: *self-interest* – usually putting one's own interests ahead of others'; *social interest* – making one's goals both personally and socially responsible; *self-direction* – taking responsibility for one's own life without depending heavily on the support of others; *high frustration tolerance* – the ability to endure discomfort and stress in one's life without becoming emotionally disturbed about it; *flexibility* – being open-minded and adaptable in one's thoughts and actions; *acceptance of uncertainty* – that one can remain relatively happy despite not knowing for sure what the future will bring; *commitment to creative pursuits* – having external interests rather than indulging in excessive introspection; *scientific thinking* – examining the evidence for and against our beliefs in order to introduce a greater self-helping objectivity into our lives; *self-acceptance* – choosing to accept ourselves unconditionally rather than linking such acceptance to external factors; *risk-taking* – making life more exciting or adventurous through calculated rather than foolish risks; *long-range hedonism* – achieving a balance between enjoying the pleasures of the moment and planning constructively for the future; *non-utopianism* – accepting what is empirically evident and achievable in life rather than pursuing the chimera of finding utopia or reaching self-perfection; *self-responsibility for own emotional disturbance* – accepting that one is largely responsible for creating one's emotional upsets instead of blaming others or environmental conditions. The above list is not meant to be definitive and no doubt will be added to.

While Ellis has always advocated the use of vigorous methods (e.g. shame-attacking exercises) to challenge clients' self-defeating ideas, Dryden (1986) introduced the concept of vivid methods for the same purpose. Vivid REBT is aimed at approaching therapy in a striking, lively, fresh and memorable way. Examples of vivid REBT include: flamboyant therapist actions – e.g. the therapist flinging herself to the floor and barking like a dog in order to teach the client that behaving stupidly does not make you a stupid person; therapist as raconteur – using stories, jokes, parables, poems, aphorisms, etc. to communicate rational concepts to clients; in-session simulation – attempting to recreate in therapy the conditions or circumstances which engender the client's problems, e.g. asking a client to maintain eye contact when he is anxious to avoid it in order to uncover his anxiogenic thinking. The indiscriminate use of vivid REBT methods can lead some clients to feel overwhelmed by such a 'dazzling' display and so it will have little or no therapeutic impact on them.

REBT therapists agree that empathy, genuineness and unconditional positive regard (or REBT's version of this last quality, unconditional acceptance) are the core conditions of therapy. Golden and Dryden (1986), influenced by the work of Bordin (1979), suggest other components which are also needed to construct a therapeutic alliance. These are: *bonds* – a bonded relationship between the therapist and client is established in the latter's preferred interpersonal and learning style in order to promote constructive change, e.g. a formal counselling approach based on the therapist's expertise; *goals* – the client's goals for change are made clear and specific rather than vague or assumed, e.g. 'I want to overcome this guilt' as opposed to 'I want to discover my true self'; *tasks* – both the therapist and the client have tasks to perform, e.g. the therapist structures the counselling process and the client carries out homework assignments. REBT hypothesizes that greater therapeutic benefits are more likely to be achieved if therapists pay attention to the requirements of these alliance domains.

REBT therapists encourage their clients to, ideally, strive for an enduring and profound philosophical change in their lives, i.e. surrendering musturbatory thinking and internalizing a rational outlook. In order to achieve a philosophical change at the specific or general level, Ellis and Dryden (1987) advise clients to recognize that they largely create their own psychological disturbances; realize that they have the ability to reduce significantly their disturbances; understand that these disturbances largely stem from irrational thinking; detect these irrational ideas and discriminate them from rational ideas; dispute the irrational ideas by using the logico-empirical methods of science; work hard to internalize their newly acquired rational beliefs through multimodal methods of change; realize that the change process is a lifelong commitment. Clients who are unable, for whatever reason, to effect a philosophical change are switched to a non-philosophical approach, e.g. challenging and changing a client's inference such as 'My wife is going to leave me' rather than the irrational belief from which it derives: 'My wife absolutely must not leave me.'

As Ellis has always been interested in providing clients with efficient therapy, he turned his attention in 1989 to the issue of consumerism in psychotherapy, i.e. the extent to which clients' interests are served by the profession of counselling. He identifies several forms of ineffective consumerism. Self-defeating consumerism of clients – they pick a therapy which will help them to feel better but not to get better, so their disturbance-creating ideas are left intact. Ineffective consumerism of psychotherapists – e.g. clients may actually get worse in therapy because therapists, who believe they need the approval of their clients, will refuse or be reluctant to push clients to undertake the hard work usually associated with constructive change. Ineffective consumerism in cognitive-behavioural therapies – e.g. unlike REBT, these approaches usually involve only disputing clients' distorted and negative inferences rather than removing the philosophical core (absolute musts and shoulds) of their emotional disturbances. Drawing upon his own practice in REBT, Ellis suggests various ways of tackling ineffective consumerism in psychotherapy, including: therapists paying attention to the counselling research literature in order to be aware of which techniques are deemed to be effective and which are not; therapists being alert to and challenging clients' desires for therapeutic methods that usually only bring relief from but not removal of their psychological problems. By following these guidelines, Ellis avers, therapists can maximize their helpfulness to clients.

During the 1980s and early 1990s REBT produced practitioner guides to tackling various clinical problems: alcohol and substance abuse (Ellis et al., 1988); anxiety disorders (Warren and Zgourides, 1991); childhood and adolescence (Ellis and Bernard, 1983; Bernard and Joyce, 1984). Guides were also produced on REBT's application to different treatment modalities: individual therapy (Dryden, 1987), couples counselling (Ellis et al., 1989), family therapy (Huber and Baruth, 1989). The self-help literature continued to flourish including Ellis's (1988) *How to Stubbornly Refuse to Make Yourself Miserable About Anything – Yes, Anything!* This book sought to teach, or at least its title reflected, a super-elegant solution to rational living (Weinrach and Ellis, 1980). This solution involves a decrease in the level of distress usually found in any presenting problem as well as individuals becoming less disturbable in the future because they have achieved an enduringly profound philosophical change. As no human being, including Albert Ellis, the founder of REBT, is expected to become totally undisturbable for any sustained period, the book is likely to help readers to make themselves less disturbable but hardly undisturbable.

A novel application of REBT was its use in underpinning the programme of rational recovery (RR), a self-help group for individuals recovering from alcoholism and a rival to the dominant approach in the field, that of Alcoholics Anonymous (AA). Differences between the two groups include the following: RR puts the locus of control for change within the individual while AA invests it in a higher power (e.g. God, the AA group); RR sees alcoholism as a self-destructive personal philosophy of living as opposed to the AA's view of it as a disease process; RR emphasizes individuals getting over alcoholism but still remaining vulnerable, while the AA stresses that they are lifelong recovering alcoholics, thereby confirming their self-image. Trimpey (1989) urges his readers in *The Small Book* to 'see how quickly we can let the nation know that it's time for a Rational Recovery (RR) program everywhere an AA group is found' (1989: 7). Although RR now focuses less on REBT methods, a new organization, Self-Management and Recovery Training (SMART), is closely involved with REBT.

The 1990s

During the late 1980s, Ellis became embroiled in a controversy when some cognitive-behavioural theorists (Guidano, 1988; Mahoney, 1988) asserted that cognitive psychotherapy could be divided into two camps: rationalist and constructivist. REBT has been placed in the rationalist camp, which Ellis takes great exception to as REBT 'is not only non-rationalist but . . . in several important respects more constructivist . . . than just about all the other cognitive therapies, including those of Guidano (1988) and Mahoney (1988)' (1990: 169). Evidence to buttress Ellis's counter-assertion includes the following: REBT 'posits no absolutistic or invariant criteria of ration-ality' (Ellis, 1990: 176) but, instead, views rationality as relative and self-helping to each person's goal-directed beliefs; Ellis (1962) has always em-phasized that thinking, feeling and behaving are interdependent processes for acquiring and validating knowledge rather than reason alone as the only source; REBT strives to effect deep personality change in individuals by encouraging them to surrender their core disturbance-creating musts and shoulds rather than focusing on disputing their distorted inferences to achieve only superficial change. Ellis suggests that this dichotomy of cog-nitive psychotherapy is neither helpful nor accurate.

The ABCDE model of the acquisition, maintenance and eventual amelioration of emotional disturbance is the cornerstone of REBT theory and practice. However, the sequential steps involved in applying this model were not always clearly delineated. In order to bring greater clarity to this process, Dryden and DiGiuseppe (1990) developed the thirteen-step REBT counselling sequence. The sequence is: ask for a problem(s) and assess its A and C elements (steps 1–5); teach the B–C connection that beliefs largely lead to emotional consequences and relate this to the client's emotional disturbance (steps 6–8); dispute the client's irrational beliefs and show him how to deepen his conviction in his newly acquired rational beliefs through homework tasks which are reviewed at the next session (steps 9–12); in order to internalize his new rational outlook, the client challenges his irrational beliefs in a variety of problematic situations (step 13). Dryden (Dryden et al., 1993: 10) states that the thirteen steps 'comprise the effective and efficient practice of RE[B]T'.

Ellis (1962) had divided emotions in REBT into 'appropriate' and 'in-appropriate' negative states (see p. 214). Not all REBT therapists agree with, and some object to, this emotional classification. Dryden (1990) offers his own taxonomy of unhealthy and healthy negative emotions (e.g. anxiety vs. concern; depression vs. sadness) as a more sophisticated account of individuals' reactions to unpleasant or stressful life events. Unhealthy nega-tive emotions interfere with or block goal attainment, decrease the ability to enjoy life, and lead to self-defeating behaviour. Healthy negative emotions, on the other hand, while still signalling some degree of emotional upset, act as a stimulus towards goal attainment, increase the ability to enjoy life, and lead to self-helping behaviour. Ellis eventually adopted Dryden's classifi-cation system in 1994 after being persuaded of its merits.

Disputing clients' irrational ideas is the principal activity of REBT thera-pists but can be undertaken, by both trainee and experienced counsellors, in a haphazard, cursory or arbitrary fashion rather than by following clearly defined disputing strategies. DiGiuseppe proposes comprehensive cognitive disputing as a method of 'provid[ing] a blueprint for the process of disputing' (1991: 173). This blueprint entails challenging clients' irrational beliefs along logical, empirical and pragmatic lines and constructing rational alternatives (the nature of the dispute); using Socratic, didactic, humorous and metaphorical interventions because the form of the argument presented is as important as its content (rhetorical disputing styles); tackling irrational beliefs held in specific contexts and at the general plane (level of abstraction); disputing clients' musts (demandingness) and the relevant derivatives from the musts without assuming that challenging one irrational idea will automatically or necessarily lead to rational changes in other irrational beliefs (multiple irrational belief processes). DiGiuseppe suggests that comprehensive cognitive disputing is a powerful addition to the therapist's armamentarium.

When the ABC model was initially presented (Ellis, 1958a, 1962) it was a relatively simple explanation of emotional disturbance. Since that time the model has been expanded and refined (DiGiuseppe, 1986; Ellis, 1969, 1973a; Wessler and Wessler, 1980); but Ellis (1985b: 313) noted that the model was still 'oversimplified and omits salient information about human disturbance and its treatment' and therefore he expanded again the ABCs of REBT. Ellis (1991), among other things, teases out the complex interactions of As, Bs and Cs, e.g. a woman who believes (B) 'I must always be approved of by others' turns a friend's mild rebuke at A into outright rejection and thereby experiences depression rather than sadness at C; a man's prior irrational beliefs (e.g. 'I must always succeed') are brought to new As (e.g. a delay in receiving his examination results) and encourage him to distort his view of them thereby strengthening his disturbance-producing ideas (in this example, his fear of failure). Ellis speculates that one day he may write a book on the ABCs of REBT in order to do full justice to them.

Rational emotive behaviour therapy: 1993–

The name change in 1993 from rational-emotive therapy to rational emotive behaviour therapy brought REBT full circle 'because it [RET] really has always been highly cognitive, very emotive and particularly behavioral' (Ellis, 1993b: 2). The new name accurately reflects REBT's long-standing trimodal approach to tackling emotional disturbance, namely, that individuals have to think, feel and act against their irrational beliefs if constructive change is to occur in their lives. Ellis suggested that some REBT practitioners would not be enthusiastic about the name change and is characteristically forthright in his reply: 'Tough – but not awful!'

In 1994 Ellis produced a collection of papers on major clinical disorders. An REBT theory of post-traumatic stress disorder (PTSD) recognizes, along with other cognitive-behavioural therapies (CBT), 'that PTSD victims (e.g. of rape, a car crash) at least partly create their severe distress by holding dysfunctional or irrational Beliefs (iBs) and that to alleviate their overwhelming fears they had better be treated with cognitive restructuring plus exposure' (Ellis, 1994b: 13). Ellis asserts that most CBT approaches to PTSD follow an information-processing model which only challenges clients' unrealistic and illogical cognitive distortions (e.g. 'Because I was out on my own late at night, it's my fault I was raped') rather than focusing on and removing the underlying rigid musts and shoulds from which these distortions derive (e.g. 'Because I was out on my own late at night, which I absolutely should not have been, it's my fault I was raped and therefore I'm a totally worthless person'). Ellis suggests that 'REBT hypotheses about the "deeper" causes of PTSD would be interesting ones for empirical investigation' (1994b: 21).

As REBT is a cognitive approach to counselling, it is recommended that some clients may need an assessment of their cognitive functioning because 'cognitive deficits [e.g. attention, memory, thought organization] may have a neurological basis which may be responsible not only for the psychological problems but social skill deficits as well' (Walen et al., 1980: 34). Working with personality disorders, particularly borderline personalities, is notably difficult because they 'almost always have cognitive, emotive [e.g. highly-strung, histrionic], and behavioral [e.g. hyperactive, impulsive] organic deficits for various reasons, including hereditary predispositions' (Ellis, 1994c: 102). Added to these existing problems, such individuals may severely denigrate themselves on the basis of these innate deficits. Besides persistently and forcefully employing the usual multimodal methods, REBT therapists are advised to employ skill training as a means of ameliorating these deficits in order to improve both cognitive competence and therapeutic outcome.

Ellis (1962) originally considered obsessive-compulsive disorder (OCD) to be largely caused by individuals' demands for certainty (e.g. in order to be absolutely certain that she is both clean and approved of, a woman engages in endless handwashing after getting her hands dirty). Ellis's (1994d) view of the causation of OCD is now much more complex. He hypothesizes that individuals with OCD, like other personality disorders, usually have biological deficits (cognitive, emotive and behavioural), 'including the strong tendency to overfocus on a particular problem and to compulsively perform ritualistic and/or other habits (such as compulsively checking, handwashing, and locking doors)' (1994d: 123). OCDers exacerbate their original problems by developing low frustration tolerance (LFT) about them and condemning themselves for having these problems in the first place; in addition, they frequently develop secondary emotional problems (e.g. anxiety, depression) in relation to their OCD. Individuals with OCD are also prone to self-denigration and LFT over non-OCD-related frustrations and failures in their lives. Such a catalogue of problems and the usually considerable persistence needed in therapy to effect change in their lives leads Ellis to call them VDCs (very difficult customers). However, the use of

REBT's multimodal methods often combined with antidepressant medication can 'help clients reduce and minimize, but rarely entirely eliminate, their OCD behaviours' (Ellis, 1994d: 132).

Conclusion

The above chronological commentary on trends in REBT over the last forty years is not meant to be exhaustive but to provide a guide to some or most of the important developments during this period. Some trends have remained constant over the decades such as REBT's strong desire to reach the widest possible audience with its psychoeducational principles and practices; others have been abandoned, e.g. its former adherence to logical positivism as a basis for challenging clients' irrational ideas; and new ones are beginning to emerge or at least be hinted at such as Dryden's observation that 'to date no one has offered an integrated model that systematically applies rational-emotive concepts to the broad area of psychology' (1994: 5). As REBT moves towards the millennium, its dynamic and innovative approach to understanding and tackling human disturbance shows no signs of diminishing.

References

Bernard, M.E. (1986) *Staying Rational in an Irrational World: Albert Ellis and Rational-Emotive Therapy*. Carlton, Australia: McCulloch.

Bernard, M.E. and Joyce, M.R. (1984) *Rational-Emotive Therapy with Children and Adolescents*. New York: John Wiley & Sons.

Bordin, E. (1979) 'The generalizability of the psychoanalytic concept of the working alliance', *Psychotherapy: Theory, Research and Practice*, 16: 252–60.

DiGiuseppe, R. (1977) 'The use of behavior modification to establish rational self-statements in children', in A. Ellis and R. Grieger (eds), *Handbook of Rational-Emotive Therapy*, Vol. 1. New York: Springer.

DiGiuseppe, R. (1986) 'The implications of the philosophy of science for rational-emotive theory and therapy', *Psychotherapy*, 23(4): 634–9.

DiGiuseppe, R. (1991) 'Comprehensive cognitive disputing in RET', in M.E. Bernard (ed.), *Using Rational-Emotive Therapy Effectively: A Practitioner's Guide*. New York: Plenum.

DiMattia, D. (1991) 'Using RET effectively in the workplace', in M.E. Bernard (ed.), *Using Rational-Emotive Therapy Effectively: A Practitioner's Guide*. New York: Plenum.

Dryden, W. (1986) 'Vivid methods in rational-emotive therapy', in A. Ellis and R. Grieger (eds), *Handbook of Rational-Emotive Therapy*, Vol. 2. New York: Springer.

Dryden, W. (1987) *Counselling Individuals: The Rational-Emotive Approach*. London: Taylor & Francis.

Dryden, W. (1990) *Rational-Emotive Counselling in Action*. London: Sage Publications.

Dryden, W. (1991) *A Dialogue With Albert Ellis: Against Dogma*. Buckingham: Open University Press.

Dryden, W. (1994) *Invitation to Rational-Emotive Psychology*. London: Whurr.

Dryden, W. and Backx, W. (1987) 'Problems in living: the Friday night workshop', in W. Dryden, *Current Issues in Rational-Emotive Therapy*. London: Croom Helm.

Dryden, W. and DiGiuseppe, R. (1990) *A Primer on Rational-Emotive Therapy*. Champaign, IL: Research Press.

Dryden, W., Neenan, M. and Doggart, L. (1993) 'Professorial rationality: an interview with Windy Dryden', *The Rational-Emotive Therapist: Journal of the Association for Rational-Emotive Therapists*, 1(1): 5–11.

Ellis, A. (1957) *How to Live with a Neurotic*. New York: Crown.

Ellis, A. (1958a) 'Rational psychotherapy', *Journal of General Psychology*, 59: 37–49.

Ellis, A. (1958b) *Sex without Guilt*. Secaucus, NJ: Lyle Stuart.

Ellis, A. (1960) *The Art and Science of Love*. Secaucus, NJ: Lyle Stuart.

Ellis, A. (1962) *Reason and Emotion in Psychotherapy*. Secaucus, NJ: Lyle Stuart.

Ellis, A. (1963a) 'Toward a more precise definition of "emotional" and "intellectual" insight', *Psychological Reports*, 13: 125–6.

Ellis, A. (1963b) *Rational-Emotive Psychotherapy*. New York: Institute for Rational-Emotive Therapy.

Ellis, A. (1965) 'Showing clients they are not worthless individuals', *Voices*, 1(2): 74–7.

Ellis, A. (1969) *Suggested Procedures for a Weekend of Rational Encounter*. New York: Institute for Rational-Emotive Therapy.

Ellis, A. (1971) *Growth through Reason*. North Hollywood, CA: Wilshire Books.

Ellis, A. (1972a) *Executive Leadership: A Rational Approach*. Secaucus, NJ: Citadel Press.

Ellis, A. (1972b) 'Helping people get better rather than merely feel better', *Rational Living*, 7(2): 2–9.

Ellis, A. (1973a) *Humanistic Psychotherapy: The Rational-Emotive Approach*. New York: McGraw-Hill.

Ellis, A. (1973b) *Emotional Education at the Living School*. New York: Institute for Rational-Emotive Therapy.

Ellis, A. (1973c) 'My philosophy of psychotherapy', *Journal of Contemporary Psychotherapy*, 6(1): 13–18.

Ellis, A. (1976a) 'The biological basis of human irrationality', *Journal of Individual Psychology*, 32: 145–68.

Ellis, A. (1976b) 'RET abolishes most of the human ego', *Psychotherapy: Theory, Research and Practice*, 13: 343–8. (Reprinted New York: Institute for Rational-Emotive Therapy.)

Ellis, A. (1977a) *Anger – How to Live With and Without It*. Secaucus, NJ: Citadel Press.

Ellis, A. (1977b) 'The basic clinical theory of rational-emotive therapy', in A. Ellis and R. Grieger (eds), *Handbook of Rational-Emotive Therapy*, Vol. 1. New York: Springer.

Ellis, A. (1977c) 'Fun as psychotherapy', *Rational Living*, 12(1): 2–6.

Ellis, A. (1977d) *A Garland of Rational Songs* (cassette recording). New York: Institute for Rational-Emotive Therapy.

Ellis, A. (1977e) 'RET as a personality theory, therapy approach, and philosophy of life', in J.L. Wolfe and E. Brand (eds), *Twenty Years of Rational Therapy*. New York: Institute for Rational-Emotive Therapy.

Ellis, A. (1978a) 'Toward a theory of personality', in R.J. Corsini (ed.), *Readings in Current Personality Theories*. Itasca, IL: Peacock. Reprinted in W. Dryden (ed.) (1990), *The Essential Albert Ellis*. New York: Springer.

Ellis, A. (1978b) 'Personality characteristics of rational-emotive therapists and other kinds of therapists', *Psychotherapy: Theory, Research and Practice*, 15: 329–32.

Ellis, A. (1979a) 'The practice of rational-emotive therapy', in A. Ellis and J.M. Whiteley (eds), *Theoretical and Empirical Foundations of Rational-Emotive Therapy*. Monterey, CA: Brooks/Cole.

Ellis, A. (1979b) 'Discomfort anxiety: a new cognitive-behavioral construct (Part 1)', *Rational Living*, 14(2): 3–8.

Ellis, A. (1979c) 'The issue of force and energy in behavioral change', *Journal of Contemporary Psychotherapy*, 10(2): 83–97.

Ellis, A. (1980a) 'An overview of the clinical theory of rational-emotive therapy', in R. Grieger and J. Boyd, *Rational-Emotive Therapy: A Skills-Based Approach*. New York: Van Nostrand Reinhold.

Ellis, A. (1980b) 'Discomfort anxiety: a new cognitive-behavioral construct (Part 2)', *Rational Living*, 15(1): 25–30.

Ellis, A. (1980c) 'Rational-emotive therapy and cognitive-behavior therapy: similarities and differences', *Cognitive Therapy and Research*, 4: 325–40.

Ellis, A. (1980d) 'The value of efficiency in psychotherapy', *Psychotherapy: Theory, Research and Practice*, 17: 414–19.

Ellis, A.(1982) 'Must most psychotherapists remain as incompetent as they now are?', *Journal of Contemporary Psychotherapy*, 13(1): 17–28.

Ellis, A. (1983) 'Failures in rational-emotive therapy', in E.B. Foa and P.M.G. Emmelkamp (eds), *Failures in Behavior Therapy*. New York: Wiley.

Ellis, A. (1985a) *Overcoming Resistance: Rational-Emotive Therapy with Difficult Clients*. New York: Springer.

Ellis, A. (1985b) 'Expanding the ABCs of rational-emotive therapy', in M. Mahoney and A. Freeman (eds), *Cognition and Psychotherapy*. New York: Plenum.

Ellis, A. (1988) *How to Stubbornly Refuse to Make Yourself Miserable About Anything – Yes, Anything!* Secaucus, NJ: Lyle Stuart.

Ellis, A. (1990) 'Is rational-emotive therapy (RET) "rationalist" or "constructivist"?', *Journal of Rational-Emotive and Cognitive-Behavior Therapy*, 8(3): 169–93.

Ellis, A. (1991) 'The revised ABCs of rational-emotive therapy (RET)', *Journal of Rational-Emotive and Cognitive-Behavior Therapy*, 9(3): 139–72.

Ellis, A. (1993a) 'Fundamentals of rational-emotive therapy for the 1990s', in W. Dryden and L.K. Hill (eds), *Innovations in Rational-Emotive Therapy*. London: Sage Publications.

Ellis, A. (1993b) Letter to mental health professionals, Catalogue of the Institute for Rational-Emotive Therapy, 1993–4, p. 2.

Ellis, A. (1994a) *Reason and Emotion in Psychotherapy*, 2nd edn. New York: Carol Publishing.

Ellis, A. (1994b) 'Post-traumatic stress disorder (PTSD): a rational emotive behavioral theory', *Journal of Rational-Emotive and Cognitive-Behavior Therapy*, 12(1): 3–25.

Ellis, A. (1994c) 'The treatment of borderline personalities with rational emotive behavior therapy', *Journal of Rational-Emotive and Cognitive-Behavior Therapy*, 12(2): 101–19.

Ellis, A. (1994d) 'Rational emotive behavior therapy approaches to obsessive-compulsive disorder (OCD)', *Journal of Rational-Emotive and Cognitive-Behavior Therapy*, 12(2): 121–41.

Ellis, A. and Abrahms, E. (1978) *Brief Psychotherapy in Medical and Health Practice*. New York: Springer.

Ellis, A. and Bernard, M.E. (eds) (1983) *Rational-Emotive Approaches to the Problems of Childhood*. New York: Plenum.

Ellis, A. and Bernard, M.E. (1985) 'What is rational-emotive therapy (RET)?', in A. Ellis and M.E. Bernard (eds), *Clinical Applications of Rational-Emotive Therapy*. New York: Plenum.

Ellis, A. and Blum, M.L. (1967) 'Rational training: a new method of facilitating management and labor relations', *Psychological Reports*, 20: 1267–84.

Ellis, A. and Dryden, W. (1987) *The Practice of Rational-Emotive Therapy*. New York: Springer.

Ellis, A. and Harper, R.A. (1961) *A Guide to Rational Living in an Irrational World*. Englewood Cliffs, NJ: Prentice-Hall.

Ellis, A., McInerney, J.F., DiGiuseppe, R. and Yeager, R.J. (1988) *Rational-Emotive Therapy with Alcoholics and Substance Abusers*. New York: Pergamon.

Ellis, A., Wilson, R.A. and Krassner, P. (1960) 'An impolite interview with Albert Ellis', *The Realist*, 16(1): 9–14; 17: 7–12. (Reprinted New York: Institute for Rational-Emotive Therapy.)

Ellis, A., Sichel, J., Yeager, R.J., DiMattia, D. and DiGiuseppe, R. (1989) *Rational-Emotive Couples Therapy*. New York: Pergamon.

Golden, W.L. and Dryden, W. (1986) 'Cognitive-behavioural therapies: commonalities, divergences and future developments', in W. Dryden and W. Golden (eds), *Cognitive-Behavioural Approaches to Psychotherapy*. London: Harper & Row.

Grieger, R. and Boyd, J. (1980) *Rational-Emotive Therapy: A Skills-Based Approach*. New York: Van Nostrand Reinhold.

Guidano, V.F. (1988) 'A systems, process-oriented approach to cognitive therapy', in K.S. Dobson (ed.), *Handbook of Cognitive-Behavioral Therapies*. New York: Guilford.

Hauck, P. (1980) *Brief Counseling with RET*. Philadelphia, PA: Westminster Press.

Huber, C. and Baruth, L. (1989) *Rational-Emotive Family Therapy: A Systems Perspective*. New York: Springer.

Jacobs, S. (1989) 'Karl Popper and Albert Ellis: their ideas on psychology and rationality compared', *Journal of Rational-Emotive and Cognitive-Behavior Therapy*, 7(3): 173–85.

Knaus, W.J. (1977) 'Rational-emotive education', in A. Ellis and R. Grieger (eds), *Handbook of Rational-Emotive Therapy*, Vol. 1. New York: Springer.

Knaus, W.J. and Haberstroh, N. (1993) 'A rational-emotive education program to help disruptive mentally retarded clients develop self-control', in W. Dryden and L.K. Hill (eds), *Innovations in Rational-Emotive Therapy*. London: Sage Publications.

Korzybski, A. (1993) *Science and Sanity*. San Francisco: International Society of General Semantics.

Mahoney, M.J. (1987) 'Psychotherapy and the cognitive sciences: an evolving alliance', *Journal of Cognitive Psychotherapy: An International Quarterly*, 1: 39–59.

Mahoney, M.J. (1988) 'The cognitive sciences and psychotherapy: patterns in a developing relationship', in K.S. Dobson (ed.), *Handbook of Cognitive-Behavioral Therapies*. New York: Guilford.

Maultsby, M.C., Jr. and Ellis, A. (1974) *Techniques for Using Rational-Emotive Therapy*. New York: Institute for Rational-Emotive Therapy.

Palmer, S. and Ellis, A. (1993) 'In the counsellor's chair: interview with Albert Ellis', *Counselling: The Journal of the British Association for Counselling*, 4(3): 171–4.

Popper, K.R. (1962) *Objective Knowledge*. London: Oxford University Press.

Popper, K.R. (1985) *Popper Selections*, ed. David Miller. Princeton, NJ: Princeton University Press.

Trimpey, J. (1989) *Rational Recovery from Alcoholism: The Small Book*, 2nd edn. Lotus, CA: Lotus Press.

Vernon, A. (1989) *Thinking, Feeling, Behaving. An Emotional Education Curriculum for Children Grades 7–12*. Champaign, IL: Research Press.

Walen, S.R., DiGiuseppe, R. and Wessler, R.L. (1980) *A Practitioner's Guide to Rational-Emotive Therapy*. New York: Oxford University Press.

Warren, R. and Zgourides, G.D. (1991) *Anxiety Disorders: A Rational-Emotive Perspective*. New York: Pergamon.

Weinrach, S.G. and Ellis, A. (1980) 'Unconventional therapist: Albert Ellis' (interview), *Personnel and Guidance Journal*, 59: 152–60.

Wessler, R.A. and Wessler, R.L. (1980) *The Principles and Practice of Rational-Emotive Therapy*. San Francisco, CA: Jossey-Bass.

Wiener, D.N. (1988) *Albert Ellis: Passionate Skeptic*. New York: Praeger.

Yankura, J. and Dryden, W. (1990) *Doing RET: Albert Ellis in Action*. New York: Springer.

Yankura, J. and Dryden, W. (1994) *Albert Ellis*. London: Sage Publications.

10

Developments in Psychotherapy Integration

Cory F. Newman and Marvin R. Goldfried

It is well known that models of psychotherapy have proliferated at a rather alarming rate since the early days of psychoanalysis and biological psychiatry over a century ago (cf. Goldfried, 1982; London and Palmer, 1988). What is less well known is that an interest in integrating the various psychotherapies has existed and grown for many decades as well. One of the reasons why this latter fact has remained rather obscure is that the issue of psychotherapy integration did not develop into a clearly delineated area of interest until the 1980s. Prior to that, it was more of a latent theme that appeared here and there in the literature.

In the present chapter, we use the phrase 'psychotherapy integration' in the generic sense, so as to include the eclectic selection of techniques from different orientations as well as efforts to pursue a theoretical synthesis of different schools of thought. Our account of the historical development of psychotherapy integration begins in the 1930s and ends in the early 1990s. As is the case with any attempt to trace the historical origins of contemporary thought, one never knows for certain where the initial, germinal idea began, nor the exact manner in which earlier contributions influenced later thinking. Our review suggests that the integration of psychotherapies was an idea that was largely ignored at first, only to become assimilated into the mainstream at a later point in time. Barber (1961) has noted that this phenomenon is common whenever innovative ideas challenge the well-accepted status quo in a given field. In the case of psychotherapy integration, it appears that its early proponents were met with silence or opposition. However, as time went on, the climate in the field of psychotherapy became a bit more hospitable, and the idea blossomed. The result has been a dramatic rise in the interest to develop a rapprochement across the psychotherapies in the past fifteen to twenty years. In fact, as a side-effect of the geometric increase in the number of publications on psychotherapy integration, we will have to omit reference to many works, some of which we have discussed in previous reviews (Goldfried and Newman, 1986, 1992).

Later, we will reflect on some of the important outgrowths of this widespread interest, including a professional organization, an annual conference, and journals, all devoted specifically to the exploration of psychotherapy integration.

Early attempts at integration

One of the earliest significant attempts to introduce the topic of psychotherapy integration was an address by French at the 1932 meeting of the American Psychiatric Association. French highlighted parallels between psychoanalysis and classical conditioning – for example the similarities between repression and extinction. When the text of French's presentation was published (French, 1933), together with comments by members of the original audience, it was clear that his notions were found to be quite provocative. A particularly negative response was by Myerson, who wrote that French's work would have caused both Pavlov and Watson to explode in opposition, while Freud would have been 'scandalized' to have one of his pupils make such an outlandish attempt to equate psychoanalytic theory with the behaviourist school. A more open-minded response was proffered by Adolf Meyer, who suggested that one should 'enjoy the convergences which show in such discussions as we have had this morning' (French, 1933: 1201). Gregory Zilboorg also was quite intrigued, writing:

> I do not believe that these two lines of investigation could be passed over very lightly. . . . There is an attempt to point out, regardless of structure and gross pathology, that while dealing with extremely complex functional units both in the physiological laboratory and in the clinic, we can yet reduce them to comparatively simple phenomena. (French, 1933: 1198–9)

In an extension of French's line of reasoning, Kubie (1934) posited that some psychoanalytic techniques could be explained in terms of the conditioned reflex. Noting that Pavlov hypothesized that certain associations might exist outside of an individual's awareness because they took place under a state of inhibition, Kubie wrote that a technique such as free association might succeed by removing the inhibition, thus allowing an unconscious association to emerge into awareness.

In 1936 Rosenzweig published a brief article in which he argued that the effectiveness of various therapeutic approaches probably had more to do with their common elements than with the apparently divergent theoretical explanations on which they were based. Rosenzweig suggested three common factors. One was the hope that caring and personable therapists inspired in their patients or clients. A second factor was that the therapists offered interpretations that permitted a better sense of self-understanding, which itself served to empower. A third factor had to do with any positive change introduced into a system. For example, even though varying theoretical orientations may focus on different areas of human functioning, they can all be effective because of the general positive ripple effect that one area of functioning may have on others.

At the 1940 meeting of the American Orthopsychiatric Association

(Watson, 1940), a small group of therapists convened to discuss points of agreement in their practice of psychotherapy. This event was a significant step away from the guarded secrecy that had been the hallmark of the psychotherapeutic process. Watson observed that 'if we were to apply to our colleagues the distinction, so important with patients, between what they tell us and what they do, we might find that agreement is greater in practice than in theory' (1940: 708).

In his book *Active Psychotherapy*, Herzberg (1945) recommended the use of systematically prescribed 'homework' assignments within the context of psychodynamic therapy. This key concept was one of the first attempts to articulate the importance of both insight and behaviour change in psychotherapy. Herzberg also proposed the use of graded tasks in order to make gradual gains in overcoming anxiety-based avoidance, thus anticipating an important behavioural contribution to the field by over a decade!

Woodworth's 1948 volume, *Contemporary Schools of Psychology*, explored the development and substantive content of the then existing schools of psychological thought, such as behaviourism, Gestalt psychology, and the psychoanalytic schools. Woodworth acknowledged the distinct advances that each orientation had made, but concluded that 'no one [school] is good enough' (1948: 255). Observing that psychotherapies were progressing on diverging paths, Woodworth wondered 'whether synthesis of the different lines of advance [might] not sometime prove to be possible' (ibid.: p. 10).

Soon thereafter, Dollard and Miller (1950) published *Personality and Psychotherapy*, a landmark work in the history of psychotherapy integration. Their tone of rapprochement was communicated early and often, as demonstrated by their dedication to 'Freud and Pavlov and their students'. Dollard and Miller's work was widely read, and remained in print for over thirty years. They described in detail how such psychoanalytic concepts as regression, repression and displacement may be understood within the framework of learning theory. For the most part, Dollard and Miller translated one language system into another, thus demonstrating how jargon can obscure communication and artificially reduce consensus in describing and explaining psychological phenomena. They also suggested that certain processes may be common to all therapeutic approaches, such as the need for the therapist to support an individual's attempts at change by expressing interest, empathy and approval for such attempts.

Even though Dollard and Miller (1950) stayed fairly close to the intervention procedures associated with psychoanalytic therapy, they made continual reference to principles on which contemporary behaviour therapy is based. For example, the authors suggested: the value of modelling procedures; the use of hierarchically arranged tasks; reinforcement of approximations towards a goal; the principle of reciprocal inhibition; the significance of the reinforcing qualities of the therapist; the importance of teaching coping skills for the individual to use after the completion of therapy; and the salience of environmental contingencies for maintaining behaviour change. Echoing a theme addressed earlier by Herzberg (1945),

Dollard and Miller also emphasized the importance of between-session assignments (e.g. 'behavioral changes must be made in the real world of the patient's current life. If benevolent changes are to occur, the patient must be doing something new': 1950: 319). As if to drive home the point that this is a universal concept (and not just a behavioural one), the authors cite Freud, who is quoted as writing, 'Actually it is quite unimportant for his cure whether or not the patient can overcome this or that anxiety or inhibition in the institution; what is of importance, on the contrary, is whether or not he will be free from them in real life' (Freud, 1924, Vol. 2: 320).

Thorne's *Principles of Personality Counseling* (1950) expressed an interest in pursuing therapeutic integration on the basis of what was known empirically about how people function and change. From the time that he was a medical student, Thorne was struck by the fact that medicine was not divided up into different schools of thought. Instead, advancements in clinical practice were made on the basis of an accumulation of knowledge about basic principles of bodily functioning. He believed that the field of psychotherapy could benefit from a similar approach.

Like Thorne, Garfield had long been interested in finding empirical bases for psychotherapeutic interventions. In 1957 he outlined what appeared to be common points among the psychotherapies. In an introductory clinical psychology text, Garfield noted such universal factors as an understanding and supportive therapist, the opportunity for emotional release in session, and the provision of enhanced self-undersanding.

Glad's (1959) *Operational Values in Psychotherapy* took issue with dogmatism and theoretical inflexibility in the practice of psychotherapy. He believed that doctrinaire approaches were inherently limited, and instead recommended that practising therapists be exposed to the systematic operations of psychotherapists across the major orientations of the time. He did not specify that therapists should be formally *trained* in all the major forms of therapy, perhaps because he recognized that this would be a formidable task to design and execute. Still, his recommendation presages the issue of integrative education, which was to come to the fore approximately twenty-five to thirty years later.

More recent trends toward rapprochement

As our overview to this point would indicate, the topic of therapeutic rapprochement, while raised surprisingly early, was seriously addressed by only a handful of writers prior to the 1960s. This may have been due, in part, to the fact that no single approach to psychotherapy had yet gained enough support to challenge psychoanalytic therapy. Perhaps the conservative social and political climate also served to discourage therapists from being paradigm challengers. By contrast, the 1960s, along with the broad array of societal changes that came with it, brought a sharp increase in the number of books and articles dealing with rapprochement.

The 1960s

The most significant contribution to the integration of psychotherapies made in the early 1960s was Frank's (1961) *Persuasion and Healing*. This influential book addressed itself to commonalties cutting across varying attempts at personal influence and healing in general. Frank observed (quite bravely!) that the process of psychotherapy shares similarities with diverse methods such as religious conversion, primitive healing, brainwashing, and the placebo effects that occur routinely in the practice of medicine. Frank reasoned that when distressed individuals are placed in any of these contexts, an expectancy for improvement and an increase in hopefulness results in a concomitant increase in self-esteem and overall functioning. It should be pointed out that although Frank continued to stress common factors across the psychotherapies in his later writings, in one of his more recent reviews of the field (Frank, 1979), he acknowledged that certain clinical problems (e.g. fears, phobias, compulsive rituals) may be effectively dealt with by methods that go beyond the general nature of the therapeutic interaction.

Thirty years after the publication of French's landmark address, a colleague of his, Alexander (1963), suggested that psychoanalytic therapy might profitably be understood in terms of learning theory. He based this opinion on his study of audiotape recordings of psychoanalytic therapy sessions, thus harkening back to Watson's (1940) contention that direct evaluation of what therapists actually *do* in session, as opposed to what they *say* that they do, will reveal more similarities than differences across theoretical orientations.

Alexander, a therapist who was dedicated throughout his career to the advancement of the field as a whole, suggested that 'we are witnessing the beginnings of a most promising integration of psychoanalytic theory with learning theory, which may lead to unpredictable advances in the theory and practice of the psychotherapies' (1963: 448). A year later, Marmor, involved in the same programme of research on psychotherapy, described in detail the learning principles that he believed to underlie psychoanalytic therapy (Marmor, 1964).

An intriguing article by Carl Rogers, published in 1963, commented on the state of the field of psychotherapy. He observed that the theoretical orientations within which therapists had typically functioned – including client-centred therapy – were starting to break down. He stated that it was essential to study more directly exactly what goes on during the course of psychotherapy, so that the field could shed the limitations inherent in specific orientations.

London (1964), in a short but insightful book entitled *The Modes and*

Morals of Psychotherapy, reflected upon both the psychodynamic and behavioural orientations, noting:

> There is a quiet blending of techniques by artful therapists of either school: a blending that takes account of the fact that people are considerably simpler than the Insight schools give them credit for, but that they are also more complicated than the Action therapists would like to believe. (1964: 39)

Marks and Gelder (1966) took the stance that, while there may in fact be identifiable differences between behaviour therapy and psychodynamic procedures, the two approaches should be viewed as potentially contributing to each other, rather than as necessarily antagonistic in nature. Wolf added that 'integration is sooner or later inevitable, however passionately some or many of us may choose to resist it' (1966: 535).

The very important concept of 'technical eclecticism' was introduced in 1967 by Lazarus, who maintained that clinicians can use techniques from various therapeutic systems based on their empirically demonstrated effectiveness, without having to be concerned with the theoretical underpinnings of these methods. His views were eventually revised and expanded into the development of multimodal therapy (Lazarus, 1992). Also appearing in 1967 were articles by Patterson, on the divergent and convergent elements across the psychotherapies; Whitehouse, on the general principles underlying a variety of therapeutic interventions; and Weitzman, regarding the useful application of systematic desensitization within a psychoanalytic context.

Brady (1968) demonstrated how, in certain cases, behavioural and psychodynamic procedures could be used in combination. He illustrated this in the treatment of a woman with a sexual dysfunction via systematic desensitization and short-term psychodynamic therapy focusing on the woman's marriage. In a similar vein, Leventhal (1968) described a case of a woman experiencing sexual anxieties who was successfully treated with combined behavioural and traditional therapeutic interventions.

Bergin (1968) asserted that systematic desensitization is made more powerful by the therapist's being warm, empathic, and active in giving moderate amounts of interpretation. He maintained that a therapy that addressed a more comprehensive set of psychological events would be less likely to lead therapists to conceptual dead-ends in the face of particularly complex cases. Along these same lines, Woody (1968) presented an integrative 'psychobehavioural' therapy that would be especially relevant to cases that were unresponsive to treatment.

In 1969, Kraft presented clinical evidence that systematic desensitization could help patients gain insight into a wealth of unconscious material via the combination of relaxation and imagery. Sloane (1969) maintained that common factors ran through psychoanalytic, behavioural and client-centred therapies, and Marmor (1969) agreed that all therapies involved some aspect of learning principles. Moreover, like London (1964), Marks and Gelder (1966), Lazarus (1967), Brady (1968), Bergin (1968) and others,

Marmor concluded that the different therapies are best viewed as complementary in nature. Brammer (1969) added that the choice of which
procedures to use from which orientation should ideally be made on
empirical grounds.

The 1970s

The year 1970 marked the inauguration of a new and important journal,
Behavior Therapy. Interestingly, the editors and contributors devoted
serious attention to aspects of theory and therapy that were not strictly
'behavioural'. For example, Birk (1970) described two clinical cases to
illustrate the potential integration of behaviour therapy with psychodynamic
theory, and Bergin (1970a) wrote that desensitization drew heavily from
cognitive and therapeutic relationship variables for its effectiveness. Bergin
(1970b) followed with another article that applauded the introduction of
cognitive methods into behaviour therapy, stating:

> The sociological and historical importance of the movement should not be
> underestimated for it has three important consequences. It significantly reduces
> barriers to progress due to narrow school allegiances, it brings the energies of a
> highly talented and experimentally sophisticated group to bear upon the intricate
> and often baffling problems of objectifying and managing the subjective, and it
> underscores the notion that a pure behavior therapy does not exist. (1970b: 207)

Prophetically, many of the behaviour therapists who became involved in the
development of cognitive procedures (e.g. Davison, Goldfried, Lazarus,
Mahoney, Meichenbaum) later moved on to an interest in therapeutic
integration.

Truax and Mitchell (1971) contended that the therapeutic relationship
played a key role in the successful application of behaviour therapy.
Further, they posited that there were certain therapist qualities that
contributed to the change process, regardless of therapeutic orientation.

Marmor's article on therapeutic integration made the following bold
comment:

> The research on the nature of the psychotherapeutic process in which I
> participated with Franz Alexander, beginning in 1958, has convinced me that all
> psychotherapy, regardless of the techniques used, is a learning process . . .
> Dynamic psychotherapies and behavior therapies simply represent different
> teaching techniques, and their differences are based in part on differences in their
> goals and in part on their assumptions of the nature of psychopathology. (1971: 26)

Responding to Bergin's (1971) clinical observations that behaviour
therapy, when used alone, was not always effective, Lazarus (1971)
described in *Behavior Therapy and Beyond* a wide array of both behavioural
and non-behavioural techniques that may be employed by broad-spectrum
behaviour therapists. In accord with Lazarus's concept of technical eclecticism, Woody (1971) suggested that clinicians could select and integrate
procedures from varying sources based primarily on pragmatic grounds.

Marks noted that therapists 'are growing less reluctant to adopt methods with pedigrees outside their own theoretical systems' (1971: 69).

Houts and Serber's (1972) edited volume *After the Turn On, What?* described the ideas that sprang from an encounter group comprised of seven researchers and practitioners whose orientations ranged from radical behaviourism to cognitive. In a provocative article on the 'end of ideology' in behaviour therapy, London noted that 'the first issue, scientifically as well as clinically, is the factual one – do [therapies] work? On whom? When? The how and why come later' (1972: 919). Feather and Rhoads (1972a, 1972b) argued that in psychology, as in the history of medicine, the existence of many competing treatments for a given disorder probably signalled a poor understanding of the disorder, and that none of the separate individual treatments was likely to be adequate.

In 1973 and 1974, some articles expounded upon the notion of the complementarity of different therapeutic methods. Birk (1973) wrote that behaviour therapy was strong in its focus on external determinants of human functioning, while psychodynamic therapy covered the relevant internal factors. Thoresen (1973) viewed behaviour therapy as providing the technology by which the philosophical goals of humanistic psychotherapy could be achieved. Woody (1973) reported that two cases of sexual deviations were successfully treated via aversion therapy and short-term psychodynamic therapy, administered concurrently by separate therapists. The complementary nature of different approaches was demonstrated by Lambley (1974) in the treatment of obsessive-compulsive disorder. Birk and Brinkley-Birk (1974) suggested that insight-oriented therapy can set the stage for change, while behaviour therapy provides some of the actual procedures to produce change. Additionally, Rhoads and Feather (1974) described cases treated with desensitization procedures that were modified along psychodynamic lines. Kaplan (1974), in her book *The New Sex Therapy*, outlined how a psychodynamic approach to therapy may be integrated with performance-based methods. Silverman suggested to his psychoanalytic colleagues that there is much to learn from 'other approaches that can make (unmodified) psychoanalytic treatment more effective' (1974: 305). Landsman also urged his humanistically oriented colleagues to attend to some of the contributions of behaviour therapy, such as 'attention to specifics, to details, careful quantification, modesty in claims, demonstrable results' (1974: 15).

Raimy's (1975) *Misunderstandings of the Self* contended that a common function of all therapies is to change clients' misconceptions of themselves and of others. Egan (1975), a humanistic psychotherapist, acknowledged that more directive measures may be necessary in order to help certain clients change. He explained that the humanistic approach has its strength in establishing a positive therapeutic relationship, while behaviour therapy may then be used collaboratively by therapist and client in order to implement specific changes. Sloane, Staples, Cristol, Yorkston and Whipple's (1975) *Psychotherapy versus Behavior Therapy*, in contrast to its title, underscored a theme of rapprochement. Sloane et al. reported that behaviour therapists and psychodynamic therapists demonstrated comparable degrees of warmth and positive regard, and that patients of both types of therapist exhibited the same depth of self-exploration.

In 1976, articles by Strupp and Grinker took issue with the practice of unchanging orthodoxy in psychoanalytic therapy, arguing instead for experimentation with newer techniques. Grinker in particular espoused the view that the field could develop through advancements made on the basis of research findings. As a practising psychoanalyst with personal experience in the human potential movement, Appelbaum (1976) suggested that some Gestalt therapy methods may complement psychoanalytic techniques. He later expanded on these ideas in his intriguing 1979 book, *Out in Inner Space: A Psychoanalyst Explores the Therapies*. Wandersman, Poppen and Ricks's (1976) *Humanism and Behaviorism* offered discussions by members of each orientation, acknowledging points of potential integration. Hunt (1976) argued that no single orientation was capable of handling all clinical material. He observed that, just as separate laser beams function together to obtain a three-dimensional holographic image, different therapeutic orientations converge to provide us with a comprehensive treatment approach. In *Clinical Behavior Therapy*, Goldfried and Davison wrote: 'It is time for behavior therapists to stop regarding themselves as an outgroup and instead to enter into serious and hopefully fruitful mutual dialogues with their nonbehavioral colleagues' (1976: 15). Along these lines, Garfield and Kurtz (1976) found that approximately 55 per cent of clinical psychologists in the United States considered themselves eclectic, and that most clinicians used a combination of psychodynamic and learning orientations. Lazarus's *Multimodal Behavior Therapy* (1976) systematically focused on many aspects of human functioning, including behaviours, emotions, cognitions and physiologic states.

The following year, Lazarus recognized the need to 'transcend the constraints of factionalism, where cloistered adherents of rival schools, movements, and systems each cling to their separate illusions' (1977: 11). The year 1977 also marked the publication of Wachtel's *Psychoanalysis and Behavior Therapy*, in which he maintained that the convergence of clinical procedures from each orientation would probably enhance the effectiveness of interventions.

In 1978 Davison delivered a talk at the Association for the Advancement of Behavior Therapy (AABT) convention in which he recommended that behaviour therapists consider using certain experiential procedures in their clinical work. At the same convention, Arkowitz chaired a symposium on the compatibility and incompatibility of behaviour therapy and psychoanalysis. A 1978 convention paper by Strupp on converging trends in the field resulted in a 1983 article provocatively entitled 'Are psychoanalytic therapists beginning to practice cognitive behavior therapy or is behavior therapy turning psychoanalytic?'

Gurman stated that 'therapy is not viewed as a reified set of procedures, but as an evolving science' (1978: 131). Diamond, Havens and Jones (1978) stressed the need for an eclectic approach to therapy that would be tied to research and theory in a broad sense, but that would be flexible enough to provide highly individualized treatments. Also in the same year, Ryle (1978) suggested that experimental cognitive psychology might provide a common language for the psychotherapies, in part to overcome the communication problems produced by disparate sets of theoretical jargon. This idea was independently supported by both Sarason (1979) and Goldfried (1979).

Prochaska (1979) made the case for ultimately developing a transtheoretical orientation that would encompass what many have found to be useful across different systems of psychotherapy. Robertson (1979) speculated on some of the reasons for the trend toward eclecticism, including the tendency for clinical experience to make a therapist more open to a wide range of procedures, and the loss of idealization of one's orientation by training. Related to this last point are the results of Mahoney's (1979) survey of leading cognitive and non-cognitive behaviour therapists. When asked the degree to which they felt satisfied with the adequacy of their current understanding of human behaviour, their average rating was *less than two* on a seven-point scale!

The 1980s

It was during this decade that psychotherapy integration made the leap from an area of interest to a fully-fledged movement. There was a significant increase in the rate of publications and presentations on the topic, making it impractical for us to review the more than 200 publications that appeared during this period. We will highlight some of these contributions in the limited space available.

Goldfried (1980), in his examination of past attempts to find commonalties across psychotherapies, argued that such comparative analyses are somewhat problematic when done at the level of either the specific technique or the general theoretical explanation. He proposed that the most fruitful level of abstraction would be the *clinical strategy* that was being employed. Goldfried posited that an important example of a transtheoretical strategy is the use of 'corrective experiences', and he went on to show how this occurs in fear-reduction interventions across orientations.

In a special issue of *Cognitive Therapy and Research*, therapists associated with different orientations answered questions about what they believed to be the most effective ingredients in therapeutic change (Brady et al., 1980). Goldfried and Strupp (1980) agreed that any attempt at finding points of commonalty must be based on what clinicians do, rather than on what they report they do. Bastine (1980) observed that a problem-solving approach to intervention would be likely to facilitate psychotherapy integration. Messer and Winokur (1980) suggested that both psychodynamic and behavioural approaches could be used in combination to help patients to translate their

insights into productive new actions. Mahoney (1980) noted that behaviourists had begun to pay attention not only to patients' conscious
thoughts, but also to their more implicit (i.e. 'unconscious'!) cognitions.
Marmor and Woods's *The Interface between Psychodynamic and Behavioral
Therapies* (1980) presented chapters from a variety of authors that
illustrated the theme that no single therapeutic stance can deal with the
entire range of human functioning. A survey by Larson (1980) found that 65
per cent of therapists who identified themselves as being practitioners of a
primary school of therapy still reported drawing on contributions from other
therapeutic approaches. Garfield's *Psychotherapy: An Eclectic Approach*
(1980) described an empirically oriented view of psychotherapy, and added
that the introduction of cognitive variables into behaviour therapy was an
advance in this direction.

In 1981 there were still more publications that supported the notion that
different orientations presented unique strengths that could be combined in
complementary fashion to form a more potent integrative treatment. For
example, Arnkoff (1981) combined cognitive therapy with the Gestalt
empty-chair technique in order to intensify affect, as well as to gain access to
meaningful ('hot') cognitions from the patient. The outcome was extremely
positive, more so than one would expect if either approach had been used in
isolation.

Landau and Goldfried (1981) spelled out how concepts from experimental cognitive psychology (e.g. schema, scripts) could offer an integrative
language system in order to bridge the communication gap between
orientations that otherwise would use their own brands of jargon. The
importance of such a unifying framework was underscored by Staats (1981),
who remarked that the field of psychology had the means to create a great
deal of empirical knowledge, but lacked the ability to organize the data into
a common conceptual model that would be enlightening to all.

Communication between psychotherapy practitioners and researchers of
diverse orientations soon became a more common, worldwide phenomenon. Examples included a small, informal two-day dialogue across
orientations held in 1981 by Garfield, Goldfried, M. Horowitz, Imber,
Kendall, Strupp, Wachtel and Wolfe, the 1982 world congress of the Adler
Society for Individual Psychology, a day-long dialogue and discussion of
actual clinical material (Mahoney and Wachtel, 1982), and an international
congress in Bogota, Colombia in 1983.

Goldfried's *Converging Themes in Psychotherapy* (1982) was a treasure
trove of old and recent articles dealing with the issue of rapprochement,
along with an overview of future directions in psychotherapy integration. In
Resistance (1982) Wachtel invited experienced, leading therapists to submit
their views on how the synthesis of psychodynamic and behavioural
therapies might shed more light on resistance to therapeutic change. In
Psychotherapy: A Cognitive Integration of Theory and Practice (1982), Ryle
used cognitive psychology as a common language in order to assimilate the
theories and methods of a heterogeneous set of orientations. In like fashion,

Segraves's *Marital Therapy* (1982) utilized the language of cognitive social psychology as an integrative communication system, as exemplified by his presentation of the concept of 'interpersonal schemas' to explain the influence of early-life attachments on a person's current perceptions of his or her spouse.

In 1983, Beutler's *Eclectic Psychotherapy* proposed that the field review what is known about the optimal matching of patients to therapists and techniques, as a means by which to maximize the effectiveness of therapy. Fensterheim and Glazer, in *Behavioral Psychotherapy* (1983), looked at the complementarity of psychoanalytic and behavioural treatment methods, an idea that was progressively receiving more attention and explication.

Reflecting the growth of the movement towards the exploration of therapeutic integration at the international level, a book on the topic in German, by Textor, appeared in 1983. Evidence of a growing rapprochement between biological and psychological orientations was seen in the work of Gevins (1983), and in the striking theme of the 1983 meeting of the Society of Biological Psychiatry, 'The Biology of Information Processing'. Along these lines, Beck (1984) and Beitman and Klerman (1984) presented guidelines for the integration of psychotherapies and pharmacotherapy.

In the search for an overarching theoretical framework for the development of a more unified paradigm, a number of authors began to suggest that the field needed to develop a better theoretical and empirical understanding of the connections between cognition, affect and behaviour (e.g. Beck, 1984; Dryden, 1984; Greenberg and Safran, 1984; Mahoney, 1984a, 1984b; Ryle, 1984; Safran, 1984).

Driscoll, in *Pragmatic Psychotherapy* (1984), substituted the vernacular for theoretical jargon as a way to bridge differing conceptual approaches to psychotherapy. He presented a method known as the 'pragmatic survey', by which any given psychological problem could be elucidated and conceptualized in a number of ways. Arkowitz and Messer's edited volume, *Psychoanalytic Therapy and Behavior Therapy: Is Integration Possible?* (1984) explored the clinical, theoretical and empirical issues and implications of a serious attempt at rapprochement.

The early 1980s also witnessed the appearance of journal issues that were devoted in part, or entirely, to the issue of psychotherapy integration. For example, a special issue of *Behavior Therapy* contained a series of articles examining the pros and cons of supplementing behavioural techniques with those of other orientations, and a 1983 issue of the *British Journal of Clinical Psychology* presented running debate and commentary on the subject of the plausibility of rapprochement.

One of the most significant events in the history of psychotherapy integration was the establishment of the Society for the Exploration of Psychotherapy Integration (SEPI) in 1983. An interdisciplinary organization that has grown to be international in scope, SEPI holds annual conferences in order to bring together the ever-growing number of professionals interested in this area. Later, SEPI members became subscribers and contributors to their own journal, the *Journal of Psychotherapy Integration*.

Prior to the creation of the above journal, there was the *International Journal of Eclectic Psychotherapy*, renamed the *Journal of Integrative and Eclectic Psychotherapy* in 1987. Also started in 1987 was the *Journal of Cognitive Psychotherapy: An International Quarterly*, which openly invites papers that explore the integration of cognitive psychotherapy with other models of treatment. We would like to review all of the progressive and thought-provoking articles that have appeared in these journals. Needless to say, that cannot be done within the scope of this chapter.

In reviewing the psychotherapy research findings to date, Stiles, Shapiro and Elliott (1986) concluded that the field needs to study the process of change, as outcome studies comparing and contrasting 'pure-form' therapies have generally failed to demonstrate the clear and consistent superiority of one approach over others. This point was similarly made by Goldfried and Safran (1986), who suggested some future research directions in psychotherapy integration.

An edited volume by Norcross (1986) aimed to define the parameters of an integrative approach to psychotherapy, and began to suggest methods and modes of teaching the therapy to trainees. For the most part, the contributing authors agreed that trainees in integrative psychotherapy would face the daunting task of pursuing the following: (1) rigorous training in the scientific method; (2) substantial exposure to a number of the major models of psychotherapy; (3) a carefully supervised clinical apprenticeship; (4) intensive training in therapeutic relationship skills; (5) extensive practical experience with a wide range of populations; and (6) training in designing and executing psychotherapy process research. Additional attention was paid to the issues of integrative training and supervision in the *International Journal of Eclectic Psychotherapy* (in 1986), as well as in succeeding years in the *Journal of Integrative and Eclectic Psychotherapy*. Another important topic given a breadth of coverage in this journal in 1987 was the problem of overcoming the theoretical language barrier between clinicians and researchers of differing theoretical training backgrounds. Authors expounded on the merits of such language systems as the vernacular (Driscoll, 1987), experimental cognitive psychology and social cognition (Goldfried, 1987; Ryle, 1987), and interpersonal theory (Strong, 1987).

The year 1987 was rich in the worldwide publication of new books on psychotherapy integration. From Italy came Guidano's *Complexity of the Self*; from English-speaking Canada, Greenberg and Safran published *Emotion in Psychotherapy*; and from French-speaking Canada we gained Lecomte and Castonguay's *Rapprochement et intégration en psychothérapie*. From the United States came Wachtel's *Action and Insight*, Beitman's *The Structure of Individual Psychotherapy*, and Norcross's *Casebook of Eclectic Psychotherapy*.

In response to the criticism that an eclectic approach is merely a 'grab-bag' or 'trial-and error' therapy, Norcross and Prochaska (1988) wrote that this viewpoint had changed considerably as the field of eclecticism and integration sought to become more systematic and data based. They observed that 'integration "by design" is steadily replacing eclecticism "by default"' (1988: 173).

Another series of articles on psychotherapy integration appeared in *Psychiatric Annals* in 1988. Topics included the complementarity of psychotherapy and pharmacotherapy (Rhoads, 1988), the emotional and cognitive insights that are provoked during a course of behaviour therapy (Babcock, 1988; Powell, 1988), the synthesis of psychodynamic and behaviour therapy principles that seems to exist in cognitive therapy (London and Palmer, 1988), and the need to look at the integration of individual therapy with marital and family therapy (Birk, 1988). This latter point was also addressed by the work of Allen (1988), Beach and O'Leary (1986), Feldman (1989), Grebstein (1986), LeBow (1984), Pinsof (1983), Segraves (1982), and Wachtel and Wachtel (1986), among others. As testimony to the momentum the cited works have gathered, a special interest group within the American Family Therapy Association has been organized to support these integrative efforts.

Toward the end of the 1980s, the call for the development of an empirical methodology for the study of psychotherapy integration became quite pronounced (e.g. Goldfried and Safran, 1986; Norcross and Grencavage, 1989; Norcross and Thomas, 1988; Safran et al., 1988; Wolfe and Goldfried, 1988). Safran et al. (1988) suggested that part of this emerging methodology involved the intensive study of successful and unsuccessful cases. Related to this suggestion, Wolfe and Goldfried (1988) stated that the establishment and growth of an accessible archive of therapy tapes and transcripts would be a major boon to the empirical study of the process of therapy, and by extension the exploration of psychotherapy integration. A sub-theme related to the need for integration to be based on empirical findings was the call for a better, more universal understanding of the aetiology, course and description of psychopathology (Arkowitz, 1989; Guidano, 1987; Wolfe, 1989; Wolfe and Goldfried, 1988).

A programme of research specifically designed to develop a methodology for the study of psychotherapy integration began to take shape as a result of the work of Goldfried and his associates (e.g. Castonguay et al., 1989; Goldfried et al., 1989; Goldsamt et al., 1992; Kerr et al., 1992). These authors developed a coding system, in the language of the vernacular, to compare and contrast the feedback that cognitive-behavioural and psycho-dynamic therapists give their patients. The database consisted of transcripts and audiotapes of actual therapy sessions from both orientations.

As part of the groundswell of support for the notion that the therapeutic relationship is a vital and central component of virtually all therapies, Beitman, Goldfried and Norcross (1989) recommended that process researchers focus more of their attention on the therapeutic alliance.

Simek-Downing's *International Psychotherapy* (1989), a book that took cross-cultural factors into account in the study of the process of therapy, examined elements of successful interpersonal helping that appear to be universal.

The Comprehensive Handbook of Cognitive Therapy (Freeman et al., 1989) surprisingly contained many chapters that seemed to create conceptual and technical bridges between cognitive therapy and approaches such as experiential therapy, Piagetian theory, behaviour therapy, psychodynamic therapy, marital therapy, pharmacotherapy, and the use of Gestalt imagery. This reminds us of London and Palmer's (1988) claim that cognitive therapy is one of the field's best integrative treatment options at this time.

The 1990s

As difficult as it would have been to review each important contribution to the field of psychotherapy integration in the 1980s, it is even more so in the 1990s. This is partly due to the fact that the burgeoning growth of publications on the topic has reached a wider audience than ever before, thus stimulating more professionals to write about their clinical, theoretical and research ideas on integration. However, it is also due to the fact that a new generation of clinicians and researchers has come of age who have been weaned on issues pertinent to rapprochement from the early days of their training, and who now may self-identify primarily as integrative in their approach to psychotherapy. We conclude by highlighting some of the broader themes that confront the field at this time, rather than review publications on an individual basis. The interested reader wanting more detail on many of these issues may wish to consult two comprehensive handbooks dealing with psychotherapy integration (Norcross and Goldfried, 1992; Stricker and Gold, 1993).

One very important and central theme is the issue of *empiricism*. It is widely acknowledged that advances in the field of psychotherapy integration will require staying close to research findings and continuing to develop methods to generate data. This will increase the likelihood that knowledge will accumulate, that the dogmatism of the past will become even less of a factor in shaping the direction that the field takes, and that the integrative movement will not fragment into its own set of idiosyncratic and divergent theories and therapies.

The following are some of the factors to which authors have pointed in their discussion of the empirical basis for psychotherapy integration: (1) the need to develop new methodologies suitable for the study of pantheoretical variables (e.g. Goldfried et al., 1989); (2) the utility of compiling centralized databases of therapy tapes and transcripts to which all researchers can gain access (e.g. Goldfried, 1991); (3) continued support for the study of the process of psychotherapy, even though economic forces are pushing for outcome data and manualized treatments (cf. Glass et al., 1993; Smith, 1995); (4) applying the findings from experimental cognitive psychology to the understanding of how people process information, learn, and change (e.g.

Coyne, 1994; Westen, 1994); and (5) utilizing research on psychopathology in order to understand better how to apply specific interventions to populations that have different deficits and needs (e.g. Arkowitz, 1989; Marten and Barlow, 1993; Millon et al., 1993; Robins, 1993).

Another theme is the importance of *cross-cultural and gender issues* in understanding psychopathology and psychotherapy. This represents an increasing awareness that the psychological functioning of the individual is set in a sociological context that must be acknowledged, examined and respected. It also alerts clinicians and researchers to beware of biases that go beyond theoretical orientation and may skew interpretation of data.

The field's heightened awareness of cross-cultural issues is both a cause and an effect of the growth of interest in rapprochement into an international movement. Authors from many different countries and ethnic backgrounds have begun to contribute publications that address psychotherapy integration in their own geographic locations, and in the context of their culturally supported belief systems.

Gender issues have come to the fore in light of decades of clinical writings and case presentations that often involve a male therapist working with a female client/patient. One implication of this observed demographic imbalance may be that gender bias and power differentials between men and women have clouded issues of psychopathology and appropriate intervention. For example, the diagnosis of borderline personality disorder (BPD) occurs far more often in women than in men. By being sensitive to gender issues, the field does not simply assume that this is a 'female disorder'. Rather, it examines how gender-based value judgements may tend to invalidate emotional reactions that are commonly associated with women in distress. For example, Linehan (1993) has presented an excellent example of an integrative approach to the treatment of BPD that takes these gender issues into account and strives to provide the client/patient with much-needed validation for her reactions.

As mentioned above, a new wave of professionals is entering the field of psychotherapy at a time when integration is a more accepted part of the *Zeitgeist*. However, being receptive to the study of psychotherapy integration is only a small part of the picture. There is also a need to find effective ways to become trained in clinical and research principles that span different orientations. Issues of *training and supervision* in integration are also hot topics in the 1990s.

Early attempts at designing prospective curricula for integrative therapists-in-training have highlighted what a massive undertaking this instruction would be (Norcross and Newman, 1992). It seems clear that it is not feasible to cram all of the requisite training into a typical course of graduate studies, even if we could achieve consensus on exactly what that training would entail. It is more realistic to consider the quest to become a well-trained integrative psychotherapist and researcher as a goal that spans one's entire career, with graduate studies serving as an introduction and as a course in 'integration appreciation'.

This requires a great deal of personal commitment, extensive continuing education, and professional organizations, journals and meetings that are conducive to stimulating discussion, collaborative networking, and moral and intellectual support. A professional context in which the various issues associated with integration may be considered is the Society for the Exploration of Psychotherapy Integration (SEPI). Since its foundation in 1983, SEPI has grown into an international network dedicated to the 'exploration' of ways that therapists from different orientations might be able to benefit from the clinical insights and research findings stemming from schools of thought other than their own. SEPI holds yearly conferences that allow for transtheoretical and interdisciplinary dialogue, also providing a venue in which clinicians and researchers from around the world can present their latest work. SEPI publishes the *Journal of Psychotherapy Integration*, a quarterly containing clinical, conceptual and empirical articles related to psychotherapy integration, as well as a newsletter that reports on the activities of regional SEPI networks, and announces forthcoming conferences and training opportunities. In addition to providing a reference group for mental health professionals seeking to expand their theoretical boundaries, the hope is that SEPI will serve a consciousness-raising function, to help the field as a whole move towards developing a more comprehensive model of therapeutic intervention.[1]

Note

1. For further information about SEPI, write to Dr George Stricker, The Derner Institute, Adelphi University, Garden City, NY 11530, USA; FAX (516) 877–4805; e-mail: STRICKER@SABLE.ADELPHI.EDU.

References

Alexander, F. (1963) 'The dynamics of psychotherapy in light of learning theory', *American Journal of Psychiatry*, 120: 440–8.

Allen, D.M. (1988) *Unifying Individual and Family Therapies*. San Francisco: Jossey-Bass.

Appelbaum, S.A. (1976) 'A psychoanalyst looks at Gestalt therapy', in C. Hatcher and P. Himmelstein (eds), *The Handbook of Gestalt Therapy*. New York: Jason Aronson.

Appelbaum, S.A. (1979) *Out in Inner Space: A Psychoanalyst Explores the Therapies*. Garden City, NY: Anchor.

Arkowitz, H. (1989) 'The role of theory in psychotherapy integration', *Journal of Integrative and Eclectic Psychotherapy*, 8: 8–16.

Arkowitz, H. and Messer, S.B. (eds) (1984) *Psychoanalytic Therapy and Behavior Therapy: Is Integration Possible?* New York: Plenum.

Arnkoff, D.B. (1981) 'Flexibility in practicing cognitive therapy', in G. Emery, S.D. Hollon and R.C. Bedrosian (eds), *New Directions in Cognitive Therapy*. New York: Guilford. pp. 203–23.

Babcock, H.H. (1988) 'Integrative psychotherapy: collaborative aspects of behavioral and psychodynamic therapies', *Psychiatric Annals*, 18: 271–2.

Barber, B. (1961) 'Resistance by scientists to scientific discovery', *Science*, 134: 596–602.

Bastine, R. (1980) 'Ausbildungen in psychotherapeutischen Methoden und Strategien', in V. Birtsch and D. Tscheulin (eds), *Ausbildung in klinischer Psychologie und Psychotherapie*. Weinheim: Beltz. pp. 71–85.

Beach, S.H. and O'Leary, K.D. (1986) 'The treatment of depression occurring in the context of marital discord', *Behavior Therapy*, 17: 43–9.

Beck, A.T. (1970) 'Cognitive therapy: Nature and relation to behavior therapy', *Behavior Therapy*, 1: 184–200.

Beck, A.T. (1984) 'Cognitive therapy, behavior therapy, psychoanalysis, and pharmacotherapy: the cognitive continuum', in J.B.W. Williams and R.L. Spitzer (eds), *Psychotherapy Research: Where Are We and Where Should We Go?* New York: Guilford.

Beitman, B.D. (1987) *The Structure of Individual Psychotherapy*. New York: Guilford.

Beitman, B.D. and Klerman, G.L. (eds) (1984) *Combining Pharmacotherapy and Psychotherapy in Clinical Practice*. New York: Spectrum.

Beitman, B.D., Goldfried, M.R. and Norcross, J.C. (1989) 'The movement toward integrating the psychotherapies: an overview', *American Journal of Psychiatry*, 146: 138–47.

Bergin, A.E. (1968) 'Technique for improving desensitization via warmth, empathy, and emotional re-experiencing of hierarchy events', in R. Rubin and C.M. Franks (eds), *Advances in Behavior Therapy*. New York: Academic Press.

Bergin, A.E. (1970a) 'A note on dream changes following desensitization', *Behavior Therapy*, 1: 546–9.

Bergin, A.E. (1970b) 'Cognitive therapy and behavior therapy: foci for a multidimensional approach to treatment', *Behavior Therapy*, 1: 205–12.

Bergin, A.E. (1971) 'The evaluation of therapeutic outcomes', in A.E. Bergin and S.L. Garfield (eds), *Handbook of Psychotherapy and Behavior Change*. New York: Wiley.

Beutler, L.E. (1983) *Eclectic Psychotherapy: A Systematic Approach*. New York: Pergamon.

Birk, L. (1970) 'Behavior therapy: integration with dynamic psychiatry', *Behavior Therapy*, 1: 522–6.

Birk, L. (1973) 'Psychoanalysis and behavioral analysis: natural resonance and complementarity', *International Journal of Psychiatry*, 11: 160–6.

Birk, L. (1988) 'Behavioral/psychoanalytic psychotherapy within overlapping systems: a natural matrix for diagnosis and therapeutic change', *Psychiatric Annals*, 18: 296–308.

Birk, L. and Brinkley-Birk, A. (1974) 'Psychoanalysis and behavior therapy', *American Journal of Psychiatry*, 131: 499–510.

Brady, J.P. (1968) 'Psychotherapy by combined behavioral and dynamic approaches', *Comprehensive Psychiatry*, 9: 536–43.

Brady, J.P., Davison, G.C., Dewald, P.A., Egan, G., Fadiman, J., Frank, J.D., Gill, M.M., Hoffman, I., Kempler, W., Lazarus, A.A., Raimy, V., Rotter, J.B. and Strupp, H.H. (1980) 'Some views on effective principles of psychotherapy', *Cognitive Therapy and Research*, 4: 271–306.

Brammer, L.M. (1969) 'Eclecticism revisited', *Personnel and Guidance Journal*, 48: 192–7.

Castonguay, L.G., Goldfried, M.R., Hayes, A.M. and Kerr, S. (1989) 'An exploratory analysis of process and outcome variables in the Sheffield Psychotherapy Project'. Paper presented at the 20th annual meeting of the Society for Psychotherapy Research, Toronto, June.

Coyne, J.C. (1994) 'Possible contributions of "cognitive science" to the integration of psychotherapy', *Journal of Psychotherapy Integration*, 4(4): 401–16.

Davison, G.C. (1978) *Theory and Practice in Behavior Therapy: An Unconsummated Marriage*. (Audiocassette). New York: BMA Audio Cassettes.

Diamond, R.E., Havens, R.A. and Jones, A.C. (1978) 'A conceptual framework for the practice of prescriptive eclecticism in psychotherapy', *American Psychologist*, 33: 239–48.

Dollard, J. and Miller, N.E. (1950) *Personality and Psychotherapy*. New York: McGraw-Hill.

Driscoll, R. (1984) *Pragmatic Psychotherapy*. New York: Van Nostrand Reinhold.

Driscoll, R. (1987) 'Ordinary language as a common language for psychotherapy', *Journal of Integrative and Eclectic Psychotherapy*, 6: 184–94.

Dryden, W. (ed.) (1984) *Individual Therapy in Britain*. London: Harper & Row.

Egan, G. (1975) *The Skilled Helper*. Monterey, CA: Brooks/Cole.

Feather, B.W. and Rhoads, J.M. (1972a) 'Psychodynamic behavior therapy: I. Theory and rationale', *Archives of General Psychiatry*, 26: 496–502.

Feather, B.W. and Rhoads, J.M. (1972b) 'Psychodynamic behavior therapy: II. Clinical aspects', *Archives of General Psychiatry*, 26: 503–11.

Feldman, L.B. (1989) 'Integrating individual and family therapy', *Journal of Integrative and Eclectic Psychotherapy*, 8: 41–52.

Fensterheim, H. and Glazer, H.I. (eds) (1983) *Behavioral Psychotherapy: Basic Principles and Case Studies in an Integrative Clinical Model*. New York: Brunner/Mazel.

Frank, J.D. (1961) *Persuasion and Healing*. Baltimore, MD: Johns Hopkins University Press.

Frank, J.D. (1979) 'The present status of outcome research', *Journal of Consulting and Clinical Psychology*, 47: 310–16.

Freeman, A., Simon, K.M., Beutler, L.E. and Arkowitz, H. (eds) (1989) *The Comprehensive Handbook of Cognitive Therapy*. New York: Plenum.

French, T.M. (1933) 'Interrelations between psychoanalysis and the experimental work of Pavlov', *American Journal of Psychiatry*, 89: 1165–1203.

Freud, S. (1924) *Collected Papers: Vols. 1–11*, 2nd edn. London: Hogarth Press.

Garfield, S.L. (1957) *Introductory Clinical Psychology*. New York: Macmillan.

Garfield, S.L. (1980) *Psychotherapy: An Eclectic Approach*. New York: Wiley.

Garfield, S.L. and Kurtz, R. (1976) 'Clinical psychologists in the 1970s', *American Psychologist*, 31: 1–9.

Gevins, A. (1983) 'Shadows of thought: toward a dynamic network model of neurocognitive functioning'. Paper presented at the meeting of the Society of Biological Psychiatry, New York.

Glad, D.D. (1959) *Operational Values in Psychotherapy*. New York: Oxford University Press.

Glass, C.G., Victor, B.J. and Arnkoff, D.B. (1993) 'Empirical research on integrative and eclectic psychotherapies', in G. Stricker and J.R. Gold (eds), *Comprehensive Handbook of Psychotherapy Integration*. New York: Plenum Press. pp. 9–26.

Goldfried, M.R. (1979) 'Anxiety reduction through cognitive-behavioral intervention', in P.C. Kendall and S.D. Hollon (eds), *Cognitive-Behavioral Interventions: Theory, Research, and Procedures*. New York: Academic Press.

Goldfried, M.R. (1980) 'Toward the delineation of therapeutic change principles', *American Psychologist*, 35: 991–9.

Goldfried, M.R. (ed.) (1982) *Converging Themes in Psychotherapy: Trends in Psychodynamic, Humanistic, and Behavioral Practice*. New York: Springer.

Goldfried, M.R. (1987) 'A common language for the psychotherapies: commentary', *Journal of Integrative and Eclectic Psychotherapy*, 6: 200–4.

Goldfried, M.R. (1991) 'Research issues in psychotherapy integration', *Journal of Psychotherapy Integration*, 1: 5–25.

Goldfried, M.R. and Davison, G.C. (1976) *Clinical Behavior Therapy*. New York: Holt, Rinehart & Winston.

Goldfried, M.R. and Newman, C.F. (1986) 'A look at what therapists actually do'. Symposium presented at the annual convention of the American Psychological Association, Washington, DC, August.

Goldfried, M.R. and Newman, C.F. (1992) 'A history of psychotherapy integration', in J.C. Norcross and M.R. Goldfried (eds), *Handbook of Psychotherapy Integration*. New York: Basic Books. pp. 46–93.

Goldfried, M.R. and Safran, J.D. (1986) 'Future directions in psychotherapy integration', in J.C. Norcross (ed.), *Handbook of Eclectic Psychotherapy*. New York: Brunner/Mazel. pp. 463–83.

Goldfried, M.R. and Strupp, H.H. (1980) 'Empirical clinical practice: a dialogue on rapprochement'. Panel presented at the convention of the Association for Advancement of Behavior Therapy, New York, NY, November.

Goldfried, M.R., Newman, C.F. and Hayes, A.M. (1989) 'The coding system of therapeutic focus'. Unpublished manuscript, SUNY at Stony Brook, Stony Brook, NY.

Goldsamt, L.A., Goldfried, M.R., Hayes, A.M. and Kerr, S. (1992) 'Beck, Meichenbaum, and Strupp: a comparison of three therapies on the dimension of therapist feedback', *Psychotherapy*, 29: 167–76.

Grebstein, L.C. (1986) 'An eclectic family therapy', in J.C. Norcross (ed.), *Handbook of Eclectic Psychotherapy*. New York: Brunner/Mazel. pp. 282–319.

Greenberg, L.S. and Safran, J.D. (1984) 'Integrating affect and cognitions: a perspective on the process of therapeutic change', *Cognitive Therapy and Research*, 8: 559–78.

Greenberg, L.S. and Safran, J.D. (1987) *Emotion in Psychotherapy*. New York: Guilford.

Grinker, R.R. (1976) Discussion of Strupp's, 'Some critical comments on the future of psychoanalytic therapy', *Bulletin of the Menninger Clinic*, 40: 247–54.

Guidano, V.F. (1987) *Complexity of the Self*. New York: Guilford.

Gurman, A.A. (1978) 'Contemporary marital therapies', in T. Paolino and B. McCrady (eds), *Marriage and Marital Therapy*. New York: Brunner/Mazel.

Herzburg, A. (1945) *Active Psychotherapy*. New York: Grune & Stratton.

Houts, P.S. and Serber, M. (eds) (1972) *After the Turn On, What? Learning Perspectives on Human Groups*. Champaign, IL: Research Press.

Hunt, H.F. (1976) 'Recurrent dilemmas in behavior therapy', in G. Serban (ed.), *Psychopathology of Human Adaptation*. New York: Plenum.

Kaplan, H.S. (1974) *The New Sex Therapy*. New York: Brunner/Mazel.

Kerr, S., Goldfried, M.R., Hayes, A.M., Castonguay, L.G. and Goldsamt, L. (1992) 'Interpersonal and intrapersonal focus in cognitive-behavioral and psychodynamic-interpersonal therapies: a preliminary analysis of the Sheffield project', *Psychotherapy Research*, 2: 266–76.

Kraft, T. (1969) 'Psychoanalysis and behaviorism: a false antithesis', *American Journal of Psychotherapy*, 23: 482–7.

Kubie, L.S. (1934) 'Relation of the conditioned reflex to psychoanalytic technic', *Archives of Neurology and Psychiatry*, 32: 1137–42.

Lambley, P. (1974) 'Differential effects of psychotherapy and behavioural techniques in a case of acute obsessive compulsive disorder', *British Journal of Psychiatry*, 125: 181–3.

Landau, R.J. and Goldfried, M.R. (1981) 'The assessment of schemata: a unifying framework for cognitive, behavioral, and traditional assessment', in P.C. Kendall and S.D. Hollon (eds), *Assessment Strategies for Cognitive-behavioral Interventions*. New York: Academic Press.

Landsman, T. (1974) 'Not an adversity but a welcome diversity'. Paper presented at the meeting of the American Psychological Association, New Orleans, LA, August.

Larson, D. (1980) 'Therapeutic schools, styles, and schoolism: a national survey', *Journal of Humanistic Psychology*, 20: 3–20.

Lazarus, A.A. (1967) 'In support of technical eclecticism', *Psychological Reports*, 21: 415–16.

Lazarus, A.A. (1971) *Behavior Therapy and Beyond*. New York: McGraw-Hill.

Lazarus, A.A. (1976) *Multimodal Behavior Therapy*. New York: Springer.

Lazarus, A.A. (1977) 'Has behavior therapy outlived its usefulness?', *American Psychologist*, 32: 550–4.

Lazarus, A.A. (1992) 'Multimodal therapy: Technical eclecticism with minimal integration', in J.C. Norcross and M.R. Goldfried (eds), *Handbook of Psychotherapy Integration*. New York: Basic Books.

Lebow, J.L. (1984) 'On the value of integrating approaches to family therapy', *Journal of Marital and Family Therapy*, 10: 127–38.

Lecomte, C. and Castonguay, L.G. (eds) (1987) *Rapprochement et intégration en psychothérapie*. Montreal: Geatan Morin Editeur.

Leventhal, A.M. (1968) 'Use of a behavioral approach within a traditional psychotherapeutic context: a case study', *Journal of Abnormal Psychology*, 73: 178–82.

Linehan, M.M. (1993) *Cognitive-behavior Treatment of Borderline Personality Disorder*. New York: Guilford.

London, P. (1964) *The Modes and Morals of Psychotherapy*. New York: Holt, Rinehart & Winston.

London, P. (1972) 'The end of ideology in behavior modification', *American Psychologist*, 27: 913–20.

London, P. and Palmer, M. (1988) 'The integrative trend in psychotherapy in historical context', *Psychiatric Annals*, 18: 273–9.

Mahoney, M.J. (1979) 'Cognitive and non-cognitive views in behavior modification', in P.O. Sjoden and S. Bates (eds), *Trends in Behavior Therapy*. New York: Plenum.

Mahoney, M.J. (1980) 'Psychotherapy and the structure of personal revolutions', in M. Mahoney (eds), *Psychotherapy Process*. New York: Plenum. pp. 157–80.

Mahoney, M.J. (1984a) 'Psychoanalysis and behaviorism: the yin and yang of determinism', in H. Arkowitz and S.B. Messer (eds), *Psychoanalytic Therapy and Behavior Therapy: Is Integration Possible?* New York: Plenum. pp. 303–25.

Mahoney, M.J. (1984b) 'Integrating cognition, affect, and action: a comment', *Cognitive Therapy and Research*, 8: 585–9.

Mahoney, M.J. and Wachtel, P.L. (1982) 'Convergence of psychoanalytic and behavioral therapy'. Presentation at the Institute for Psychosocial Study, New York, NY, May.

Marks, I. (1971) 'The future of the psychotherapies', *British Journal of Psychiatry*, 118: 69–73.

Marks, I.M. and Gelder, M.G. (1966) 'Common ground between behavior therapy and psychodynamic methods', *British Journal of Medical Psychology*, 39: 11–23.

Marmor, J. (1964) 'Psychoanalytic therapy and theories of learning', in J. Masserman (ed.), *Science and Psychoanalysis*, Vol. 7. New York: Grune & Stratton.

Marmor, J. (1969) 'Neurosis and the psychotherapeutic process: similarities and differences in the behavioral and psychodynamic conceptions', *International Journal of Psychiatry*, 7: 514–19.

Marmor, J. (1971) 'Dynamic psychotherapy and behavior therapy: are they irreconcilable?', *Archives of General Psychiatry*, 24: 22–8.

Marmor, J. and Woods, S.M. (eds) (1980) *The Interface between Psychodynamic and Behavioral Therapies*. New York: Plenum.

Marten, P.A. and Barlow, D.H. (1983) 'Implications of clinical research for psychotherapy integration in the treatment of the anxiety disorders', *Journal of Psychotherapy Integration*, 3: 297–311.

Messer, S.B. and Winokur, M. (1980) 'Some limits to the integration of psychoanalytic and behavior therapy', *American Psychologist*, 35: 818–27.

Millon, T., Everly, G. and Davis, R.D. (1993) 'How can knowledge of psychopathology facilitate psychotherapy integration? A view from the personality disorders', *Journal of Psychotherapy Integration*, 3: 331–52.

Norcross, J.C. (ed.) (1986) *Handbook of Eclectic Psychotherapy*. New York: Brunner/Mazel.

Norcross, J.C. (ed.) (1987) *Casebook of Eclectic Psychotherapy*. New York: Brunner/Mazel.

Norcross, J.C. and Goldfried, M.R. (eds) (1992) *Handbook of Psychotherapy Integration*. New York: Basic Books.

Norcross, J.C. and Grencavage, L.M. (1989) 'Eclecticism and integration in counseling and psychotherapy: major themes and obstacles', *British Journal of Guidance and Counseling*, 17: 227–47.

Norcross, J.D. and Newman, C.F. (1992) 'Psychotherapy integration: setting the context', in J.C. Norcross and M.R. Goldfried (eds), *Handbook of Psychotherapy Integration*. New York: Basic Books.

Norcross, J.C. and Prochaska, J.O. (1988) 'A study of eclectic (and integrative) views revisited', *Professional Psychology: Research and Practice*, 19: 170–4.

Norcross, J.C. and Thomas, B.L. (1988) 'What's stopping us now? Obstacles to psychotherapy integration', *Journal of Integrative and Eclectic Psychotherapy*, 7: 74–80.

Patterson, C.H. (1967) 'Divergence and convergence in psychotherapy', *American Journal of Psychotherarpy*, 21: 4–17.

Pinsof, W.M. (1983) 'Integrative problem-centered therapy: toward the synthesis of family and individual psychotherapies', *Journal of Marital and Family Therapy*, 9: 19–35.

Powell, D.H. (1988) 'Spontaneous insights and the process of behavior therapy: cases in support of integrative psychotherapy', *Psychiatric Annals*, 18: 288–94.

Prochaska, J.O. (1979) *Systems of Psychotherapy: A Transtheoretical Analysis*. Homewood, IL: Dorsey.

Raimy, V. (1975) *Misunderstandings of the Self*. San Francisco: Jossey-Bass.

Rhoads, J.M. (1988) 'Combinations and synthesis of psychotherapies', *Psychiatric Annals*, 18: 280–7.

Rhoads, J.M. and Feather, B.W. (1974) 'The application of psychodynamic to behavior therapy', *American Journal of Psychiatry*, 131: 17–20.

Robertson, M. (1979) 'Some observations from an eclectic therapist', *Psychotherapy: Theory, Research, and Practice*, 16: 18–21.

Robins, C.J. (1993) 'Implications of research in the psychopathology of depression for psychotherapy integration', *Journal of Psychotherapy Integration*, 3: 313–30.

Rogers, C.R. (1963) 'Psychotherapy today or where do we go from here?', *American Journal of Psychotherapy*, 17: 5–15.

Rosenzweig, S. (1936) 'Some implicit common factors in diverse methods in psychotherapy', *American Journal of Orthopsychiatry*, 6: 412–15.

Ryle, A. (1978) 'A common language for the psychotherapies?', *British Journal of Psychiatry*, 132: 585–94.

Ryle, A. (1982) *Psychotherapy: A Cognitive Integration of Theory and Practice*. London: Academic Press.

Ryle, A. (1984) 'How can we compare different psychotherapies? Why are they all effective?', *British Journal of Medical Psychology*, 57: 261–4.

Ryle, A. (1987) 'Cognitive psychology as a common language for psychotherapy', *Journal of Integrative and Eclectic Psychotherapy*, 6: 168–72.

Safran, J.D. (1984) 'Assessing the cognitive-interpersonal cycle', *Cognitive Therapy and Research*, 8: 333–47.

Safran, J.D., Greenberg, L.S. and Rice, L. (1988) 'Integrating psychotherapy research and practice: modeling the change process', *Psychotherapy*, 25: 1–17.

Sarason, I.G. (1979) 'Three lacunae of cognitive therapy', *Cognitive Therapy and Research*, 3: 223–35.

Segraves, R.T. (1982) *Marital Therapy: A Combined Psychodynamic-Behavioral Approach*. New York: Plenum.

Silverman, L.H. (1974) 'Some psychoanalytic considerations of non-psychoanalytic therapies: on the possibility of integrating treatment approaches and related issues', *Psychotherapy: Theory, Research, and Practice*, 11: 298–305.

Simek-Downing, L. (ed.) (1989) *International Psychotherapy: Theories, Research and Cross-cultural Implications*. New York: Praeger.

Sloane, R.B. (1969) 'The converging paths of behavior therapy and psychotherapy', *American Journal of Psychiatry*, 125: 877–85.

Sloane, R.B., Staples, F.R., Cristol, A.H., Yorkston, N.J. and Whipple, K. (1975) *Psychotherapy versus Behavior Therapy*. Cambridge, MA: Harvard University Press.

Smith, E.W.L. (1995) 'A passionate, rational response to the "manualization" of psychotherapy', *Psychotherapy Bulletin*, 30(2): 36–40.

Staats, A.W. (1981) 'Paradigmatic behaviorism, unified theory construction methods, and the Zeitgeist of separatism', *American Psychologist*, 36: 239–56.

Stiles, W.B., Shapiro, D.A. and Elliott, R. (1986) 'Are all psychotherapies equivalent?', *American Psychologist*, 42: 165–80.

Stricker, G. and Gold, J.R. (eds) (1993) *Comprehensive Handbook of Psychotherapy Integration*. New York: Plenum.

Strong, S.R. (1987) 'Interpersonal theory as a common language for psychotherapy', *Journal of Integrative and Eclectic Psychotherapy*, 6: 173–83.

Strupp, H.H. (1976) 'Some critical comments on the future of psychoanalytic therapy', *Bulletin of the Menninger Clinic*, 40: 238–54.

Textor, M.R. (ed.) (1983) *Integrative Psychotherapies*. Munich: Schobert.

Thoresen, C.E. (1973) 'Behavioral humanism', in C.E. Thoresen (ed.), *Behavior Modification in Education*. Chicago: University of Chicago Press.

Thorne, F.C. (1950) *Principles of Personality Counseling*. Brandon, VT: Journal of Clinical Psychology.

Truax, C.B. and Mitchell, K.M. (1971) 'Research on certain therapist interpersonal skills in relation to process and outcome', in A.E. Bergin and S.L. Garfield (eds), *Handbook of Psychotherapy and Behavior Change*. New York: Wiley. pp. 299–344.

Wachtel, P.L. (1977) *Psychoanalysis and Behavior Therapy: Toward an Integration*. New York: Basic Books.

Wachtel, P.L. (ed.) (1982) *Resistance: Psychodynamic and Behavioral Approaches*. New York: Plenum.

Wachtel, P.L. (1987) *Action and Insight*. New York: Guilford.

Wachtel, E. and Wachtel, P.L. (1986) *Family Dynamics and Individual Psychotherapy*. New York: Guilford.

Wandersman, A., Poppen, P.J. and Ricks, D.F. (eds) (1976) *Humanism and Behaviorism: Dialogue and Growth*. Elmsford, NY: Pergamon.

Watson, G. (1940) 'Areas of agreement in psychotherapy', *American Journal of Orthopsychiatry*, 10: 698–709.

Weitzman, B. (1967) 'Behavior therapy and psychotherapy', *Psychological Review*, 74: 300–17.

Westen, D. (1994) 'Implications of cognitive science for psychotherapy: promises and limitations', *Journal of Psychotherapy Integration*, 4(4): 387–99.

Whitehouse, F.A. (1967) 'The concept of therapy: A review of some essentials', *Rehabilitation Literature*, 28: 238–347.

Wolf, E. (1966) 'Learning theory and psychoanalysis', *British Journal of Medical Psychology*, 39: 1–10.

Wolfe, B.E. (1989) 'Phobias, panic, and psychotherapy integration', *Journal of Integrative and Eclectic Psychotherapy*, 8: 264–76.

Wolfe, B.E. and Goldfried, M.R. (1988) 'Research on psychotherapy integration: recommendations and conclusion from an NIMH workshop', *Journal of Consulting and Clinical Psychology*, 56: 448–51.

Woodworth, R.S. (1948) *Contemporary Schools of Psychology*. New York: Ronald.

Woody, R.H. (1968) 'Toward a rationale for psychobehavioral therapy', *Archives of General Psychiatry*, 19: 197–204.

Woody, R.H. (1971) *Psychobehavioral Counseling and Therapy: Integrating Behavioral and Insight Techniques*. New York: Appleton-Century-Crofts.

Woody, R.H. (1973) 'Integrated aversion therapy and psychotherapy: two sexual deviation case studies', *Journal of Sex Research*, 9: 313–24.

The Editor and Contributors

The Editor

Windy Dryden is Professor of Counselling at Goldsmiths College, University of London. He has authored or edited over 100 books including *Facilitating Client Change in Rational Emotive Behaviour Therapy* (Whurr, 1995) and *Daring to be Myself: A Case of Rational-Emotive Therapy*, written with Joseph Yankura (Open University Press, 1992). In addition, he edits twelve book series in the area of counselling and psychotherapy including the 'Brief Therapy and Counselling' series (Wiley) and 'Developing Counselling' (Sage Publications). His major interests are in rational emotive behaviour therapy, eclecticism and integration in psychotherapy and, increasingly, writing short, accessible self-help books for the general public.

The Contributors

Marvin R. Goldfried is Professor of Psychology and Psychiatry at the State University of New York at Stony Brook. In addition to his teaching, clinical supervision and research, he maintains a limited practice of psychotherapy in New York City. He is a diplomate in clinical psychology, Editor-in-Chief of *In Session: Psychotherapy in Practice*, editorial board member of professional journals and author of several books. Dr Goldfried is co-founder of the Society for the Exploration of Psychotherapy Integration.

Judith Hemming, formally a teacher and teacher trainer, has been in private practice as a Gestalt psychotherapist for the past ten years, having trained in a variety of Gestalt and other approaches in Britain and America since 1980. She is an Associate Teaching and Supervising Member of the Gestalt Psychotherapy Training Institute and offers training and supervision for several institutes in Britain and abroad. She specializes in and has written about Gestalt Couples Therapy and her current research interest lies in integrating Bert Hellinger's family systemic work with Gestalt practice. She is Associate Editor of the *British Gestalt Journal*.

Joel M. Martin is a doctoral student in clinical psychology at the University of Memphis, Memphis, Tennessee. He received his Bachelor of Science degree from the University of Pittsburgh in 1993 with a major concentration in psychology and minor concentrations in biology, philosophy and English literature. Since that time, his graduate studies have involved examination of issues related to the history, theory, practice and research of personal construct theory. His current research interests include psychotherapy outcome, behavioural medicine, and ethical issues of psychotherapy practice.

Michael Neenan is senior tutor (part-time) at the Centre for Rational Emotive Behaviour Therapy, Blackheath, London and Co-Chair of the Association of REBT therapists (United Kingdom). As well as writing a number of articles on REBT, he has co-authored with Windy Dryden *A Dictionary of Rational Emotive Behaviour Therapy* (Whurr, 1995) and *Dealing with Difficulties in Rational Emotive Behaviour Therapy* (Whurr, 1996). His major interests are in promulgating REBT and cognitive-behaviour therapy (CBT) including using these approaches to teach stress management in industry.

Robert A. Neimeyer is a Professor at the Department of Psychology, the University of Memphis, Memphis, Tennessee, where he also maintains an active private practice. Since completing his doctoral training in clinical psychology at the University of Nebraska in 1982, the majority of his research has drawn on concepts and methods in personal construct theory and related constructivist approaches to personality and psychotherapy. He has published fourteen books, including *The Development of Personal Construct Psychology* (University of Nebraska Press, 1985), a *Personal Construct Therapy Casebook* (Springer, 1987), *Advances in Personal Construct Theory*, vols 1–3 (JAI Press, 1990, 1992, 1995), and *Constructivism in Psychotherapy* (American Psychological Association, 1995). The author of over 150 articles and book chapters, he is currently conducting research in the areas of depression, suicide, and psychotherapy process and outcome. Dr Neimeyer is the co-editor of the *Journal of Constructivist Psychology*, and serves on the editorial boards of a number of other journals. In recognition of his scholarly contributions, he was granted the Distinguished Research Award by the University of Memphis in 1990.

Robert Newell has been involved in behaviour therapy for the past fourteen years, as clinician, teacher and researcher and describes himself as a radical behaviourist. He is currently Lecturer in Nursing at Hull University where his most recent areas of clinical interest have included work with challenging behaviours, body image and the teaching of interviewing skills, examining these issues from the cognitive-behavioural perspective. Particular interests include the application of cognitive-behavioural strategies to nursing interventions and the evaluation of outcomes in nursing. He is the author of *Interviewing Skills for Nurses and Other Health Professionals* (Routledge, 1994), co-editor of the series *Routledge Essentials in Nursing* and editor of the journal *Clinical Effectiveness in Nursing*. In addition, he is the author of numerous book chapters and academic papers related to behaviour therapy and to nursing.

Cory F. Newman is Clinical Director of the Center for Cognitive Therapy and Assistant Professor of Psychology in Psychiatry at the University of Pennsylvania's School of Medicine.

He earned his doctoral degree from the State University of New York at Stony Brook, where he worked with Marvin R. Goldfried. After completing an internship at the Palo Alto Veterans Administration Medical Center, and a postdoctoral fellowship at the Center for Cognitive Therapy in Philadelphia, Dr Newman became the Assistant Director of Education and Training at the Center for Cognitive Therapy in 1989, and then Clinical Director in 1990. His current activities include seeing patients in individual and marital therapy, supervising and teaching postdoctoral Fellows and psychiatric residents, performing research on cognitive therapy of drug-resistant depression, and acting as a clinical administrator for the Center. Dr Newman has co-authored three books on cognitive therapy, working with Drs Aaron T. Beck, Fred D. Wright and Bruce S. Liese on *Cognitive Therapy of Substance Abuse* (Guilford, 1993), with Drs Mary Anne Layden, Arthur Freeman and Susan Morse on *Cognitive Therapy of Borderline Personality Disorder* (Allyn and Bacon, 1993), and with Dr Thomas E. Ellis on *Choosing to Live: How to Defeat Suicide through Cognitive Therapy* (New Harbinger, in press).

Malcolm Parlett is a Gestalt psychotherapist, clinical supervisor, trainer and organizational consultant in private practice, resident in Bristol. He is editor of the *British Gestalt Journal*. He has a background in qualitative research in education and has held visiting professorships at three universities. He has been centrally involved in the development of Gestalt therapy training and professionalization in Britain since the early 1980s and one of his major interests is in new applications of the Gestalt philosophy and methods. His chief research interests are in field theory, about which he has written several articles, and in mind–body relationships and Gestalt bodywork.

Simon du Plock is an Associate Fellow of the British Psychological Society and Director of the BA in Counselling and Mental Health Programme at Regent's College School of Psychotherapy and Counselling. He is a registered psychotherapist and chartered counselling psychologist with a background which includes experience in the NHS, the independent sector, and therapeutic communities. He is the author of a number of papers and journal articles, primarily on existential-phenomenological therapy (in which he maintains a private practice), and is co-editor of the *Journal of the Society for Existential Analysis*.

Nathaniel J. Raskin is Professor Emeritus of Psychiatry and Behavioral Sciences at Northwestern University Medical School in Chicago, where he taught and did research in a clinical psychology doctoral programme for thirty-four years. He received a PhD from the University of Chicago in 1949. He is a Fellow of the American Psychological Association, a diplomate in clinical psychology of the American Board of Professional Psychology, and a past president of the American Academy of Psychotherapists. He has studied, researched, practised, taught and written about client-centred therapy with children and adults for over fifty years, and was a student, associate and friend of Carl Rogers from 1940 to 1987, the year of Rogers's death. The author of over fifty publications, he has also made a similar number of presentations at conventions of the American Psychological Association, and other national, regional and international groups. He has taught in client-centred programmes in Italy, France, England, Switzerland, Slovakia, Hungary and Portugal and been an invited speaker at professional associations or universities in Rome, Messina, Amsterdam, Cork, Moscow, St Petersburg, Bratislava, Lisbon and Oporto. Dr Raskin has maintained a part-time psychotherapy practice for more than forty years.

John Rowan teaches at the Minster Centre in London, and is the author of a number of books, including *The Horned God: Feminism and Men as Wounding and Healing* (Routledge, 1987), *Ordinary Ecstasy: Humanistic Psychology in Action* (2nd edn., Routledge, 1988), *Subpersonalities* (Routledge, 1990), *Breakthroughs and Integration in Psychotherapy* (Whurr, 1992) and *The Transpersonal in Psychotherapy and Counselling* (Routledge, 1993). He is on the editorial board of *Masculinities, Self & Society*, the *Journal of Humanistic Psychology* and the *Transpersonal Review*. He is a Fellow of the British Psychological Society. His particular interests are in men and the transpersonal, and these two themes come together in his forthcoming book *Healing the Male Psyche: Therapy as Initiation*, to be published by Routledge in September 1996 .

Ian Stewart is Co-Director of The Berne Institute in Kegworth, Leicestershire. He is a Teaching and Supervising Transactional Analyst (ITAA/EATA), a Professional Member of the Institute of Transactional Analysis, a UKCP registered psychotherapist, and a practitioner in neuro-linguistic programming. His publications include *TA Today* (Lifespace, 1987, as co-author with Vann S. Joines); *Transactional Analysis Counselling in Action* (Sage Publications, 1989); the volume on *Eric Berne* in the series 'Key Figures in Counselling and Psychotherapy' (Sage Publications, 1992); and *Developing Transactional Analysis Counselling* (Sage Publications, 1996).

Marjorie E. Weishaar is Clinical Associate Professor of Psychiatry and Human Behavior at Brown University in Providence, Rhode Island. She has written numerous chapters on cognitive therapy and is author of the book *Aaron T. Beck* (Sage Publications, 1993). Her other articles and book chapters concern suicide risk assessment and cognitive therapy for suicidal behaviour. Her interests include teaching cognitive therapy to psychiatrists and psychologists in training.

Index